D1715668

THE ROLLING STONES
OFF THE RECORD

THE ROLLING STONES
OFF THE RECORD

MARK PAYTRESS

OMNIBUS PRESS

London / New York / Paris / Sydney / Copenhagen / Berlin / Madrid / Tokyo

Exclusive Distributors:
Music Sales Limited,
8/9 Frith Street,
London W1D 3JB, UK.

Music Sales Corporation,
257 Park Avenue South,
New York, NY 10010, USA.

Macmillan Distribution Services,
53 Park West Drive,
Derrimut, Vic 3030,
Australia.

To the Music Trade only:
Music Sales Limited,
8/9 Frith Street,
London W1D 3JB, UK.

Front cover photograph: Gered Mankovitz

Every effort has been made to trace the copyright holders of the photographs in this book but one or two were unreachable. We would be grateful if the photographers concerned would contact us.

Typeset by Galleon Typesetting, Ipswich.
Printed in Great Britain by Creative Print & Design, Wales.

A catalogue record for this book is available from the British Library.

www.omnibuspress.com

Contents

Acknowledgements   vii

Bibliography   ix

Sources   xi

Introduction   xv

1   Start Me Up   1

2   Good Times, Bad Times   12

3   Respectable   186

4   Dirty Work   295

5   No Expectations   363

6   On With The Show   429

Acknowledgements

To the Rolling Stones and their associates, whose utterances form the basis of this book; to the writers and interviewers who prompted them to 'tell the story'; to the newspapers and magazines, the television and radio stations and, more recently, the websites, that have kept us gripped and informed for more than 40 years.

While I have made every effort to trace the source of every moth-eaten clipping and wildly flickering videotape from some hitherto unknown television broadcast, it is likely that one or two credits may have got lost in the mix. So, to those unknown reporters, a special thanks.

Particular thanks, too, go out to Clive Crump, who gave me the opportunity to rummage through his amazing video archive, which helped enlarge the scope of this book considerably. Also to Andy Neill, for trawling through the back issues of various magazines on my behalf, to Julie Fraser for transcribing some Sixties clips I'd not seen in years, and to Matt Lee, for the long discussions about Stones minutiae.

On a personal level, I am eternally grateful to Erika and Norman, for whom the words 'Rolling' and 'Stones' were usually hideously entwined with the phrase, 'Turn that DOWN!' Also, to my sister Julie-Anne, who became Keith's youngest fan and is still able to recite Charlie Watts quotes from mid-Seventies radio broadcasts; to Zulema Gonzalez, for a little help in transcription and a whole lot of everything else; to Chris Charlesworth and Andy Neill at Omnibus Press for their skilful editing and continued passion for their work. And, of course, to everyone who's shared my enthusiasm for the Rolling Stones over the years – from the tearful girls at Brian Jones' graveside in 1974 to my colleagues at *Record Collector*, *Mojo Collections* and *Mojo*. Special mention must go to Karen Pearce (alias Langley), the Brian Jones devotee who became a lifelong friend, to the intrepid Stones collector Chris Eborn, and to the late Alan Barton, whose enthusiasm for and knowledge of Brian Jones' work surprised those who otherwise knew Alan as the cheery bloke who sang 'Agadoo' with Black Lace. It certainly surprised me.

Mark Paytress, London, April 2003.

Bibliography

The following books have been sitting on my shelves for years. While useful in yielding the occasional quote, their contribution has more often been in leading me back to various original sources.

Rolling Stones, ed. David Dalton, Amsco Music Publ., 1972
The Rolling Stones Story, George Tremlett, Futura, 1974
Mick Jagger, Anthony Scaduto, Mayflower Books, 1975
The Rolling Stones, ed. David Dalton, Star Books, 1975
The Rolling Stones: An Illustrated Record, Roy Carr, New English Library, 1976
Keith Richards, Barbara Charone, Futura, 1979
Up and Down With the Rolling Stones, Tony Sanchez, NEL, 1979
The Rolling Stones: The First Twenty Years, David Dalton, Thames & Hudson, 1981
Death Of A Rolling Stone: The Brian Jones Story, Mandy Aftel, Sidgwick & Jackson, 1982
The Stones, Philip Norman, Hamish Hamilton, 1984
Jagger, Carey Schofield, Futura, 1984
The Life And Good Times Of The Rolling Stones, Philip Norman, Century, 1989
Blown Away: The Rolling Stones and the Death of the Sixties, A.E. Hotchner, Simon & Schuster, 1990
Rolling Stones: Complete Recording Sessions 1963–1989, Martin Elliott, Blandford, 1990
The Rolling Stones Chronicle, Massimo Bonanno, Plexus, 1990
Stone Alone: The Story Of A Rock'n'Roll Band, Bill Wyman with Ray Coleman, Viking, 1990
Mick Jagger: Primitive Cool, Christopher Sandford, Gollancz, 1993
The Rolling Stones In Their Own Words, Omnibus Press, 1994

The Rolling Stones – A Visual Documentary, Miles, Omnibus Press, 1994

Faithfull, Marianne Faithfull with David Dalton, Michael Joseph, 1994

The Complete Guide to the Music of the Rolling Stones, James Hector, Omnibus, 1995

The Rolling Stones: 1962–1995 – The Ultimate Guide, Felix Aeppli, Record Information Services, 1996

Not Fade Away: The Rolling Stones Collection, Geoffrey Giuliano & Chris Eborn, Paper Tiger, 1996

Good Times Bad Times: The Definitive Diary Of The Rolling Stones 1960–1969, Terry Rawlings, Keith Badman, with Andrew Neill, Complete Music, 1997

Phelge's Stones – The Untold History Of The Rolling Stones, James Phelge, Buncha Asshole Books, 1998

The Rolling Stones Files, Mark Paytress, Bramley Books, 1999

Various fanzines have invariably been useful, including:

Shattered! International, The Spirit, It's Only Rock'n' Roll, Basement News, Sticky Fingers, and *Tumbling Dice*. Most have websites that are worth checking out, as do the Stones themselves at www.stones.com, www.mickjagger.com and www.keithrichards.com. Best of all, perhaps, is Nico Zentgraf's extraordinary online database, which you'll find at www.nzentgraf.de.

Sources

(by chapter)

PRE-60s

Start Me Up

Pete Goodman, *Our Own Story* (Beat Publications), Janice James, ATV's *Seeing Sport*, *Everybody's* magazine, Peter Doggett.

1960s

Good Times, Bad Times

Ronald Hudson (head Dartford Grammar), *Rolling Stone, Melody Maker*, Scott E. Kutina, *Guitar Player*, Radio 4, *Everybody's, Today* magazine, Peter Doggett, John MacGillivray & John Kirkham, *Shattered!* magazine, Richard Green, *New Musical Express, The Rolling Stones Story*, BBC Radio 1, *Phelge's Stones*, Alan Freeman, Robert Greenfield, *Jazz News*, Pat Andrews, *Richmond And Twickenham Times*, Barry May, Kevin Howlett, Pete Goodman, Patrick Doncaster, *Daily Mirror*, Decca Records, *Record Mirror*, Norman Jopling, Brian Matthew, *Hit Parader, New Record Mirror, Beat Monthly*, Ian Dove, Ray Coleman, Judith Simons, *Daily Express, Disc*, Maureen Cleave, *Evening Standard, Ready, Steady, Go!*, Peter Jones, *Charlie Is My Darling*, Peter Whitehead, Bob Dawbarn, Mike Nevard, *Daily Herald*, Chris Hayes, *Rave*, David Bailey, *Vogue* (US), Peter Dacre, Jimmy Savile, *Sunday People*, Reuters, Associated Press, *Les Crane Show, Hollywood Palace*, Jack Hutton, Linda Lawrence, *Daily Sketch*, Alan Whittaker, *The News Of The World*, Channel Television, *Rolling Stones Monthly, New York Herald Tribune*, Tom Wolfe, *Fabulous, Taylor & Cutter* magazine, Klaes Burling, Jim McKenna, *Shindig!*, Jack Good, Cynthia Plastercaster, *Newsweek*, Ron Grevatt, *Disc Weekly*, Ed Rudy, Jacqui Swift, *Washington Post*, Sue Mautner, *The Ed Sullivan Show*, Keith Altham, *Hit Parader*, *Houston Chronicle*, *Hullabaloo*, *Village Voice*, Richard Goldstein, *Datebook*, Kenneth Eastaugh, *The Eamonn Andrews Show*, *Sunday Telegraph*, *Sunday Express*, Brion Gysin, *The Look Of The Week*, Robert Robinson, *Private Eye*, *The Times*, William Rees-Mogg, John Gordon, *The New Law Journal*, Stephen Jessel, *World In Action*, *Sunday Mirror*, Jack Bentley, Leslie Perrin PR, Miles, *International Times*, Jon Landau, *Sounds Of The City*, Jonathan & Sue Cott, *Los Angeles Free Press*, *New York Times*, Roger Greenspun, Jann Wenner, Der Spiegel, *Rolling Stones' Rock'n'Roll Circus*, M.C. Escher, Jo Bergman, *Disc*, *Daily Sketch*, Anthony Scaduto, *Disc & Music Echo*, Philip Norman, Don Short, Jim Morrison, Patrick McCarville, Ritchie Yorke, Ralph Gleason, Albert Goldman, K-SAN-FM radio, KFRC News, *Brian Jones, The Rolling Stone – A Story Of Our Time*, BBC Radio 4, Michael Wale, *Gimme Shelter*.

1970s

Respectable

Gimme Shelter, Bud Scoppa, Les Perrin PR, Rolling Stones Records, Jonathon Cott, *Rolling Stone*, Warner Brothers Films, Derek Malcolm, *The Guardian*, Tony Elliot, *Time Out*, Anthony Hayden-Guest, *Frij Nederlands* newspaper, *Melody Maker*, *New Musical Express*, Atlantic Records, *Brian Jones, The Rolling Stone – A Story Of Our Time*, BBC Radio 4, *Daily Telegraph*, Derek Taylor, John Peel, Tom Donahue, Pete Townshend, Robert Greenfield, Richard Neville, *Oz*, *Sounds*, *Beaton By Bailey*, Chris Charlesworth, Michael Wale (*Vox Pop*), Radio Luxemburg, Kid Jensen, Richard Williams, *The Old Grey Whistle Test*, BBC TV, Radio 1, Michael Watts, Danny Holloway, Caroline Boucher, *Disc*, Chris Welch, Truman Capote, *The Dick Cavett Show*, Chet Flippo, Steve Peacock, Billy Walker, Jack Hutton, Barbara Charone, Nick Kent, Pete Erskine, Roy Carr, *Record & Radio Mirror*, Keith Altham, Roderick Gilchrist, *Daily Mail*, Bob Harris, Elly de Waard, James Fox, *ZigZag*, Andrew Tyler, Martin Hayman, Bob Hart, Steve Turner, Peter Dignam, *Sunday Times*, Karl Dallas, *International Musician & Recording World*, Steve Rosen, Lisa Robinson, Steve Dunleavy, *National Star*, Janice James, *Record Mirror & Disc*, John Blake, *The Sun*, Chris Ingham, Charles Shaar Murray, Bob

Hart, Bill Hagerty, Steve Clarke, *Woman's Own*, *Daily Mirror*, David Lewin, David Wigg, *Daily Express*, Gordon Burn, *Men Only*, *Hit Parader*, *Andy Warhol's Exposures*, Geraldo Rivera, *Today* Show, John Pidgeon, Richard Samuels, NBC News, Anne Nightingale, Robert Hilburn, *Honey*, Rick Sky.

1980s

Dirty Work

Ray Bonici, *Melody Maker*, Victor Bockris, Andy Peebles, Radio 1, *Playboy*, *Daily Star*, Chris Welch, *Record Mirror*, Glenn A. Baker, *Goldmine*, *Woman's World*, MTV, *Newsnight*, Robin Denselow, *The Tube*, Paula Yates, Tempo TV, Alan Bangs, *Cheltenham Echo*, David Albino, *Evening Standard*, *The Times*, Muriel Gray, *Friday Night Videos*, *The Sun*, Lisa Robinson, *All Night Long*, *International Musician & Recording World*, Tim Bouquet, *The Guardian*, *New Musical Express*, *Daily Mirror*, Sunie, *Whistle Test*, David Hepworth, Mat Snow, *Music Box*, Nick Kent, *Spin*, *The Meldrum Show*, *My Top Ten*, Radio 1, *Q*, *Daily Mirror*, Chris Evans, *The News Of The World*, *The Star*, *Musician*, Rien A Declarer, *Rolling Stone*, Simon Kinnersley, Adrian Deevoy, Kenichi Yamakawa, Richard Ellis, Craig Mackenzie, Anthony DeCurtis, Peter Hilmore, *The Observer*, Johnny Waller, *Record Mirror*, Francesco Adinolfi, *Top*, *Musician*, Charles M. Young, Bill Milkowski, Steve Turner, *You*, Boudewijn Büch, Kurt Loder, Maurice Packer, *Saturday Morning Live*, Rona Elliot, Robin Eggar, David Thomas, *Night & Day*, Rudi Dolezal, *Daily Express*, Sticky Fingers Restaurants, *The Sun*, Kevin Sessums, *The Telegraph* magazine, *20/20*, Steve Grant.

1990s

No Expectations

25 x 5: The Continuing Adventures Of The Rolling Stones, BBC Television, Robert Sandall, *Sunday Times*, Chris Jagger, *Hello!*, Henrietta Knight, *TV Times*, *Stone Alone* (Bill Wyman), *Q*, Mat Snow, Neil Spencer, *The Observer*, Steve Turner, *The Times*, Ira Robbins, *Pulse!*, *Vanity Fair*, Christian Kammerling, Andreas Lebert, *Rien A Declarer*, David Fricke, Robin Eggar, Robert Sandall, *The Times*, *Spotlight*, *Kerrang!*, *Maclean's*,

London Tonight TV, *Saturday Night Live*, *Rolling Stone*, *Daily Mail*, Nina Myskow, Adam Sweeting, *The Guardian*, *Hot Press*, Don Was, *New Musical Express*, Paul Sexton, Virgin Records, Salman Rushdie, Anthony DeCurtis, VH-1, Jane Stevenson, *Toronto Sun*, Nicky Campbell, Radio 1, *Sunday Times*, Richard Williams, David Sinclair, Matthew Fort, Sophie Grigson, *NME*.com, Dominic Pedler, *Total Guitar*, Harvey Kubernick, *Musician*, Chris Heath, Barney Hoskyns, *Mojo*, Steve Lamacq, Radio 1, Martin Newell, *The Independent*, B.C. Pires, *The Guardian*, *Daily Mirror*, Chris Lander, AOL, Laister-Dickson PR, Bernard Doherty PR, Jonathan Freedland, Victoria Newton, *The Sun*, Ernst Hofacker, *Musik Express*, *Guitar*, Mike Ross, *The Express* (Canada), Karen Bliss, Jam! Music, Radio 2, Mark Hagen, Barbara Ellen, Chris Evans, Linda Lee-Potter, Marianne McDonald, *Night & Day*.

2000s

On With The Show

The Independent, *Daily Mail*, *The Spirit – The Brian Jones Fan Club*, *The Sun*, Maria Croce, *Sunday Mail*, Susie Cormack, *Daily Record*, Rick Fulton, Alison Boshoff, *New York Post*, *Daily Mirror*, Alun Palmer, mickjagger.com, Bill Ribas, *New York Rock*, Angela Hagen, *Daily Mirror*, *Being Mick*, Jagged Films, Channel 4, Kieron Grant, *Toronto Sun*, David Fricke, *The Observer*, Sabine Durrant, *Boston Herald*, Sarah Rodman, David Thomas, *Daily Mail*, Vanessa Thorpe, Ed Helmore, *Rolling Stone*, Dotmusic, Adam Woods, *Saga*, Elizabeth Vargas, ABCNews.com, Will Hodgkinson, *The Guardian*, *Guitarist*, *Uncut*, Philip Norman, Tom Moon, *Philadelphia News*, *Evening Standard*, Hugh Dougherty, Bernard Weinraub, *New York Times*, *The Herald*, *The Scotsman*, Robert Webb, Kieron Grant, *Toronto Sun*, Lester Middlehurst, *Daily Express*, HBO cable TV.

Introduction

According to Mick Jagger, now into his fifth decade as rock's quintessen-
tial icon, "so many books on the Rolling Stones are mostly garbage . . .
untrue". At last, then, here's one he may have a little less trouble digesting.

Forty years into their career, the Stones have yet to tell their story.
There's been the coffee-table memoir, *A Life On The Road*, and, at the
onset of their career, the ghost-written *Our Own Story*. Best of all, at least
in terms of factual detail, is *Stone Alone*, the first volume of Bill Wyman's
autobiography. While Jagger, too, had once been commissioned to write
his own history, the project stalled when he became bored by the weight
of his own past.

Perhaps it's Mick's keen interest in the panoramic canvas of political
history that undermines the feeling that his own story is of any genuine
worth. After all, he's contested on countless occasions that he's merely a
performer who sings and writes songs. But I think he's wrong. Anyone
with a keen interest in the cultural history of the late 20th century will
invariably be drawn to The Rolling Stones, whose work, whose lives and
whose meaning to others lies at the heart of it.

There's still plenty of room on the Rolling Stones bookshelf. The
further one travels from the era that witnessed their birth and development, the easier it will be to unlock the extraordinary meeting of pop and
politics, of post-war neatness and the drift towards psychedelia, narcissism
and nihilism that the band at once reflected and embodied. The best books
– necessarily wider and more speculative – have yet to be written.

This book, though, falls firmly into the opposite camp. The sole voices
heard in it – with a few carefully chosen exceptions – are those of the
band. More important still, the textual tapestry that unfolds allows virtually
no room for reflection, revisionism or lapses in memory. That's because
the material has – by and large – been drawn from contemporary sources.
This is the story of the Rolling Stones as it happens, a vérité account that

gives the band's extraordinary tale immediacy and, perhaps, a convincing ring of truth.

I was concerned that in trawling back through the range of sources I'd meticulously been assembling since the early Seventies, the early years would yield much detail about the Stones' favourite colours, actresses and food, but very little about the mechanics of music-making and their relationship with their times. It's a testament to the journalists of that era – and I would cite Keith Altham (*New Musical Express*), film-maker Peter Whitehead and television journalist Robert Robinson as among those who helped elevate the art of the pop interview – and, perhaps an indictment of today's PR-dominated times, that I was pleasantly surprised by much of what I uncovered.

Invariably, no historical study of popular music can ignore Britain's two leading music weeklies, *New Musical Express* and *Melody Maker*, especially during the Sixties, when both had a virtual monopoly on quizzing pop stars on (sometimes) serious musical matters. But on this occasion, I have attempted to stretch out far beyond the familiar sources, to rare and sometimes never previously transcribed interview material from one-off television and radio broadcasts, to long-forgotten conversations buried in public archives and to various private collections. From Sixties court depositions to modern-day audiences shrieking "Charlie, Charlie!", fly-on-the-wall accounts of studio sessions to food menus, this is the Rolling Stones' own story and how it has managed to touch virtually every aspect of contemporary life.

A few personal thoughts . . . I first saw the Rolling Stones on 8 September 1973, at an afternoon show at the Empire Pool, Wembley. I was 14 years old, and had travelled 200 miles in order to catch what was only my third rock concert. I'd swallowed a little too much of all that 'Is This The Last Time?' publicity, which meant that the climax of 'Street Fighting Man' was blurred by a few lonely tears. More happily, the occasion did inspire my first proper piece of non-fiction writing, which was deemed acceptable enough for my Beckett-loving English teacher to award me a prize – a ticket to any concert of my choice. (Hawkwind, Bournemouth Winter Gardens, 1974, actually.)

I never imagined that what I'd seen would ever be regarded as early-to-mid-period Rolling Stones. Brian Jones was dead and gone, and the band were exiled and – despite the magnificent performance – seemingly under threat from glam and progressive types. After three more sightings during 1976 – at Earl's Court, Paris and Knebworth, the latter experienced in mind-altering fashion thanks to some particularly potent punch passed round by a nearby group of Hell's Angels – I started to see the Stones through a thrilling new prism called punk. Incredibly, the band managed to survive that upheaval, largely through, I suspect, Jagger's remarkable resilience and commercial/critical nous.

I must confess that for much of the next decade, though, the Stones succumbed to the Eighties key pitfall of allowing themselves to defer to new technology and the cloth-eared boffins that operated it. As the Nineties arrived, they skilfully metamorphosed once again, this time to embrace a rootsier sound inspired by Nirvana and the 'Unplugged' aesthetic. Today, the Rolling Stones have passed their 40th anniversary after a remarkable revival in fortunes. Commercially, they're still the world's biggest concert attraction; but as *Voodoo Lounge* and *Bridges To Babylon* have proved, they're also capable of knocking out songs ('You Got Me Rocking', 'Out Of Tears' and that long-time-coming cover of Dylan's 'Like A Rolling Stone' for starters) destined to sit alongside their best work.

I've dined with Bill Wyman, swapped tales with Mick Taylor, enjoyed the same Thames-side vistas as Mick Jagger and Ronnie Wood and concurred with Keith's unswerving belief in Chuck Berry. But I can't say I've ever shared much with Charlie Watts. Perhaps there is one thing. The drummer, who today epitomises the group's longevity-with-dignity qualities, always appeared to be on the cusp of retiring to his private world of American Civil War literature, Charlie Parker discs and his beloved wife, Shirley. But even gentleman Charlie cannot help but concede that the Rolling Stones are more than the soundtrack to our lives. For him, and for us, they are, as Andrew Oldham once insisted, "A way of life". He'd miss them terribly, and so would we all.

1

Start Me Up

MICK JAGGER

• "My mum is very working class, my father bourgeois, because he had a reasonably good education, so I came from somewhere in between that. Neither one nor the other."

• "The war didn't leave much impression on me. The only thing I can remember was my mum taking down the blankets from the windows when all the fighting was over."

• "I had a very good and easy relationship with my mother. I liked her and I could talk to her. There were no hang-ups. It wasn't an intense relationship. I wasn't a mother's boy. I've a brother, Chris, so we were a perfectly normal family with just the usual ups and downs."

Mrs Eva Jagger: "I always had the feeling that Mike would be something. He was a very adventurous boy when he was younger, but then later he became interested in money. It always struck us as odd. Money doesn't usually interest little boys, but it did Mike. He didn't want to be a pilot or an engine driver – he wanted a lot of money!"

• "(Keith and I) went to school together when we were about seven . . . We lived in the same block. We weren't great friends, but we knew each other. We also knew each other when we left school . . . I went to Grammar School while Keith went to another school in the same village, so I used to see Keith riding to school on his bike."

• "I asked (Keith) what he wanted to do when he grew up. He said he wanted to be a cowboy like Roy Rogers and play a guitar. I wasn't that impressed by Roy Rogers, but the bit about the guitar did interest me."

• "When I was 13 the first person I really admired was Little Richard. I wasn't particularly fond of Elvis or Bill Haley . . . I was more into Jerry Lee Lewis, Chuck Berry and a bit later Buddy Holly. There was a lot of TV

1

then, *Cool For Cats, 6.5 Special, Oh, Boy!,* and I saw a lot of people on those shows."

On Monday, 14 September 1959, a more familiar face appeared on the Jagger family's television screen. It was 16-year-old 'Mike' himself, making his TV debut on ATV's Seeing Sport, *an educational programme that revealed the pleasures and the pitfalls of rock climbing. His father, Joe, was Technical Adviser for the programme.*

John Disley (presenter): "Here's Michael, wearing a pair of gym shoes."

Mr Joe Jagger: "Mick had natural agility. It was just a matter of not having the right application. I feel that if he had had a different temperament, he could have been a really great athlete. Apart from basketball, he was a useful cricketer. He was certainly good enough for the school teams, but I suppose he rebelled against all the practice that was necessary."

• "My father was quite ambitious in his way. He broke out from where he came from, in the way that I broke out from where I came from."

• "I started performing in front of people when I was about 14. A lot of our family did. My mother's family were very working class and, in England, working-class people all play and sing. My father's family were from a different background but they played and sung Victorian type of music. Everyone mimicked. It was almost vaudeville. Music hall, copying their idols."

Mrs Eva Jagger: "He was always interested in pop music and used to play records for hours. After leaving a song on the record player only a couple of times, he knew the words and could sing it . . . he could have been a very good impersonator."

Unnamed classmate: "Mick wanted to be hip, and to be American. There was a TV detective series at the time called *77 Sunset Strip*, which had a character called 'Cookie' who used all the latest West Coast slang. Cookie's job was parking cars – or, as he put it, he was a fender bender. Mick was very impressed by all that, and every Monday morning after he'd seen the latest episode, he'd come into school and start reeling off Cookie's latest hip jargon."

• "Everyone was dreamin' about America. That whole American dream was in vogue then."

• "I was crazy over Chuck Berry, Bo Diddley, Muddy Waters and Fats Domino, not knowing what it meant, just that it was beautiful. My father used to call it 'jungle music' and I used to say, 'Yeah, that's right, jungle music, that's a very good description.' Every time I heard it, I just wanted to hear more. It seemed like the most real thing I'd ever known. (Blues) was never played on the radio and, if it was, it was only by accident. I subsequently became aware that Big Bill Broonzy was a blues singer and Muddy Waters was also a blues singer and they were all really the same and it didn't matter. There were no divisions and I'd realised that by the time I was 15."

Unnamed classmate: "There was a small band of music enthusiasts in the school, including Mick and myself, who were bowled over by the initial wave of American rock'n'roll. Then around 1959, when Buddy Holly died, we thought that music was going down the pan. Some of us got into jazz . . . Mick hated jazz, though. He used to call it 'chink-chink' music, after the sound of the banjo."

'Mike' was also prone to writing memos to himself in his school exercise books . . .

• "Before any group is started up, there should be someone who can sing really well and a couple of guitarists who can play good strong chords."

Unnamed classmate: "Mick was always flamboyant at school, always keen to be a character. He was well known for stretching the rules about school uniform to the absolute limit. And his temper could be nasty at times if you got on the wrong side of him. Everyone knew he was on a short fuse."

Mrs Eva Jagger: "He was a leader even when he was at school. If he believed in something, he would defend it against anyone . . ."

FRIDAY, 8 DECEMBER 1960

Ronald Hudson, headmaster of Dartford Grammar, signs a report intended to assist Jagger's bid to go to university.

"Michael Philip Jagger has been a pupil at this School since September 1954. His general record has been satisfactory and he passed the General Certificate of Education in seven subjects in the summer of 1959 with the following marks: English Language 66, English Literature 48, Geography 51, History 56, Latin 49, French 61, Pure Mathematics 53.

"In the sixth form he has applied himself well on the whole and has shown a greater intellectual determination than we had expected. He should be successful in each of his three subjects though he is unlikely to do brilliantly in any of them.

"Jagger is a lad of good general character though he has been rather slow to mature. The pleasing quality which is now emerging is that of persistence when he makes up his mind to tackle something. His interests are wide. He has been a member of several School Societies and is a prominent member in Games, being Secretary of our Basketball Club, a member of the First Cricket Eleven and he plays Rugby Football for his House. Out of School, he is interested in Camping, Climbing, Canoeing, Music and he is also a member of the local Historical Association.

"Jagger's development now fully justifies me in recommending him for a Degree Course and I hope that you will be able to accept him.

"Head Master."

SEPTEMBER 1961

Leaving school with two A-levels, Mick starts his university course.

Mrs Eva Jagger: "For a long time, Mick seemed destined for a steady office job. That was why he went to the London School of Economics to study accountancy."

KEITH RICHARDS

Mrs Doris Richards: "I was one of a family of seven girls, and Keith was the first boy. With six aunts, he was a bit spoiled, and he really was a sweet-looking kid. Chubby and sturdy – and always with a red nose. He was a bit of a mother's boy, really. When he started school, he used to get panic-stricken if I wasn't there waiting for him when they all came out."

• "I knew Mick when I was really young . . . five, six, seven. We used to hang out together. Then I moved and didn't see him for a long time. I once met him selling ice creams outside the public library. I bought one. He was tryin' to make extra money."

• "Moved into a tough neighbourhood when I was about ten. Just been built. Thousands and thousands of houses, everyone wondering what the fuck was going on. Everyone was displaced. They were still building it and already there were gangs everywhere. Coming to Teddy Boys. Just before rock'n'roll hit England. But they were waiting for it . . . Rock'n'roll got me into being one of the boys. Before that I just got me ass kicked all over the place."

Mrs Doris Richards: "Actually, he was too sensitive to be a Ted."

• "I was into Little Richard. I was rockin' away, avoidin' the bicycle chains and the razors in those dance halls. The English get crazy. They are calm, but they were really violent then, those cats. Those suits cost them $150, which is a lot of money. Jackets down to here. Waistcoats. Leopard-skin lapels . . . amazing. It was really, 'Don't step on mah blue suede shoes.' It was down to that."

Mrs Doris Richards: "Keith was always worrying for a guitar of his own. When he was 15, I bought him one for ten pounds. From that day, it has been the most important thing in his life. My father, who used to run a dance band before the war, taught Keith a few chords, but the rest he has taught himself."

• "But then I started to get into where it had come from. Broonzy first. He and Josh White were considered to be the only living black bluesmen still playing. So let's get that together, I thought, 'That can't be right.' Then I started to discover Robert Johnson and those cats. You could never get their records though. One heard about them. On one hand I was playing all that gold stuff on the guitar. The other half of me was listenin' to all that rock'n'roll. Chuck Berry, and sayin' 'Yeah, yeah.'"

• "When I started at Sidcup Art College in 1959, I acquired a guitar from a fellow student. It was virtually a home-made affair, assembled from bits and pieces of various damaged instruments. It was, however, fitted with a pick-up and I just had to have an amplifier – and again I bought one from another student. It was no bigger than a small radio set, but at least it was an amplifier. It worked, too – especially when I kicked it!"

• "It was a place where everybody learned to play guitar. There were lots of guys in various stages of learning (though) I probably learned more off records. I'd spend hours and hours on the same track. I'd learn the chords and how songs were put together . . . People (were) very conscious of music at art school. There was a lot of jazz as well as blues and folk music. So I learned two or three different sorts of things all at once, some old Woody Guthrie and Ramblin' Jack Elliott. I was also trying to pick up rock'n'roll riffs and electric blues – the latest Muddy Waters. I probably never would have heard of those people if I hadn't gone to art school."

Dick Taylor (fellow student): "I thought Keith was a bit of a layabout at art school. His interest was in playing guitar – nothing else counted. In that sense, Mick was much more hard working as a student."

Mrs Doris Richards: "There were three times when it was a waste of effort trying to talk to Keith. When he got up in the morning, when he was playing records and when he was playing his guitar. But his main trouble was that he was so shy."

BRIAN JONES

Keith: "Brian was from Cheltenham, a very genteel town full of old ladies, where it used to be fashionable to go and take the baths once a year at Cheltenham Spa. The water is very good because it comes out of the hills; it's spring water. It's a Regency thing. You know, Beau Brummell. Turn of the 19th century. Now it's a seedy sort of place full of aspirations to be an aristocratic town. It rubs off on anyone who comes from there."

Mrs Louisa Jones: "He had always been keen on music and started piano lessons when he was six or seven. When he was 12, Brian joined the school orchestra and learned clarinet . . . He was very keen on sports at school, particularly cricket, table tennis and judo, and one thing he really excelled at was diving, although he wasn't particularly interested in swimming itself . . . Brian did so well at school. He passed nine subjects in his GCE at ordinary level when he was only 16, and two years later gained advanced level chemistry and physics."

Mr Lewis Jones: "He always was musical, church music he was always fond of, hymns, but it wasn't really until he came into his teens that he began to develop this liking, in the early days, rather an insufficiently strong word perhaps – which became an absolute religion with him. He played the piano quite nicely. He'd had quite legitimate lessons from a very good teacher. But all the time his fanaticism for jazz music was coming to the fore. It was a great disappointment to us and a source of considerable anxiety that he became so wrapped up in his love of jazz music, and that in spite of everything we could do or say, he went off and did it . . .

"Up to a certain point, Brian was a perfectly normal, conventional boy who was well behaved and was well liked, and he was liked because he was well behaved. He was quite a model schoolboy. And then there came this peculiar change in his early teens, at the time I suppose when he began to become a man. He began to get some resentment against authority. It was a rebellion against parental authority; it was certainly a rebellion against school authority. He often used to say, 'Why should I do something I'm told just because the person telling me is older?'"

• "My father wanted me to go to university, but I didn't fancy that. And I didn't like the idea of working for anyone who could boss me around."

• "I started drifting and got interested in drink, girls and things, so I jacked it all in and did exactly what I pleased. I went against everything I had been brought up to believe in. I just went from place to place (hitchhiking abroad), spending a little time in each and doing hardly any work. I was happy going where I fancied and . . . lived the life of Riley just kicking around doing nothing."

In 1961, during a brief spell as a junior assistant in the architects department of Gloucestershire County Council, Brian was renting a room from bus driver Bernard Taylor for £3 per week. But when Jones' girlfriend Patricia Andrews fell pregnant with Brian's son, the landlord kicked them out and Brian left owing three weeks rent. Taylor contacted a solicitor, who in turn contacted Jones who responded thus . . .

• "I must explain that my fiancée, who is your client's sister-in-law, was expecting a baby. I am at present applying for a student apprenticeship with a large contracting company and if I am successful my fiancée and I are planning to marry. We are of course keeping the child."

They did, and Mark Julian – the third already fathered by Jones – was born on 22 October 1961.

Alexis Korner: "I was playing occasional dates with the Chris Barber Band, which at that time was very popular. One of the towns we visited during a tour was Cheltenham. After the performance, Brian came up to me together with a friend of his and started talking about blues. I gave him my phone number and address if he ever came up to London, because he was thoroughly miserable as an assistant in an architect's office. He was there because there was absolutely nothing else to do in Cheltenham, he maintained. He was also playing with a small local jazz band at the time."

Brian's rapidly growing network of fellow R&B enthusiasts also included future Manfred Mann vocalist Paul Pond (alias Jones).

• "We used to have ideas for forming a band when I was in Cheltenham and (Paul) was at Oxford. We actually made some blues tapes and sent them to Alexis Korner, but I don't think he ever got them."

• "I got a few jobs here and there when I needed money, but I was not interested in things – I had no real ambition. As long as I was not absolutely broke, I was okay. I used to go to clubs and listen to R&B bands. I came to London at the instigation of Alexis Korner."

CHARLIE WATTS

Mrs Lilly Watts: "He loved games, especially football, and was forever coming home with dirty knees and muddy clothes. Charlie was a big boy with strong legs. We often thought he would become a footballer. Charlie always wanted a drum set, and used to rap out tunes on the table with pieces of wood or a knife and fork.

• "I was just a teenager when I first got interested in drums. My first kit was made up of bits and pieces. Dad bought it for me and I suppose it cost about £12. Can't remember anything that gave me greater pleasure and I must say that the neighbours were great about the noise I kicked up."

Mrs Lilly Watts: "We bought him his first drum set for Christmas when he was 14. He took to it straight away, and often used to play jazz records and join in on his drums. The neighbours were very good; they never complained. Charlie used to play for hours. Sometimes it nearly drove me mad."

• "The first record I ever got interested in was 'Flamingo' by Earl Bostick. My uncle bought me that."

• "My dad bought me suits and I wore them as smartly as I could. I was a kind of Little Lord Fauntleroy, I suppose. But I do remember that I didn't like jeans and sweaters in those days. I thought they looked untidy and I didn't feel somehow as good as I did in my little suits with the baggy trousers."

BILL WYMAN

• "The only music when I grew up was ballad singers and big band stuff."

• "I couldn't stand wearing a school uniform. I mean, what fun was there in being turned out exactly the same as everybody else. You felt just like the others and that didn't suit my attitude to things. I hated suits, too. But my mum made me wear them."

Mrs Kathleen Perks: "I can't remember him ever losing his temper. We found out later that when something annoyed Bill, he would go up to his bedroom and read the Bible. He was closely connected with our local church, and a member of the choir for ten years."

• "When I was in junior school, I always wanted to be a musician, to be in a band. But I knew it was so impossible, so unlikely, that I just dismissed it completely from my mind."

• "When I left Beckenham Grammar School, I hadn't the faintest idea what I wanted to do. I didn't excel at anything, except maths. I went to a firm in Lewisham and started as nothing in a little office job. I really was nothing. I got all the odds and ends that other people didn't want to do. I'd been there two years when I decided to pack it in. I left and went to work for a big department store in Penge."

• "The first person I heard who I thought was really amazing was Les Paul. He was the one who turned me on to the sound of guitar music. I was listening to singers before that . . . Johnny Ray was one of the first to make me really open my ears. That was like two or three years before Elvis. Then rock'n'roll appeared, and it was a whole other thing. Just about then, when I was 18, I was called up for the National Service and had to serve two or three years in the Royal Air Force in Germany. When I got there I started listening to American broadcasts, which we used to pick up in the British sector. Suddenly I was hearing things like the Grand Ole Opry show when I'd never heard country music before . . . all the great singers like Roy Acuff and Flatt & Scruggs. Then we started to hear things by Bill Haley and Elvis, and then Little Richard and Chuck Berry. (They) really blew me away. I saw Berry in a film called *Rock, Rock, Rock* where he was playing 'You Can't Catch Me' and I was completely won over."

Mrs Kathleen Perks: "I remember telling them that if they learned to play an instrument, they would never be short of a pound."

• "I became inspired, bought an acoustic guitar from a local German shop, and came back to the camp and put a little band together."

• "I left just after that and returned to England as a civilian and tried to put another band together with local friends. We played in South East London and Essex and Surrey and we were playing all the kind of R&B/rock'n'roll stuff, all the black stuff really – Sam Cooke, Jackie Wilson, Lloyd Price, Fats Domino, Chuck Berry – as opposed to the white pop music."

In 1961, Bill, by now playing with The Cliftons, switched from guitar to bass.

• "I built my own bass guitar because we didn't have money to buy guitars in those days. And bass guitars weren't that common anyway. I got an old guitar, completely chopped it up, took it to bits, changed the shape of it, put different electrics in, and just made myself a mini bass guitar way before fretless basses were invented."

• "I had a couple of bands, formed from local kids, people I was working with or lived round the corner. None of us could play very well. All the local bands were playing Shadows stuff, Ventures stuff, all those semi-instrumental groups, because there were never really any good singers about. So most of the bands had an echo chamber and a good lead guitarist who could play 'FBI' and all that shit, and experiment and try and play some American music, but it was always the wrong stuff – it was 'Poetry In Motion' and 'Personality' and all those things – whereas the band I was trying to get together, we were trying to play the R&B kind of American music that was coming over, more like Little Richard, the Coasters, Chuck Berry, Fats Domino, black artists, not the Pat Boones and the Bobby Vees."

9

2

Good Times, Bad Times

Summer 1961: Mick joins his first band, Little Boy Blue & The Blue Boys – a name inspired by Bobby 'Blue' Bland. According to a custom-made press release, the line-up consists of: "Vocals – Mike Jagger, Drums – Dick Taylor, Guitar – Bob Beckwith, Miscellaneous background noises – Alan Etherington."

TUESDAY, 25 OCTOBER 1961

Mick and Keith bump into each other on the platform on Dartford Station. Among the records under Mick's arm are two recently released American R&B sets, Chuck Berry's Rockin' At The Hops *and* The Best Of Muddy Waters.

Keith: "I was going to Sidcup Art College, and it just so happened that the particular train I had to take was the same one as Mick caught to go to the London School of Economics, although we didn't normally catch the same train . . .

"Under his arm he has four or five albums. I haven't seen him since the time I bought an ice cream off him and we haven't hung around since the time we were five, six, ten years. We recognised each other straight off. 'Hi, man,' I say. 'Where ya going?' he says. And under his arm, he's got Chuck Berry and Little Walter, Muddy Waters. 'You're into Chuck Berry, man, really?' That's a coincidence . . ."

Mick: "We're very close, and always have been. He was born my brother by accident by different parents . . ."

Mrs Doris Richards: "I remember the night Keith came in from art school and told me he'd met Mick at the station that morning. He was really excited about that meeting. He'd been playing guitar for ages, but always on his own. He was too shy to join in with anybody else, although Dick Taylor had often asked him."

10

AUTUMN 1961

Keith joins Little Boy Blue & The Blue Boys.

Mick: "I used to go round his house and play records and guitar, then after that we'd go to other people's houses. We just used to play anything . . . Chuck Berry stuff."

Dick Taylor: "Keith sounded great – but he wasn't flash. When he came in, you could feel something holding the band together."

Mrs Eva Jagger: "I don't think Mick considered making music his career until he started practising with Keith Richard and Dick Taylor. I was very worried when Mick first started out. Sometimes they all came around here to practise. A nice bunch of lads. There seemed no future to it at all, and it was taking up all his time."

Chris Jagger: "When Keith and Dick came, Mick gave up the guitar and thought more about playing the harmonica and singing."

Dick Taylor: "We never even *thought* of playing to other people. We thought we were the only people in England who'd ever *heard* of R&B."

Mrs Eva Jagger: "We used to sit in the next room listening to their band play and just crease up with laughter. It was lovely but so loud. I always heard more of Mick than I saw of him."

In May 1995, a 13-song reel-to-reel tape, recorded by Little Boy Blue & The Blue Boys during the winter of 1961, was auctioned at Christie's in London. Among the songs included, in glorious mono, were two versions apiece of Chuck Berry's 'Beautiful Delilah', 'Little Queenie' and 'Around And Around', Berry's 'Down The Road Apiece' and 'Johnny B. Goode', two attempts at Billy Boy Arnold's 'I Ain't Got You' and a take on Richie Valens' recent novelty hit, 'La Bamba'. The tape's 'mystery' buyer, for a sum in excess of £60,000, was none other than one-time Blue Boy vocalist, Mick Jagger. The vendor, a Blue Boy who preferred to remain anonymous, spoke to writer Peter Doggett about this historic slice of pre-Stones history.

"They wanted to know what they sounded like, so that they could get better. I had access to my parents' reel-to-reel recorder, so I volunteered to tape some of their rehearsals. 'La Bamba' was a favourite record of Mick's. He got all the words off the record, in pseudo-Spanish – they sounded like Spanish, but weren't real words at all. Keith struck me very much as an introvert when I first met him. He seemed to be more interested in his guitar than anything else."

THURSDAY, 15 MARCH 1962

Tucked away in the Melody Maker *classified ads section is the following advert.*

ALEXIS KORNER'S BLUES INCORPORATED
The Most Exciting Event Of This Year!
Rhythm And Blues Club
Ealing Club. Ealing Broadway Station. Turn left, cross at Zebra,
and go down steps between ABC Teashop and Jewellers.
Saturday at 7.30 p.m.

Dick Taylor: "One day Keith and I were at art school and we picked up *Melody Maker* and saw an advert announcing that this jazz club in Ealing had started one night a week with Alexis and his musicians, and there was a picture of the group. We showed it to Mick as fast as we could and his reaction, all our reactions, was, 'This can't be happening. This can't be true. Let's go and see what it's all about.'"

Mick: "The Ealing Club was dripping off the roof all the time. It was so wet that sometimes we had to put a thing up over the stage, a sort of horrible sheet which was revoltingly dirty, and we put it up over the bandstand so the condensation didn't drip directly on you. It was very dangerous, too, 'cause of all this electricity and all these microphones. I never got a shock . . ."

Keith: "Alexis was packin' 'em in, man. Jus' playing blues. Very similar to Chicago stuff. Heavy atmosphere. Workers and art students, kids who couldn't make the ballrooms with supposedly long hair then. Just when we were getting together, we read this little thing about a rhythm and blues club starting in Ealing. 'Let's get up to this place and find out what's happening.' There was this amazing old cat playing harp – Cyril Davies . . . So we went up there."

Alexis Korner: "We began playing at the Ealing Club, which was a drinking club. The Ealing Club was Mick and Keith's first appearance on the scene. We played R&B there, which always had one night a week of trad jazz, and the jazz people didn't like us at all . . . The club held only 200 when you packed them in, and there were only about 100 people in all of London into the blues, and all of them showed up at the club that first Saturday night . . . Our membership lists had gone up to 800 at the end of the fourth week with more people showing up than could get in. The word started getting around London that there was something strange happening at this club in Ealing."

Charlie: "Paul Jones used to come down from Oxford, Brian Jones from

Cheltenham, and Eric Burdon from Newcastle – just to hear Blues Incorporated."

SUNDAY, 7 APRIL 1962

Alexis Korner's Blues Incorporated are joined onstage by Brian Jones, then going under the pseudonym Elmo Lewis, in homage to slide guitar blues master, Elmore James.

Alexis Korner: "We got a guest to play some guitar. He comes from Cheltenham, all the way up from Cheltenham, just to play for ya!"

Keith: "The first or the second time, Mick and I were sittin' there. Suddenly, it's Elmore James, this cat, man. And it's Brian, man, he's sittin' on his little . . . he's bent over . . . da-da-da, da-da-da . . . I said, 'What? What the fuck?' Playing bar slide guitar. We get into Brian after he finishes 'Dust My Blues'. He's really fantastic and a gas. We speak to Brian. He's been doin' the same as we'd been doin' . . . thinkin' he was the only cat in the world who was doin' it."

Charlie: "The first time I met Brian he had a guitar in his hand. My first impression of him was just of a very good guitar player."

Jones also had an occasional spot at the Ealing Club with his old pal from Oxford.

Dick Taylor: "They were a duo, Brian and Paul Jones. Paul wore sunglasses and sang. Brian played slide guitar. Cyril Davies introduced them as Elmo Lewis and P.P. 'Perpetually Pissed' Jones."

Pianist Ian 'Stu' Stewart, was another familiar face at the Ealing Club's jam sessions.

Keith: "I never heard a white piano like that before. Real Albert Ammons stuff. He blew my mind, too."

Charlie: "I met Alexis in a club somewhere and he asked me if I'd play drums for him. A friend of mine, Andy Webb, said I should join the band, but I had to go to Denmark to work in design, so I sort of lost touch with things. While I was away, Alexis formed his band, and I came back to England with Andy. I joined the band with Cyril Davies, and Andy used to sing with us. We had some great guys in the band with us, like Jack Bruce. These guys knew what they were doing. We were playing at a club in Ealing and they, Brian, Mick and Keith, used to come along and sometimes sit in."

Alexis Korner: "Brian used to appear and sleep on our floor and come round the clubs if I was playing anywhere, and then go back again on Sunday night. At the same time I was getting visits from Mick Jagger and

Keith Richard, and Brian met them at our flat one night. Charlie Watts was my drummer at the time, so that was the Stones."

Chris Barber: "Alexis is a guy who makes a living; his *raison d'être* in life is to bring people together. To get groups together . . . He's made a lot of things happen."

Alexis Korner: "Mick Jagger sent me some tapes, I think that's how we made contact, and I told him to come on over. So he came up from Dartford and we talked about Chuck and Bo Diddley, and I talked about Muddy (Waters) and Slim (Harpo) and Robert Johnson, people like that. We decided we dug each other and he used to come up with Keith and talk."

Keith: "It was really Mick and myself that turned Brian onto rhythm and blues because before that he was primarily into jazz. He hadn't heard people like Slim Harpo, Jimmy Reed and Bo Diddley, he was into T-Bone Walker and that sort of scene and he'd been in a Dixieland jazz band before. Mick and I were more into the Chuck Berry thing."

Brian: "Alexis Korner started the whole thing off . . . He introduced me to Mick and Keith at a club in West London and it's really true that he is responsible for the birth of The Rolling Stones inasmuch as he introduced us."

Keith: "It was Brian's band in the beginning. When we met Brian, he was the only one around really interested in forming a band. Mick and I were just interested in playing. We hadn't got to the point of thinking about putting a real band together."

Long John Baldry: "Lots of kids used to come down for a blow, people like Mick Jagger, Brian Jones, Keith Richards, and that's basically how The Rolling Stones started. Mick worked with us for a while as a vocalist, and Charlie Watts was on drums. We were called Blues Incorporated. Mick was basically all lips and ears, 'cause he had short hair and he has got quite big ears."

Alexis Korner: "By the end of the fourth week (at Ealing), Harold Pendleton, who managed the Marquee, came round to take a look. He had a spare Thursday night at the Marquee, where nothing worked to bring in the audience, so he offered it to us. We took it. What happened on that first Thursday night was the original 120-odd members of the Ealing Club showed up, but the Marquee was bigger and they didn't look like many people. But bit by bit . . . the people who started coming in were young kids who didn't dig the trad jazz scene or the pop scene, and who wanted the excitement of something pretty raw. And that's exactly what we provided. They used to stand on the tables and rock and dance and shout, and by the eighth week or so, we were doing 350 on Thursday nights and feeling pretty good."

SATURDAY, 19 MAY 1962

"SINGER JOINS KORNER"

Disc magazine carries a small story from the margins of the mainstream music world:
"A 19-year-old Dartford rhythm and blues singer, Mick Jagger, has joined Alexis Korner's group, Blues Incorporated, and will sing with them regularly on their Saturday night dates at Ealing and Thursday sessions at the Marquee Jazz Club, London. Jagger, at present completing a course at the London School of Economics, also plays harmonica."
Mick: "I remember the first time I played with Alexis Korner, I made a pound or ten bob."
Alexis Korner: "Mick used to sing three songs a night. He learned more but was only really sure of three, one of which was a Billy Boy Arnold song, 'Poor Boy', I think it was, and he used to sing one of Chuck's songs and a Muddy Waters song."
Mick: "I wouldn't ever get in key. That was the problem. I was quite often very drunk 'cause I was really nervous . . . The first night I was with Alexis in Ealing I was incredibly nervous 'cause I'd never sung in public before and the second time was singing the first time at the Marquee with Alexis, which was like the same thing only a bit bigger. He used me Thursdays. We used to sing 'Got My Mojo Working'. John Baldry, Paul Jones, they were much taller than me. I was very small."
Alexis Korner: "The thing I noticed about him wasn't his singing. It was the way he threw his hair around. He only had a short haircut, like everyone else's. But, for a kid in a cardigan, that was moving quite excessively . . .
"Round about June, the BBC asked us to do a broadcast. There were seven of us in the band, including Mick, but they'd only pay for six for this broadcast. We had a band meeting and I said to Mick, 'Look, we'll turn it down.' And he said, 'No, no, don't turn it down, because if you do that broadcast we'll have twice as many people in by next week.' . . . So we decided that we'd go ahead with the broadcast and Mick, Brian, Keith, Ian Stewart and a friend – I don't remember who – would get together a group to work the Marquee that night as a support group; John Baldry would get together the lead band. The support group called themselves

The Rolling Stones, the first time the Stones ever played publicly in London."

WEDNESDAY, 11 JULY 1962

"MICK JAGGER FORMS GROUP"

Jazz News *reports on a new development on the close-knit scene:*
"Mick Jagger, R&B vocalist, is taking a rhythm and blues group into the Marquee tomorrow night (Thursday) while Blues Inc. is doing its *Jazz Club* gig.

Called 'The Rolling Stones' ('I hope they don't think we're a rock'n' roll outfit,' says Mick), the line-up is: Jagger (vocal), Keith Richards, Elmo Lewis (guitars), Dick Taylor (bass), 'Stu' (piano), Mick Avery [*sic*] (drums).

A second group under Long John Baldry will also be there."

Mick: "I didn't really expect to go on the broadcast because I was only one of (Korner's) singers . . . Alexis used to sing, so did Cyril (Davies), Long John Baldry, Ronnie Jones, Paul Jones. But the thing is, we didn't have any gigs at all. We had a gig that night but it was the one that Alexis had given us. I think that must have been our very first gig."

Ian Stewart: "The Rolling Stones? I said it was terrible! It sounded like the name of an Irish show band or something that ought to be playing at the Savoy."

Mick: "We only played down the Marquee about half a dozen times. As to who was the leader . . . Well, Brian used to want to be, but nobody really wanted to be the leader of the band – it seemed a rather outmoded idea. Even though we were all working together, Brian desperately wanted to be the leader, but nobody ever accepted him as such. I don't mean with the band, I mean with the kids."

Nicky Hopkins: "In 1962, I joined Cyril Davies, who'd split from Alexis Korner because Korner's band was rather insipid; it wasn't solid Chicago blues, which was what Cyril wanted to get into. We formed the first authentic Chicago blues band and we went down a storm – had the Marquee packed out every Thursday. We had the Stones on as our support band on the 20 minute interval spots. They were good, but I never dreamed they were going to become as big as they did later. Cyril didn't like them because they were playing too modern for him. They were doing Chuck Berry and Bo Diddley – he was doing Muddy Waters and early people. I was with Cyril from October 1962 until May 1963."

LATE SUMMER 1962

The group continues its residency at the Ealing Club, though with future Kinks drummer Mick Avory and bassist Dick Taylor replaced by Cliftons stickman, Tony Chapman and, occasionally, a rhythm section borrowed from an infamous club act.

Mick: "Eventually Alexis got some more work together and we got a group together. We got a drummer from Screamin' Lord Sutch called Carlo (Little) and a bass player from Screamin' Lord Sutch called Ricky and we used to play on Saturday, occasionally under the paternal auspices of Alexis. It got very crowded, incredibly hot, and all kinds of rakes came down and demanded these strange rock'n'roll numbers which they thought we ought to play . . . Drunken people came up wanting to sing 'Ready Teddy'. I used to sing 'Don't Stay Out All Night', 'Bad Boy', 'Ride 'Em Down' sometimes, not mostly, with Keith."

AUTUMN 1962

Avid readers of the Classified Ad pages in various trade publications are greeted with this regularly placed notice:

A shot of rhythm and blues?
THE ROLLIN' STONES
Every Saturday at the Ealing Club
7.30 p.m.–11 p.m.
Opposite Ealing Broadway Station

Meanwhile, the band – or at least its three key members, Brian Jones, Mick Jagger and Keith Richards – move into a two-room flat at 102 Edith Grove, at the down-market end of Chelsea. James Phelge, who was soon to share the flat with the trio, recounted the parlous state of the residence in Phelge's Stones, *his fascinating memoir of life with the band in its infancy.*

Phelge: "The hallway was gloomy and everything seemed brown and dismal as I climbed the lino-covered stairs to the first landing. The kitchen was straight ahead and as I turned left I had my first glimpse of the communal toilet and continued up a few more steps to the next landing. The bedroom was on the right opposite more stairs to the bathroom and the flat above. The lounge was straight ahead . . . it was a complete shambles. Over in the far right-hand corner was an unmade bed looking as if it had just been dumped there. A table covered with dirty plates, cups, knives and other crap stood in the bay window. To my immediate right stood a dark coloured radiogram, the kind where you pulled a flap down on the top half to gain access to the deck and the radio. The flap was down now, sagging under the weight of a pile of records. There were more records on top of the gram and yet more on the floor. The carpet had probably been coloured once but now it was just grime, an almost perfect match for the wallpaper, which was hanging off in places."

Keith: "Brian was the one who kept us all together then. Mick was still going to school. I'd dropped out. So we decided we'd got to live in London to get it together. Time to break loose. So everybody left home, upped and got this pad in London, Chelsea. Just Mick and myself and Brian.

"We had the middle floor. The top floor was two schoolteachers trying to keep a straight life. God knows how they managed it. Two guys trainin' to be schoolteachers; they used to throw these bottle parties. All these weirdos, we used to think they were weirdos havin' their little parties up there, all dancing around to Duke Ellington. Then when they'd zonked out, we'd go up there and nick all the bottles. Get a big bag, Brian and I, get all the beer bottles and the next day, we'd take 'em to the pub to get the money on 'em."

Brian: "We weren't layabouts. We were so genuinely dedicated to our music that everything we did had to be connected with rhythm and blues. We starved, of course. Mick Jagger had a little cash because he had a grant to attend college. Sometimes during the day, when the money had run out, Keith Richard and I would swipe food from our friends' flats in the building. An egg here, some bread there. It all helped. My nerves suffered from all this, but at least it meant we could dig R&B all day."

Brian was especially productive during these early months at Edith Grove . . .
Keith: "I went out one morning and came back in the evening and Brian was blowing harp, man. He's got it together. He's standing at the top of the stairs sayin', 'Listen to this,' whooooow, wooow. All these blues notes comin' out. 'I've learned how to do it. I've figured it out.' So then he started to really work on the harp. He dropped the guitar. He still dug to play it and was still into it and played very well, but the harp became his thing."

WEDNESDAY, 31 OCTOBER 1962

Jazz News *publishes a letter sent in by an earnest young R&B fan.*
"It appears there exists in this country a growing confusion as to exactly what form of music the term 'Rhythm & Blues' applies to. There

further appears to be a movement here to promote what would be better termed 'Soul Jazz' as Rhythm & Blues. Surely we must accept that R&B is the American city Negro's 'pop' music – nothing more, nothing less.

"Rhythm & Blues can hardly be considered a form of jazz. It is not based on improvisation as is the latter. The impact is, and can only be, emotional. It would be ludicrous if the same type of pseudo-intellectual snobbery that one unfortunately finds contaminating the jazz scene were to be applied to anything as basic and vital as Rhythm & Blues.

"It must be apparent that Rock'n'Roll has a far greater affinity for R&B than the latter has for jazz, insofar as Rock is a direct corruption of Rhythm and Blues, whereas jazz is Negro music on a different plane, intellectually higher, though emotionally less intense."

Brian Jones
London, SW10
(Brian Jones plays guitar with The Rollin' Stones)"

Keith: "We certainly didn't wanna be rock'n'roll stars. That was just too tacky."

FRIDAY, 7 DECEMBER 1962

Having completed their first proper recording session in October, the Rollin' Stones audition Bill Wyman at the Wetherby Arms, World's End, Chelsea with a view to him becoming the group's bassist.

Bill: "My drummer Tony Chapman had answered an ad from Mick, Keith and Brian in one of the music papers, and he came back the next day and said, 'It's not bad actually, it's a very different kind of music. I've made a tape copy and I thought you'd like to hear it, because they haven't got a bass player either' – it must've been just after Dick Taylor split. So I listened to this stuff and there were about four or five Jimmy Reed tracks, and I thought it was very interesting and unusual, and it gave me a weird feeling to listen to it, but an excited feeling. But I thought, 'It's *so* slow,' because we were playing all the uptempo, semi-black stuff. So I said, 'All right, I'll go up . . .

"I didn't know whether I should put my best suit on or not . . .

"It was snowing and cold, but I turned up at this horrible pub where there was a rehearsal hall, and nobody spoke to me for two hours. Mick said 'Hello' to me when I arrived and Stu, who was playing piano, was nice, but Brian and Keith never spoke to me until they found out I had some cigarettes. They never had any money so I bought them each a drink and we were all mates . . .

"I practised with them and sat in for a few numbers. We went through loads of tunes and messed about a lot. It wasn't a real audition . . . They didn't like me, but I had a good amplifier, and they were badly in need of amplifiers at that time! The two they had were broken and torn inside. I had a good amp, a Vox AC-30. But quite honestly I didn't like their music very much. They were into pure R&B. I had been playing hard rock. Anyway, they kept me on. Later, when they were going to get rid of me, I think I clicked or something and I stayed. I must have just fitted in."

Brian: "When Bill first joined us he wasn't like the rest of us. He had greasy hair and dressed rather peculiarly. Keith and I used to laugh at him and not take him too seriously."

Mrs Kathleen Perks: "When he met up with the other Stones, we weren't too happy at first, because he had a wife and baby to support, though all that was a secret at the time."

WEDNESDAY, 2 JANUARY 1963

Brian Jones once again puts pen to paper on behalf of the Stones in a bid to secure the interests of BBC Radio.

"Dear Sir,

I am writing on behalf of the 'Rolling Stones' Rhythm and Blues band. We have noticed recently in the musical press that you are seeking fresh talent for *Jazz Club*.

"We have West-End residencies at the Flamingo jazz club on Mondays, and at the Marquee jazz club on Thursdays, as well as several other suburban residencies. We already have a large following in the London area and, in view of the vast increase of interest in Rhythm and Blues in Britain, an exceptionally good future has been predicted for us by many people.

"Our front line consists of: vocal + harmonica (electric), and two guitars, supported by a rhythm section comprising bass, piano, and drums. Our musical policy is simply to produce an authentic Chicago Rhythm and Blues sound, using material of such R&B 'greats' as Muddy·Waters, Howlin' Wolf, Bo Diddley, Jimmy Reed, and many others.

"We wonder if you could possibly arrange for us an audition.

"We look forward eagerly to hearing from you.

Yours faithfully, Brian Jones."

Eager to expand the band's repertoire on a tight budget, Brian isn't averse to asking favours from the odd friend, as evidenced by this letter to blues and soul enthusiast Dave Godin . . .

"102 Edith Grove, London SW10.

Dear Dave,

Herewith the tape on which you very kindly agreed to stick some Reed gear. Couldn't put the blank side on the outside, as I didn't have a spare reel. The one side has Bo Diddley on most of it – it is an Extra Play tape, so you should easily be able to stick *Rockin' With Reed, I Can't Hold Out* and flip (Elmore) and your Reed singles (only ones which aren't duplicated on LPs) on it.

Also, Dave, if you possibly could grab hold of one, could you tape *Just Jimmy*, the latest Reed LP <u>over</u> Bo Diddley. But please don't record over Bo unless it is *Just Jimmy*.

This is really very good of you mate – if there's anything we can do for you – let us know.

Cheers, Brian Jones.

PS. Was it you who wrote to *Disc* some time ago about R&B and mentioning the Savages and us? We never saw it, but we were talking to Ricky Fensen [*sic*] and Carlo Little the other night and they told us about it. We can't think who can have wrote [*sic*] it. Incidentally, Carlo and Rick should be doing quite a few dates with us in the near future. We can do with a solid rockin' rhythm section.

Hope you had a good Christmas."

Mick is also writing letters. However, these are of a more passionate persuasion, directed at Cleo Sylvester, a 17-year-old backing singer with Cyril Davies' band . . .

Mick: "I want somebody to share everything with, someone to respect, not just someone to sleep with. Please make me happy. It's the one thing that's missing in my life right now . . ."

WEDNESDAY, 9 JANUARY 1963

Charlie Watts turns up to see the Stones perform at the Red Lion, Sutton, and is invited to join.

Keith: "We were all a bit in awe of Charlie then. We thought he was much too expensive for us."

Bill: "They asked Tony Chapman, who wasn't a very good drummer, if he would leave, and asked Charlie if he would join permanently."

Alexis Korner: "Charlie Watts, who was still not blowing regularly with anybody, came up to my old lady and said, 'The Stones have asked me to join them, what do you think I should do?' And she said, 'Well, if you're not doing anything else, why don't you? What have you got to lose?' So Charlie joined the Stones."

Charlie: "I liked their spirit and I was getting very involved with rhythm'n'blues. I figured it would be a bit of an experiment for me and a bit of a challenge, too. So I said yes. Lots of my friends had thought I'd gone stark raving mad."

Mrs Lilly Watts: "I was worried when he gave up his job to join The Rolling Stones. He lived at home and we had to keep him. Of course, I hoped that the group would do well – but I never imagined they would be big."

WEDNESDAY, 6 FEBRUARY 1963

Brian Jones introduces himself to Giorgio Gomelsky, who runs a club at the Station Hotel, Richmond, Surrey.

Giorgio Gomelsky: "Brian used to come up to me and say, 'Giorgio, you must come up and hear this band, best band in London, we play rhythm and blues.' I went to see them in Sutton, at the Red Lion. I liked what they were doing. I said, 'Listen, I promised this guy I would give him a job but the first time he goofs, you're in.' And then came that famous day. (Resident band) Dave Hunt had a terrible problem getting everybody together, he just wasn't together, and the next Sunday they didn't turn up. I was there, it was snowing, and they didn't show up. So Monday I called Ian Stewart: 'Tell everybody in the band you guys are on next Sunday.'"

Keith: "The first cat we had who looked after the band was Giorgio Gomelsky. He was a kind person was Giorgio, because we really didn't care about anybody – just took advantage of everybody. We thought everybody was against us."

Giorgio Gomelsky: "I had a verbal agreement with them to be their manager – and that agreement suited me fine. I worked as hard as I could for the boys for a number of reasons. First they were doing a great job for my club. Second, they were playing a brand of music that appealed to me personally and had fired me with an ambition to see it better appreciated here in Britain. And third, I was fed up with a lot of the insipid rubbish that was making the Top 20."

SATURDAY, 23 FEBRUARY 1963

Giorgio Gomelsky places the first of a series of extravagantly worded small ads in the listing pages for jazz clubs in Melody Maker.
"Sunday . . . RICHMOND, Station Hotel: RHYTHM 'N' BLUES with the inimitable, incomparable, exhilarating Rollin' Stones."

Subsequent hyper-excitable descriptions include:
"The unprecedented, incontestable, inexhaustible purveyors of spontaneous combustion The Rollin' Stones"
"Hyperheterodox Rhythm'n'Blues Voluptuousness from Tempestuously transporting Rollin' Stones"
"Unrepressed Rhythm 'n' Blues with unmitigating, ebullient, perturbing Rollin' Stones"
and . . .
"Warning – R&B sound barrier to be broken by Rolling Stones"

Pat Andrews, mother of Brian's son Julian, remembered the journeys from Edith Grove to Richmond – and the band's dashing new manager.
"We used to get to the Crawdaddy by train. The instruments usually went by van, which Stu used to drive . . . I used to think Giorgio Gomelsky was wonderful, so tall and exuberant, like he'd just stepped out of a Hollywood movie."
Giorgio Gomelsky: "The Stones weren't the first people into the blues in England. Alexis Korner and Cyril Davies were, but the Stones were the first ones who were young."

SATURDAY, 13 APRIL 1963

The group's first press profile appears in the Richmond and Twickenham Times. *Brian Jones carries the clipping with him for months.*
"Barry May writes about the 'new' rhythm and blues
JAZZ
Nowadays it means the music that goes round and around – or the Rollin' Stones are gathering them in . . .
"A musical magnet is drawing the jazz beatniks away from Eel Pie Island, Twickenham, to a new Mecca in Richmond.
"The attraction is the new Crawdaddy Rhythm and Blues club at the Station Hotel, Kew Road – the first club of its kind in an area of flourishing modern and traditional jazz haunts.
"Rhythm and blues, gaining more popularity every week, is replacing

'traddypop' all over the country, and even persuading the more sedate modernists to leave their plush clubs. The deep, earthy sound produced at the hotel on Sunday evenings is typical of the best of rhythm and blues that gives all who hear it an irresistible urge to 'stand up and move' . . .

". . . Rhythm and blues has been described as 'pepped-up' blues and 'original American Negro pop-music'. But the sound also has its modern-ist leaning . . .

"Rhythm and blues can claim to provide a happy medium for young jazz fans. Modernists and 'traddies' can be seen side by side at the Station Hotel, listening to resident group, the Rollin' Stones.

"From a meagre 50 or so on the club's first night, less than two months ago, attendances have rocketed by an average of 50 a week to last Sunday's record of 320 . . .

"The Rollin' Stones, a six-piece group, were formed just 10 months ago.

"Since then they have played in more than a dozen London rhythm and blues clubs, as well as appearances at the West End Marquee Club.

"Semi-professionals now, although the average age is only 20, the day-time occupations of its members are as varied as the instruments they play.

"Driving force behind the group is London School of Economics student Mick Jagger, vocal and harmonica. He is backed by architect Brian Jones (guitar, harmonica, maracas), guitarist Keith Richards, an art student, bass guitarist Bill Wyman, a representative, drummer Charlie Watts, a designer, and, on piano, Ian Stewart.

"Although 'pop' numbers are sometimes played, songs written and recorded by the American rhythm and blues guitarist Bo Diddley are the Rollin' Stones' favourites. Their appreciation of him is carried to the extent of naming the club after a dance Bo Diddley has invented, the 'craw-daddy'.

"The 300 and more in their late teens and early 20s who pack the club on Sunday nights do a dance similar to the craw-daddy. But most impro-vise on a wildly remote form of the hully-gully similar to the twist.

"For those less inclined to express their feelings for the music, physi-cally, the Rollin' Stones also provide visual entertainment.

"Hair worn Piltdown-style, brushed forward from the crown like the Beatles pop group – 'We looked like this before they became famous' – the rhythm section, piano, drums and bass guitar provide a warm, steady backing for the blues of the harmonicas and lead guitars.

"Save for the swaying forms of the group on the spotlit stage, the room is in darkness. A patch of light from the entrance doors catches the sweating dancers and those who are slumped on the floor where chairs have not been provided . . .

"Outside in the bar the long hair, suede jackets, gaucho trousers and Chelsea boots rub shoulders with the Station Hotel's 'regulars' resulting in whispered mocking, though not unfriendly remarks about the 'funny' clothes.

"The Rollin' Stones and the Crawdaddy Club have put the Station Hotel on the map, as far as youngsters are concerned.

"How sad and unfortunate that it is destined to be soon wiped off the map. Demolished, flattened to the ground and replaced with a brand new public house.

"THE CRAWDADDY CLUB WILL BE FORCED TO LOOK FOR ANOTHER WEEKLY STAGE – AND THE ROLLIN' STONES WILL GO ON ROLLIN'."

Giorgio Gomelsky: "The Crawdaddy in Richmond was 12 miles away on the outskirts of London . . . It was in a pub. You just had to walk out of the room and buy a drink at the bar in the front. What we used to call a club was really the back room of a pub . . .

"The last 45 minutes used to be the ritual, tribal thing. They would do, like, 'Pretty Thing' or 'The Crawdad' for 20 minutes, it would be hypnotic . . . The Stones were nothing but ritual really. In the end people just went berserk . . . I cannot tell you the excitement that place was in those months. It was, like, all of a sudden. Man, you hit the fucking civilisation right on the nail!"

Mick: "The twitch business really comes from a regular club session we do at Richmond, near London. It gets so crowded that all the fans can do is stand and twitch. They can't dance because there isn't much room. We believe that there is a lot of room for the rhythm'n'blues sound broadly patterned on the type of music put down by Chuck Berry."

SUNDAY, 14 APRIL 1963

The Beatles, who had been filming nearby at Teddington Studios earlier in the day, drop by at the Station Hotel to see what all the fuss is about.

Giorgio Gomelsky: "I said, 'You've got to come and see this band when you finish recording the show. It's on your way back.' I didn't tell the Stones until that night. The Stones had been doing their afternoon stint at Studio 51 and arrived, as usual, at the Crawdaddy around six, where they'd have a beer and a sandwich. That's when I told them, 'Hey, something nice might happen today. The Beatles might come . . .'"

Midway through the first set, four darkly dressed figures appear at the club doorway.

James Phelge: "I saw Giorgio fuss them past his entrance table into the hall and they then stood at the left-hand side of the stage and watched the Stones. Very soon the word spread around the hall: 'The Beatles are here.'"

Pat Andrews: "Brian told me they were coming down, and asked me if I could put them somewhere where they could see. It was one of the scariest moments of my life. I remember seeing this leather cap coming round the door. I think it was Ringo. They were all dressed in black leather, and I hid them in the shadows."

Bill: "They were dressed identically in long leather overcoats. I became very nervous, and said to myself, 'Shit, that's the *Beatles*.'"

Charlie: "I don't suppose they came down just to see us. They can't like our faces. They must like the music."

George Harrison: "It was a real rave. The audience shouted and screamed and danced on tables. They were doing a dance that no one had seen up till then, but we now all know as the Shake. The beat the Stones laid down was so solid it shook off the walls and seemed to move right inside your head. A great sound."

Pat Andrews: "After the show, we all went back to the Edith Grove flat. That was when John Lennon told me that he also had a son called Julian, the same name that Brian had given to our son."

TUESDAY, 23 APRIL 1963

The group auditions for BBC Radio, with Ricky Fenstone and Carlo Little sitting in for Bill and Charlie, who are still committed to their day jobs. David Dore, assistant to BBC Light Booking Manager, later breaks the bad news:
". . . After being played to our Production Panel with a view to General Broadcasting, the performance was not considered suitable for our purposes."

SUNDAY, 28 APRIL 1963

Andrew Loog Oldham – who'd already made the decision to become "a nasty little upstart tycoon shit" – catches the Rolling Stones at the Station Hotel, Richmond.
Andrew Oldham: "I was working for (Brian) Epstein at the time. I was handling the press side for him from the record after the Beatles' 'Love Me Do', (which was) 'Please Please Me'. Then I did the publicity for the Beatles' next single ('From Me To You'). One evening I was drinking with an

editor of one of the pop papers (Peter Jones of *Record Mirror*) down in Shaftesbury Avenue and he told me I should go and see this group down in Richmond. It was as simple as that. I was probably 48 hours ahead of the rest of the business in getting there. But that's the way God planned it . . .

"They made an immediate impact on me and my first reaction was, 'This is it!' I felt they were magic. I saw that they had a unique style. The combination of music and sex was something I had never encountered in any other group, and the surprising thing was that you could take them as they were, without asking them to change their clothes, hairstyle or anything else . . . In just a few months the country would need an opposite to what the Beatles were doing."

WEDNESDAY, 1 MAY 1963

The Stones sign a three-year management deal with Oldham and business partner Eric Easton. At Oldham's prompting, sixth Stone Ian Stewart is quietly dropped from the line-up.
Ian Stewart: "I left for one or two reasons that aren't worth going into now, but those early days were odd mixtures of frustration and elation. I've a feeling I wasn't cut out to be a pioneer. I never looked upon the group as being a long-term proposition for me as a musician."
Norman Jopling: "I wasn't surprised when Andrew (Oldham) threw Ian Stewart out. He was a beautiful guy, but you could see he didn't fit visually."

The new management team forms the Impact Sound production company.
Eric Easton: "This wasn't a vote of no confidence in the existing companies. But Andrew and I felt that the Stones *were* ahead of their time and therefore it was expecting a lot for ordinary A&R men to see eye to eye with the sounds they were producing. By doing the whole thing ourselves, we had complete control."

MONDAY, 6 MAY 1963

The group signs a two-year deal with Decca Records.
Eric Easton: "Dick Rowe, at Decca, was obviously going to be our man. He'd heard about the boys in advance, anyway – and he was anxious to find a new star group for the company, especially as he had put up with a lot of kidding because he had failed to sign the Beatles."

Dick Rowe: "As I had turned down the Beatles, I didn't want to make the same mistake again."

FRIDAY, 10 MAY 1963

The band records their first single, 'Come On', at Olympic Studios, central London. Andrew Oldham is the record's producer:
"Look, this is the first recording session I've ever handled. I don't know anything at all about music, but I'm sure I know the right sort of sound which might prove commercial. Let's just play it by ear and not get too panicky about it all. Let's also remember that we've got the studio for three hours – and that it's all costing money (to the engineer) . . . You mix it. I'll drop in and pick it up in the morning."
Mr Lewis Jones: "I clearly remember (Brian) ringing me up almost speechless with excitement, saying that they were going to have a record produced. I didn't really realise the significance of it. But of course this was the record 'Come On', which started the snowball which got bigger and bigger."

SATURDAY, 11 MAY 1963

"THE ROLLING STONES – GENUINE R&B"

Record Mirror's Norman Jopling writes the first proper music press profile of the band:
"As the Trad scene gradually subsides, promoters of all kinds of teen-beat entertainments heave a sigh of relief that they've found something to take its place. It's Rhythm and Blues, of course. And the number of R&B clubs that have suddenly sprung up is nothing short of fantastic.

"At the Station Hotel, Kew Road, the hip kids throw themselves about to the new 'jungle music' like they never did in the more restrained days of Trad.

"And the combo they writhe and twist to is called The Rolling Stones. Maybe you haven't heard of them – if you live far from London, the odds are you haven't.

"But by gad you will! The Stones are destined to be the biggest group in the R&B scene, if that scene continues to flourish. Three months ago only fifty people turned up to see the group. Now (Giorgio) Gomelsky has to close the doors at an early hour – with over four hundred fans crowding the hall . . .

"Those fans quickly lose their inhibitions and contort themselves to truly exciting music. Fact is that, unlike all the other R&B groups worthy of the name, The Rolling Stones have a definite visual appeal. They aren't like the jazzmen who were doing trad a few months ago and who had converted their act to keep up with the times. They are genuine R&B fanatics themselves and they sing and play in a way that one would have expected more from a coloured US group than a bunch of wild, exciting white boys who have the fans screaming and listening to them.

". . . They can also get the sound that Bo Diddley gets – no mean achievement. The group themselves are all red-hot when it comes to US beat discs. They know their R&B numbers inside out and have a repertoire of about eighty songs, most of them ones which the real R&B fans know and love.

"But despite the fact that their R&B has a superficial resemblance to rock'n'roll, fans of the hit parade music would not find any familiar material performed by The Rolling Stones. And the boys do not use original material – only the American stuff. 'After all,' they say, 'can you imagine, a British-composed R&B number – it just wouldn't make it.'"

Eric Easton: "I'd only just moved into our offices when a journalist told me about this young publicist, Andrew Oldham. He thought Andy could use a little help, find somewhere to park his feet in London. It seemed he was a very lively young man, so I told him to come round and see me. We had a spare room in the office and I reckoned that it wouldn't do any harm to give this character a helping hand. It worked out fine. I talked over the business with him and we felt we might be in at the start of a useful partnership on the agency and management side."

Eric Easton: "Are you the leader?"

Brian: "Yes."

Eric Easton: "Well, would you be interested in having a chat about what can be done for the group?"

Norman Jopling: "Brian was very much the leader. He continued to do much of the PR for months afterwards. He was a whirlwind of energy, absolutely charming."

Brian may have given the group its name, and been the prime mover in the Stones' formation, but the rest of the Stones no longer regard him as leader. However, Alexis Korner remembers Jones possessing a special magic during the group's early days:

"He'd learned how to *bait* an audience long before anything like that occurred to Mick. You should have seen those kids' reaction when Brian picked up a tambourine and gave it one tiny little shake in their faces."

JUNE 1963

Brian Jones describes fellow Stone Bill Wyman in less than flattering terms to fan club secretary Doreen Pettifer: "Bass, works during the day as storekeeper or something equally horrible. Only member of band married, only one who'll ever be married."

Weeks later, Bill quits his job and turns pro.
Bill: "I was in line for a good job. There was one person above me, then the manager. I had a good future, and they all asked me not to leave when I began to get on The Rolling Stones kick."

. . . and Mick tells his mum he's not going back to college.
Mrs Eva Jagger: "He told me he was throwing up his university course. For months on end, I seemed to lose touch with him . . . He suddenly realised that though he could still become a lawyer or a politician, which was what I thought he would be, the rewards would come so late in life that he'd be too old to enjoy them. Mick suddenly wanted to join the 'get-rich-quick' stakes."

The press soon begins to notice that The Rolling Stones don't dress in the manner of traditional showbiz acts.
Brian: "If people don't like us as we are, well that's too bad. We're not thinking of changing, thanks very much. We've been the way we are for much too long to think of kowtowing to fancy folk who think we should start tarting ourselves up with mohair suits and short hair."

FRIDAY, 7 JUNE 1963

The first Rolling Stones single, 'Come On', is released in the same week that the Chuck Berry Twist LP (which includes 'Come On') features in the Top 20 LP chart. Press reaction is essentially favourable, with one or two reservations . . .
"There's such a rush on for this sort of group noise that I believe this quintet will be making plenty of room for themselves," says *Disc*. "I particularly like Brian Jones' work on mouth organ."
In *Record Mirror*, Norman Jopling says, "The disc doesn't sound like the Rolling Stones. It's good, punchy and commercial, but it's not the

fanatical R&B that audiences wait hours to hear. Instead, it's a bluesy commercial group that should make the charts in a smallish way."

However, Craig Douglas, singer and compere of On The Scene with – apparently – "a strong knowledge of Hit Parade trends" begs to differ.
"Very, very ordinary. Can't hear a word they're saying and I don't know what all this is about. If there was a Liverpool accent it might get somewhere, but this is definitely no hit. I dislike it, I'm afraid. Take it off!"
BBC Radio DJ Brian Matthew disagrees and describes the Stones as "A wildly exciting group who deserve to have a big success with their first disc."

The single makes a brief foray into the British Top 30.
Brian: "To be perfectly frank, we were a little surprised ourselves when the record got into the charts. For a time it is hard to associate yourself with the disc when you hear it played on the radio. I suppose you get over this kind of thing in time, but at the moment we are fresh enough to the business to enjoy all the little kicks."

SATURDAY, 8 JUNE 1963

Brian explains the group's devotion to Chuck Berry.
"The ones we do are 'Bye Bye Johnny', 'Down The Road Apiece' and Chuck's interpretation of the Nat 'King' Cole oldie, 'Route 66' – contained on his *Juke Box Hits* LP. But we also do a lot of Bo Diddley numbers. Things like 'Diddley Daddy', 'Pretty Thing' and, of course, 'Bo Diddley' all go down tremendously well."

Keith is asked why American R&B stars have yet to really take off in popularity.
"They don't make it big over in Britain. I reckon there are three reasons why they don't click with the British teenager fans. One, they're old; two, they're black; three, they're ugly. This image bit is very important – though I must say it doesn't matter to us. But the Americans have helped get things going in Britain . . . their influence is big if their popularity isn't."

THURSDAY, 13 JUNE 1963

"TWITCHING THE NIGHT AWAY"

Patrick Doncaster ("The Daily Mirror's DJ") gives the band their first national press exposure.
"In the half-darkness, the guitars and the drums start to twang and bang. A

31

pulsating rhythm and blues. Shoulder to shoulder on the floor stood 500 youngsters, some in black leather, some in sweaters. You could have boiled an egg in the atmosphere.

"They began to dance. They just stood as they were. Their heads shook violently in what I can only describe as a paroxysm. 'A sudden attack' says the dictionary of this word.

"That's what it looked like in a sweating jazz club that meets in the Station Hotel at Richmond, Surrey. Their feet stamped in tribal style. If they could, the dedicated occasionally put their hands above their heads and clapped in rhythm. In its fervour it was like a revivalist meeting in America's Deep South.

"Responsible for this extraordinary scene in suburban Surrey are five long-haired lads known as The Rolling Stones . . ."

ROLLING STONES GATHER NO MISS . . .

"Rhythm and blues. That's the £ s. d. sound of today. This music with the insistent drum-beat. Driving guitars, and the wild, exciting voices that compel you to go! go! go! has been very popular in America for years. But it's only since the beginning of this year that there has been an amazing increase of rhythm and blues fans, particularly in the Merseyside area . . .

"Liverpool has been named as the Mecca of R&B, closely followed by Manchester. But what has happened to the music-infested streets of London – is there no one in the Smoke to contribute to this 'new' sound?

"We think there is; and we're not alone in this thought.

"A new group was noticed recently at an ordinary dance hall in the ordinary London borough of Battersea. They were more than noticed – they were chased! The crowd raved about them so much that by the end of the evening three record companies were chasing after them with contracts!

"Their names? The Rolling Stones. That's London's answer to the Merseyside Marvels!

"Who would have thought that a name like the Beatles would have become a household word? So what are the chances for The Rolling Stones?

"Their first disc has been rushed out and it's now on sale. It's called 'Come On' – a rocking rhythm and blues number written by Chuck Berry."

SATURDAY, 29 JUNE 1963

It is announced that the band have been added to the bill of a nationwide package tour, beginning in September, together with three visiting American acts – Little Richard, Bo Diddley and The Everly Brothers. The group already has a few ideas on stage presentation.

Mick: "We'll just go wild. Yes, we're having stage gear made, but we don't know what it is yet. We've never worn a uniform in the clubs. It's going to be something very different, though."

Brian: "We won't be going on to do Muddy Waters stuff. We'll stick to Chuck Berry and Bo Diddley. There'll be plenty of beat there."

Brian: "This is a wonderful break for us and we're looking forward to meeting the American duo. For the present, we are coping with plenty of dates in and around the London area and we're very pleased with the way our début disc is selling. We don't hear enough about the London scene in these days of Liverpool domination but we're hoping we'll fly the flag of the capital when we get out on tour."

But, boys, what about all that hair?

Mick: "Art students and college people have had these haircuts for years. They were around when the Beatles were using Brylcreem."

And this 'Beat bandwagon' that everyone's talking about?

Mick: "Some groups are jumping on the bandwagon . . . They're more familiar with The Coasters, The Shirelles and Chuck Berry than with Jimmy Reed or Muddy (Waters). But it doesn't worry us. We'll play the stuff we like for as long as people come to hear it."

SUNDAY, 7 JULY 1963

The Rolling Stones make their television début on ATV's Thank Your Lucky Stars. *Despite exchanging their cardigans and slacks for matching dog-toothed jackets and smart trousers, the performance prompts a deluge of letters to newspapers and television producers.*

"It is disgraceful that long-haired louts such as these should be allowed to appear on television. Their appearance was absolutely disgusting."

"The whole lot of you should be given a good bath, then all that hair should be cut off. I'm not against pop music when it's sung by a nice clean boy like Cliff Richard, but you are a disgrace. Your filthy appearance is likely to corrupt teenagers all over the country."

"I have today seen the most disgusting sight I can remember in all my years as a television fan. The Rolling Stones . . ."

SATURDAY, 10 AUGUST 1963

Three months after his original piece in Record Mirror, *which helped secure the Stones a deal with Decca, Norman Jopling returns with a piece headlined, with no false pride, 'Are We Clairvoyant?'*

Mick: "We don't intend to change our sound now. And although a lot of people have accused us of 'going commercial' by employing a group vocal, we certainly had no thoughts of that when we deviated from our original style. We changed because we found we could embrace a lot more R&B material into our act by having a group vocal as well as a lead supported by a group."

Elsewhere, Mick is a little less defensive.

Mick: "I suppose you could say we've made some concessions, but we still play what we like. We consider ourselves professional amateurs. We still have the enthusiasm to treat the business as an enjoyable pastime, but also the professionalism to realise that you can't turn up late for dates and that sort of thing."

But what does the band think of the 'London versus Liverpool' debate that's been prompted by their success?

Brian: "It's all a load of rubbish. It's all a big thing invented by the news-papers. We are on very friendly terms with the Northern groups and think they've added a lot to the pop scene. Obviously we prefer the Americans, but there hasn't been anything beatier in Britain for a long, long time."

TUESDAY, 10 SEPTEMBER 1963

The Beatles donate a new song, 'I Wanna Be Your Man', to the Stones. A con-temporary fan magazine imaginatively recounts the historic liaison.

"Andrew happened to be walking along Jermyn Street, near London's Piccadilly Circus. Hands in pockets, quick-striding, brow furrowed as he tried to recall the melody line of a song which might be the answer. And a taxi pulled up by the traffic lights. Inside: Paul McCartney and John Lennon, no less. They rammed down the window and yelled to their erstwhile publi-cist. 'Get in, Andy,' they roared. 'We've got something to tell you.' Andrew leapt in. The Beatles had been to a Variety Club Of Great Britain lunch and had a bit of time to kill before they had to start work again.

"'We've got some numbers which might be right for the Stones,' they said. Andrew brightened up. He knew that the Beatles had heard the Stones' work, and knew for sure that they were pretty keen on the sounds created by the boys from the South. 'What's it called?' he asked. Said the Beatles: 'I Wanna Be Your Man'.

"They went on to say that they wondered if the Stones would mind using material written by a 'rival group'. Said Andrew: 'If it's right for the boys, I couldn't care less if it was written by Dorothy Squires. Let's have a listen . . .'"

Mick: "We were rehearsing and Andrew brought Paul and John down. They said they had this tune – they were real hustlers then. So they played it and we thought it sounded pretty commercial, which is what we were looking for, so we did it like Elmore James or something. It was completely crackers, but it was a hit and sounded great onstage."

SATURDAY, 21 SEPTEMBER 1963

Melody Maker announces its 1963 Pop Pollwinners. The Stones make an appearance in the Brightest Hope (British Section) listing.
1. Billy J. Kramer
2. Beatles
3. Freddie & The Dreamers
4. Gerry & The Pacemakers
5. Billie Davis
6. The Rolling Stones
7. Hollies
8. Susan Singer
9. Heinz
10. Julie Grant

SUNDAY, 29 SEPTEMBER 1963

The Stones' first nationwide tour with The Everly Brothers gets underway with two shows at London's New Victoria Theatre.
"Having seen the current Everly Brothers and Bo Diddley package, I think it was a great mistake to put these two acts on the same bill. Many R&B fans left the theatre after The Rolling Stones and Diddley had appeared, and those who stayed chanted for the reappearance of Bo and the Stones – much to the annoyance of the Everly fans . . ."

– B.A. Woodbridge, London SW6

Brian, too, has his misgivings.

"We get the atmosphere going in a club. That is not so easy in a vast theatre, especially when you've got contrasting types of performers on the bill."

Although the tour does have its compensations with the fledgling Stones learning from the greats:
Brian: "Actually playing harmonica with the great Bo Diddley. You don't forget the day when a long-standing dream comes true."

WEDNESDAY, 16 OCTOBER 1963

As the group travels across the Pennines for two shows in Manchester, Brian finally finds time to write to his Home Counties sweetheart, Linda Lawrence.
"My darling Linda,

"I'm so very, very sorry I haven't written until now . . . The tour is proving a great laugh but playing in theatres is definitely a drag. We played in Hull last night at a concert with Johnny Kidd & The Pirates and Heinz. The girls were mad – the screaming nearly split my eardrums – we stole the show. Do you remember The Mindbenders – Wayne Fontana's mob? Well, do you remember the coats they had that night they came to see us? The grey check ones with black collars, pockets, etc – I bought one today – it's real gear. I like it better than my leather one and that's good!

". . . Please be good and faithful and don't forget all about me. I love you more than ever, darling, and I always will."

FRIDAY, 1 NOVEMBER 1963

The Stones' second single, 'I Wanna Be Your Man', is released. Even the Lennon and McCartney connection isn't enough to convince DJ Pete Murray.
"The backing is wild but too prominent. The voices are lost. This may have been the intention but it was not a good one. Well, at least it's a different sound. Is it the boys with the haircuts, The Rolling Stones? This isn't as good as 'Come On' . . ."
Mick: "It's been said we've deserted the original R&B material we did. Let's be honest – we did for a while, especially on 'Come On'. But that was our way of getting accepted. We're back on the good wildies now."

The flip, 'Stoned', credited to the band's Nanker-Phelge publishing company, was, Keith later admits, "nothing more than just a nick off Booker T's 'Green Onions'."

TUESDAY, 17 NOVEMBER 1963

The Stones are introduced to singer Gene Pitney while promoting their latest single on the Thank Your Lucky Stars *television show.*

Mick: "He was singing a number called 'If I Didn't Have A Dime' when we wandered in. We got talking and Gene said he was really brought down by his lack of success in Britain. We'd watched him rehearse the *Stars* show and were all knocked out because he was so professional. This was just before 'Tulsa' started happening so big for him. Eventually we started fooling around with some of our numbers. One in particular Gene dug very much – 'That Girl Belongs To Yesterday'. He told us: 'That's a very nutty thing.' Apparently that was a compliment! We thought no more about it then."

Gene Pitney: "I'd heard The Rolling Stones, been told they were a wild crew and I must say they looked it, with all that long hair. But their song wasn't earthy rhythm'n'blues by any means . . . It's also good for the American scene because it's different from 'Tulsa' . . .

"It took about one hour for the Stones and myself to form what we call our M.A.S. . . . that's our Mutual Admiration Society. I arrived at the TV studios in Birmingham . . . to appear on *Thank Your Lucky Stars*. When my agent told me that The Rolling Stones were also on the bill, I said, 'What's that? A team of acrobats?' The boys made me feel like a million dollars right away. 'Hi! You are Gene Pitney! One American pop singer we really dig.' 'Grab a stool and see what you think of this number we are thinking of recording,' said Mick Jagger. After the TV show we all travelled back to London. I don't think we stopped talking once . . . music, music, music. I mentioned that I hadn't a follow-up to 'Tulsa'. Mick and Keith said, 'Could we try and write you one?' You can imagine how thrilled, and I might add surprised I was when they later sang 'That Girl Belongs To Yesterday' to me.

"One of the main reasons the Stones have become so very successful, apart from having soul, is that they are self-styled and copy no one. They are imitated, and always will be, by others but that's to be expected when you are as big as they are. When you switch on the radio in the middle of a disc, you know right away it's the Stones. And that goes for any stars who have lasting power, from Bing Crosby to the Beatles."

As a promising year for the band ends, the Stones take stock of what they've achieved, not least the scenes of hysteria that have begun to greet their arrival in otherwise tranquil British towns . . .

Brian: "We've been shaken at the mob scenes we've caused. There've been times when we've nearly been torn to pieces. Course we love it. The only thing is that we didn't want to change our image, if you see what I mean. We could afford the tidy trim nowadays. But the hair, well, it's sort of us, isn't it? Without it, we wouldn't look like The Rolling Stones.

"Even at a concert, we'd just go on in our ordinary clothes. We feel more comfortable that way and anyway we don't want to conform to the usual group type of uniform. We don't like looking scruffy but we don't want to look like tailor's dummies either."

Mick: "In the trad boom a couple of years ago, only British bands made any real impression, but look what is happening to R&B today. British and American acts are getting into the charts, and everywhere you go groups are playing it. Even with the trad boom, none of the bands did all that well as far as the hit parade went."

Brian: "We've just provided the right thing at the right time. We've come along with a very raw sort of music where everything was rather sweet, and a new tough element seems to be growing up and we provide a music that has the same sort of vitality. We've come along at the right time with the right thing . . . it's just happened."

And, with their diary for 1964 already filling up, the Stones' bandwagon looks set to continue rolling well into the spring . . .

Brian: "We are going on tour with the Ronettes soon, and after that, there is talk of a continental tour, and a television series. We don't want to play at the Star Club, though. This is because British groups are only booked there to fill in . . . It is all right for experience, but that is all."

SATURDAY, 14 DECEMBER 1963

The Rolling Stones, "the first London group to break through the powerful Liverpool beat barrier", give their verdict on the latest crop of singles in Melody Maker's *regular Blind Date column.*

Elvis Presley – 'Kiss Me Quick'
Keith: "I don't think Elvis cares any more. This isn't much good."
Brian: "Since he left the army he has turned out poor stuff."
Chuck Berry – 'Run Rudolph Run'
Bill: "Marvellous."
Brian: "He's the guv'nor. This will be as big as 'Memphis'."
Keith: "It won't be as big as 'Memphis', but I loved it."

Charlie: "Marvellous record."
Mick: "It hasn't got time before Christmas to be as big as 'Memphis'. Shame."
Danny Delmonte – 'John Kennedy'
Bill: "They didn't waste much time with that."
Brian: "I think it's quite a sincere tribute but the idea is a bit sick."
Keith: "It hasn't a hope of being a hit."
Mick: "Horrible."
Charlie: "In very bad taste."
Interviewer: "Your latest disc is a Lennon-McCartney job. How is the Stones' songwriting team coming along?"
Brian: "Keith and Mick have written a song for Gene Pitney called 'The [*sic*] Girl Belongs To Yesterday'. We're doing fine."

TUESDAY, 7 JANUARY 1964

The Stones' 'Group Scene' tour begins with two shows in Slough, Buckingham-shire. Their co-headliners are US vocal group the Ronettes, protégés of noted US producer Phil Spector, who sends an urgent telegram to the band that simply states: "STAY AWAY FROM MY GIRLS."

And for good reason . . .
Mick: "Those Ronettes just stopped us dead in our tracks. We were just knocked out – by their looks, their sense of humour, everything . . . You couldn't really say the girls have different personalities. Ronnie and Estelle are friendly. In fact, they're all right little darlings!"
Phil Spector: "Those oddballs are just great – get an incredible sound going. Wait till they see them in the States . . . the kids'll flip. If they don't like the sound, they just look at them. That hair, boy, is gonna be one great big asset."

SATURDAY, 11 JANUARY 1964

In a Melody Maker *feature titled 'The Beat Pursuers – The Beat Boys chasing the Beatles', Mick explains the subtle changes in the Stones' musical policy:*
"We have always favoured the music of what we consider the R&B greats – Muddy Waters, Jimmy Reed and so on – and we would like to think that we are helping to give the fans of these artists what they want, as well as doing more commercial numbers."

FRIDAY, 17 JANUARY 1964

The group's début EP, The Rolling Stones, *is released.*

A New Musical Express *critic suggests that:* "Perhaps the most requested number on the EP is the slowest – 'You Better Move On'. But a lot of people have been decrying it as not R&B."

Mick's response is persuasive.

"It is an Arthur Alexander number, and as much R&B as 'Memphis' or 'Road Runner'. We have been using it in our act for ages and it has always gone down well. That's why we decided to record it."

There was little doubt over the style of the other songs on the EP.

Mick: "I can remember buying Barrett Strong's 'Money', which was a really big R&B hit in America, but didn't happen when it came out in England. When we saw that those things were popular, we said, 'Well, let's do that.' So we did."

SATURDAY, 25 JANUARY 1964

Among the "new pop records" reviewed by Paul McCartney in this week's Melody Maker *is George Bean's 'Will You Be My Lover Tonight?', the first official Jagger-Richard composition.*

"It appears to me that they're trying to get that sound like American groups like The Crystals. The song doesn't mean an awful lot. Don't think the voice is very distinctive . . . The record will not be a hit because it is samey . . ."

SATURDAY, 8 FEBRUARY 1964

The band begins a third British tour at the Regal, Edmonton, coming third on the bill behind hit soloists John Leyton and Mike Sarne.

"Welcomed by a tremendous barrage from girls and boys alike, the Stones opened with 'Talkin' 'Bout You' but it was almost lost in the noise from the fans, who quietened down for Mick Jagger's harmonica break in 'Road Runner' which followed.

"The screams did not let up for the slower 'You Better Move On', or 'I Wanna Be Your Man', with which the caveman-like quintet ended."

The same week, Brian Jones of the Rolling Stones answers a few typical questions . . .

Q: "Why Rolling Stones?"

Brian: "We got the name from the words of an old R&B number by Muddy Waters."

Q: "How long have you been a Rolling Stone?"

Brian: "Since we started! Seriously, though, we have been professionals since about last Easter, but of course we were playing the clubs long before that."

Q: "Any word of an LP?"

Brian: "Well, our EP features numbers we used to play at Eel Pie Island and other clubs. I expect our LP will follow the same pattern. New material as well, though. On the whole, the LP is on a 'rhythm-kick with beat supreme'."

Q: "Have you settled on any distinctive Rolling Stones uniform?"

Brian: "No. We just wear what we want to wear. We like to be as casual as possible."

Q: "All bachelors?"

Brian: "Yes!"

Q: "And now for the most important question of all. Your ideas about girls?"

Brian: "I like girls one by one, but not so much in screaming masses. I like them to be intelligent. I also like long, dark hair."

Q: "And the other fellas?"

Mick: "All girls. They must be bright and gay, though."

Keith: "I like them all."

Bill: "Any sort of girl, especially those who like me."

Charlie: "All girls. We all like girls who wear the latest fashions like all this leather gear. I don't like them too way out, though. My own favourites are intelligent blondes."

"REBELS WITH A BEAT"

Ray Coleman begins his profile of the Stones by detailing an encounter with a 42-year-old London cabbie, who asks him . . .

"Was that the Rolling Stones you just left?"

Coleman: "Yes. What do you think of them?"

Cabbie: "A bunch of right 'erberts! 'Ere, aren't they the boys they say are trying to knock the Beatles off the top?"

Coleman adds: "Their image is perfect . . . five dishevelled rebels who have already made a firm imprint on the hit parade, who have gained a huge following among young people, who never wear stage uniforms, and who JUST DON'T CARE!"

Q: "Are you jealous of the Beatles' success?"

Mick: "Yes!"
Rest of group: "No!"

And your image . . .
Mick: "If you've got an image, you sell the records on the image, if you see what I mean and you can always rely on a following whatever you do. But we didn't all sit down and say, 'Right, let's be untidy and not have uniforms and let's grow our hair long like the Beatles,' or anything like that."
Bill: "The image was a thing that just happened. We always carried on like this. People thought when we started that we were so strange to look at. Now we're lumbered with the image."
Keith: "We've always been careless . . . We had a set of uniforms on, but everyone kept losing his suit, so we decided to call it a day and go on as we liked."

The Beatles?
Mick: "Well, I reckon the Beatles have wider acceptance now. They're liked by old people. We could never hope for such acceptance."
Bill: "Do you know, some places we go, they bill us as London's answer to the Beatles. They don't like it when we say we don't do 'Twist And Shout'."
Mick: "Whatever you do, don't say we're knocking the Beatles. They're good mates of ours. We like 'em and they've done so much good for the whole scene."

Are you rebels?
Keith: "We're not deliberately untidy. I think a lot of this 'rebel' thing has been brought up by people thinking too much about it. People like you come up to us and say, 'Are you rebels?' The answer's no."
Charlie: "We like it this way – we like to please ourselves what we do. We don't do this 'big star' bit. We get treated by the fans as just ordinary blokes, and that's good. There's none of this 'fab gear' and all that."

Money?
Andrew Oldham: "About £1,500 a week for personal appearances, that's between them, and excluding record royalties."

Are they sporting 'Beatle' hairstyles?
Keith: "Look, these hairstyles had been quite common down in London long before the Beatles and the rest of the country caught on. At art school, and years ago, ours had always been the same."

Mick: "Look at Jimmy Savile. He had his like it long before others started that style. It's the same with us."

Bill: "And Adam Faith. He had hair like the Beatles years ago, didn't he?"

Keith: "I dunno. I reckon our style came direct from The Three Stooges."

Musical tastes?

Mick: "Charlie likes jazz. He's the only one in the group who does, really."

Bill: "Chuck Berry, Jerry Lee Lewis and Fats Waller."

Mick: "I go for singers like Ben E. King."

Keith: "So do I. And Muddy Waters."

Are the Rolling Stones still an R&B group?

Keith: "We claim to be R&B as much as anyone. We were playing R&B material long before this beat craze got going. You know, the beat craze that's going on at the moment will last longer than a lot of people think. Kids realise that having four or five stars, like a group, is better than having one star and groups are improving tremendously all the time. The Searchers' 'Needles And Pins' is the best record they ever made."

Do you ever experience prejudice from concert promoters?

Keith: "Sometimes. They used to have this attitude of 'That scruffy lot from London who don't turn up on time and are nasty to look at.' "

Bill: "They just think we're layabouts. They call us the ugliest pop group in the country."

Mick: "We could name a few uglier people in the business."

You all smoke . . .

Bill: "The cancer business doesn't scare me."

Keith: "We're not boozers, but we enjoy a drink and fags like anybody else."

Bill: "Let's face it, if you have got to go, you have got to go."

Keith: "I'll probably die of electric shock."

FRIDAY, 14 FEBRUARY 1964

"GROUP PARENTS HATE MAKE BIG HIT"

The Stones' third single, 'Not Fade Away', is released to great success on what is fast becoming dubbed 'The Beat Parade'.

Andrew Oldham: "As far as I'm concerned, when Keith sat in a corner and played those 'Not Fade Away' chords, that was the first song the Stones ever 'wrote' . . . They picked the concept of applying that Bo Diddley thing to it. The way they arranged it was the beginning of the shaping of them as songwriters."

Keith: "We had been working on the number for about five minutes when two of The Hollies turned up, then Gene Pitney arrived. Phil Spector was already there, so everything came to a halt while everyone started talking. When we got around to recording again, Phil had grabbed hold of Mick's maracas and was shaking the daylights out of them. He really had a ball, and it's him you hear on the disc."

Mick: "I suppose I suggested it. I have the song on an EP by Buddy Holly – he always seemed to go in for these Bo Diddley things. For some reason or other, I mentioned it to the rest of them when we started talking about a new single. Well, we all tossed the idea around, and in the end, we thought it was a good 'un because it had a vague tune – which does help commercially, and that's more than you can say for a lot of the tunes in that Diddley style, isn't it?"

Chris Barber: "The Rolling Stones do a splendid job of country blues in the Bo Diddley style. I quite like them."

"The melody is insignificant, but the sound's sensational," reckons *New Musical Express*.

On the flip is a song intriguingly credited to 'Phelge/Spector'.

Andrew Oldham: "After we had done 'Not Fade Away', Phil and Mick disappeared. Nobody noticed they had gone until about five minutes later when they returned, looking very pleased with themselves. They sat down, told me to listen, and played the number they had just written in the outside corridor. It was very good so we decided to use it as the B-side. Mick took hold of his harmonica, Phil found the maracas again, and Gene Pitney and the Stones road manager, Ian Stewart, sat down at the same piano. It was a fantastic scene."

Charlie: "We were well away, with Phil Spector and Mick composing like lunatics and then who should come charging through the door but old Gene Pitney who had stopped off in London for the day on a trip to Italy. And then Graham and Allan of The Hollies turned up. Well, after that nobody could get any work done. We were all bashing away, and carrying on. Gene on the piano, Phil charging around, and Andrew Oldham, our publicity man, waving his arms around conducting and everyone laughing – even me. We just hope you can't hear what was going on during 'Little By Little', because it's a great composition by

Phil and Mick with musical accompaniments by whoever happened to be around at the time."

Another session yields an expletive-filled jam known as 'Andrew's Blues', alias 'Fucking Andrew'. Phil Spector contributes a few choice ad-libs, including the distinctly audible:
"I thought the Rolling Stones were full of shit, then I heard the group. Now I know they're full of shit."

The band see quite a bit of Spector during his British visit . . .
Brian: "We went to this great party our recording company flung in aid of that fab A&R man from the States, Phil Spector. As you know, we certainly go for his sort of sound so it was very interesting talking to him. The Ronettes were along to keep things swinging and we had quite a time talking about the tour we'd just finished with them. After the party, the rest of the boys went off to the theatre, but I was going on with a load of friends to the Scene in Wardour Street for a couple of Shakes and then out again and off to the Flamingo Club. That part of the evening was really the greatest. They had the Cyril Davies Memorial Concert down there with all the really great R&B groups, like Georgie Fame & The Blue Flames and Manfred Mann, The Yardbirds, and The Animals. I can't explain the excitement and the atmosphere down there. All I can say is that in the early hours of the morning we were still digging this real music. That's the sort of music we like playing and it's the sort of music we could listen to all night – and do. People think that when you're playing the scene with this sound every evening yourself, you want to forget about it when you have any free time. But it's not true. We live the music, we really do. And to listen to it being played by people who really know what they're doing and in the right sort of surroundings is the most terrific thing."

FRIDAY, 28 FEBRUARY 1964

News of the 'Stones effect' begins to trouble the popular press, although Judith Simons in the Daily Express *tries the tongue-in-cheek approach.*
"They look like boys whom any self-respecting mum would lock in the bathroom! But The Rolling Stones – five tough, young, London-based music makers with doorstep mouths, pallid cheeks and unkempt hair – are not worried what mums think! For now the Beatles have registered with all age groups, The Rolling Stones have taken over as the voice of the teens."

SATURDAY, 29 FEBRUARY 1964

In the music press, the central debate continues to revolve around questions of authenticity. "Where does Beat begin and R&B end?" Melody Maker demands to know.

Mick: "Rhythm and blues covers such a wide area. It stretches from original stuff, from people like John Lee Hooker, to the more 'produced' material, as from Arthur Alexander and The Drifters. We are not original R&B, but if you are referring to R&B as it's referred to in Britain, then yes, we're R&B."

Not forgetting the question everyone needed to ask . . .
Q: "How long can the Beatles last?"
Mick: "Two years."

FRIDAY, 6 MARCH 1964

Backstage at the Gaumont, Wolverhampton – and that hair issue just won't go away.

Brian: "We're dirty and scruffy because of the hair, they reckon. They call us tramps. It's getting back to army discipline, you know, the barrack-room thing. Short hair makes you clean, they say. That doesn't follow at all. How would girls or women who have long hair like it if we said they were dirty? I don't see why we shouldn't grow our hair as long as we like. Why don't women get it cut, then? Presumably because they prefer it long. So do we."

Despite the hair, the Stones still manage to get themselves mistaken for others.

Brian: "Can I get one thing straight? I am not the brother of Paul Jones, who sings with Manfred Mann."
Mick: "And me, I am Mick Jagger and I don't like fans grabbing my hair at stage doors saying, 'Brian, Brian'."

SATURDAY, 7 MARCH 1964

The Stones' gruelling, two-shows-a-night, month-long UK package tour ends with two shows at the Winter Gardens, Morecambe.

Mick: "I don't like touring at the best of times, but as tours go this one has been quite good. The audiences are good. One thing I find about touring the country is that it's hard to find somewhere to eat. One night, somebody suggested we went to a nightclub and that was all right, but usually we wind up having Chinese chop suey – not because we like Chinese food but because the English stuff is so bad."

Charlie: "Sure, there's a lot of screaming and that. They scream because we're popular, I think, and because they want to let us know it. They get excited, too, and so do we when we're playing to 'em. It's the atmosphere, you know. Gets all hot and sticky, and everybody's having a great time. Riot's the wrong word. Enthusiasm is more like it . . . ."

SATURDAY, 14 MARCH 1964

"WOULD YOU LET YOUR SISTER GO WITH A ROLLING STONE?"

This Melody Maker *headline is subsequently taken up – and adapted – in all sections of the press. Despite the air of sensationalism that was beginning to engulf the band, Mick Jagger is keen to rebut accusations that the Stones are merely band-wagon jumpers.*

Mick: "Two years ago, I was an R&B purist. I used to write thousands of letters to Pye Records pleading with them to release Chuck Berry and Bo Diddley records long before this beat thing got commercial. I don't know if the people at Pye remember my name, but they ought to. They sent me back catalogues and they were very sympathetic. To the critics, then, who think we're a beat group who came up overnight knowing nothing about it, we invite them to examine our record collection. It contains things by Jimmy Reed, Elmore James, (John Lee) Hooker and a stack of private tapes by Little Walter. That's a good start. My big point is that these legendary characters wouldn't mean a light commercially today if groups were not going round Britain doing their numbers. It's made them all popular again – particularly Berry and Diddley . . .

"I cringed years ago when groups did remakes of stuff by artists I loved. Now I see it differently, and don't anybody write in saying the Stones have gone commercial. We're still doing the same music today that we did when we started. Of course, it's the system that's sometimes wrong. Girl fans, particularly, would rather have a copy by a British group than the American version – mainly, I suppose, because they like the British blokes' faces and they feel nearer to them . . . We feel strongly about our music in The Rolling Stones. We love what we play. I get niggled about all this talk of desecration of real rhythm-and-blues. We don't claim to play real R&B."

"BUT WOULD YOU LET YOUR DAUGHTER MARRY ONE?"

Maureen Cleave tailors the headline to instil fear among readers of the Evening Standard.

"Parents do not like The Rolling Stones. They do not want their sons to grow up like them; they do not want their daughters to marry them.

"Never have the middle–class virtues of neatness, obedience and punctuality been so conspicuously lacking as they are in The Rolling Stones. The Rolling Stones are not the people you build empires with; they are not the people who always remember to wash their hands before lunch.

". . . The Stones cause many adult males to gibber with rage. Brian Jones, the most talkative Stone, thinks some of this is jealousy. 'They seem,' he says, 'to have a sort of personal anxiety because we are getting away with something they never dared to do. It's a sexual, personal, vain thing. They'd always been taught that being masculine meant looking clean, cropped and ugly.'

"Mick Jagger was at the London School of Economics. He has an enormous mouth and soft curling hair. He does the singing. This is more like baying at the moon. On stage he sort of shudders all over.

"Brian Jones has hair that is silky, straight and yellow. His father is an aeronautical engineer and intended his boy to be one, too. But he left Cheltenham Grammar School prematurely. He became obsessed by the music.

"Bill Wyman, the married one, bears a marked resemblance to both Charles I and Charles II.

"If apes were handsome, they would look like Charlie Watts. His managers think Steve McQueen looks like him. He is a bit of a dandy.

"Keith Richard is the only one I would have ever dreamed of making into a pop singer. He has a pert Oliver Twist face and likes doing potty things like building walls round people's front doors in the night."

Around this time, the Rolling Stones become a staple part of any self-respecting comedian's repertoire . . .

"There's absolutely no truth in the rumour that Fred Flintstone was the first ever Rolling Stone!"

"The Rolling Stones? They're the ones who look like five shots of Hayley Mills!"

FRIDAY, 20 MARCH 1964

The new Beatles 45, 'Can't Buy Me Love', is released.
Charlie: "It's gonna be a hit."

Mick: "I like it but it's not their best. The B-side is better in my opinion . . . We won't remember it in years to come like some of the other John and Paul things. But it's good."

Brian: "I'm surprised. They sound more like The Searchers. But they're clever, you know, the Beatles. I reckon everybody expected something more sophisticated for the new single and they've gone and rocked it up. They're shrewd. I like it, but as Mick says, it's not their best."

Keith: "The B-side has got more about it – it's more interesting."

Keith then replaces the record with a Jimmy Reed LP.
Keith: "*That's* our kind of music."

FRIDAY, 27 MARCH 1964

Mick Jagger meets Marianne Faithfull at a press reception to launch Oldham protégé Adrienne Posta.
Marianne Faithfull: "The day I was introduced to them I thought to myself, 'What a shame.' I didn't feel a thing except sorrow for the Stones."
Mick: "'Ello darling, 'ow yer doin'?"
Marianne Faithfull: "God, those Rolling Stones are horrible. They're all greasy and spotty."
Andrew Oldham: "I'm interested in you. You have a contemporary face. You are today."
Marianne Faithfull: "(Andrew Oldham) came up to me and said, 'I would like to make a record with you.' I thought he was kidding me, but it turned out he was telling me the truth. I was very concerned about the whole thing, because I think it's so bad for anyone to stand in front of a microphone and ask for everybody's attention."

SATURDAY, 28 MARCH 1964

"THE HAIR STAYS LONG SO HARD LUCK!"

Melody Maker seems to adopt the Stones as their virtual 'house band' during spring 1964, providing them with a mouthpiece in order to get back at their detractors.
Brian: "My hair is not a gimmick. I've had it like this for a couple of years. It doesn't strike me as dirty, scruffy or effeminate. To be honest, I think it looks good. I think I look right with longer hair. So I'll tell you all this much: my hair's staying as it is. If you don't like it – hard luck."

Turning to musical matters, Brian was emphatic about his tips for the top . . .
Brian: "The Yardbirds and The Barron Knights. The Yardbirds are a London group playing just our kind of stuff, and they are really fantastic. All they want is a hit record and they'll be very, very big. The Barron Knights are great musicians and the best stage act I've seen."

Meanwhile, Mick is bemused, though not duly concerned, by the public outcry.

"WHY DO PARENTS HATE US?"

Mick: "I don't particularly care either way whether parents hate us or not. They might grow to like us one day – then they'll like us for some reason. It's a thing you can't make out. I reckon some of them think we are ugly cavemen and others think we are cuddly, like teddy bears. We don't set out to try to be grizzly. And, well I can tell you this much, my parents like me! We're getting to understand the things they say about us a bit better. But some stupid things have been said. For a start, we're not shy, as some people have said."

MONDAY, 30 MARCH 1964

Mods and Rockers clash violently on Clacton beach. Many suspicious fingers are pointed at the example set by beat groups like the Stones.
Brian: "Every time something like this happens, they blame music. They did it with rock. Beat music does not build up tension. It allows young people to let off steam, and they usually do so by dancing. You will never stamp out teenage violence. We've only seen three or four fights in ballrooms, and we rarely see violence. The Rolling Stones do not incite violence. I deny it categorically."

WEDNESDAY, 8 APRIL 1964

The Stones play the Ready, Steady, Go! *Mod Ball at the Empire Pool, Wembley. They mime to several songs, including a version of Tommy Tucker's recent hit, 'Hi-Heel Sneakers'. Mick talks about the record in* Melody Maker*:*
Mick: "He's a 25-year-old negro from Chicago and this is his first record, I believe. Frankly, I didn't imagine for a minute that a record like this would get in the chart over here. It's such a great, honest blues track that I can't understand why it's there in the hit parade. It's amazing. Before I found out from a friend about this being his first record, I had a sneaking

suspicion he was an old blues singer making a record under a different name. This is great."

Brian: "Did you see the calamity that happened at the *Ready, Steady, Go!* Mod Ball a few weeks back? There was poor old Keith falling, well, actually, he was pulled off the rostrum, twice, in fact. It was supposed to be that Charlie would be sitting at the drums at the beginning, playing away, and we would all walk on to the stand singing and playing our guitars 'like wandering minstrels,' as Keith says. But it didn't go quite that way! And to top it all, the rostrum was being pushed all over the place, which wasn't in the script at all. Of course, I was all right. I just hid behind Mick and he defended us both with his maracas."

FRIDAY, 17 APRIL 1964

The group's début LP, titled simply The Rolling Stones, *is released. Decca circulates a press release that stops short of 'favourite colour' territory – just.*
"MICK JAGGER . . . likes money and spends it like water . . . BRIAN JONES . . . smokes 60 cigarettes a day . . . wants to be President of the Dr Beeching Fan Club . . . BILL WYMAN . . . is often called 'The Ghost' due to his pale complexion . . . KEITH RICHARD . . . has one romance in his life – his guitar! . . . CHARLIE WATTS . . . is the 'Beau Brummell' of the group. Has over 100 pocket handkerchiefs."

Top pop critic Peter Jones is one of the first to hear it . . .
"I went along to Decca's offices on Monday for a preview of the disc that thousands of fans are screaming for. Believe me, it is fantastic! I will go as far as to say that if it doesn't take over from the Beatles at the top of the LP chart I will eat my chocolate-flavoured record player."

Brian: "Though Keith Richard takes the Chuck Berry-style leads with The Rolling Stones, I like getting unusual sounds from my guitar. It's much more important to me than just knowing a sequence of different chords. I use steel guitar a lot and people seem surprised that I use the conventional tuning for it . . . To be honest, I prefer playing harmonica to guitar. It's that *sound* business all over again – I just like getting soulful sounds without worrying about simple sequences of notes."

Melody Maker *writer Bob Dawbarn notices something else . . .*
"A curious sidelight is shown by the one original tune on the album 'Tell Me'. The Negroid mask slips away and both tune and lyric are second-hand Liverpool."

Mike Nevard of the Daily Herald *isn't convinced at all.*
"Their singles have a strange appeal, but the LP is a stinker."

WEDNESDAY, 22 APRIL 1964

"CROP OF THE POPS"

Mr Wallace Scowcroft, President of the National Federation of Hairdressers, offers a free haircut to the next successful pop group.
"If pop groups had their hair well cut the teenagers would copy them – instead of just asking for a bit off the neck. The Rolling Stones are the worst. One of them looks as if he has got a feather duster on his head."

A few days later, the nationals had even worse to report – the Stones in full 'Nanker' mode . . .
"As if by a pre-arranged signal, all five simultaneously pulled down the skin under their eyes and pushed up their noses. Believe me, it's frightening . . ."

Andrew Oldham and most within the band lap up the publicity, but not everyone welcomes it.
Diane Perks (Bill's wife): "It really upset me when, especially in the early days, the boys were called 'cavemen' and dirty. You don't spend hours washing and ironing shirts to have people turn round and call your husband dirty . . . He's always a family man and he loves his son, Stephen."

Some members even make light of their beloved craft . . .
Keith: "R&B is a bit of a giggle. It's hard to say what R&B is. So many people say Chuck Berry is R&B, then he says he is rock'n'roll, so where do you go from there? . . . Still, I don't mind what you call it at the moment and for the next ten years. I'm happy."

Others aren't quite ready to take the flippant approach . . .
Brian: "The truth is that we take our music very seriously indeed. Older folk get the impression that we're a gang of clowns. Well, that's too bad. We study American musicians' work in every spare moment and we rehearse very hard indeed. And I would like to say that the actual musical standard of many of the British beat groups is exceptionally high. Too many people deride the scene. Even some of the older musicians. I say that there are guitarists in the pop groups who are every bit as good, techni- cally, as some of the older hands who've been around for years. I think some people are simply jealous of the money that a successful beat group

can make. They don't stop to think about the sheer hard work, the travelling and the expenses."

Charlie: "I like negro music mainly for its influence on non-negro artists. For example, The Everly Brothers have got that coloured feel. Coloured artists who stand out for me include Miles Davis, Louis Armstrong and another trumpeter from way back, Freddie Keppard. And I'm also very keen on Charlie Mingus, whom I met recently at the airport in Switzerland. I also like American country music – not country and western but music of the American country, Hillbilly music, for example. And I'm very fond of classical music."

Brian: "Favourite musicians? Django Reinhardt, for sure – not that I'd ever try to model myself on him. Then there's Elmore James, who's a beautiful player. I like Robert Johnson, too. But there are two players with Muddy Waters who I dig a lot – Pat Hare, and someone called Jimmy Rodgers, who is not to be confused with the folk singer of the same name."

Mick: "My collection isn't large but it's quite varied. I don't usually buy more than a couple of LPs a week because that's about all I like in an average week. I don't like light-hearted films – they don't interest me. I like quite heavy films usually. I'd like to make films, but I'd also like to write – novels as well as songs – and produce records. Only time will tell how many of these things I'll be able to do."

Mick isn't the only cinema buff in the band.
Bill: "If I do have any free time I love going to the cinema because I love action films and big spectaculars. 78s are fascinating. I'll go and buy hundreds of old records – they're about sixpence each – and tape any decent ones. Then I give them all away."

Brian: "Occasionally I go to the cinema and see films that have been recommended. I liked *Dr Strangelove*, which was very funny and also had something to say for itself. I wouldn't say I had a huge record collection – I mean, I don't make a hobby of collecting records or anything like that."

When they aren't touring or going to the cinema, Mick, Keith and Andrew Oldham retire to their shared first-floor flat in Mapesbury Road, Hampstead.
Keith: "This is how we like the place to be. We spend most of our time here when we aren't touring, rarely going out . . . most nights we just concentrate on writing new songs, often staying up until four or five in the morning. Mind you, we don't get up until midday – and some days not until tea-time."

SPRING 1964

The group record a jingle extolling the virtues of the popular children's breakfast cereal, Rice Krispies.

> Wake up in the morning/There's a snap about the place,
> Wake up in the morning/There's a crackle in your face,
> Wake up in the morning there's a pop that really sends
> Rice Krispies to you . . . and you . . . and YOU!

The jingle, 'Wake Up In The Morning', is written by Brian Jones to words supplied by ad agents J. Walter Thompson Co. Ltd, according to Chris Hayes' answer in his 'expert advice' column in Melody Maker.

MAY 1964

As the Stones continue to tour the country, Rave *magazine catches up with them on the road.*

Brian: "For us a rave starts pretty quietly. As we drive into town, we stop to ask someone the way to the ballroom.

"We like to case the joint first, to see how big the crowd is outside. If it looks large and a bit mad, we shoot off to a phone box and lay on an emergency service.

"Police and officials bundle us through a secret door. With a bit of luck, our car remains unscratched and unlipsticked, our clothes stay in one piece and we still have as much hair as we started with.

"We wander round backstage to scout out the scene. Already we can hear the screams.

" 'What's the audience like?' we ask. 'Wild,' someone else says. And that's great, because that's how we like it.

". . . Standing in the wings, waiting for the curtains to part, you get your first real glimpse of all the excitement. Stage hands frantically beat off girls who are trying to wrench back the stage drapes.

"The atmosphere is more than electric by now – it's something tangible, like a vast elastic band, ready to snap at any moment!

"And then we're off. Keith roars in to 'Talkin' About You'. The curtains slowly part. The Stones are rolling!

"As our music gains momentum, the kids sway like palm trees in a hurricane. A huge Hampden roar swamps our overworked amplifiers. We feel as if we're really in there with the fans.

"As the excitement mounts, the girls surge down off the footlights and start showering us with gifts – sweets, peanuts, cuddly toys. We're feeling very good.

"Suddenly it's all over. The curtains close quickly, shutting off the faces behind that ear-splitting roar.

"Back in the dressing room, we swallow Cokes to get that sandpaper taste out of our throats. We start to unwind as we wait for the police to arrange our getaway."

THURSDAY, 21 MAY 1964

The Stones' short tour of Scotland with Freddie & The Dreamers reaches an ugly head after a show at the ABC, Edinburgh.
Freddie Garrity: "I've not been pleased with the billing at all during the show's Scottish tour. The public have been led to believe they were seeing 'The Rolling Stones and supporting cast'. This is not the case. We are the bill-topping act, not the Stones."

Meanwhile, the sound of 2,700 fans chanting "We want the Stones!" continues to reverberate through the building.

SATURDAY, 23 MAY 1964

"STONES SET TO INVADE"

It's announced that the Stones will leave for a three-week tour of the States at the start of June. A London-based press agency helps to fan the flames of controversy.
"Americans – brace yourselves.

"In the tracks of the Beatles, a second wave of sheepdog-looking, angry-acting, guitar-playing Britons is on the way.

"They call themselves The Rolling Stones and they're due in New York Tuesday.

"Of The Rolling Stones, one detractor has said: 'They are dirtier, and are streakier and more dishevelled than the Beatles and, in some places, they are more popular than the Beatles.'

"Says Mick Jagger: 'I hate to get up in the morning. I'm not fond of being hungry either.'

"From Keith Richard: 'People think we're wild and unruly. But it isn't true. I would say that the most important thing about us is that we're our own best friends.'

"More than the others perhaps, Brian Jones likes clothes. He puts his philosophy this way: 'It depends on what I feel like really. Sometimes I'll wear very flamboyant clothes like this frilly shirt. Other times I'll wear very casual stuff. I spend a lot of my time buying stuff.'

"Then he adds: 'There's really not much else to it.'"

Brian: "Now we're going to America next month, I think I've finally proved to those people who said I was always doing the wrong thing that I've been right all along. I've got somewhere by doing things my own way. It's been fun and we've had some laughs."

Meanwhile, at home, the onslaught continues . . .

WEDNESDAY, 27 MAY 1964

"BEATLE YOUR ROLLING STONE HAIR"

"A headmaster ruled yesterday: Beatle haircuts are IN – but Rolling Stones haircuts are OUT. The head, Mr Donald Thompson, has suspended eleven of his boys from Woodlands Comprehensive School, Coventry, because they wear their hair like Mick Jagger and Co. of The Rolling Stones pop group. 'Long and scruffy,' Mr Thompson calls it. But yesterday he said they could return if they cut their hair neatly – like the Beatles."

Brian sips lager outside a London pub with tabloid journalist Peter Dacre and attempts to set the record straight.

Brian: "I know the image of us is that we are hooligans and unwashed layabouts, but as a matter of fact we're all very interested in clothes. I would love to be a fashion designer – but I never will be, of course. On stage we dress like we do because we feel more comfortable that way. They say we're dirty and scruffy because we've long hair. Short hair makes you clean, they say, but that doesn't follow at all.

"We went out to please teenagers with our kind of music, which we are very sincere about. We have a very, very fanatical following, but this is not only due to our music. We've become kind of figureheads for all the kids who would like to rebel against authority. We are expressing something *they* cannot say or do. It has happened quite unintentionally on our part. We have been accused of antagonising parents so that the kids would follow us, but to us that seems a Chinese way of going about it."

DJ Jimmy Savile, whose hair is even longer than the Stones', comes to their defence in his column in the Sunday People.

"The Stones are a great team for having a laugh and dress very clean and smart when they relax, contrary to what lots of people think."

In a bid to elevate the tone of the Stones' appeal, photographer David Bailey primes readers of American Vogue *with an insight into the sexual appeal of Mick Jagger.*

"To the inner group in London, the new spectacular is a solemn young man, Mick Jagger, one of the five Rolling Stones, those singers who set out to cross America by bandwagon in June. For the British, the Stones have a perverse, unsettling sex appeal with Jagger out in front of The Pacemakers, The Searchers, The Breakaways, and Freddie & The Dreamers. To women, Jagger looks fascinating, to men, a scare."

As the group arrive mid-afternoon at New York's Kennedy Airport on Monday, 1 June, to be met by 500 fans and 20 police, the Daily Express *expresses its doubts.*

"What sort of picture of British youth will they create across the Atlantic?"

"STONES SHAKE STATES"

Brian: "It looks like a big Balham."

There is one question on every reporter's lips . . .

Q: "How do you compare your group with the Beatles?"

Mick: "I don't know. How do you compare it with the Beatles? I don't compare it at all. There's no point."

Q: "Now let's get down to brass tacks. Do you think you're better than they are?"

Mick: "At what? You know, it's not the same group, so we just do what we want to do and they do what they want, and there's no point just going on comparing us. You can prefer us to them or them to us. This is diplomatic, you see!"

Q: "But do you feel that you do what you want to do better than they do what they want to do?"

Mick: "I don't know what they want to do, you see. Very diplomatic!"

TUESDAY, 2 JUNE 1964

The Stones début on American television with an appearance on The Les Crane Show.

Crane: "This is your first appearance on American television?"

Keith: "Yeah."

Crane: "Isn't it exciting?"

Keith (sarcastically): "Yeah, it knocks me out."

Crane: "You wouldn't be sending me up, would you?"

Keith: "No, I wouldn't dare . . ."

WEDNESDAY, 3 JUNE 1964

The group film a slot for Hollywood Palace, *hosted by Dean Martin, where their co-stars are Rosie and Suzie, a pair of performing elephants.*
Dean Martin: "Now something for the youngsters, five singing boys from England who've sold a lot of albums. They're called The Rolling Stones. I've been rolled when I was stoned myself! I don't know what they're singing about, but here they are . . ."

A little later on the show, Dino plays for a few more cheap laughs . . .
"Their hair is not that long. It's just smaller foreheads and higher eyebrows . . . Now don't go away, anybody. You wouldn't leave me with these Rolling Stones, would you?! . . . Actually the boys are soon back in England to have a hair-pulling contest with the Beatles! That (referring to a trampoline artist) is the father of the Rolling Stones. He's been trying to kill himself ever since!"

Fuming quietly, the Stones prove no match for their host.
Mick: "It's nice to have you on our show, Mr Martin."

SATURDAY, 6 JUNE 1964

After two successful shows in San Bernardino, California, the previous night, the band take off for San Antonio, Texas, from where Jack Hutton files this report for The Daily Mirror.
"Britain's Rolling Stones got 'the bird' when they appeared at a show in San Antonio, Texas, last night. Local singers were cheered wildly. A tumbling act and a trained monkey were recalled to the stage for encores. But the long-haired Rolling Stones – Mick Jagger, Keith Richard, Brian Jones, Charlie Watts and Bill Wyman – were booed. After the show, at the Teen Fair of Texas, one seventeen-year-old girl said: 'All they've got that our own school groups haven't is hair.'

"Britain's Rolling Stones group are being treated as freaks in America. People gasp in amazement when they appear at airports, in hotel lobbies and in the streets.

"Shouts of 'Where are your razors?' and 'Get your hair cut' are commonplace. Men have whistled at Mick Jagger and Co., and one girl asked: 'Do they wear lipstick and eye make-up and carry purses?' When I assured her they didn't she seemed disappointed!

". . . One man was heard to say: 'Shucks, I thought they were girls wearing one-piece bathing suits.'

"How do the Stones reply to all these cracks? As if by a pre-arranged signal, all five simultaneously pull down the skin under their eyes and push up their noses. Believe me, it's frightening."

MONDAY, 8 JUNE 1964

After four shows in San Antonio, the Stones go sightseeing.
Bill: "What a funny country America is! In the afternoon, we went shopping downtown and saw the Alamo from outside, but didn't go in to look. Things haven't changed much since the Alamo days, because there is a bit of feeling, to put it mildly, between the Texans and the Mexicans – and quite a bit of actual shooting goes on! This particular day 15 Mexicans were shot – so we didn't stay out too long! In the evening, I visited a few local haunts with two Texans. Their pubs have swing doors just like the old western saloons, but the jukeboxes play Sam Cooke and Jimmy Reed all the time."
Mick: "The coloured people have a ropey time here. You know, they wouldn't take us through the coloured section of San Antonio. I kept asking them to let me see it, but they'd never take me through."

WEDNESDAY, 10 JUNE 1964

The group spend the first of two days recording at the home of Chicago's R&B scene, Chess Studios, at 2120 South Michigan Avenue.
Jack Hutton (*Daily Mirror*): "The session got underway right into a verbal punch-up between co-manager Andrew Oldham, Charlie Watts and Mick Jagger about the intro. Curses flew between them thick and fruity. Outsiders grew concerned. Then suddenly it was settled with laughs all round. Take after take came and went. Charlie Watts' face went through painful-looking emotions as he thrashed away on drums, Keith bent double as he worked on his swinging guitar solo. And in the cubicle at the back, Mick shouted and clapped his hands as he yelled out the vocal. Finally, they were satisfied at the 14th take. Then they dubbed on extra voices and Charlie added tambourine. We sat back and listened to the playback. People from all over the building, mostly coloured, joined us. The playback came crashing through the huge speakers at top volume. Then Mick's vocal, and the pretty coloured chicks started to jive. In seconds, everybody in the studio was moving. Mick and the boys were shaking and twisting. It was like a scene from a film."

THURSDAY, 11 JUNE 1964

Bill: "That afternoon we paid our second visit to the Chess label's recording studios. We visited them the day before and cut four tracks, including our next single, 'It's All Over Now'. It was a big thrill for the boys and myself to be recording in the same studio as used by Muddy Waters, Chuck Berry and Bo Diddley.

"We met friendly Buddy Guy, and that great bass player and songwriter Willie Dixon there for the first time. And on the Thursday, who should walk into the studio while we were working but Chuck Berry and Muddy Waters. They both seemed most enthusiastic with the numbers we did – and the way we did them. It meant a lot to us!"

Chuck Berry: "Swing on gentlemen, you are sounding well, if I may say so."

Bill: "We were advised not to go down the South Side area of Chicago (where all the blues clubs are), as there were bad scenes between the negroes and whites. As I say, what a funny country this is!"

Muddy Waters: "They're my boys. I like their version of 'I Just Want To Make Love To You'. They fade it out just like we did. One more trip (to America) and they'll have it. Believe me, I'll come back (to Britain) one more time and then I won't need to come back no more."

FRIDAY, 12 JUNE 1964

The band roll into Minneapolis for a hastily arranged ballroom date.

Bill: "Nobody had heard of us. I think the reaction was the same as we first experienced in England a year ago – complete disbelief and curiosity. There weren't many people there because the tickets were three dollars."

SATURDAY, 13 JUNE 1964

As the Stones roll into Omaha, Nebraska, Mick discusses his future with Jack Hutton.

Mick: "I want to stay in show business. Write songs, too. And maybe go into management. I could handle money all right. That wouldn't worry me. Remember, I spent two years at the London School of Economics and passed all my exams. I know this won't last. I give the Stones about another two years. I'm saving for the future. I bank all my song royalties, for a start."

Meanwhile, Brian sends two postcards to girlfriend Linda Lawrence.
Brian: "I really miss Texas. The weather was so hot and everything was great. I killed a rattlesnake, too! I've got his rattler for you! I'm looking forward to seeing you. Bye, Brian."
Brian: "This is where I am now. Life is so happy here. I don't want to come back to England ever – except to get you and Pip and Billy (a poodle and goat, both gifts from Brian). Love, Brian."

WEDNESDAY, 17 JUNE 1964

As the group prepare for the evening's show in Pittsburgh, fatigue and despondency is clearly evident.
Mick: "It's been a real drag. We feel we've been given the business here in America. We would never get involved in this kind of tour again."
Keith: "The reaction has been great where there have been people to give a reaction. But really this tour was all a farce . . . Nobody even knew we were coming."

Brian is still smarting over Dean Martin.
"We're going to get on a show of ours one day and really let him have it. He was just a symbol of the whole tour for us . . . It has been an experience to meet some of the Americans. The fans are much the same, but they seem to take longer to grow up here, especially the boys. I've seen some of these fellows 20 and 21 acting like they're 14. It's amazing."
Keith: "They looked at us like we were Martians. Complete strangers, and they all hated us and wanted to beat the shit out of us."
Mick: "Hair questions drove us potty in America. Why do they always pick on me? I got cheesed off with the whole thing over there."

FRIDAY, 26 JUNE 1964

'It's All Over Now', the group's fourth single, is released.
Mick: "I don't care a damn if our new record has reached number one. I reckon it will do half a million in this country and in others altogether, and I'd rather have a sale like that than sell five hundred and fifty thousand in Britain alone and have the number one thing. What's it matter, anyway? 'It's All Over Now' has reached the top, that's great. But I can tell you none of us has been worrying about it."
Brian: "I didn't like the number when I heard it on the radio, but I like it now."

Keith: " 'It's All Over Now' is the best single we've done. I like the overall sound on it more than I did on anything before."

SATURDAY, 4 JULY 1964

The group cause a stir when they make up the panel for the latest episode of Juke Box Jury. *The reviewer from* The Daily Sketch *was clearly not amused.*
"I report with no regret the death of a sacred cow on TV. A group of Neanderthal young men who call themselves The Rolling Stones sat in judgment as the jury men. It was a mockery of a trial as the gum-chewing, ill-mannered, ill-humoured, illiberal and illogical jurors indicated their pleasure or displeasure by catarrhal grunts that an ear, trained in the illiterate school of young people, could sometimes distinguish as, 'Well, yeah, er, I, er, mean, like, well it's, ha-ha, awful then. Naw, definitely not, in'nit?' "
Keith: "I think the whole programme's very old hat. We weren't great, but the records they played us were nothing! There didn't seem anything to say about them. We were all lost except for Charlie and maybe Mick . . . I'm sure it helped us reach number one, if nothing else; it kept our image up. People thought the worst of us before they saw us. *Juke Box Jury* was confirmation that we were a bunch of idiots."

FRIDAY, 10 JULY 1964

The Beatles' 'A Hard Day's Night' single is released.
Mick: "Quite good, but not their best. As a song, it's quite good, and they play it really well, but I expected a bit more out of the ordinary. I still reckon 'I Want To Hold Your Hand' was the best A-side they've had. My personal favourite is 'You Can't Do That'."

AUGUST 1964

Marianne Faithfull's début single, 'As Tears Go By', written for her by Mick Jagger and Keith Richard, is released by Decca.

"GREENSLEEVES GOES POP"

Andrew Oldham: "I told them, Marianne's a convent girl. I want a song with brick walls all around it, and high windows and no sex."
Marianne Faithfull: "I'm not really an extrovert, but I seem to have

landed myself an extremely extrovert manager. As much as I like Andrew, it worries me . . . I hate the star cult and I don't want the big star treatment . . . I like my record now much better than I did when I first heard it. Another thing I didn't like was people's dishonesty. They told me it was great. They tried to convince me pop is a great art. It is not. My record is all right, and that's just about all there is to say . . . But there is so much better. Dusty's songs are marvellous. Mine is a bit wet – a bit drippy and languid."

Marianne Faithfull: "Some critics have said it's folksy. Well, I'm a folk fanatic. People like Joan Baez impress me – and I know I could never sing in the same class as her. So for me there's something phoney about my disc."

The sweet natured song does little to assuage the fury of tabloid commentators, whipped into a moral panic by unruly hair and seaside punch-ups. Alan Whittaker, in The News Of The World, *is one of many who relishes the opportunity to stick the knife in.*

"There are few mothers who wouldn't welcome a Beatle into the family. The Beatles bubble with laughter. They make jokes, wear neat clothes, get along with royalty. Even long hair has become acceptable after a time. But it's different with the Stones. They leer rather than smile. They don't wear natty clothes. They glower. Nobody would accuse them of radiating charm. And the extraordinary thing is that more and more youngsters are turning towards the Stones. The Beatles have become too respectable. The five Stones – and their young manager, Andrew Oldham – are symbols of a rebellion against authority, against the boss, the clock, the clean-shirt-a-day routine. How true is this carefully nourished picture of five indolent morons? The Stones give one the feeling that they really enjoy wallowing in a swill tub of their own repulsiveness. They flick ash everywhere. Charlie Watts, the zombie-eyed drummer, has a habit of dropping cigarette ends in other people's coffee cups – before they've finished drinking."

SATURDAY, 1 AUGUST 1964

Andrew Oldham's plan to pitch the Stones against the Beatles in the youth stakes was exceeding his personal expectations. Complaining that the Stones are now suffering from overexposure, he says:

"We are picking and choosing interviews now. We don't want all the usual questions. The boys like to be people . . ."

SATURDAY, 8 AUGUST 1964

A Dutch concert at the Kurhaus, Scheveningen, The Hague, is halted when the audience riots.
Manfred Mann: "People are blaming The Rolling Stones for causing trouble. This is rubbish. I think the Stones have been terribly misrepresented. They are nice, ordinary blokes. Some of the rumours they say about them – they say they don't wash – are a lot of rubbish."

FRIDAY, 14 AUGUST 1964

Andrew Oldham marries 18-year-old Sheila Klein at a secret ceremony in Glasgow. He reveals in Melody Maker *that he too is suffering from the pressures of the job, and claims that he intends to bow out of management and move abroad.*
Andrew Oldham: "The main reason is health. I think I've aged four years in the last year, all because of the pop rat race . . . I didn't come into the pop business to make money. Money can't buy you happiness, although you can't have happiness without money . . . I plan to get away from the scene for a while. I'll buy a joint in Portugal and spend some time there. It's cheap. I'm in a bit of a state, really. Don't know what I want. The doctor says I've got an ulcer. That's from no sleep and worrying about perfection. Failure in anything is terrible. Success, that's everything . . . The boys can take care of themselves. They know the score now . . . I'll still advise them on records.

"I must stress that I'll continue to make records, will still produce the Stones' records, Marianne's records and others, including some by my orchestra. One of the reasons I'm doing this is to get loose from the chores of the day-to-day handling of the Stones so it will leave me free for producing records. In America, a record producer does only that. That's what I'm going to do."

At the same time, the group members retreat briefly into their own private sanctuaries.
Brian: "Mick and Keith now have a two-storey flat in Hampstead (10a Holly Hill) with all mod cons, two telephones, two big bedrooms, a big lounge and they've just bought themselves a big 21″ TV set. I've been moving backwards and forwards in the past few days. I left Belgravia, went to St John's Wood and then back to Belgravia again. I must say, though, that I never pay any rent. I've got so many friends in town who are always offering me a place in their abodes that I really don't need a place of my own . . . Sometimes I go out of London to the Windsor-Maidenhead area. It's really lovely out there, quiet and peaceful."

64

Mick: "The whole British music scene is dead boring now. There hasn't been anything new or exciting for ages . . . First there was the Beatles, then us, now there's nothing."

Andrew Oldham: "The group boom has broken every law that people applied to pop. What we're seeing is not a pop music phenomenon, but a social phenomenon. Rhythm and blues was not promoted into a big thing by record companies. It was made big by the public, and that's the healthiest thing of all, which everybody seems to have ignored."

During this brief hiatus in media relations, 'Sixth Stone' Ian Stewart gives a rare interview.

"I joined before Charlie or Bill and when we wanted a new drummer, I suggested Charlie to Brian . . . I left because of one or two things, and the Stones stayed as just five blokes instead of six . . . I don't want to be pointed at in the street and get torn to pieces, so I'm better off like this."

THURSDAY, 20 AUGUST 1964

During a five-night season in the Channel Islands, Mick gets doorstepped by the local television station.

Q: "How do you feel about the reception you got in the Channel Islands?"

Mick: "Oh, it's been very good."

Q: "Are you worried by the constant attention you get from fans?"

Mick: "It's one of those things that you get used to all the time. It's part of your life."

Q: "One of the criticisms of your music is that you only appeal to 13-year-olds. Do you envisage any more changes that might make it more of a family show?"

Mick: "No one's ever asked me that before! I've seen lots of age groups at our show. It's a pop act. It's not meant to be a family show – although a lot of parents do come."

SATURDAY, 12 SEPTEMBER 1964

The results of the 1964 Pop Poll in Melody Maker, *voted by readers of the magazine, confirms The Rolling Stones as genuine contenders for the Beatles' crown. British Section: Top Group – 1 Rolling Stones; Vocal Disc – 1 'Not Fade Away'; Male Singer – 3 Mick Jagger ; Musician – 9 Brian Jones.*

The poll provokes an even bigger outbreak of Beatles versus Stones rivalry. Time for John Lennon to wade in . . .

John Lennon: "There comes a point where the only thing left to do to a group like us is to knock it. I get on all right with Jagger, but ask him where the hell's their new record? They need one out now!"

But wasn't this clear evidence that the Beatles were indeed slipping?

John: "I think there probably was a moment a few weeks ago when the Stones had it over us just a bit. Jagger's the one, of course. He is the Stones, isn't he? Well, about the time everyone went potty for Jagger, that's when it could have meant something about them 'taking over'. But I don't know about now. I just don't know."

WEDNESDAY, 14 OCTOBER 1964

Charlie Watts marries Shirley Ann Shepherd in a secret ceremony at Bradford Registry Office.

Charlie: "She was one of the audience when I spotted her. I liked her and asked her for a date. We've been courting ever since, except for a short break. I proposed six months ago and she accepted. That's it, I suppose. Now everyone will know. I tried to keep it a secret. I wanted it to be a secret. But I suppose if Khrushchev can't keep a secret, neither can I."

TUESDAY, 20 OCTOBER 1964

The Stones conquer Paris with another riot-splattered show at L'Olympia. The venue's owner, Bruno Coquatrix, says it is "the best reception an English group has had here. The Rolling Stones made even more impact than The Beatles."

Charlie was characteristically unfazed: "I dunno. Was it good? I was too far back to hear!"

SATURDAY, 24 OCTOBER

"STONES HIT STATES: THEY'VE STARTED STONE-MANIA"

"The Rolling Stones, who haven't bathed for a week, arrived here for their second US tour yesterday."

After the Stones disembark at Kennedy Airport, New York, they sit down to talk to Independent News Service journalist Ed Rudy for a series of widely syndicated interviews.

Ed Rudy: "Mick is the lead singer on most songs for The Rolling Stones and is sometimes called 'Old Stone Face' because he rarely smiles. He has also uniquely been said to be similar in appearance to British film star, Hayley Mills. He was born on 26 July 1944 [*sic*] in Dartford, Kent, England, and was christened Michael Philip Jagger. Mick is five feet 10 inches tall and attended the London School of Economics and prepared to be an accountant. He never had any formal musical training and is self-taught on the harmonica and piano, which he plays when he is not acting as lead singer for The Rolling Stones. Mick *are* you the leader of The Rolling Stones?"

Mick: "Not really. No, there isn't a leader."

Ed: "Do you sing lead on most of the songs?"

Mick: "Yes."

Ed: "Do you also write some of the material?"

Mick: "Yes, with Keith."

Ed: "A great deal of it has been previously out some years ago in America by the down-home rhythm and blues groups."

Mick: "Yeah, a lot of it has. We find that these American songs are better for ourselves than the songs that Keith and I write. Most of the songs we write we give to other people 'cos they're mostly ballads and things like that."

Ed: "Do you think if I started singing and you gave me a song you could turn me into a success?"

Mick: "Dunno, we'd have to get your hair a bit longer than that, wouldn't we?"

Ed: "Do you find that the American girls are any different to the British girls in their reaction to you?"

Mick: "No, not in their reaction at all. They look different because they wear different clothes and talk differently, the things they say are different."

Ed: "Do you find they're more precocious?"

Mick: "Not more precocious. They're probably more outspoken."

Ed: "I know that you're single, I know that four of the five Stones are single. Do you have any particular type of girl in mind as the type you'd like to marry, Mick?"

Mick: "Well, I like ones that are intelligent and ones that carry on a decent conversation. And they've got to look pretty, too, of course."

Ed: "A-ha-ha! I was waiting for that last comment! Do you find that there's a great affinity between the Stones? Do you fellas get along well or do you have frequent arguments? How does your life together go?"

Mick: "It goes along very well. We have our arguments. Every group has arguments, you know, about what records we're gonna do and general things like that. But on the whole we get on fine."

Ed: "When you date, Mick, do you generally date in conjunction with the other fellas. Do you double, triple, quadruple or quintuple date, or is it singly?"

Mick: "Sometimes we go out on double dates, not very often. Mostly just single dates."

Ed: "Is one of the reasons you do not double or triple date the fact that you're so easily spotted because of your rather unique style of dress and your long hair."

Mick: "Yeah, you find it's much easier if you go by yourself. Though you get recognised badly enough then. But if you go in twos or threes, it's terrible."

Ed: "Uniquely, your faces are extremely well known in America now. As a matter of fact, I think that at this point, appearance-wise, each of you individually is better known than the Beatles were when they first started really hitting in America."

Mick: "I think the Beatles are much more of a group than we are. We're five individuals who happen to play together and we look different – we've got different colour hair, we've all got different features."

Ed: "Yes, that was also true of the Beatles. They don't really look alike . . ."

Mick: "They've all got black hair, you see. You can pick Brian out or me 'cos we're not so sort of conventionally looking because we've got funny features. Bill looks like Charles II! He can't help it . . ."

Bill: "In America, it's a rather young Abraham Lincoln. In France, it's a rather young Louis XIV. And in Penge . . .?!!"

Ed: "He's an old married man at home! Now we'll get back to Mick. Do you have any particular kind of girl in mind? Or are you going with anyone special? Are you engaged?"

Mick: "No, I'm not engaged. I don't find that much time to go out with girls, really. It's very difficult, especially when you're on tour for weeks and you're away from home. I go out with lots of different girls . . . all pretty!"

Ed: "Haha! You don't sound too unhappy about that at all!"

Mick: "No, I'm not. I'm very pleased!"

Ed: "Do you find the appearance of American girls is any different than the British girls?"

Mick: "The clothes are different. I think the hair is longer . . ."

Ed Rudy: "Brian Jones is sometimes called 'Rolling Jones' by his fans and he plays rhythm guitar and harmonica with the group though he has had no musical training. He was born 22 February 1944 [*sic*] in Cheltenham, England, and his father is a former school principal, or, as they say, head-master. He is quite extroverted and extremely exuberant when anything happens that makes him happy, or that he considers funny. He is very friendly and, most likely, the most outspoken of The Rolling Stones."

Ed: "What specific difference would you say there is between The Rolling Stones and the other British groups as of this point?"

Brian: "Well, the essential difference between ourselves and the British groups that are well known in the United States at the moment is really that we are the first to really have a strong Negro rhythm and blues influence. We haven't adapted our music from a watered-down form of rhythm and blues or rock'n'roll such as the white American rock'n'roll. We've adapted our music from the early blues forms and, actually, most of the groups in England now are copying us whereas they used to copy the Beatles."

Ed: "I can't help but agree with you. There are a great many rhythm and blues sounds coming out of England at this point. Do you write any of the material that you sing?"

Brian: "Yes, we write a lot of it, actually. The ones that appear under the pseudonym Nanker-Phelge are written by all of us together, and Mick and Keith write a lot. And others of us do write but we haven't had anything recorded by this group."

Ed: "Could you account for the phenomenal success that you've had here in America and around the world. Why specifically have The Rolling Stones become such a fantastic success?"

Brian: "We've just provided the right thing at the right time. We've come along with a very raw music where everything was rather sweet. Things were getting sloppy and sentimental. In England they were anyway, and I believe so in America, too . . . a Cliff Richard sort of thing. A new tough element seemed to be growing up. I don't mean tough kids, but a new vital urge seemed to be growing up amongst young people and we provided a music that had the same sort of vitality. And we came along at the right time with the right thing. So it's just . . . happened. It hadn't happened all that quickly. We've been around in England for about 18 months now. Some groups make big records with

69

their first ones. We haven't. Like in America, it's taken time to build."

Ed: "Yes, I'm aware of that. As a matter of fact, there seemed to be a great deal of resistance to the group at the start. How would you account for that?"

Brian: "There's always resistance to something new, isn't there? Always. To every action there's a reaction."

Ed: "I read many, many magazine articles on The Rolling Stones that, very uniquely for a British group, were practically libellous. I've never seen any British group described in the way that The Rolling Stones have been. Now I've met the fellas, they're clean-cut looking boys, you've got very long hair but you certainly don't look dirty, and this is an allegation that I've have read so many times in the magazines and I just can't understand it. Would you make an attempt to explain this to me and to our listeners?"

Brian: "It's very difficult. All I can do really is deny it and personally – I'm speaking for myself – I resent it very much being called dirty. And if anyone called me dirty to my face, I wouldn't take it lying down. When you read it in magazines, there's very little you can do. You're really at the mercy of magazine writers: what they write, people believe. And they've written so much dirty rubbish about us, I do feel very resentful about it, but I just hope that this time around we can show people we're not dirty, we're not really scruffy and we're not thick."

Ed: "As a matter of fact, appearance-wise, your mode of dress is not unlike the Beatles."

Brian: "It's English. We're English."

Ed: "The length of your hair is longer, is it not?"

Brian: "A lot of people have long hair this way in England. Not everybody, not all the young people do. It's pretty well accepted, so if people want to grow their hair long, they're not laughed at any more in England."

Ed: "They say that the way to tell the difference between a boy and a girl in England since they both have long hair and tight pants is that if the pants are tighter and the hair is longer, it's a girl!"

Brian: "There you go."

Ed Rudy: "Charlie Watts is the drummer for the Stones and he is very likely the most conventional of the group. He was born on 2 June 1941 in London and named Charles Robert Watts. He is generally very carefully attired and the best educated of The Rolling Stones. He attended Tyler's Croft School and graduated from Harrow Art College. Charlie Watts is five feet eight inches tall and goes in for continental style clothes. He is undoubtedly the Beau Brummell of The Rolling Stones."

Ed: "Are the Rolling Stones rebels of any type?"

Charlie: "No, people say we are but we're not really. We're just sort of kids of today. I think that any kid of any day is a rebel, he's gotta be."

Ed: "They say that your fans are classed by sizes of stone. Like your real little fan is a pebble and he gets bigger until he's a boulder. Was this started by the group or the fan clubs?"

Charlie: "Yeah, I should imagine the fan clubs. I would never have even thought of it. I think it's very novel, actually."

Ed: "Do you write any of the songs that you sing?"

Charlie: "No, I just contribute my bit. Which is not writing. It's a collective thing. If we ever write a Nanker-Phelge thing which . . . they're our own songs, Mick has a line, Keith does a rhythm, I do a rhythm, it just happens."

Ed: "Do any of the Stones have musical training?"

Charlie: "Er, I'm not sure. I think Brian has, and Keith might have as well."

Ed: "Do you read music?"

Charlie: "Not very well, I'm sorry to say."

Ed: "Would you consider yourself a Beatle fan to any degree?"

Charlie: "I met Ringo when he came back from here, very tired. Er, yeah, you know, I think they're very talented fellas. Lennon and McCartney, yeah. I am a Beatles fan if you can call it that."

Ed Rudy: "Keith Richard is the lead guitarist for the Stones and started playing when he was a very young child. He is five feet ten inches tall and was born on 18 December 1943 in Dartford, England. His family name is Richards but Keith dropped the 's' because he thought that Keith Richard sounded better. He was a good student and attended Sidcup Art School where he won many prizes. He is quite quiet offstage, but a stand-out performer on stage with The Rolling Stones."

Ed: "Would you join a 'Stamp Out the Beatles' club?"

Keith: "No, I wouldn't."

Ed: "Are you a Beatle fan?"

Keith: "I'm not a fan; I appreciate some of their stuff. I like them; I think they're good."

Ed: "What would you say is the difference between the Beatles' sound and The Rolling Stones' sound?"

Keith: "We've got a more coloured sound, a more rock'n'roll sound."

Ed: "A rhythm and blues thing, an R&B sound. They call it in America, a down-home blues."

Keith: "Yeah, that's right. You got it."

Ed: "Have any American groups in particular influenced The Rolling Stones' style?"

Keith: "Yeah, lots. A lot of people: Chuck Berry, Jimmy Reed, The Miracles' stuff, Marvin Gaye, people like that, you know."

Ed: "Strangely enough, while the Beatles sound and The Rolling Stones sound is nowhere near the same, they claim to have been influenced by the very same groups. How would you account for that?"

Keith: "I dunno. We've got different ideas on what happens. We interpret it differently. I think it's a good thing. Maybe it is, maybe it isn't, I dunno."

Ed: "The Beatles are in between rockers and mods. How would you determine what The Rolling Stones are?"

Keith: "I don't bother with that, quite honestly. We don't class ourselves as anything."

Ed: "Do you have any specific reaction to the type of publicity that you've received in America?"

Keith: "I don't really care what they write about us, so long as they write about us. But, we do bathe, that's all I've gotta say."

Ed: "Why do you think this publicity came about?"

Keith: "I think everybody associates long hair with dirtiness; I don't know why. Maybe it's a Victorian thing or something."

Ed: "Either that or just not taking a haircut often enough. That is not the case. Actually, the length of your hair is almost standard in Great Britain at this point, is it not?"

Keith: "I should say so. It's a lot shorter than some people's."

Ed: "Yeah, but those girls don't count!"

Keith: "You're being cheeky!"

Ed: "I was teasing. How would you account for the success of The Rolling Stones?"

Keith: "I think it's a cross between the music, the image and the time that we came along. I think we came along just at the right time. It was luck, among other things."

Ed: "This rhythm and blues sound that you have. Have you ever had another sound? Would you say that this is a particularly British sound? Does it sound to you like the people who originated this sound?"

Keith: "We hope it does. We're trying. Maybe, it doesn't sound the same, you know, but that's because of what we are. I think at least we're trying, you know?"

Ed Rudy: "Bill Wyman is best known as the Married Rolling Stone, and his gaunt appearance and very long hair makes him stand out. Bill plays

72

bass guitar for the group and the piano for his own enjoyment. He is five feet eight inches tall and was born on 29 October 1941 [*sic!*] in Lewisham, just south of the Thames river, near London. He is the father of a baby boy. Bill Wyman enjoys reading poetry and his hobby is studying the stars, but he hasn't had much time for it since he became a star himself."

Ed: "One of you is married? Who is that?"

Bill: "Me."

Ed: "I knew it! That's why I asked. Do you find that your fans are any different than the rest of the fellas? Do you attract a unique type because you're the married Stone?"

Bill: "No, I think it's the same. It doesn't seem to make a difference to 'em too much, not in England, anyway. I don't know too much about America. In England, the fans are fans – whether you're married, single . . . it's horrible!"

Ed: "Do you find a great deal of difference between American girls and British girls as fans? We're not gonna ask you anything else because you're a married man, I'm sure you wouldn't know. But as fans . . ."

Bill: "No, they seem just as interested in you. They scream just as loud and they like your records just as much. I think they're about the same."

Ed: "Are the 'pebble people' here wilder than they are in England?"

Bill: "No, about the same."

Ed: "You mean you get this fantastic response practically any place in the world that you go?"

Bill: "Yeah, all except for Switzerland. They're a bit old-fashioned there."

Ed: "Gee, that country's been there so long I imagine there's a shortage of teenagers."

Bill: "Shortage of something, I don't know what it is."

Ed: "What's your reaction to some of these horrible magazine articles?"

Bill: "As far as what they say about us, it doesn't bother me because I think the true fans know what we're like and as far as they're concerned, the writers writing them, it only shows up their lack of writing well, that's all. If they've got nothing better to write about, I think they should give up."

Ed: "Bill, how did this thing come up, writing miserable articles about the Stones? Did this originate in Europe? Did it start here? How did it come about?"

Bill: "It started when we started in England, but by now in England, everybody knows what we're really like so they don't write things that are untrue. But of course, when you go to a new country, and we're fairly new to America, you get the same thing starting again. And after a certain period, it will wear off."

SUNDAY, 25 OCTOBER 1964

The band début on what is probably the most influential light entertainment show on American television.

Mick: "Another rehearsal for *The Ed Sullivan Show* in the first half of the day. Then did the actual performance. Fantastic welcome. Ed told us it was the wildest, most enthusiastic audience he'd seen any artist get in the history of his show. Got a message from him a few days later saying: 'Received hundreds of letters from parents complaining about you, but thousands from teenagers saying how much they enjoyed your performance.'"

The host tells a different story elsewhere.

Ed Sullivan: "I promise you they'll never be back on our show . . . Frankly, I didn't see The Rolling Stones until the day before the broadcast. They were recommended by my scouts in England. I was shocked when I saw them. Now the Dave Clark Five are nice fellows. They are gentlemen and they perform well. It took me seventeen years to build this show. I'm not going to have it destroyed in a matter of weeks."

Writing in The New York Herald Tribune, *Tom Wolfe waxes lyrical on the Great Stones Debate.*

"The five Rolling Stones, from England . . . are modelled after the Beatles, only more lower-class deformed. One, Brian Jones, has an enormous blonde Beatle bouffant . . .

"The girls have Their Experience. They stand up on their seats. They begin to ululate, even between songs. The look on their faces! Rapturous agony! There, right up there, under the sulphur lights, that is them. God, they're right there! Mick Jagger takes the microphone with his tabescent hands and puts his huge head against it, opens his giblet lips and begins to sing . . . with the voice of a bull Negro."

Those "giblet lips" are back in action with a vengeance during the tour . . .

Mick: "On the whole the Americans are very generous people, but they're very rude. The police are unbelievable. In the south they look like cowboys, wearing Stetsons and carrying guns and riding motorbikes. In towns they look like they do on the films. And they're not quietly spoken like they are in Britain. In fact, they're loud-mouthed. In Britain I think they're a bit fed up with knocking us. The knockers here are madder than in Britain and more demonstrative. They're just twisted out of their minds. Because they think everything that is ever said about us is serious, lots of people think we're being hit around and are pawns in the hands of publicity men. You've only got to give a joke answer to a question and

74

they make it into a serious statement of fact. We go everywhere by car. Even then in the hotel lobby the other day, an 80-year-old woman asked me if I was one of The Supremes! She wasn't kidding."

MONDAY, 26 OCTOBER 1964

The Stones tour rolls into the Memorial Auditorium, Sacramento, California. A poster outside the venue proudly proclaims:
"Now . . . No. 1 in England
Why Have Thousands of European Teenagers Rioted?
Because of THE ROLLING STONES."

In Cleveland, Mick is asked whether the band's club appearances are behind them.
Mick: "Nobody plays clubs when they get anywhere because if you go to a town where about 5,000 people want to see you, what's the point of playing a club which can only hold around 500?"
Q: "You started in clubs though?"
Mick: "Yeah, in the Crawdaddy Club in Richmond, Surrey."
Q: "Will clubs come back into the picture when you're a little older?"
Mick: "Oh, no."
Q: "What's in the offing in five years' time musically? How about it, Charlie?"
Charlie: "We'll probably be deaf by then."

MONDAY, 2 NOVEMBER 1964

The Stones spend a day recording at RCA Victor's new studios in Hollywood – the first of two sessions squeezed in during the American tour.
Mick: "We are recording in the US solely because we believe we can produce our best work there. We can record right through from six o'clock in the morning over there without so much as a tea break, and the engineers are first class."
Brian: "Los Angeles is definitely my number one place. I'm not impressed by America as a whole – there's still a terrible rat race, and the people can be rather stupid in a crowd. I hated New York, but Keith liked it."

THURSDAY, 5 NOVEMBER 1964

The band return to New York, where Mick and Keith meet up with James Brown.
Mick: "Keith and I went to see him live at the Apollo in Harlem, and his

show was great. The audience work with him, and respond to everything he does. But even so you can hear everything he's singing. We were the only white people in the audience, and they announced from the stage that two Stones were there, and girls at the back started shouting and screaming. Afterwards, we visited James in his dressing room and the scene was fantastic. He sits there like a lord. Someone puts a phone in his hand when he wants to call somebody, and somebody else is combing his hair for him at the same time. He laughs all the time – I can't really work out what at – and he gives you champagne from a big tub in the corner."

Towards the end of the tour, in mid-November, another television crew catches up with the band.

Q: "Well, you've now been on your second tour of the United States for three weeks. How was it?"

Mick: "It was really enjoyable, a very successful tour."

Q: "That was not true of the first one, was it?"

Mick: "Oh, no, but we only came over on the first one so that we could get ourselves known, so to speak. And then, when we went back, things started to happen for us."

Q: "Why did they start happening?"

Mick: "I don't really know. Something sort of chemical . . . reaction seemed to have happened."

Q: "What do you think happened?"

Charlie: "I really don't know, quite honestly. Press relationships seem to have been much better over here."

Q: "Do you think perhaps the general public started getting a little tired of the Beatles and have been looking for something new?"

Keith: "I dunno about that. What could you say to a thing like that? Yes, I suppose so, perhaps."

Q: "You've been number two to the Beatles, but you're catching up fast, I'm told."

Bill: "What, in America, you mean? Probably, yeah."

Q: "What about in England?"

Bill: "Yeah, we're number one. We have been for about six months now."

Number one and, according to Daily Express *gossip columnist William Hickey, beginning to move in unlikely social circles.*

"There's no harm these days in knowing a Rolling Stone . . . And pop people do not seem to mind who *they* mix with. Some of their best friends, in fact, are fledglings from the upper classes."

FRIDAY, 13 NOVEMBER 1964

'Little Red Rooster' is released in the UK.

Marianne Faithfull: "Excellent, this will be a fantastic hit. It's interesting because Mick Jagger seems more gentle and pleasant on this. One thing I didn't like was their affected hardness. It always annoyed me. I wish they would use Brian Jones' qualities with the harmonica more."

Some critics feel that the Willie Dixon song, a slow blues, isn't commercial enough.

Mick: "I don't see why we should have to conform to any pattern. After all, wasn't 'Not Fade Away' different from 'It's All Over Now'? We try to make all our singles different and so far every one has been in a different tempo. This time, I didn't want to do a fast beat number. It's a straight blues and nobody's ever done that, except on albums."

FRIDAY, 20 NOVEMBER 1964

After miming to the new single on Ready, Steady, Go!, *Brian is asked about the group's plans.*

Brian: "We're all having a holiday and we all need a holiday. We have about six weeks off, I think, and we've been working very hard and my resistance was very low, so the doctors tell me. When in America I picked up this virus which they still don't know what it is. They're just growing cultures."

THURSDAY, 26 NOVEMBER 1964

"DUKE WAS A LONG HAIR LIKE MICK, COURT TOLD"

Mick Jagger pleads guilty to three motoring offences at Tettenhall, Staffordshire, and is fined £16.

Dale Parkinson (Jagger's solicitor): "Put out of your minds this nonsense talked about these young men. They are not long-haired idiots but highly intelligent, university men. The Duke of Marlborough had much longer hair than my client, and he won some famous battles. His hair was pow-dered, I think because of fleas – my client has no fleas! The Emperor Caesar Augustus was another with rather long hair. He won many great victories. Long hair is worn by barristers in court curled up at the ends . . . This unhappy country suffers from a perennial disease called the balance of payments crisis and it needs every dollar it could earn. The Rolling Stones earn more dollars than many professional exporters."

FRIDAY, 27 NOVEMBER 1964

Mick gives his verdict on the new Beatles single, 'I Feel Fine'.
"I like the backing more than anything . . . it's very good. I don't like the lyrics all that much."

As the year draws to a close, the novelty seekers demand to know what might be the first craze of 1965.
Brian: "Why does there always have to be a next craze? I couldn't give a damn about any beat boom. I am interested in The Rolling Stones, and we have nothing to do with beat booms. I know this much – there's a Rolling Stones boom, though of course, that will die one day."

Nevertheless, news that a folk/protest boom has been sweeping the States, and is likely to arrive in Britain in the New Year, inspires Fabulous *magazine to ask Mick and Brian to describe their 'Brave New World'.*
Brian: "My world would be a world without sickness . . . a world where sickness of the body and of the mind would cease to exist. I'd like lots of money spent on neuro-research – to find out what causes mental illness. When man can understand the human brain, he'll understand everything. A world without sickness would be a world without cruelty, and that's everything."
Mick: "A perfect world would be a drag. Think, if everyone was nice to you, what a bore. But I want to see poverty wiped out. And I want a peaceful world where everyone isn't walking around in fear of something or someone. I wouldn't like to see everyone the same. I don't like seeing the adoption of a political system or culture by people when they don't really want it . . . when it's pushed onto them by other people. We should all have the right to choose which way to live our lives . . . whatever world we live in."

Television interviewers are not always so sensitive with their questioning . . .
Q: "Keith, it's obvious that you don't get your hair cut. But do you get it trimmed from time to time?"
Keith: "Yes, last night."
Q: "It's certainly grown a lot since then. What sort of brand image do you think your group gives to the average mums and dads?"
Keith: "Er, I dunno."
Q: "Brian, what did you do before you joined the group?"
Brian: "Just bummed around, waiting for something to happen, really."
Q: "How much do you earn?"
Charlie: "Thousands!"

Q: "Brian, you have many hobbies. One of them includes antiques."
Brian: "This question always embarrasses me because I know nothing whatsoever about antiques."
Q: "I understand you use pop bottles to give some of the effects in your recordings. Is that right?"
Charlie: "No. I never heard of it."
Q: "Mick, the Beatles gave you your first hit record did they not?"
Mick: "No."
Q: "You have said, 'We don't even care if parents hate us or love us, most of them don't know what they're talking about anyway.' Can you recall making that statement?"
Mick: "No. Don't believe everything you read in the press."

SATURDAY, 9 JANUARY 1965

Mick Jagger reviews the new pop singles in Melody Maker.

Manfred Mann – 'Come Tomorrow '
"No! I don't like it at all . . . it's a terrible new record for Manfred."

Jan & Dean – 'Sidewalk Surfin' '
"All right if you like that sort of thing. But I don't! It won't be a hit."

Cheetahs – 'Soldier Boy'
"No! No! They've lost all the simplicity of the Shirelles original. And I reckon somebody's singing flat."

Rolf Harris – 'The Five Young Apprentices'
"Oh, that's awful. Terrible. Take it off."

Ronnie Hilton – 'Dear Heart'
"I can't stand it."

Novas – 'The Crusher'
"It's the best so far. And that's not saying much."
"Well, that wasn't a load of good stuff today, was it? I'm not generally like this, but really, it was a bit of a drag. Manfred's got the only certain hit there – and I didn't even like that."

FRIDAY, 15 JANUARY 1965

The band's second album, Rolling Stones No. 2, *is released. The sleevenote, penned by Andrew Oldham, appears to be inspired by Anthony Burgess' recent novel,* A Clockwork Orange.

"Cast deep into your pockets for loot to buy this disc of groovies and fancy words. If you don't have bread, see that blind man, knock him on the head, steal his wallet and lo and behold, you have the loot. If you put in the boot, good. Another one sold."

This doesn't go down well with Mrs Gwen Matthews, Secretary of the Bournemouth Blind Aid Association.
"They're horrible. It's putting ideas into people's heads. I'm writing to Decca to ask them to change the cover."

Two months later, the matter is raised in the House of Lords by Lord Conesford, who is told that the Director of Public Prosecutions has ruled that the published words do not constitute a criminal offence. Lord Stoneham, Joint Parliamentary Under-Secretary, at the Home Office, seeks to placate him.
"If it is any consolation to the noble lord, research I made at the weekend supports the view that even when they are intelligible the words of a pop song are not considered important and teenagers have even less regard to the blurb on the envelope."

Nevertheless, Decca, who initially dismissed Oldham's text as "a giggle", relents.
"We deleted these words off goods from the factory a week ago, before notice of the question was given in the Lords. They were written by Andrew Oldham, who records The Rolling Stones. What was meant to be a joke misfired. He is most apologetic. There is some talk of doing something for the blind. They are most hurt. This is the jargon of the kids today. He did not wish to cause any offence to anybody."

As for the music . . .
Mick: " 'Under The Boardwalk' had us all going out of our minds. For two hours we had a series of minor catastrophes that ruined every take. We really mucked things up. My voice cracked on the high notes and Bill's amp packed up. Charlie missed a beat. Brian and Keith made mistakes. We all broke up. Kept apologising to each other all the time. It turned out to be one of the most successful things on our second LP."

TUESDAY, 26 JANUARY 1965

"STONES GAS AUSSIES"

Brian Jones phones home from Brisbane, Australia, midway through the band's first tour Down Under.

Brian: "Australia is a gas. We didn't think it would be anything like this. They seem to like us. We were worried, to be truthful – we thought it would just be Beatles, Beatles and nothing else. But it's Beatles and Stones. Five shows so far – all sell-outs. The most popular number is 'Little Red Rooster' – funny considering we didn't want it released in any country except England! The audiences are marvellous – the whole scene is much hipper than we expected. There's only been one slight rough side to everything here and that's been press reaction. The papers have been having terrible 'go's' at us. But we made some vitriolic remarks about the papers during radio and television interviews and that seems to have brought a lot of people round to our side . . . Just heard that the Righteous Brothers have got to the top with 'You've Lost That Lovin' Feelin''. That's knockout news. We've plugged it like mad since it came out because it's such a terrific record."

SATURDAY, 30 JANUARY 1965

Don Short talks tough with the Stones in what appears to be the band's favourite magazine outlet, Melody Maker.

Q: "Have the Stones any moral obligation to teenagers?"

Mick: "Everyone has their own moral code. I conduct myself as I see fit and what I do is my affair. In the same way I feel this should be the right of every teenager today. If they want to smoke, drink, swallow purple hearts and pills, then the decision is theirs. It is not for me to criticise them. Stars and celebrities should not try to set any lead in morals. Who are we to say what is right and what is wrong? . . . It was once considered detrimental for a star to be seen smoking or drinking in photographs. That is all different today. Everyone accepts we smoke and drink, and so do other young people. They are nobody's fools."

Q: "How do The Rolling Stones view religion?"

Keith: "What is religion anyway? Does it mean you are a bad sinful guy if you don't go to church? We're atheists and we're not ashamed to admit it. We wouldn't stop anyone else from going to church. But people who go to church just for the sake of it, to keep up appearances and smile at the vicar, are idiots."

Q: "Has The Rolling Stones' attitude to life changed?"

Bill: "I would never work for anyone else now. I was once in diesel engineering and I couldn't stick a 9–5 again. I would like to stay in this business, and I'm now preparing plans to do just this. I've got to be ready for when the Stones die – as ultimately they must. The glamour has never worried me much and I enjoy being a family man. The money, I must admit, has made a big difference. If there's anything we want in the home we can have it. But has it all changed me materially? Very little, I would say."

Q: "There have been frequent rumours of disharmony among the Stones. Is there any chance of them splitting?"

Charlie: "We would not be human if we occasionally didn't have the odd word to say to one another. But there has never been any major row between us. Rumours came thick and fast that we were splitting when we were in America last time and Brian went into hospital. To us, rumours like this are just a big bore. The truth is we are probably the most closely knit group in the whole country. There's no chance of the Stones splitting."

Q: "Are the majority of your fans the breed of teenager rebellious to parental control?"

Brian: "Certainly our fans are most demonstratively dedicated. That's because we have come out on the side of the kids. They find in us themselves. They are searching for new ideas and new things in their adolescence. An outlet in self-expression. That's why they come to us . . . adolescent youth must be given the chance to think for itself. Teenagers seek their own niche in life – and when they do, parents may quite naturally regard it as a rebellious streak. Every generation brings a fresh wave of ideas – and if the age of adolescence was stifled, then society and culture would be drowned. Our children will be rebelling against us in 20 years' time in just the same way."

MONDAY, 1 FEBRUARY 1965

Mick phones home from Christchurch, New Zealand.

Mick: "Our Australian tour has been very, very good – better than we ever imagined it could be. We now have four records in the Top 10 – and we didn't have any when we arrived. 'Under The Boardwalk' from our album is the number one single in Sydney, and 'Walking The Dog', 'Heart Of Stone,' and 'Little Red Rooster' are all doing well. We have been getting up at 8 a.m. and then going straight out to the beaches. And we haven't been getting home to bed until around 3 a.m. . . . Everybody is marvellously sunburned – I have never seen the Stones look so healthy."

Australian paper reports . . .

"Shockers! Ugly looks, ugly speech, ugly manners . . . They speak as they look – rough. There is none of the musical twang of the Beatles' speech in the Stones' harsh London accents."

Despite the press, Brian continues to praise the country on his return home . . .
Brian: "I was so impressed with Australia. No one takes them seriously over here: we send up the accent, and laugh at jokes about kangaroos and gum trees, but I tell you their standard of living is much higher than we have. I'm not being anti-British, but Australians are so nice, friendly, relaxed and happy-go-lucky. In London, the streets are filled with neurotics . . . If the majority of English people could see what Australia is like, there could be a mass exodus next week. Singapore was a fantastic place too . . . Everybody was so polite in Singapore, including the press. I can't stand press conferences in America and Australia. The reporters try to be funny and rude, just to impress each other, and we're just their guinea pigs."

. . . where audiences are growing ever more hysterical.
Keith: "This tour is pretty mad and it's doing ridiculous business. Fans have pulled down curtains, crashed through barriers and jumped on the stage. They have got a new thing going – the suicide wish. Girls have started jumping out of the balconies now!"

FRIDAY, 26 FEBRUARY 1965

'The Last Time', recorded a month earlier in Los Angeles, is released.
Mick: "We've written, arranged and recorded things in a matter of minutes. Yet when we came to do 'The Last Time' we tried so hard that it took seven or eight hours in America to get what we set out to do."

MONDAY, 1 MARCH 1965

The Stones talk to Brian Matthew during a break while recording a radio session for the BBC.
Q: "Mick, you've achieved so very much on the international scene. What is there left to make you want to go on?"
Mick: "What drives us on? If you've ever got to do anything that you haven't done before. Or if you look forward to something, like going to a new country or perhaps making a film or making new records – always something new."
Q: "Brian, do you visualise the group going on for a long time, or do you think you'll get to the stage where you'll say, we've made it, let's get out of it."
Brian: "Well, it's very difficult to say, but certainly things seem to be as

big now as they were . . . I mean, there's no lessening of interest. Reactions everywhere are good. At the moment, I'm not worried. But I can't give any long-term answer."

Q: "From your own point of view, you'd like to go on for a long time?"

Brian: "Oh, I think so. As long as things keep on happening, as Mick says, as long as there's always something new to look forward to."

THURSDAY, 11 MARCH 1965

Michael Parkinson grills Mick Jagger in a Granada TV studio.

Q: "Mick, we've had the normal sort of Stones-type reception for you today, girls swarming round the taxi. What's it like being a Stone, having this 24 hours a day?"

Mick: "It's something you get used to. After two years of it, it just becomes part of your life. You might think it's unusual, or you think you couldn't stand it, but you get used to it. I could say the same thing to anybody in any job: how could you do that all the time?"

Q: "Have you ever thought about what kind of an adulation it is? Why do they do it?"

Mick: "It's sexual completely."

Q: "How much longer do you give yourself doing this?"

Mick: "I never thought I'd be doing it for two years. When we started off, I never thought we'd make it very big anyway. Now we've been making records for two years and everybody still goes round calling us a new group. I don't know, quite honestly. I think we're pretty well set up for at least another year."

Q: "Do you ever think of a future?"

Mick: "Well we've climbed a ladder really. We've gone up . . . When it looks like it's gonna go down, I'm gonna pack up. It all depends on how much money I've got and exactly what my financial position is. If I don't have to worry about money I can do exactly what I like."

Q: "If you had enough money, what would you do?"

Mick: "I'd try and write songs and just produce records and things. I'd also like to do films but that's something that's really gotta be worked hard at."

Q: "As an actor?"

Mick: "Yeah."

Q: "You are in a curious position in the pop world as far as groups are concerned. The Beatles are adored by mums and most everybody. You are not adored by mums generally are you? Mums tend to look at you and say, 'Would you let your daughter marry a Rolling Stone?' "

Mick: "Well, maybe. There are lots of mums and dads that turn up at our concerts. I'm not sure really what they come for! But they do, they turn up without any kids and things. The other night there were half a dozen people – they must have been 80! They didn't come with any grandchildren or anything like that. Lots of mums and dads like us and lots of them don't."

Q: "You've been in a bit of trouble recently over the dress you wear in restaurants. You weren't allowed into the Midland Hotel in Manchester. There was a story in the paper this morning about the manager at a hotel in Yorkshire, the Scotch Corner, complaining about biscuits being trod into your carpets and your hotel bedroom and telephone numbers being scribbled on the walls. Do you think you are badly behaved in public?"

Mick: "Well, sometimes. Most of the things are exaggerated and why this particular hotel manager got so upset was that he was trying to be a little over-officious as some of them do. He turned round to Brian and said, 'I'm giving you an order to get out of your rooms!' It got very nasty. And this is why it got exaggerated. I dropped a biscuit and I got up in the morning and got out of bed and trod in it. Which is most unfortunate but I'm sure other people do that. I'm sure commercial travellers tread on biscuits sometimes. We're not the only people."

Q: "What about this other business of not wearing a tie going into a restaurant. You're worldly enough surely to realise that there are restaurants that you can't go into without ties. Do you do it deliberately?"

Mick: "Naah. I don't honestly have a tie. I've never liked ties much and I haven't got one. If it was the Duke of Edinburgh he'd get in."

Q: "Do you wish you were the Duke of Edinburgh?"

Mick: "No, quite honestly I wouldn't like to be the Duke of Edinburgh!"

FRIDAY, 19 MARCH 1965

"SAVE TIE MAKERS"

Taylor & Cutter *magazine suggests that Mick and the Stones are responsible for the bleak employment prospects of the nation's tie makers.*

"This article is triggered by the sartorial discrepancies of Mr Mick Jagger (lead singer of The Rolling Stones) but the trend towards disregard for proper clothes for proper occasions is one shared in its instigation by other celebrities in the show business world. The Stones are not the only pebbles on the beach, but an authoritative lead from the number one spot on the

Top 20 would be clearly welcome. It might do more for the necktie than all the tie weeks from here to forever."

Mick: "The trouble with a tie is that it could dangle in the soup . . . it is also something extra to which a fan can hang on when you are trying to get in and out of a theatre. As for having a purse at the end of a tie – this would lead to a nation of rich hunchbacks!"

SATURDAY, 27 MARCH 1965

It's Brian Jones' turn to play Blind Date *in the popular* Melody Maker *singles review column.*

Miracles – 'Ooh, Baby Baby'
"I'm trying to make my mind up if this is really coloured, because there are a lot of records now with a coloured feeling."

Temptations – 'It's Growing'
"I don't think there's going to be a big Tamla-Motown thing. Let's face it, Marvin Gaye came over here, but he never had a hit record – which is a great shame because he's really one of my favourite artists. The Temptations could make it, though."

Stevie Wonder – 'Kiss Me Baby'
"He's a good harmonica player, but I don't reckon him much. He plays a chromatic harmonica and you can't get a really bluesy feeling."

Beach Boys – 'All Summer Long'
"They usually sing better than this. Oh, God, no! This is corny. I wouldn't have been surprised if this was a British group trying to get a surf sound."

Peter & Gordon – 'True Love Ways'
"It's pretty soulless, but it's nice. All the Buddy Holly fans are going to be wringing their hands in anguish. Me and Paul McCartney played on some of their LP tracks – just for a laugh."

FRIDAY, 2 APRIL 1965

While the group tour Scandinavia, reporter Klaes Burling reprises a few familiar questions.
Q: "Brian, you get a lot of bad publicity. How come?"
Brian: "The whole thing started really with bad publicity. It just became the thing to write certain things about us such as, 'Oh, The

Rolling Stones never wash, The Rolling Stones are rude, they're scruffy.' We don't take any notice of it because our fans know it's not true anyway. The press write what they want. Anything controversial is bound to be good. If the press ignored us completely, we'd worry about it."

Q: "What kind of music do you prefer?"

Brian: "I like all sorts of different music. I know more about American rhythm and blues music than I do about any other sort of music, because that was the particular music I became interested in in a very practical way; I wanted to play it. But I like classical music, and I like good pop music."

Q: "What kind of artists do you like?"

Brian: "My favourite artists are American coloured artists such as James Brown, Muddy Waters, Jimmy Reed, Bo Diddley, Chuck Berry."

Q: "You still like records by Muddy Waters?"

Brian: "Oh yeah. I think Muddy Waters is fantastic. He created a whole new style of folk singing, he really did."

Q: "What do you think of English groups and artists?"

Brian: "I like very few. Let's face it, nearly all the English groups have got their original inspiration from coloured American music, so they're not original to such a great extent. But some of them are, I think, very bad. What *we* have is what the American's call soul, and I think the Beatles are very good musically; in fact, they're my favourite British group. Apart from them, there are very few English groups that I do like. The Animals are good musicians, but apart from that, I can't think of very many people I like at all."

Q: "What do you think of Elvis Presley?"

Brian: "I think Presley got a whole thing going . . . I'm not very interested in Elvis Presley. I think he made some very good records early on when he was still interested in his profession. He lost interest in his career a long time ago. Presley's records are very impersonal and he has no feeling behind them. I just wouldn't bother to listen to Elvis Presley these days. As far as I'm concerned, he's of no importance in the pop music world whatsoever."

Back home, the Stones dispense advice for budding 'Beat' players . . .

Keith: "I do not believe in having lessons. You only learn how some old geezer in their thirties wants you to play — a few Django (Reinhardt) chords and that's that. Nobody can teach you this music. Either you've got it or not . . . Don't start this game unless you really want to. You've got to really want to play around every spare minute. If you just fancy yourself as being a big star, don't bother."

Bill: "The bass guitarist must learn to knit together perfectly with the drums. Keep going all the time. Never lag behind. I don't think anybody sets out in life to be a bass guitarist. People start learning the guitar then find there are more vacancies for bassists than any other instrument."

Brian: "I play a lot of lead guitar and I am not really interested in rhythm guitar. Rhythm guitar is a very functional instrument, and it's a drag. In the Stones, we often have two lead guitar patterns going and we never use straight rhythm as in the old Shadows days. We also use a heavy bass riff pattern – a Chuck Berry thing. If we have got two guitars, we might as well use them to full advantage."

Charlie: "Just play with a good beat and use a lot of bass drum. Get a big back beat. I use the hi-hat a lot – Ringo does as well. If you have got a quiet passage in the tune, then you play the hi-hat closed. For the other cymbals, have a big crash and a ride. Most of my playing is volume, and I use a heavy stick."

Mick: "In an all-guitar group, harmonica helps make for variety of sound. But it's no good trying to teach people. Years ago, I asked Cyril Davies if he'd teach me, and he just replied: 'There's nothing to teach.' He said the same as I say now – go and blow it and suck it, but know when to do it. And you can't teach that. My favourite player is Little Walter; Keith Relf of the Yardbirds is just about the best in this country. When you've learned to play harmonica well, don't leave it alone for a long time. It's easy to forget things about it. It's a good noise and sounds dead right if it's played okay."

Not everyone welcomes the advice . . .

"It's a pity (Keith Richard) doesn't know a few Django chords, then we wouldn't have to listen to 16 bars of one major chord as on 'It's All Over Now' " (letter to *Melody Maker*).

A disgruntled Brian Jones is already envisaging a life beyond the confines of the Rolling Stones.

Brian: "I want to produce records. At the moment, I'm just soaking in the feel of the business. When I was in America, I saw Phil Spector and Brian Wilson of the Beach Boys, and it was great to watch those people at work. There's not one record producer in this country who's as good as the Americans. Who would I record? Well, any sort of pop artist. I'd love to produce in America."

Even the gossip columns begin to sense Jones' unease.
"How does Mick Jagger feel about Brian Jones' constant statements that he thinks Eric Burdon Britain's best singer?"

Brian quickly repents.
"I reckon Mick's twice as good as Burdon."

FRIDAY, 16 APRIL 1965

The first of three nights at the Paris Olympia. Melody Maker's *Jack Hutton joins them and notes that . . .*
"Françoise Hardy attended all three Stones concerts . . . French boys leaving concerts wore Donovan-type hats and shouted, 'En bass Yeh Yeh', which apparently means down with the 'Yeh-Yeh' type singing . . . One far-out French 'singer' on the Stones bill had wilder hair than Ken Dodd and walked on stage with two chickens on a lead . . . Mick was by far the most popular Stone in Paris . . . Jagger speaks French quite well when he wants to . . . The police even guarded the Stones' hotel when they weren't in it."

THURSDAY, 22 APRIL 1965

The Stones arrive in Quebec for their third North American/Canadian tour.
Q: "Have you worked here before, Mick?"
Mick: "We've never worked here before. We tried to get in here once but Keith didn't have a passport."
Brian: "Keith lost it."
Keith: "They said it was very doubtful they'd let us back in again. And we had to play in Detroit that night."
Q: "Who are some of your favourite groups, Brian?"
Brian: "We all like virtually the same American artists. We like James Brown, Solomon Burke, Wilson Pickett and people like that, don't we fellas . . ."
(muted approval)
Q: "What were you doing before music and The Rolling Stones came along, Charlie?"
Charlie: "I was a designer."
Q: "In what field, fashion?"
Charlie: "Advertising."
Q: "Would you like to get back into this field eventually?"

Charlie: "No. Perhaps Mick would like to answer."

Mick: "What? Charlie. Used to be in advertising, apparently. He just told you. Doesn't wanna to go back into it, though."

Q: "You had a formal education at the London School Of Economics, didn't you?"

Mick: "A misfortune, yes."

Q: "Why a misfortune? Is formal education not a good thing, Mick?"

Mick: "I'm glad I went because now I know how to draw curves."

Q: "Have the Rolling Stones learned a lot about life being on the road?"

Brian: "Oh yes. We've been practically all over the world and we've seen things that we've read about in books. I'd better not go any further . . . we've learnt a lot about life!"

Q: "What problems do you run into on the road?"

Keith: "Dirty shirts. Laundry takes at least a day to do."

FRIDAY, 30 APRIL 1965

Bob Dylan's British tour kicks off in Sheffield. While in the States, the Stones discuss the man whose name is on everyone's lips.

Brian: "I think Dylan's probably out of his mind sometimes, but he's great. We've got a lot of albums, and we've been playing his more than any other. He's a little frustrating because you don't always understand what he's really saying, but some of his lyrics are unbelievable. We've been watching Donovan too. He isn't too bad a singer but his stuff sounds like Dylan's. His 'Catch The Wind' sounds like 'Chimes Of Freedom'. He's got a song, 'Hey Tangerine Eyes' and it sounds like Dylan's 'Mr Tambourine Man'."

Mick: "Dylan is the darling of the sweet young things now. And they latch onto him not really because they really like him, but because it's suddenly the 'in' thing to do. We used to be the hip, 'in' thing too and R&B was the same way."

Brian: "Then the hard core dropped and started moaning in ecstasy about Muddy Waters, John Lee Hooker and some of the others. Now they've gone right down the line till they're off R&B altogether. This is what probably will happen to Dylan. It's the old familiarity breeds contempt idea."

MONDAY, 10 MAY 1965

The band take a break midway through their US tour to spend another day at Chess Studios in Chicago.

Brian: "It's not so much the studio itself as it is the engineer. We could spend half a day in any other studio getting our proper balance, but that man (Ron Malo) is terrific. He knows what we want and he gets it right away. It's a great place to cut a record, and America is a great place to be generally. You see these albums all around the suite? We've picked them all up since we got here. You can't get a lot of this blues stuff back home."

Mick: "We all love to dig the real sounds of R&B, to hear the groups and the bands that have something to say. But there isn't really anything in England today that any of us would go to see expecting to learn something. It's all right here in America. You've got to come here to get the real thing."

Q: "Mick, you've recorded two or three discs in America. What's the reason for this?"

Mick: "We've done most of our later recordings in America because we find the studios are better – better facilities and you can get a better sound quicker."

Q: "In other words, you're saying that the American engineers contribute a great deal to the sound you want to achieve?"

Mick: "Yes, they're bound to. They try out all sorts of different things."

During the Chess sessions, the Stones make their first attempt at recording a song written by Mick and Keith a few days earlier in Clearwater, Florida . . .

Keith: "A week later we recorded ('Satisfaction') again (at the RCA Studios) in Los Angeles. This time everything went right. Charlie put down a different tempo and, with the addition of a fuzz box on my guitar which took off all the treble, we achieved a very interesting sound."

Mick: "We cut 'Satisfaction' in Los Angeles when we were working there. We cut quite a lot of things and that was just one – contrary to some newspaper reports, it only took us just half an hour to make. We like it, but didn't think of it as a single. Then London said they had to have a single immediately because 'The Last Time' was long gone and we had a *Shindig* TV date and had to have something to plug. So they released 'Satisfaction' as a single (on 5 June, 1965)."

THURSDAY, 20 MAY 1965

The Stones début '(I Can't Get No) Satisfaction' on the ABC-TV show, Shindig!, produced by Jack Good. They also introduce Howlin' Wolf, who performs 'How Many More Times' on the show.

Jack Good: "Tell us about him, Brian."

Brian: "Well, when we first started playing together, we started playing because we wanted to play rhythm and blues, and Howlin' Wolf was one of our greatest idols. And it's a great pleasure to find he's been booked on this show tonight. So I think it's about time you shut up and we have Howlin' Wolf on stage."

FRIDAY, 11 JUNE 1965

The Stones' third UK EP, Got Live If You Want It!, *is released. Material for the record had been recorded at the Liverpool Empire and the Palace Theatre, Manchester in early March. It is reported that the final tracklisting was whittled down from a selection that originally included 'Everybody Needs Somebody To Love', 'I'm Alright', 'Pain In My Heart', 'Down The Road Apiece', 'Time Is On My Side', 'Little Red Rooster', 'Route 66', and 'The Last Time'.*

Mick: "All the numbers taped, except one, have already been issued before, but we feel that the fans, even if they already have them, may well buy the EP as a souvenir of a live performance. The whole operation cost around £1,000 but we are hoping that the result proves worthwhile. Whether the EP will be finally taken from these four sessions we just don't know until we have all listened to the results. We may use four of the tracks, or even three – a couple of the numbers are rather long. The number that's not been recorded before, 'I'm Alright', is a fairly long one and 'Everybody Needs Somebody To Love', which we use as a sort of opening signature, is also lengthy when we play the full version later in the show."

On the same day, the press announces that the Beatles are to get MBEs.
Mick: "Isn't it funny to think of the Beatles meeting the Queen and having a medal pinned on them. I think the funniest thing is these stupid old geezers sending their medals back. I met John the night before the award was announced in the papers. He told me about it and he seemed a bit embarrassed."

The Beatles story fills the letters pages right across the press. Carol Lindsey from Stoke-on-Trent quietly notes that:
"The Stones won't get MBEs because they don't wear ties."

Mick is also asked whether he'd ever write a song for the Beatles . . .
Mick: "We've already done that. A long time ago, me and Keith wrote something called 'Give Me Your Hand And Hold It Tight', but the

Beatles wouldn't do it. They wrote one for us as well, called 'Outside 109' (*probably a reference to 'One After 909' that the Beatles finally released on* Let It Be). We said we wouldn't do the song until they did ours. So nothing happened on either side. We're still waiting."

SATURDAY, 12 JUNE 1965

"JAGGER SWIPES AT FOLK FAKERS"

The folk and protest boom that threatens to knock the Beatles and the Rolling Stones off the front pages is obviously bothering Mick . . .
Mick: "The Dylan and Donovan thing is very refreshing, but I shudder to think of the tenth-rate beat groups playing rotten folk music just because it's the 'in' thing of the moment. I don't dislike folk music, but I hate it when people move in on a thing like that and do it for the sake of it. The folk thing at the moment threatens to be more pretentious than the whole R&B thing of a year ago . . . I don't think it will become huge, actually . . . A couple of years ago, there were people we'd heard of but not heard. Now everybody's been to Britain who we need to see, and the personality seems to have gone. It might take a long time before anything new happens. I can't really see it being folk."

Ian Campbell, of the Ian Campbell Folk Group, responds angrily:
"It seems comical to hear Mick Jagger talking about folk 'fakers'. Is there nothing fake about an English ex-grammar school boy trying to sound like a Southern Negro farmhand?"

Jagger's 'folk' credentials take a further knock when he talks to the press from a phone in Auchterarder, Perthshire, during a whistle-stop tour north of the border.
Mick: "It's funny in Scotland . . . I mean, they're all a bit uncivilised up here."

Even the usually reticent Keith finds his voice . . .
Keith: "Whatever these sweet young things who dig Dylan say, I bet they don't understand much of what he is doing. We play a lot of his LPs, Brian and I, and quite a lot of his lyrics don't mean anything to us. I have nothing against Dylan or Donovan, but I'm sick to the back teeth of the characters who are just climbing on a craze, that think they can make quite a fortune."

THURSDAY, 22 JULY 1965

"ROLLING STONES FINED FOR A 'PUBLIC INSULT'"

Bill Wyman, Mick Jagger, and Brian Jones are each found guilty and fined £5 for 'insulting behaviour' during an incident at the Francis Service Station in Romford Road, Forest Gate, East London in March.

Mr Kenneth Richardson (prosecutor): "The three stopped at the service station late at night, Wyman used disgusting language in asking an attendant if he could use the toilet. After being told the public toilets were being reconditioned and being refused permission to use the private toilet, they urinated against the boundary wall of the service station . . . They assumed they had the right to treat the property of others with the utmost contempt."

"The court heard of the night a Daimler car pulled into a petrol station in Romford Road. Mr Kenneth Richardson, prosecuting, said that eight or nine boys and girls got out and Wyman asked if he could go to the lavatory, but was refused. A mechanic, Mr Charles Keeley, asked Jagger to get the group off the forecourt of the garage. He brushed him aside, saying, 'We will piss anywhere, man.' This was taken up by a group in a chant as one of them danced. Wyman, Jagger and Jones were seen to urinate on a wall of the garage. The car drove off with people inside sticking their hands through the windows in a well-known gesture."

Keith: "Bill has probably got one of the biggest bladders in human existence. When that guy gets out of a car to take a pee, you know you aren't going to move for 15 minutes."

"LONG-HAIRED MONSTERS"

Magistrates' Chairman: "Because you have reached the exalted heights in your profession, it does not mean you have the right to act like this. On the contrary, you should set a standard of behaviour which should be a moral pattern for your large number of supporters. You have been found guilty of behaviour not becoming of young gentlemen."

SUNDAY, 1 AUGUST 1965

The Stones play two shows at London's principal showbiz venue, the Palladium.
Eric Easton (Co-manager): "We felt it was time the Stones were brought into the West End."
Melody Maker *reviewer Nick Jones left with mixed feelings:* "The impact of their huge sound and the visual effect was fantastic. But Brian Jones, all in

white, was much too loud and completely drowned the others – to the extent that one didn't hear a single word that Mick Jagger sang all night."

MONDAY, 2 AUGUST 1965

The infamous 'Plastercasters' of Chicago eye up Keith for a 'fitting' when the Stones next roll into town.

"Dear Keith,

"We watched you on TV the other night and the first thing that grabbed our eyes was your lovely Hampton Wick. After that we did little besides studying it. We're not kidding: you've got a very fine tool, as a friend of ours puts it. From the way your pants project themselves at the zipper, we figure you've got a beauty of a rig . . . Hey, tell Mick he doesn't have to worry about the size of his either; we noticed that already (well, who could help but?). Our favourite names for you are Keith the Giant Meat and Hampton Mick.

". . . We can hardly wait till you come into town in November, maybe then we can find out more about what's inside your pants . . . If you're interested, drop by awhile, why don't you, when you're in Chicago or give us a ring. We're both 18 and like to wear tight-fitting sweaters.

Reach us at: Cynthia Plastercaster, Chicago, Ill."

FRIDAY, 20 AUGUST 1965

'(I Can't Get No) Satisfaction' finally gets a British release.

Mick: "In England, we already had the EP all pressed up, the covers done and the plugs lined up before we knew that 'Satisfaction' was going to be a single. But now, of course, we are happy. Anyway, after the EP, the Beatles had 'Help!' and it seemed silly to issue 'Satisfaction' then. If 'Help!' hadn't come out, then we would have brought it out a month ago."

Mick: "I get the idea for a lyric quite separately from the songs. And Keith gets his ideas quite separately from my lyrics. In the case of 'Satisfaction', we thought of a phrase and the riff first, and worked from there.

"Keith and I wrote it – half in Canada, half in Florida. It is quite fast and very danceable. I think it has very funny sounding guitar on it. Eric Easton (co-manager) thought it was a saxophone. But it's not – it's Keith's lead guitar. Actually, there's only one electric guitar on the track."

Q: "Mick, I've read in the papers that you took 38 hours to record it ('Satisfaction'). Is this true?"

Mick: "God, no. Not even with a hamburger break in the middle! No, it only took us about two hours to do it, and that included arranging it 'cause not everybody knew the song, and then another hour to mix it. But it actually took two hours to make the record."

Q: "What's 'Satisfaction' about?"

Mick: "Frustration."

Burt Bacharach, reviewing the single for Melody Maker, *is less than impressed:*
"So violent, so rude. Why can't they be polite, like Paul and John? Or at least write poems, like Bob?"

Bob Dylan (in conversation with Keith): "I could have written 'Satisfaction' but you cats could never have written 'Tambourine Man'."

SATURDAY, 21 AUGUST 1965

Newsweek *describes The Rolling Stones as a "leering quartet with tasteless themes and lyrics".*

Keith: "It's a lot of rubbish and typical America now, isn't it? It's like the old Mothers' legion banning Elvis again. There are some weird people who stand up on their soapbox and preach that you are undermining the morals of young America and all that sort of crap . . . I think maybe the article could help us. They printed our picture and you know they always say it doesn't matter what the writer says as long as he spells the name right."

SATURDAY, 28 AUGUST 1965

It is announced that the Stones' management partnership of Andrew Oldham and Eric Easton has split. Allen Klein will become the group's co-manager, and will work alongside Oldham. It is also announced that a deal has been struck with Decca for five films, and that Tito Burns will become the band's UK agent and that William Morris will handle the band in the US.

Andrew Oldham: "I manage the Stones, and Allen Klein manages the Stones and me. I met Allen two months ago through Mickie Most, and I think this will be a tremendous help to the Stones career."

Allen Klein: "Andrew, how'd you like to be a millionaire?"

Andrew Oldham: "Of course."

Klein: "Okay, whaddya want for now?"

Oldham: "I want a Rolls-Royce."

Klein: "You got it . . ."

Andrew Oldham tells Daily Express writer Judith Simons:
"Under the terms of a deal concluded by our American business manager, Mr Allen Klein, the Stones are guaranteed three million dollars over the next five years. It isn't all profit, of course. Expenses are high. Each guitarist owns about eight instruments, and the total cost of their present equipment was £4,000. When the Stones are on tour hotel bills are about £700 a week. Salaries for secretarial and other staff accounts for £200 a week."

THURSDAY, 2 SEPTEMBER 1965

The group pre-tape a special Stones edition of Ready, Steady, Go!*, during which they reveal their favourite singles of the year.*
Mick – Wilson Pickett's 'In The Midnight Hour'
Keith – Bob Dylan's 'Like A Rolling Stone'
Brian – The Four Tops' 'It's The Same Old Song'
Bill – Bo Diddley's 'Hey Good Lookin''
Charlie – Ramsay Lewis Trio's 'The In Crowd'

FRIDAY, 3 SEPTEMBER 1965

The Stones leave for a two-day Irish tour accompanied by filmmaker Peter Whitehead. The initial idea is to shoot footage for a promotional film to accompany their next single.
Mick: "We feel that this is a progressive step. Something has to be done to try and breathe new life into the pop shows. This is a step towards a new approach to television pop."

Whitehead also shoots a series of one-to-one interviews with each band member.
Mick: "You're not the same person on stage as you are the rest of the time."
Q: "What sort of person do you think you are on stage?"
Mick: "I don't really know. I don't really know what I am on stage. It's very different because you have to treat everybody differently. You have to be very egotistical 'cos you're acting, you're doing an act for them. It's not really you."
Q: "What do you set out to do in your act?"
Mick: "Entertain people."
Q: "Why take up music?"
Charlie: "I didn't look upon it as taking up music. I just took up the drums, and a musician to me . . . I play music that doesn't need an art form . . . If

someone said to me, 'You're playing with Shostakovitch next week,' I'd say, 'How wonderful,' but how could I play with Shostakovitch? I can't read [music]."

Q: "Shostakovitch is not only reading music. He's feeling music."

Charlie: "I don't know how to put half of what I feel down. Maybe it doesn't matter. Maybe it's just an inferiority complex. Maybe I'm great after all."

Q: "Do you think you're imaginative with your work?"

Charlie: "Yes."

Q: "Do you ever feel that you're evolving something new that hasn't been done before?"

Charlie: "What, when I play? No."

Q: "Do you ever try?"

Charlie: "No."

Q: "Would you like to?"

Charlie: "I couldn't because I think the limitations are pretty strict."

Q: "What, you mean the instruments?"

Charlie: "Just popular music is restricting in a way."

Brian: "Let's face it, the future as a Rolling Stone is very uncertain."

Mick: "In the last two or three years, young people – this especially applies to America which is the biggest and most important country in the western world, therefore the young people in America are the most important – have gone through a transition. Instead of just carrying on in the way their parents told them to, they've started a big thing where they're anti-war and they love everybody and their sex lives have become freer. And they want to change society, a lot of them. It could be changed, the whole basis of society and values, and it definitely could be changed for the better. But it's up to them when they reach the age of 21 to carry on those ideals they have, or at least to keep them in the back of their minds, instead of just falling into the same old routine that their parents have fallen into, which is just grabbing as much money as they could and not knowing what to do with it."

Mick: "Popular music wasn't a real thing at all. It was very romantic in so far as every song was about boy/girl relationships which is romantic in one sense. If you listen to popular songs from ten years ago, very few of them actually mean anything, or have any relationship to what people were doing. Songs didn't have any relation to what people were actually spending their lives doing, like getting up, washing, going to work, coming back and feeling very screwed up about certain things. They were just about being unhappy because your girl had left you, or being very happy because you'd just met somebody. That's all they were about – 'the moon in June' and 'the sky is blue' and 'I love you'."

MONDAY, 6 SEPTEMBER 1965

The Stones return to RCA Studios in Los Angeles where they complete work on eight songs. One, tentatively titled 'Hey You, Get Off My Cloud', is tipped as the band's next 45. Mick continues to praise American studios.

Mick: "Recording-wise, they're way ahead. I much prefer to cut our records in an American studio, although I don't particularly like America. Touring over there is a drag. It's like playing a different country every night."

He also confirms that the group is changing – in several ways.

"I think our image is softening. People don't hate us as much as they used to. We're becoming more accepted, mainly because people are getting used to us . . . We like to think we're progressing musically, too. The difference between our first record 'Come On' and 'Satisfaction', which we cut in the States, is fantastic."

THURSDAY, 9 SEPTEMBER 1965

Barry McGuire's controversial 'Eve Of Destruction' enters the British chart. Mick is not impressed.

Mick: "Oh, take it off . . . please! I can't stand any more. I've never heard such awful rubbish in my life. It's all about hating war, but it's written because it's commercial and it's so phoney: Americans like it because of the lyrics. Any record with a sort of protest in it is going to be a hit, including 'Satisfaction', Bob Dylan, Sonny & Cher and other wonderful things . . . But you have to point out the difference between this and Dylan and Donovan. This is crap."

SATURDAY, 18 SEPTEMBER 1965

Mick announces that he intends to team up with photographer David Bailey in a comedy film – and that "none of the other Stones will be in it". Inevitably, the declaration prompts 'Mick to quit the Stones' rumours.

Mick: "Why should I? I'm happy with the group as it is. I've always been happy to be a member of the Stones and I've certainly no intention of going solo. We get on very well, always have, so why split a successful partnership?"

And as for the Stones' much-fancied film project . . .

Mick: "It's such a bore. I won't say anything about it. People have been reading about the Stones film for two years now and it's still non-existent, it still hasn't been made."

FRIDAY, 24 SEPTEMBER 1965

Out Of Our Heads, *the third UK Rolling Stones LP, is released.*

Mick: "One person who reviewed our LP kept saying, 'It's got bits of Dylan or bits of Donovan,' and things like that. What does it matter if it sounds a bit like something else? It's better in the States. There, they treat every record as a separate thing and only ask, 'Will it sell?' That's the important thing. Everyone says there are trends in pop music. The youth trend, the R&B trend, the ballad trend. It's a load of rubbish. We used to do a couple of folky numbers, but we've had to drop them because people were saying, 'The Stones are doing a Dylan or a Donovan.' It's crazy."

SATURDAY, 2 OCTOBER 1965

Disc Weekly announces that Bill Wyman is to manage a new band, The End. Once again, rumours that all is not well within the Stones camp, and that Wyman is about to leave, are rife.

Bill: "It's the first I've heard of it. I don't know if any of the boys know about it. I'm certainly not quitting. If I'm thrown out I still get my money, but if I leave of my own accord, I don't. I'm not stupid."

WEDNESDAY, 27 OCTOBER 1965

The Stones fly out from London Airport for North America.

Andrew Oldham: "This is the boys' fourth American tour, but the first one that is going to pay dividends. During this six-week period of concerts and TV appearances, we will gross an unprecedented £1,500,000."

Once again, the band delights the nation's youth but enrages much of Middle America. They are "slightly simian," says Newsweek *in a piece titled 'Pop's Bad Boys'. And as for that "liver-lipped" singer . . . Jacqui Swift in the* Washington Post, *tries to restore some balance.*

"The United States has been faced with war, depression, racial discrimination, murders, disease, rapists, natural disasters – and if we fall apart just

100

because five men from England perform in an unusual manner, then I feel this country is in great need of help."

In the wake of mass demonstrations against the Vietnam War on 17 October, the topic that appears to be mobilising the nation's youth against the establishment begins to crop up in pop interviews.

Keith: "What does Vietnam have to do with me? They fight, they don't fight – I don't care."

Mick: "I wouldn't live in America. I don't like the country enough. I prefer England. The atmosphere is too much for me. Life is too fast here with everyone rushing around like a lot of idiots. I don't like the food because menus lack variety. The transport cafes are better than the transport cafes in England but the good restaurants here are not anywhere near as good. All the food tastes pre-packed . . ."

TUESDAY, 9 NOVEMBER 1965

During the infamous New York 'black-out', harmonica-blowing Brian Jones jams with Bob Dylan at the Warwick Hotel until his lips bleed. The friendship prompts speculation that Brian is the 'Mr Jones' referred to in Dylan's 'Ballad Of A Thin Man'.

Q: "Who is Mr Jones?"

Bob Dylan: "Mr Jones, I'm not going to tell you his first name. I'd get sued."

Q: "What does he do for a living?"

Bob Dylan: "He's a pinboy. He also wears suspenders."

TUESDAY, 7 DECEMBER 1965

New Musical Express *reports that "Rumours have been sweeping London for the past ten days that Brian Jones of The Rolling Stones is about to marry. His wife-to-be is 20-year-old German model, Anita Pallenberg. At a recent Chelsea party, Jones said, 'The wedding is definitely on, and Bob Dylan will be best man.'"*

Meanwhile, a Stones version of 'As Tears Goes By', taped in London, is released as a single in the States.

Andrew Oldham: "In America, each record is judged purely on whether it will sell or whether it's a good record. If we released this here, we'd only be accused of copying and people would say it was another 'Yesterday'."

The same week, the Stones were in California recording a batch of songs for a new album, including ' 'Goin' Home' – that was rumoured to last for up to 12 minutes.

Charlie: "We did ten numbers altogether . . . They are all originals written by Keith and Mick, and although I don't say they are the best songs the Stones have ever written, I think that musically they are the best things we've ever done."

THURSDAY, 13 JANUARY 1966

"THE GIRL WHO LOVED A ROLLING STONE"

A paternity order was made against Brian Jones in relation to a four-year-old boy, Julian Mark, whose mother Patricia Andrews had issued a summons. Jones, who did not attend the hearing, held at South West London Magistrates' Court, due to illness, was ordered to pay 50s per week maintenance plus £60 costs.

Sir John Cameron: "The Bench finds it deplorable that the child is now four years old and has not been recognised and helped by his father up to the present date. We find it impossible to understand the father's attitude. If we could make a larger order we would do so."

Pat Andrews: "When I met Brian I was as green as anything. At the time I was so madly in love with Brian that I didn't think of the consequences. To be honest, even when I was about seven months pregnant, I wouldn't believe that I was pregnant. It wasn't until the actual time that I had Mark that I knew I had to be. I would never tell anyone else to go out and do the same thing I did unless they know they've got some money to support them.

"I went to work, and Brian was working. But his main interest was his guitar. He never bought very much food, he paid the rent and that was it. I had to find the food and the money to buy clothes and odds and ends. It was really rough going. We used to starve quite often. Mark didn't but Brian and I did. The first few months were all right, Brian was quite proud of Mark; he would carry him about and take him everywhere. Then his manager said that due to the publicity, he shouldn't go round with Mark. Finally, when they did make a record and they became pretty well known, he just seemed to drift away. He wasn't interested in Mark anymore. He was just interested in the people he'd met, the big names they were going around with.

"When I'm walking down the road with Mark and he sees some toy he wants, I just can't afford to get it for him, and I ask myself, 'Well, Brian's got enough money, why can't he give me some to buy him something.' I think if he was turned out on the streets, I think nobody would want to know Brian. He's not the kind of person that you'd take to because he's so cynical. He's got no feelings for anybody, he just uses people for his own good and when he's finished he throws them aside."

FRIDAY, 4 FEBRUARY 1966

'19th Nervous Breakdown' is released. Mick gives a rather spurious account of the song's inspiration to Rolling Stones Monthly *magazine.*
Mick: "We had just done five weeks hectic work in the States and I said, 'Dunno about you blokes, but I feel about ready for my nineteenth nervous breakdown.' We seized on it at once as a likely song title. Then Keith and I worked on the number at intervals during the rest of the tour. Brian, Charlie and Bill egged us on – especially as they liked having the first two words starting with the same letter."
Keith: "It's alliterative."
Mick: "We're not Bob Dylan, y'know. It's not supposed to mean anything. It's just about a neurotic bird, that's all. I thought of the title first – it just sounded good."

"So where," asks Sue Mautner, "do you get your inspiration for the lyrics?"
Mick: "Things that are happening around me – everyday life as I see it. People say I'm always singing about pills and breakdowns, therefore I must be an addict – this is ridiculous. Some people are so narrow-minded they won't admit to themselves that this really does happen to other people besides pop stars."

FRIDAY, 11 FEBRUARY 1966

Disc magazine gets each Stone to describe another.
Mick by Bill: "He's changed a lot – he was a lot quieter and less confident. He was very friendly when I first met the group. Now he's more difficult to get on with. He's automatically on guard with people he's not sure about – if they're trying to hang on. He's always been very close to the rest of the group and at no time have we been scared that he was going to quit and turn solo.

"Why does Mick send people up? I think he puts these send-ups on as a way of being a comedian. He's not a born comedian and so he finds it's a way out for him to make people laugh.

"He gets depressed sometimes and we have to bear with it. He's a bit careful with money – not extravagant like Keith. I also think Mick's a romantic – very much so. When the group breaks up, I think he'll do something completely different."

Keith by Mick: "Very untidy and very forgetful – that's Keith. I've known him longer than anyone else in the group. I still don't know what he's thinking at any time and he really is one of my closest friends. We live close to each other. From time to time, we've had little arguments. In fact we disagree quite a lot, but we usually come to a compromise. There's never any hard feeling. He's forgetful and so he doesn't remember to bear a grudge. He's very good at his songwriting now and we've got a relatively efficient way of going about it.

"Keith's so awful in the mornings. But occasionally he changes and is so bright. That's a drag because it's out of character! The rest of the time he's so lively . . . He's very good about the group. Very optimistic. This cheers me up when I'm feeling low. I think people find it difficult to know Keith. Sometimes he's shy, other times he can't be bothered to take an interest in people."

Brian by Charlie: "He's basically a very quiet bloke. He likes being left alone – not on his own, though. He's really a very soft person. His biggest fault is the same as mine – people don't know him. I know him really only as someone I play with. He can be very funny, though – when he feels like it. He's fairly quick-tempered but he gets over it. Like all of us, he's a bit moody. He's generous to people he wants to be generous to. He's very wary of people he doesn't know. This business makes people that way.

"At the start, in particular, he worked very hard with great determination for the success of the group. When the only place he could learn and rehearse was from records, he used to sit there for hours listening to LPs."

Bill by Brian: "I'm very fond of Bill. In fact I often feel very paternal towards him. He gets drunk more easily than the rest of us. He's more difficult to understand than the rest of us because he's married and, until recently, lived a very reserved home life. But now he and his wife are coming out more.

"I think I'm considered the mad raver of the group and he's the opposite. He's older than the rest of us and more stable. Rather matter of fact. He's a very likeable guy and an excellent musician. He picks things up more easily than the rest of us. Bill is very concerned with money and he's very precise with things."

Charlie by Keith: "You don't have to partake in the whole affair of the pop business – I don't anyway. I think Charlie fits in the group and the business as much as anyone. He fits in well really because you only don't fit in if you're awkward. And Charlie ain't awkward. He hasn't changed much since I first met him except he's a lot happier since he got married.

"Charlie's a very deep thinker. It's hard to tell if he's listening to a conversation or thinking about something else. Then, when you think he hasn't heard a thing you've been talking about, he'll start discussing the subject. But he's not that deep that we don't know him – although he still surprises us . . . he's a good bloke."

Meanwhile, Rave *magazine gets at least as close to the truth with its own 'Analysis of the Stones'.*
"Brian Jones – He is subtle, hypersensitive and the intellectual of the group. He has great artistic talent and is capable of creation of a highly original and personal level. Loves to shock, lives at a very fast pace, almost as though he doesn't want time to think. He has an aggressive quality, is inwardly anxious and a little vulnerable – slightly afraid of life. But he has a tremendous charm, a great deal of personal magnetism, and a devilish streak which is unconsciously revealed in his answers."
"Mick Jagger – He's got loads of personality, but isn't as free as he'd like to be in expressing it. Plenty of creative talent, spontaneous kindness and an easy-going nature. He has an amazing talent for communicating with people. Mick is the soul of the Rolling Stones."
"Charlie Watts – He gives the impression of being slow, but his presence visibly strengthens the rest of the group. He is a person who lacks the creative talent of the others."
"Keith Richard – If the Stones' popularity wanes, Keith will find it a little more difficult to adjust than the others. He's an anxious, affectionate person who tends to shy away from reality. His identification with the group protects him. He's very sensitive and artistic, and lives spontaneously."
"Bill Wyman – A craftsman and something of a buccaneer. He has the hands of a practical man and his writing shows technical aptitudes. He dislikes intellectuals yet, to a certain extent, he is one himself. He's rational, cool and calculating with a very strong will. He enjoys dramatic situations in which he can play a dominating role."

SUNDAY, 13 FEBRUARY 1966

As the Stones plug three singles – '(I Can't Get No) Satisfaction', 'As Tears Go By' and '19th Nervous Breakdown' – on The Ed Sullivan Show, *Brian Jones is excited by the change in mood Stateside.*

Brian: "America is a great scene for us at present. We've never been so powerful there. I think we've reached a peak in Britain but things are still opening up for us in the States . . . There's one interesting development in the US, which does not exist for us here any more. That is, we've built up a type of intellectual following among the hippies. The Greenwich Village crowd all dig us. There was a terrible scene out there just before I left. The police were stopping and searching everybody on sight – looking for drugs, I suppose, but it was frightening. Worse than a police state."

Mick isn't convinced by the tone adopted by a new breed of American journalist . . .
Mick: "They (the press) don't like most of the groups any more. They quite like us, but they have this ridiculous attitude towards us – a sort of intellectual approach towards the group."

SATURDAY, 26 MARCH 1966

The band land at Schipol Airport for a show that evening in the Kurhaus, Scheveningen, The Hague, Holland.
Q: "Are you still runners-up for the Beatles?"
Brian: "I dunno. We've got different scenes going. I've got no idea who's more popular in what part of the world. I don't sort of worry about that."
Q: "How's your popularity in Europe at the moment?"
Brian: "Very good, I think. Very healthy."
Q: "Why did England become the pop centre?"
Brian: "I think England had the right type of sound and the right sort of visual image that kids around the world wanted at that particular time. It could have happened anywhere . . ."

TUESDAY, 29 MARCH 1966

Two sell-out shows at the Paris Olympia confirm that basic instincts are as much part of the Stones' appeal as the search for a deeper meaning.
Mick: "They were ripping the seats apart and beating up the gendarmes. The kids were going bonkers. Even hitting the police with their own truncheons. I kept out of it as much as possible. I don't like seeing police being thumped."

'The Generation Gap'
Mick: "Once the mums and dads start saying to their daughters, 'Now why can't you find someone nice and polite like Mick Jagger?' The Stones will be finished."

Brian: "We never deliberately went out to antagonise parents as many suspected, although I will confess here and now, we are not particularly interested in pleasing parents."

THURSDAY, 7 APRIL 1966

Otis Redding's version of '(I Can't Get No) Satisfaction' enters the British singles chart. A rumour spreads that the song might not have been a bona fide Jagger/Richard original after all.

Steve Cropper: "As far as the story that Otis wrote 'Satisfaction', it's completely false because we took The Rolling Stones' record and then cut our version of what we thought we heard."

Otis Redding: "They really groove on 'Satisfaction'. It's too much. I like their original things better. But they can't do anybody else's songs."

FRIDAY, 15 APRIL 1966

The Stones' first self-composed album, Aftermath, *is released.*

Brian: "I don't like the new LP cover (that Andrew) did, but I don't think it was really his fault."

Andrew Oldham: "Everyone's grown older and become more mature. Mick and Keith write about everyday things that are happening and their songs reflect the world around them."

Some feel that the album includes a surfeit of songs – 'Under My Thumb', 'Out Of Time', 'Stupid Girl' for starters – that adopt an unhealthy misogynistic attitude toward women.

Mick: "When I write our songs, I never think about boy–girl relationships."

SATURDAY, 23 APRIL 1966

Brian Jones is the subject of this week's 'Pop Think-In' in Melody Maker.

Money: "I hate reading about John and Paul's £150,000 and all their money. It makes me jealous."

Alcohol: "I got quite a reputation a couple of years ago for being the youngest alcoholic in London. But I drink very little now."

Charlie Watts: "A very good friend. I admire Charlie a lot. He's managed to remain serene and calm through all the chaos of the last couple of years."

Birth control: "I'm all for it. I'm all for legalised abortion as well."

Mick Jagger: "He's the best pop performer Britain's ever had. A great inspiration to the Stones. He made the group, really. Without Mick, The Rolling Stones would have been nothing. He's inspired us as a group."

National newspapers: "I read them every day, but the national newspaper reporters I've met have been in rather unfortunate circumstances. I hate the lot, the bastards."

LSD: "Money, I love it."

TUESDAY, 10 MAY 1966

It is announced that the Stones have finally nailed a suitable film project in which to star – based on a novel where, reckons The Daily Mirror, *"the grown-ups commit suicide and teenagers turn Britain into a fascist jungle".*

"In a major acquisition the film rights to the novel *Only Lovers Left Alive* was purchased by Allen Klein for The Rolling Stones. The Stones are to join that affluent acting society peopled by such chosen few as Richard and Elizabeth Burton who command $1 million per film. The group, already surrounded with astronomical earnings from concerts and records, will receive $1 million for their film début *Only Lovers Left Alive*. This is a novel by Dave Willis dealing, in essence, with an imaginary conquest of England by its violent and rebellious youth. Andrew Loog Oldham, the Stones' 22-year-old manager, chose the novel for them . . . Oldham and Klein will co-produce the film."

Keith: "Guess you've heard of the plans for our movie. We're all pretty excited about that, right now. It seems to be all we ever talk about. Mick's been running around seeing every movie he can. Trying to pick up some new ideas, or something, I guess. Mick will play a guy named Ernie, who is a kind of hero, you know what I mean, and I am sort of his right-hand buddy. We hope to begin around October if we can. We're trying to get Nicholas Ray (*Rebel Without A Cause*) to direct . . . Mick and I are working on (the music) right now!"

By November 1966, this project, too, had been quietly abandoned.

FRIDAY, 13 MAY 1966

'Paint It Black' released.

Q: "Is 'Paint It Black' about blindness?"

Mick: "It's about somebody dying, a funeral."

The record introduces the exotic sound of the Indian sitar to the British singles chart.
Brian: "I love the instrument. It gives a new range if you use an instrument like that. It has completely different principles from the guitar and opens up new fields for a group, in harmonics and everything."
Keith: "Sitars are made out of watermelons or pumpkins or something smashed so that they go hard. They're very brittle and you have to be very careful how you handle them. Brian's cracked his already. As we had the sitars, we thought we'd try them out in the studio. To get the right sound on 'Paint It Black' we found the sitar fitted perfectly. We tried a guitar but you can't bend it enough."
Jack Nitzsche: "They didn't know what to play on the back-up and I started playing the piano gypsy style and they just picked it up. I thought it was just a joke."

Oddly, Decca advertise the single with a superfluous comma in the title: 'Paint It, Black' . . .
Keith: "Don't ask me what the comma is in the title; that's Decca. I suppose they could have put 'black' in brackets."

. . . and circulate a press release that concentrates on the Stones' domestic front.

"A MOAT FOR KEITH"

"Stone Keith has recently bought a house (Redlands) in Sussex. 'It's gorgeous,' he says, 'and has a moat around it.' He's the third member of the group to emigrate from London to Sussex – Bill and Charlie bought houses there last year. Brian and Mick still live in London flats. Mick's latest possession is a week-old dark blue Aston Martin sports car. 'My pride and joy,' he says."

THURSDAY, 23 JUNE 1966

As the Stones return to the States for their fifth tour there, a new generation of rock critics sharpens its pens.
Village Voice *critic Richard Goldstein:* "Their names are Bill Wyman, Charlie Watts, Keith Richard, Brian Jones and Mick Jagger. All approximately 21, and together the recipients of $8 million in hard pop star cash. Pete Hamill, a journalist who knows about such things, says they come on like an open switchblade. He means for real. 'We are not nice, but we are honest,' says the image. 'We are not respectable, but we are genuine. We are evil but cool.'"
A groupie: "Aren't they adorable?"

Q: "What's the difference between the Stones and the Beatles?"
Mick: "There are five of us and four of them (or vice versa)."

THURSDAY, 30 JUNE 1966

The Stones temporarily halt a show in Montreal, Canada, when security guards continue to attack members of the audience. Mick telephones Disc *magazine back in London to express his annoyance.*
Mick: "It was unbelievable. We've never seen anything like it before. I was disgusted. There were about 30 bouncers when we appeared – all of them huge blokes, wrestlers, I think. They were punching people up for no reason at all and then throwing them out. One fight broke out at the front of the theatre while we were playing and six of the chaps set on one kid. It was terrible. It was going on in front of 12,000 people, too. In the end we stopped playing because the fans were booing and hissing and pointing at the bouncers. We joined in – and after the show had to run for our lives because the wrestlers tried to get up on the stage after us. I was scared out of my life. I thought we were going to get it that time."

MONDAY, 25 JULY 1966

Violence of a more purposeful kind is preached by a group of radicals in Los Angeles, who greet the Stones with the following leftist manifesto.
"We welcome the Rolling Stones, they themselves are our fellows in the desperate struggle against the mad people who got the power. We fight in guerrilla groups against the imperialist invader in Asia and South America. We make noise at every rock'n'roll concert. In Los Angeles, we set on fire and raid everywhere and the bulls know that our guerrillas will be going back there . . . Fellows, you'll come back to this land when it is free from state tyranny and play your wonderful music in the factories which will be led by workers among one million red flags fluttering above an anarchic community of two million people. Rolling Stones, the young people of California listen to your message. Long live the revolution!"

FRIDAY, 23 SEPTEMBER 1966

No less intemperate is the Stones' next single, the clumsily titled 'Have You Seen Your Mother, Baby, Standing In The Shadow?'.
Mick: "I'm not going to burst into tears if this doesn't go to number one."

he Rolling Stones' first photo session, Chelsea Embankment, May 1963. "We certainly didn't wanna' be
ck'n'roll stars," said Keith Richard. "That was just too tacky." (*Redferns*)

London R&B zealots, September 1962, (l-r) Brian Jones, Mick Jagger (holding a photo of Bo Diddley), Graham Ackers, Keith Richards (with a photo of Chuck Berry) and Harry Simmonds.
(*copyright unknown*)

The original six-man Rolling Stones with Ian Stewart (far left) at the Crawdaddy Club, Richmond, May 1963. "I've a feeling I wasn't cut out to be a pioneer" said 'Stu.' "I never looked upon the group as being a long-term proposition for me as a musician."
(*Dezo Hoffman/Rex*)

Vox Pops, mid-1963. Brian Jones: "We've been the way we are for much too long to think of kowtowing to fancy folk who think we should start tarting ourselves up with mohair suits and short hair." (*Dezo Hoffman/Rex*).

"Scowl!" Andrew 'Loog' Oldham directs his charges to be even more objectionable at a Hyde Park photo-shoot, summer 1964. (*Rex*)

California Dreaming? The Stones at Malibu Beach during their first US tour, June 1964. "Britain's Rolling Stones group are being treated as freaks in America," wrote the *Daily Mirror*. "People gasp in amazement when they appear at airports, in hotel lobbies and in the streets…" (*Mirrorpix*)

Safe in the arms of the law, while leaving a gig in Hastings, Sussex, August 1, 1964. Within three years, police would be escorting the Stones for different reasons. (*Associated Press*)

Charlie, Mick, Andrew Oldham and engineer Glyn Johns listen to playbacks backstage at the Liverpool Empire, March 6, 1965. The recordings were for the Stones' live EP *Got Live If You Want It*. (*Music Sales*)

Arriving to answer charges of insulting behaviour at Romford court, Essex, July 22, 1965. Court prosecutor: "A mechanic, Mr Charles Keeley asked Jagger to get the group off the forecourt of the garage. He brushed him aside, saying, 'We will piss anywhere man'." (*Corbis*)

"... never thought I'd be doing it for two years," said Mick in 1965. "When we started off, I never thought we'd make it very big anyway... I don't know, quite honestly. I think we're pretty well set up for at least another year." *(Gered Mankowitz)*

Royal Albert Hall concert, September 23, 1966 with Peter Whitehead (right) filming a promo for 'Have You Seen Your Mother, Baby…'. Some of the concert was later used on the *Got Live If You Want It* album. (*Pictorial Press*)

Between The Buttons. The 'Swinging London' Stones hold a photo session in Green Park, Mayfair, January 11, 1967. Keith Richard: "You can't suddenly become accepted overnight by cutting your hair, putting on a suit and saying, 'Look, aren't I nice?' It's not us, it's not honest, and why should we?" (*Music Sales*)

Mick and Keith leave Chichester court following their arraignment on drug charges with Stones publicist, Les Perrin (centre) and business manager, Allen Klein (rear middle), May 10, 1967 (*Redferns*)

The same day, Brian Jones was arrested for unlawful possession of cannabis. When shown a phial containing cocaine, Jones reacted, "Not me. I am not a junkie. It is not me at all." (*Camera Press*)

The Stones return to the stage as surprise guests at the NME Pollwinners Concert, May 12, 1968. "If you really want us to cause trouble, we could do a few stage appearances," said Keith Richard. "We are more subversive when we go on stage." (*copyright unknown*)

A *Beggars Banquet* photo session in the Derbyshire countryside, June 8, 1968 (*Camera Press*)

Eric Clapton: "Really, I just didn't think this was good enough a record to reach number one. It wasn't as well constructed or as commercial as other records they've made, but I really can't see this affecting them in any way at all. The Stones are big enough to cope."

Keith: "We don't ask ourselves what is most commercial. We simply say – we like this one best. What we have liked over the past few years has proved to be what the young people like, so this is how to choose a single. This is probably the way that Mozart wrote. He wrote for himself. So do we. And it is a happy coincidence that what we like should also be what our public likes."

Bobby Elliott (The Hollies): "The record was basically above the fans' heads. It was too hippy and those photos showing the Stones in drag put the youngsters off a bit."

Keith: "Progression in music can even go backwards. Look at The Troggs. They are experimenting with simplicity – it's a form of progression. Dylan is a progressive writer. You only have to listen to *Blonde On Blonde* and then his early albums to see how far he has gone. People just aren't sympathetic to Bob Dylan. They said that 'Rainy Day Woman' was rubbish, but if you'd been stoned and listened to the disc you would have understood."

That same day, the Stones begin their last British tour for five years.

Brian: "Certainly things seem to be as big now. There's no lessening of interest, reaction everywhere's been good so at the moment I'm not worried."

Keith: "It's been an enormous success because it's brought the young people back again. In the 'It's All Over Now' era we were getting adults filling up half the theatre and it was getting all 'draggy' and quiet. We were in danger of becoming respectable! But now the new wave has arrived, rushing the stage just like the old times!"

Brian: "A new generation came to see us. Youngsters who had never seen us before, from the age of about 12, were turning up at the concerts. It was like three years ago when the excitement was all new."

OCTOBER 1966

"BRIAN JONES FORECASTS: FREER OUTLOOK ON LIFE MUST FOLLOW NEW WAVE. NEW POP GENERATION'S REVOLUTION IS AT HAND"

With his role within the Rolling Stones ever diminishing, Brian Jones finds his forte as the band's most erudite spokesman.

Brian: "Censorship is still with us in a number of ugly forms. But the days when men like Lenny Bruce and artist Jim Dine are persecuted are coming to an end. Young people are measuring opinion with new yardsticks and it must mean greater individual freedom of expression. Pop music will have its part to play in all of this. When certain American folk artists with important messages to tell are no longer suppressed maybe we will arrive nearer to the truth. The lyrics of 'Satisfaction' were subjected to a form of critical censorship in America. This must go. Lennon's recent piece of free speech (that the Beatles were 'more popular than Jesus') was the subject of the same bigoted thinking. But the new generation will do away with all this – I hope."

Brian still harbours many unfulfilled musical ambitions, as NME *journalist Keith Altham reveals:*

"Brian played me some of the experiments in sound he has been conducting in the privacy of his new home. He impressed on me that they were purely personal attempts and that the mixing and dubbing were far from perfect. He seemed enthusiastic but embarrassed about his efforts. One tape was astoundingly effective with a weird, psalm-like chant going on in the background like an electrified Black Mass. Some further electronics sounded like The Who after a few drinks!"

There is more controversy, during this period, when Brian poses satirically in a Nazi uniform with his girlfriend Anita Pallenberg.

Brian: "The recent pictures of me taken in Nazi uniform were a put-down. Really, I mean with all that long hair in a Nazi uniform, couldn't people see that it was a satirical thing? How can anyone be offended when I'm on their side? I'm not a Nazi sympathiser.

"I noticed that the week after the pictures of me taken in that uniform appeared there were photographs of Peter O'Toole in the same newspaper wearing a German uniform for a film he's making. But no one put him down for wearing that."

FRIDAY, 7 OCTOBER 1966

The Stones play Colston Hall, Bristol. Marianne Faithfull attends at the request of support act Tina Turner, and – as recounted in her autobiography Faithfull *– she spends the night watching Roman Polanski's* Repulsion *with Mick before going out for a dawn walk in a nearby park.*

Marianne Faithfull: "It was sunrise and my boots had got wet in the dew. When we got back to the room I remember he unlaced my boots and put them to dry by the heat. He was sweet that night, I was completely moved by his kindness. And then we made love. And then I left. But, of course, I was beginning to think, 'This guy is pretty amazing!'"

SATURDAY, 15 OCTOBER 1966

Mick and Marianne 'come out' at the launch party for underground magazine International Times *at the Roundhouse in Chalk Farm.*
Mick: "I went to one of those 'smashing happenings' at the London Roundhouse a few weeks back. I thought everyone would be freaking out and wearing weird clothes but they were all wandering around in dirty macs. It was the most boring thing I've ever seen. Paul McCartney thought everybody would be wearing weird clothes and he went as an Arab, which must have been very lonely for him, because when I went, there wasn't another Arab in sight."

MONDAY, 19 DECEMBER 1966

Mick announces that his three year romance with Chrissie Shrimpton is over.
Mick: "We just couldn't get along together, for two people so close to one another. Three years is a long time to be with someone. But I don't feel as cut up about it as you may imagine. Although we were unofficially engaged, we hadn't set any date for a wedding. I don't dig the marriage bit at the moment."
Chrissie Shrimpton: "We just grew out of each other. This was the only solution. We had been unofficially engaged for some time. We were very much in love. The strange thing is we argued the whole time. As time goes on, you begin to feel differently about life – and about each other. There was no explosive row or anything like that. We broke up by mutual agreement. If anyone asked how I feel now – I don't. I feel nothing."

A few days later, Mick's ex is admitted to a nursing home suffering from stress.

WEDNESDAY, 28 DECEMBER 1966

It is reported that the Stones will appear on ITV's Sunday Night At The London Palladium *show in the New Year, to promote their forthcoming single, 'Let's Spend The Night Together'.*

Mick: "Times are changing. And with the changing times comes a different market – one market. We think the Palladium is ready for the Stones, and the Stones are ready for the Palladium."

Kenneth Eastaugh, TV critic for the Daily Mirror *is delighted by the news.*
"On too many occasions, I have begun to feel they should advertise this show as: 'The Only Show That Gives You That Monday Morning Feeling on Sunday Night' . . . It is time for the Palladium Show to come up to date."

SATURDAY, 21 JANUARY 1967

It is announced that Brian Jones has been commissioned to write and record the soundtrack for a new film by a young new German director, Volker Schlondorff.
Brian: "It's been something I've been working on for a long time and I've got my first offer within the last few days. It's very new and I haven't had the chance to talk to anybody about it. That's why I have to be vague. There's really nothing more I can say because you must realise that everything we do exists within the framework of The Rolling Stones."

SUNDAY, 22 JANUARY 1967

The group appear on The All New Sunday Night At The London Palladium *show – and reaffirm their bad boy reputation by refusing to join the other artists on the revolving stage at the end of the programme.*
Mr Albert Locke (producer): "Who do the Stones think they are? Every artist that's ever played the Palladium has done it. They are insulting me and everyone else."
Mick: "Anyone would think that this show is sacred or something. That revolving stage isn't an altar. It's a drag . . . Anyone who thought we were changing our image to suit a family audience was mistaken."
Brian: "Why should we have to compromise with our image? You don't simply give up all you have ever believed in because you've reached a certain age. Our generation is growing up with us and they believe in the same things we do. When our fans get older, I hope they don't require a show like the Palladium."
Mick: "It was a mediocre show, and it made us the same. It was all terrible . . . We were dreading the Palladium performance and we will never do a programme there again."

Keith: "You can't suddenly become accepted overnight by cutting your hair, putting on a suit and saying, 'Look, aren't I nice?' It's not us, it's not honest, and why should we?"

MONDAY, 30 JANUARY 1967

New Musical Express feature writer Keith Altham interviews Brian and Keith in a bar off Kensington High Street. While Keith remains fairly mute, boisterous Brian – drinking Guinness and flicking ash into his untouched oxtail soup – speaks with remarkable eloquence and prescience.

Brian: "Our real followers have moved on with us – some of those we like most are the hippies in New York, but nearly all of them think like us and are questioning some of the basic immoralities which are tolerated in present-day society – the war in Vietnam, persecution of homosexuals, illegality of abortion, drug taking. All these things are immoral. We are making our own statement – others are making more intellectual ones.

"Our friends are questioning the wisdom of an almost blind acceptance of religion compared with total disregard for reports related to things like unidentified flying objects which seems more real to me. Conversely, I don't underestimate the power of influence of those, unlike me, who do believe in God.

"We believe there can be no evolution without revolution. I realise there are other inequalities – the ratio between affluence and reward for work done is all wrong. I know I earn too much but I'm still young and there's something spiteful inside me which makes me want to hold on to what I've got.

"I believe we're moving toward a new age in ideas and events. Astrologically we are at the end of the age called the Pisces Age – at the beginning of which people like Christ were born. We are soon to begin the Age of Aquarius, in which events as important as those at the beginning of Pisces are likely to occur. There is a young revolution in thought and manner about to take place."

Eventually, he manages to add a few words about the contemporary music scene.
"I'd like to see the Move. They are really an extension of our idea of smashing conventions. Those kind of smash-ups they have – destroying TV sets, cars, etc., are all a part of dissatisfaction with convention. Pete Townshend's tendency to smash guitars is a physical reproduction of what is going on in his mind. I wish he'd write a book!"

SUNDAY, 5 FEBRUARY 1967

"POP STARS AND DRUGS – FACTS THAT WILL SHOCK YOU"

The second part of The News Of The World's *special series on 'Pop Stars and Drugs' turns its attentions to pop's perennial bogeymen.*
"Another pop idol who admits he has sampled LSD and other drugs is Mick Jagger of The Rolling Stones . . .

"He told us: 'I don't go much on it (LSD) now the cats (fans) have taken it up. It'll just get a dirty name. I remember the first time I took it. It was on our first tour with Bo Diddley and Little Richard.'

"During the time we were at Blaises (a Kensington club), Jagger took about six Benzedrine tablets. 'I just couldn't keep awake in places like this if I didn't have them,' he said . . .

"Later at Blaises, Jagger showed a companion and two girls a small piece of hash (solid marijuana) and invited them to his flat for 'a smoke'."

In fact, the ill-informed investigator had actually been speaking to Brian Jones. Unsurprisingly, Mick Jagger issues a hasty statement later that day.
Mick: "I am quite shocked that a responsible newspaper can publish such a defamatory article about me."

Coincidentally, he is booked to appear on The Eamonn Andrews Show *that night.*
Q: "What's this we've been reading about you, Mick?"
Mick: "Oh, I can't discuss that. It's all untrue, inaccurate and misleading. I am issuing a writ and suing *The News Of The World*."

It was perhaps less of a coincidence when, one week later, as Keith Richard threw a weekend party . . .

SUNDAY, 12 FEBRUARY 1967

"DRUG SQUAD RAIDS POP STARS' PARTY"

It isn't until the following weekend that news of the bust becomes public. Even then details are restricted to the fact that shortly after 8 p.m., a team of 15 policemen and women, led by Chief Inspector Gordon Dineley, raided Keith's country home in Redlands Lane, West Wittering, near Chichester.
Keith: "Look, there's lots of little ladies and gentlemen outside. They're coming in. They have this funny piece of paper, all sorts of legal rubbish."
Chichester Police: "Officers entered the house under the authority of a warrant issued by a magistrate under the Dangerous Drugs Act. As a result,

several persons were questioned and certain articles were brought away from the house. We have to wait until we get the analysis before possible further action can be taken."

Sgt Cudmore (to Keith): "Should laboratory tests show dangerous drugs have been used on the premises and not related to any individual, you will be held responsible."

Keith: "I see. They pin it all on me."

A week later, The News Of The World *coyly reveals that . . .*

"Several stars, at least three of them nationally known names, were present at the party. It was held at a secluded country house near the South Coast."

The report in The Sunday Telegraph *tells it straight.*

"Police have raided the country mansion of Keith Richard, one of The Rolling Stones pop group, in West Wittering, Sussex, and searched the house and all the people present for drugs. Among some 12 guests at the weekend houseparty was Mick Jagger, leader of the group."

Mrs Eva Jagger: "I don't think Mike takes drugs. But if they have been having a lark they will have to take the consequences . . . If he knows there is going to be something sensational about him in the newspapers he always phones to warn us and tell us not to worry. It infuriates me that some people regard him as a moron. He is a very intelligent, sensitive boy . . . I just wish he would stay out of trouble."

Mick: "You sit at home and you think you are safe because you are not in South Africa or some other police state. But when suddenly the police move in it's very disturbing and you begin to wonder just how much freedom you really have . . . There are only about a thousand real addicts in Britain and nobody is going to make a fortune peddling heroin because the addicts can get it on prescription. But if you stop this, the Mafia will move in and we're going to have the same problem as America."

SATURDAY, 25 FEBRUARY 1967

Brian, Keith and Anita Pallenberg leave London for Morocco via Paris. On the journey, Brian falls ill.

Anita Pallenberg: "It was Brian who suggested that we drive on without him to Tangier. That meant that Keith and I could be alone. By the time we reached Valencia we could no longer resist each other and Keith spent the night in my room. In the morning, I realised, as did Keith, that we were creating an unimaginable situation . . ."

117

Mr Lewis Jones: "What I firmly believe to be the turning point in Brian's life was when he lost the only girl he ever really loved. I think this was a very severe blow to him. He changed quite suddenly, and alarmingly, from a bright, enthusiastic young man to a quiet, morose and inward-looking young man, so much so that when his mother and I saw him for the first time for some months after this happened, we were quite shocked by the changes in his appearance, and in our opinion, he was never the same boy again. It was that time, I think, that he got mixed up with drugs. I'll always be convinced that that was the turning point in Brian's life rather than the pop scene generally."

TUESDAY, 14 MARCH 1967

While in Marrakesh, Morocco, Mick, Keith and Brian meet socialite photographer, Cecil Beaton.

Mick (to Beaton): "Have you ever taken LSD? Oh, I should. It would mean so much to you; you'd never forget the colours. For a painter it is a great experience. One's brain works not on four cylinders but on four thousand. You see everything aglow. You see yourself beautiful and ugly, and other people as if for the first time. Oh yes, you should take it in the country, surrounded by all those flowers. You'd have no bad effects. It's only people who hate themselves who suffer."

Cecil Beaton: "Brian Jones with his girlfriend Anita Pallenberg – dirty white face, dirty blackened eyes, dirty canary drops of hair, barbaric jewellery – Keith Richard in eighteenth-century suit, long black coat and the tightest pants . . . Mick very gentle with perfect manners. He has much appreciation and his small, albino-fringed eyes notice everything . . . The very strong sun reflected from white ground, made his face look a podgy, shapeless mass; eyes very small, nose very pink, hair sandy dark. He is sexy . . ."

Also enjoying the local hospitality is beat writer Brion Gysin.

Brion Gysin: "We take over the top floor of this hotel for a playpen hanging ten storeys over the swimming pool. The action starts almost at once. Brian and I drop acid. Anita sulks and drops sleepers. Goes off to sleep in the suite she shares with Brian. Keith has plugged in and is sending some great throbbing sounds winging after her and out into the moonlight over the desert. Robert [Fraser] puts on a great Elmore James record out of his collection. Gets Mick doing little magic dances for him. For the first time, I see Mick really *is* magic. So, as the acid comes up on me, Brian recedes into Big Picture. Looks like a tiny celluloid kewpie doll, banked all around by choirs of identical little girl dolls looking just like him, chanting his hymns. Tom [Keylock] the sinister chauffeur shows up, rolling his eyes, hovering over Brian, whispering in his ears like a procurer. Brian wants me to translate something for Tom. With a finger I wigwag: I can't make it. No! Room Service arrives with great trays of food in which we toboggan around on the floor, I am sorry to say. Food? Who wants it? Who needs it? How very gross."

THURSDAY, 16 MARCH 1967

Keith and Anita leave Tangier.
Brian: "They've left me. They've taken everything – my cash, credit cards, even my cameras. I'm stranded . . ."

MONDAY, 27 MARCH 1967

On the second date of the Stones' European tour, around 2,000 fans riot at a concert in Orebro, Sweden, throwing stones, chairs, bottles and fireworks at the stage, causing the group to flee.
Mick (to police): "Why do you have to hit girls on the head with your batons?"
Mick: "People talk about the riots that happen when we play. Of course there is a certain violent element, and, to a certain extent, the kids are conforming to what is expected of them. But there is more to it than that . . . I've seen this wild behaviour in so many countries and the pattern is always the same. Because it is the same symptom. Frustration . . . You can't solve the problem by locking them up – you have to find out why it is that kids are discontented. They are not all morons just spoiling for a fight with the police."

TUESDAY, 11 APRIL 1967

Mick gets held up at customs at Orly Airport, Paris.
Mick: "Of course they are after me. In the last two months there have been about four occasions when, on landing at London, I have been taken to a private room and searched – obviously for drugs . . . I feel as if I am being treated as a witch."

He's no more impressed by the state of contemporary pop.
Mick: "Since the peak of the Beatles and Stones there have been a lot of big groups but none with any real flair – except for The Who and the Jimi Hendrix Experience."

FRIDAY, 14 APRIL 1967

As the tour winds down, fans riot again, this time at a concert in Zurich.
Mick: "It was a very strange concert really, considering it was in Switzerland. I always thought that Swiss people were very cool and they didn't really show their emotions very much. It was this enormous stadium, about 12,000 people. Instead of us being on a level with the audience, we were really high up, 30 to 40 feet up, so it was really quite dangerous for us. We had to keep back from the edge all the time. And we'd just got on the stage and there were all these people yelling, a lot of noise going on. Then somebody jumped out and gave me a rugby tackle. I nearly went over the edge, I was down on the floor with about ten people on top of me with the crowd seething underneath. I'm never normally frightened by that. But on this occasion I was."

This experience, combined with the incipient flowering of the Love Generation, inspires Mick to take a wider view, as he tells the Daily Mirror.
Mick: "Teenagers are not screaming over pop music any more, they're screaming for much deeper reasons . . . Teenagers the world over are weary of being pushed around by half-witted politicians who attempt to dominate their way of thinking and set a code for their living. They want to be free and have the right of expression; of thinking and living aloud without any petty restrictions. This doesn't mean they want to become alcoholics or drug takers or tread down on their parents. This is a protest against the system. I see a lot of trouble coming in the dawn."

MONDAY, 24 APRIL 1967

The annual Cannes Film Festival opens. The German entry is A Degree Of Murder *(Mord Und Totschlag) scored by Brian, who also plays sitar, organ, dulcimer, autoharp and harmonica.*
Volker Schlondorff (director): "Brian's music has worked out so marvellously . . . His special music fits the film wonderfully – and I do not think anyone but he could have done it. He visited Munich three times to see the film for timings."

Brian: "I ran the gamut of line-ups – from the conventional brass combination to a country band with Jew's harp, violin and banjo. In the main the musicians were established session men – though some of the boys from the groups also played . . .

"I'm very hung up on electronic music at present. If there's no room to include it on our album, I would like to do something separately."

SATURDAY, 29 APRIL 1967

Mick and Marianne attend The 14-Hour Technicolor Dream 'Be-In' at Alexandra Palace, North London.
Mick: "I thought it was fantastic. The awareness of colour and light and dressing up – much of it was brought on perhaps through LSD, which has done something towards becoming more aware of that kind of spectacle . . . Everybody wants to be with other people who believe in more or less the same things as they do, and show affection for each other. It's about being with a lot of people and having a good time, to be with a lot of people or perhaps with someone you've never seen before, and do things together . . . throw things and colours at him."
Charlie: "There's a fish shop near my home – they've got 'Herrings Are Flower Power' in the window. Ridiculous. People just don't know what it's all about."

WEDNESDAY, 10 MAY 1967

"POP STARS CHEERED AND BOOED"

Mick Jagger and Keith Richard plead 'Not Guilty' to various drug offences at a hearing in Chichester Magistrates' Court, West Sussex. Around 600 fans – and a few detractors – are there to meet them outside the courthouse. The pair, together with art dealer Robert Fraser, are committed for trial at West Sussex Quarter Sessions, commencing 27 June, and each is released on £100 bail.
Mr Anthony McCowan (prosecutor): "When officers arrived they noticed a strong sweet unusual smell. Other officers found sticks of incense but no sign that any had been burned. The burning of incense can be used as a means of masking the smoking of hemp, which gives off a very unusual smell."

A green jacket, which Jagger admits had belonged to him, was found to have a plastic phial with four tablets in the pocket.
Mick (to police): "My doctor prescribed them."

When asked why he had them, he replies:
Mick: "To stay awake and work."
Detective Sergeant Cudmore (cross examined): "Both Mr Jagger and Mr Richard behaved in a thoroughly adult manner. The whole party was well behaved in so far as we were concerned in our investigations."

While Mick and Keith are being driven back to London, another Stone receives an unwelcome knock at the door . . .

"BRIAN JONES ON DRUGS CHARGE"

Brian, together with Prince Stanislaus Klossowski de Rola ("a Swiss-born entertainer", according to the police report, 'Stash' to his friends) are arrested at Jones' flat at 1 Courtfield Road and charged at Kensington Police Station with unlawful possession of dangerous drugs. The police report later reveals:

"The ensuing search of the flat produced some 29 exhibits . . .

Item No. 1 – A wallet containing herbal material.
Item No. 2 – One cardboard box containing herbal material, a white tablet, cigarette papers and cotton wool.
Item No. 3 – Milk bottle containing ash and cigarette ends.
Item No. 4 – An earthenware pot containing ash and cigarette ends.
Item No. 5 – A cigarette holder.
Item No. 6 – Two black and red capsules.
Item No. 7 – A water pipe.
Item No. 8 – A plastic jar containing herbal mixture.
Item No. 9 – Brown wallet containing herbal mixture.
Item No. 10 – Two sheath knives.
Item No. 11 – One pipe.
Item No. 12 – One hookah pipe.
Item No. 13 – One packet of joss-sticks.
Item No. 14 – One yellow metal ashtray containing ash, cigarette ends and a small bottle.
Item No. 15 – One bottle containing tablets.
Item No. 16 – A box containing a cigarette end and an empty glass ampoule.
Item No. 17 – A cigarette end and a white tablet.
Item No. 18 – White metal tin containing herbal mixture.
Item No. 19 – A yellow tin containing tablets.
Item No. 20 – One white tablet.
Item No. 21 – A cigarette end.

Item No. 22 – Jar containing traces of crystalline powder.
Item No. 23 – A part empty phial marked Methedrine.
Item No. 24 – One ornamental pipe.
Item No. 25 – One white cigarette box containing ash and herbal mixture.
Item No. 26 – A blue tablet.
Item No. 27 – A chair castor containing cigarette ends and herbal mixture.
Item No. 28 – A white metal container containing herbal mixture.
Item No. 29 – Two Trancopal capsules.

Subsequent analysis of these items showed 12 of them to be innocuous and the remaining 17 to contain mainly cannabis – resinous and herbal. A small quantity of methedrine and traces of cocaine were also revealed . . . With the exception of Item No. 24, all these items contain cannabis."

According to police notes, when questioned Brian admits:
"Yes, it is hash. I do smoke it, but not cocaine, man. That is not my scene."

When shown a phial that appears to contain cocaine, Jones adds:
"Not me. I am not a junkie. It is not me at all."

FRIDAY, 19 MAY 1967

At a conference of the Justices' Clerks' Society, Mr Dick Taverne, QC, joint Parliamentary Under-Secretary, of the Home Office, criticises the massive publicity surrounding the Stones' case.
"One cannot anticipate what the outcome of these proceedings will be. But whatever happens elsewhere, can one really say there will be no prejudice in the minds of the public against these defendants, even if they are acquitted?"

SUNDAY, 21 MAY 1967

BBC-TV's The Look Of The Week *focuses on the relationship between audiences and performers in pop. Robert Robinson hosts.*
Mick: "It's a very strange feeling being on the stage and feeling all this energy coming from the audience directed straight into you. You can feel it, but you don't really understand it. I sometimes get perplexed by what they are trying to say to me, or what they want from me as a performer or as a person. I just stand there and really don't understand what they want to say, and I have nothing to say back."

Q: "But when the girls get excited there's a good deal of violence in the affection. (They) clamber all over you. At the same time they look as if they were menacing you, as if they want to tear you apart."

Mick: "I dunno. I don't really understand. Perhaps someone else can understand human behaviour better than I can. It's a very strong sexual thing, and sexual things are often violent. I think that's half the explanation of that."

Q: "Do you ever get the impression that the audience is banding together to say something when they behave like that?"

Mick: "Yes. They all band together and when you're on stage you feel it very strongly giving you this energy. You don't really understand what they're trying to say, what they want from you, from life. You just feel that they need something, and they're giving it to you."

Q: "What's your feeling when you confront an audience. Is it affection?"

Mick: "Normally, yes. I mean, most audiences are affectionate, they come and see us because they like us. And we do the show because we like doing shows and we like audiences so there's a tremendous affection, a basic affection. On top of that lots of other things . . ."

Q: "What things?"

Mick: "Well, on top of that affection there's violence. On top of that there's sex, there's everything."

Q: "Do you yourself ever feel any kind of aggression seeping up from underneath your own affection for the audience as you confront them? Do you ever feel that you're going to do the work and they're just going to prey upon you?"

Mick: "I do feel quite violent sometimes, and lots of groups have taken it much further than we have – being violent on stage, smashing things up. I quite often feel like smashing microphones up because I really don't feel like the same person as I am normally when I'm on stage."

At this point, Professor John Cohen, Professor of Psychology at Manchester University, joins the debate.

"When these boys or mostly girls pounce upon Mick, and seem to want to tear him to pieces, it's not essentially an act of aggression but rather an act of devouring him. They want to incorporate his essence. It is a sort of fetishism which has more in common with people collecting the relics of saints. When James Dean's car was put up as an emblem of his sanctity and his mystique, his fans and devotees would pay any amount of money for screws and bolts at $20 or $50 to have as amulets. These are incorporations of the mystical, magical quality of the idol, the hero that they worship. And that's why they would like to tear him to pieces and eat bits of him, (obtain) bits of his clothes, locks of his hair, his autograph. I'm sure you must get thousands of people who want your picture. Your image is the double of you, your soul, and they want to incorporate it into themselves."

Q: "This sounds as though you regard this whole phenomenon as religious."

Professor Cohen: "Yes, well I do . . ."

Q: "It would be interesting to hear if Mick wonders why he wants to get up in front of people. Most people, I suppose, are happy enough to stay private. Yet performers seem to need to get up in front of audiences. Is it something you've thought about?"

Mick: "Yes, I've only thought about it because I keep being asked about it. I never asked myself the question, 'Why?' until people would say, 'Why do you do this?' I don't really know. I know it helps me in a certain way and I think it helps me to get rid of my ego. I enjoy getting rid of my ego in that way. It's much better because I have no ego problems once I've left the stage. I don't have to keep proving myself over and over again because I suppose I do it then; that's when I try and concentrate it all. I don't think one can really understand that, because when you start off as a performer, you really want to do it for something to do. It seems very simple at the time. But the more it goes on the more involved it gets. You just get more drawn into it, drawn into a pattern of behaviour."

Q: "Do you ever feel frightened, ever suddenly become transfixed with the thought that you are isolated on that stage, and that so much emotionally is at that moment required of you?"

Mick: "No, I don't feel isolated because I'm not, because I have other people with me because I'm part of a group of people. I'm not on my own and we all experience more or less the same things. It's very good and it's always funny. We always have a laugh, and we always enjoy ourselves on stage. I don't feel alone on the stage and I also don't feel alone because I feel a sympathy for the audience, sympathy in the true sense of the word."

Q: "It seems to be mostly girls who respond at these concerts . . ."

Mick: "That's very true. But in this country the audience is mainly all girls; in the rest of the world this isn't true. It's a completely different audience, and in lots of places they're nearly all boys. And this leads to a completely different kind of, well, it's the same kind of phenomenon but it's very different. You get this great big sexual thing with the girls but with the boys it erupts much more aggressively. And boys, being much more aware of their future role in society, will use this – 10,000 or 20,000 of them – to enjoy themselves and also to have a great fight with the police, who of course they'll outnumber. At one of our concerts, in Berlin, this happened. They just beat the police up as a show of strength, of dissatisfaction with something. It's completely different to the girls and the sexual thing."

THURSDAY, 1 JUNE 1967

The Beatles' latest album, Sgt. Pepper's Lonely Hearts Club Band, *is officially released to instant acclaim.*
Mick: "The music that's being done now – not only *Pepper* – has been influenced by drugs, LSD, pot. That's damned obvious. A lot of freaky people are playing a lot of freaky music without LSD, but the drug has had an influence on the music. Take 'A Day In The Life'. Nothing in there is specifically about drugs, yet it's all about drugs."

SUNDAY, 18 JUNE 1967

Brian Jones introduces the Jimi Hendrix Experience as the trio makes its US début at the International Pop Festival at Monterey, California.
Lou Adler: "He's all the way over from London – Brian Jones of the Rolling Stones!"
Brian: "I'd like to introduce a very good friend, a fellow countryman of yours . . . he's the most exciting performer I've ever heard – the Jimi Hendrix Experience."

TUESDAY, 27 JUNE 1967

"MICK JAGGER IS FOUND GUILTY"

Mick and Keith attend court at West Sussex Quarter Sessions in Chichester to answer various drugs-related charges arising from the Redlands bust in February. Mick ("an entertainer") is found guilty of possessing four tablets containing amphetamine sulphate and methylamphetamine hydrochloride – despite the fact that their use had been sanctioned by his doctor.
Mr Malcolm Morris, QC (prosecutor): "Are you really saying that after a patient came to you, as Mr Jagger did, and said, 'I have some pep pills,' you would say, 'All right, you can take them if you need them but not too many'?"
Dr Dixon Firth: "Yes, providing I was satisfied after discussion that they were appropriate for him."

126

This verbal agreement is not adjudged to constitute a formal prescription.
Judge Block: "It therefore follows that the defence open to Mr Jagger is not available to him. I therefore direct you that there is no defence to this charge."

As he is driven away, a crowd bangs on the van and chants: "We want Mick!"

WEDNESDAY, 28 JUNE 1967

"YOUNG WOMAN WEARING ONLY FUR RUG AT GUITARIST'S PARTY"

At the next day's hearing, the case is made against Keith, who pleads 'Not Guilty' to allowing his home to be used for the purpose of smoking cannabis resin. Much of the case against him relies on a moral issue, specifically the behaviour of an unnamed "young woman" who is not named in court on the judge's instructions. That doesn't prevent several newspapers from running the story alongside a prominent photograph of Marianne Faithfull arriving at court.
Mr Malcolm Morris, QC: "The behaviour of one of the guests may suggest that she was under the influence of smoking cannabis resin in a way which Richard could not fail to notice . . . In the drawing room where Richard was entertaining his guests one of them had a large supply of cannabis resin. Brooding over it all was that sweet, strong smell which no one could fail to notice. You cannot have any doubt at all that Richard was permitting his house to be used for the purpose of smoking cannabis resin."

After a drug squad officer is called to illustrate the liberating effects of the drug, Morris continues:
"You may think it may have had exactly that effect upon one of Richard's guests. This was the young lady sitting on the settee. All she was wearing was a light-coloured fur skin rug which from time to time she allowed to fall, disclosing her nude body. She was unperturbed and apparently enjoying the situation. We are not in any way concerned with who that young lady was or may have been, but was she someone who had lost her inhibitions and had she lost them because she had been smoking Indian hemp?"

Defence lawyer Mr Michael Havers then switches tack, insinuating that the bust had clearly been a set-up initiated by a national newspaper.
"When you hear the paper you will have a difficulty in accepting them as guardians of the public's morals."

He adds that, after publishing an alleged libel in an article in relation to Jagger on 5 February, a writ was duly served on the paper in question, The News Of The World.

"For the next five days, this man was followed and observed wherever he went or whatever he did. A van or car was constantly outside his flat. Within a week, this well-known national newspaper tipped off the police to go to West Wittering, not for anything but for drugs. We know it was for drugs because the warrant was for drugs. If a newspaper publishes a story and it is found to be untrue, how many thousands of pounds would a jury like you award?"

Havers also names the man likely to have been involved in the set-up.
"In that party was a man not known to The Rolling Stones as a group, conveniently from across the seas and loaded to the gunwales with cannabis. (David) Schneiderman was the only man on whom was found any cannabis. He has gone out of England."

Outside the court, protesters wear "Free The Stones" and "Mick Is Innocent" T-shirts.

THURSDAY, 29 JUNE 1967

"JAIL SENTENCES ON 2 ROLLING STONES"

After Keith Richard is found guilty of allowing his home to be used for the consumption of cannabis, the pair are sentenced. Mick receives a three-month jail term, Keith gets one year. A third defendant, Robert Fraser, is found guilty of possessing 24 tablets of heroin and is sentenced to six months in jail.
Michael Havers, QC (defence lawyer): "What has success meant to you?"
Keith: "There was a complete lack of privacy from 1963 onwards and continual work for four years."
Havers: "Do you need any sort of protection against fans?"
Keith: "Oh, yes. I need an army."

When asked about Mr David Henry Schneiderman, alias Britton, Keith recalls a brief meeting with him in New York, then adds, "I next met him a week before the raid on my house."

And exactly how did the weekend party materialise?
Keith: "It was suggested to me a week previous by a friend of mine and I agreed. The next thing I knew when I got back from Munich is that I was

128

telephoned on Saturday, 11 February and told that a party had been arranged."

He was then quizzed about the incense which police found burning at the house.
Keith: "Well, I picked it up from fans who used to send me joss sticks over the last three years and I quite liked the smell of them."
Havers: "Is there anything sinister in that? Is it done to cover up the smell of cannabis?"
Keith: "No, sir."

Oh, and about that girl . . .
Havers: "Do you know why she was clothed in that rug?"
Keith: "As far as I understand she had been upstairs to have a bath and must have taken off her dirty clothing, because we had been in the country the whole of the day and she had not brought any fresh clothes with her. She must have gone downstairs to get a cup of tea or something."
Havers: "Did she let fall that rug?"
Keith: "Absolutely not."

Then came the cross-examination.
Mr Malcolm Morris, QC: "(Your counsel) spoke about various things and in the course of that opening speech made it quite clear that your defence was that Schneiderman had been planted in your weekend party as part of a wicked conspiracy by *The News Of The World*. Is that any part of your defence or not?"
Keith: "Yes, it is, sir."
Morris: "Is your defence that Schneiderman was planted by *The News Of The World* in an attempt to get Mick Jagger convicted of smoking hashish? Is that the suggestion?"
Keith: "That is the suggestion."
Morris: "So if you are seriously suggesting that this was part of a plot, it is a curious plot in that nothing in fact was done to associate Jagger with Indian hemp."
Keith: "He was associated with the whole raid, which is enough, I am sure."
Morris: "The jury will want to know that because *The News Of The World* did not want to pay libel damages to Mick Jagger, which they might have to pay if what they published was untrue, then what you are saying is that it was they who arranged to have Indian hemp planted in your house?"

Keith: "Yes."
Morris: "Is that really your suggestion?"
Keith: "It is, sir."
Morris: "There was, as we know, a young woman sitting on a settee wearing only a rug. Would you agree in the ordinary course of events you would expect a young woman to be embarrassed if she had nothing on but a rug in the presence of eight men, two of whom were hangers-on and the third a Moroccan servant?"
Keith: "Not at all."
Morris: "You regard that, do you, as quite normal?"
Keith: "We are not old men. We are not worried about petty morals."
Morris: "After she had gone upstairs with the woman police officer, did it come as a great surprise to you that she was prepared to go downstairs to the drawing room still only with a rug, where there were about a dozen police officers."
Keith: "No, sir. She had taken off her dirty clothes, which she had been wearing all day."
Morris: "You do not think it was because she was smoking Indian hemp and had got rid of her inhibitions and embarrassment?"
Keith: "No, sir."
Morris: "May I ask you this. This is right, you were all sitting round in the drawing room doing nothing in particular?"
Keith: "Yes, sir."
Morris: "Was anyone there smoking hashish or hemp?"
Keith: "Not to my knowledge."
Morris: "Would you have objected if anyone had been smoking Indian hemp?"
Keith: "Yes, sir. I knew if the police had come over, I would be standing here – and I am."

Others were called to further deliberate upon the 'mystery girl' at Redlands.
Sgt John Cudmore: "I saw the young lady come upstairs with a policewoman. She allowed the fur rug to fall down. She had her back to me. She was naked. I heard a man in the bedroom, using the telephone, laugh."
Michael Havers: "Was it a large rug?"
Sgt Cudmore: "Quite large."
Q: "Was it bigger than a fur coat?"
A: "Yes."
Michael Havers: "It's a bed-cover, isn't it? It's *enormous*. You can see – it's about eight-and-a-half feet by five."

130

A rumour soon spreads that an act involving Mick's appetite, Marianne Faithfull's nakedness, a Mars Bar and a watching room was also recorded by the detectives.
Private Eye couldn't resist: "A Mars Bar fills that gap."
Keith succinctly puts the record straight. "The fur rug – yes. The Mars Bar – no. We were out of Mars Bars."
Malcolm Morris, QC: "The issue you have to try is a comparatively simple one. You have to be satisfied that cannabis resin was being smoked in the house when the police went there, and you have to be satisfied that Richards knew of it . . . Finally, I would ask you to disregard the evidence as to the lady who was alleged by the police to be in some condition of undress, and not to let that prejudice your minds in any way."

One hour later, the jury returns with its verdict.
Judge Block: "Keith Richards, the offence for which you have, very properly, been convicted carries a maximum sentence, imposed by Parliament of up to ten years. That is a view of the seriousness of the offence . . . As it is, you will go to prison for one year . . ."

"Michael Philip Jagger, you have pleaded guilty to possessing a highly dangerous and harmful drug . . . You will go to prison for three months . . ."
(Overheard in the gallery): "Poor Mick."
According to the Daily Telegraph *reporter,* "Jagger almost broke down and put his head in his hands as he was sentenced. He stumbled out of the dock almost in tears."

Outside the court, there are hysterical scenes as the news filtered out.
"He's been sent to prison! Mick's been sent to prison!"
Les Perrin (publicist): "A certificate of appeal has been granted for Jagger and Richard."

Later that evening, 200 protesters gather outside the offices of The News Of The World *and chant "Free The Stones".*

FRIDAY, 30 JUNE 1967

After Mick and Keith are released on £7,000 bail, pending appeals against their sentences, the pair celebrate with a drink in a pub off Fleet Street.
Keith: "The publicity will not break up the group. There are definitely no plans to split up. We hope our fans will remain loyal."

Mick: "We were treated very kindly and everyone was helpful. We do not bear a grudge against anyone for what has happened."

Michael Havers: "There is no question of peddling, no question of vast quantities and there is all the difference in the world between this case and the case of the person who has large quantities for gain as a peddler or pusher."

Meanwhile, the sense of outrage at the severity of the sentences spreads.

"The trial proved to be a show trial in which the prurient press coverage played an essential and predictable part," *writes Hugo Young in* The Times.

"CAN THE STONES SURVIVE A SPELL IN THE WILDERNESS?"

"Financially, they are all in a position to turn down money-spinning stage concerts. The group have earned more than £1,000,000 since 1963 and their recording contracts guarantee them another £1,000,000 over the next ten years . . . The Beatles went five months without a record. Like them, the Stones have an aura of glamour and glitter which will still appeal to those who buy their discs . . . Pop stars of world-class calibre – and their popularity puts the Stones into this category – can come back after delays in their careers. Frank Sinatra has been in and out of fashion several times. Elvis Presley spent two years in the US Army, but he is still the biggest single money-earning pop singer in the world. Recently the Tremeloes hit back with two massive selling records after splitting up from lead singer Brian Poole . . ."

SATURDAY, 1 JULY 1967

"STONES – PROTEST AT 2 A.M."

In the early hours of the morning, around 400 protesters gather around the statue of Eros in Piccadilly Circus and hand out leaflets complaining about the sentences.

"Calm down police. Calm down Sunday papers. Calm down outraged magistrates. The laws will change and we'll all die soon, and we will win – why not get things in perspective? We are not a threat to government or the law and order – we just don't like our people hurt."

As morning breaks, the questions posed by the case are taken up by The Times, *which deems the matter worthy of a* sub judice *editorial statement from William Rees-Mogg.*

"WHO BREAKS A BUTTERFLY ON A WHEEL?"

"Mr Jagger has been sentenced to imprisonment for three months. He is appealing against conviction and sentence, and has been granted bail until the hearing of the appeal later in the year. In the meantime, the sentence of imprisonment is bound to be widely discussed by the public. And the circumstances are sufficiently unusual to warrant such discussion in the public interest.

"Mr Jagger was charged with being in possession of four tablets containing amphetamine sulphate and methyl amphetamine hydrochloride; these tablets had been bought perfectly legally in Italy, and brought back to this country. They are not a highly dangerous drug, or in proper dosage a dangerous drug at all. They are of the benzedrine type and the Italian manufacturers recommend them both as a stimulant and as a remedy for travel sickness.

"In Britain it is an offence to possess these drugs without a doctor's prescription. Mr Jagger's doctor says that he knew and had authorised their use, but he did not give a prescription for them as indeed they had already been purchased. His evidence was not challenged. This was therefore an offence of a technical character, which before this case drew the point to public attention any honest man might have been liable to commit. If, after his visit to the Pope, the Archbishop of Canterbury had bought proprietary airsickness pills at Rome airport, and imported the unused tablets into Britain on his return, he would have risked committing precisely the same offence. No one who has ever travelled and bought proprietary drugs abroad can be sure that he has not broken the law.

"Judge Block directed the jury that the approval of a doctor was not a defence in law to the charge of possessing drugs without a prescription, and the jury convicted. Mr Jagger was not charged with complicity in any other drug offence that occurred in the same house. They were separate cases, and no evidence was produced to suggest that he knew that Mr Fraser had heroin tablets or that the vanishing Mr Schneiderman had cannabis resin. It is indeed no offence to be in the same building or the same company as people possessing or even using drugs, nor could it be reasonably be made an offence. The drugs which Mr Jagger had in his possession must therefore be treated on their own, as a separate issue from the other drugs that other people may have had in their possession at the same time. It may be difficult for lay opinion to make this distinction clearly, but obviously justice cannot be done if one man is to be punished for a purely contingent association with someone else's offence.

"We have, therefore, a conviction against Mr Jagger purely on the grounds that he possessed four Italian pep pills, quite legally bought but not legally imported without a prescription. Four is not a large number. This is not the quantity which a pusher of drugs would have on him, nor even the quantity one would expect in an addict. In any case Mr Jagger's career is obviously one that does involve great personal strain and exhaustion; his doctor says that he approved the occasional use of these drugs, and it seems likely that similar drugs would have been prescribed if there was a need for them. Millions of similar drugs are prescribed in Britain every year, and for a variety of conditions.

"One has to ask, therefore, how it is that this technical offence, divorced as it must be from other people's offences, was thought to deserve the penalty of imprisonment. In the courts at large it is most uncommon for imprisonment to be imposed on first offenders where the drugs are not major drugs of addiction and there is no question of drug traffic. The normal penalty is probation, and the purpose of probation is to encourage the offender to develop his career and to avoid the drug risks in the future. It is surprising therefore that Judge Block should have decided to sentence Mr Jagger to imprisonment, and particularly surprising as Mr Jagger's is about as mild a drug case as can ever have been brought before the Courts.

"It would be wrong to speculate on the judge's reasons, which we do not know. It is, however, possible to consider the public reaction. There are many people who take a primitive view of the matter. They consider that Mr Jagger has 'got what was coming to him'. They resent the anarchic quality of the Rolling Stones' performances, dislike their songs, dislike their influence upon teenagers and broadly suspect them of decadence, a word used by Miss Monica Furlong in the *Daily Mail*.

"As a sociological concern this may be reasonable enough, and at an emotional level it is very understandable, but it has nothing at all to do with the case. One has to ask a different question: has Mr Jagger received the same treatment as he would have received if he had not been a famous figure, with all the criticism and resentment his celebrity has aroused? If a promising undergraduate had come back from a summer visit to Italy with four pep pills in his pocket, would it have been thought right to ruin his career by sending him to prison for three months? Would it also have been thought necessary to display him handcuffed to the public?

"There are cases in which a single figure becomes the focus for public concern about some aspect of public morality. The Stephen Ward case, with its dubious evidence and questionable verdict, was one of them, and that verdict killed Stephen Ward. There are elements of the same emotions in the reactions to this case. If we are going to make any case a symbol of the conflict between the sound traditional values of Britain and the new hedonism, then we must be sure that the sound traditional values include those of tolerance and equity. It should be the particular quality of British justice to ensure that Mr Jagger is treated exactly the same as anyone else, no better and no worse. There must remain a suspicion in this case that Mr Jagger received a more severe sentence than would have been thought proper for any purely anonymous young man."

SUNDAY, 2 JULY 1967

"A MONSTROUS CHARGE"

The newspaper at the centre of the case fights back . . .
"The defence assertion was that this newspaper, faced with a libel action by Mick Jagger, planted a man called Schneiderman, 'with all the trappings and kit of someone interested in drugs', in a weekend party at Keith Richards' home in an attempt to get Mick Jagger convicted of smoking hashish . . . that we took part in a 'criminal conspiracy' to pervert the course of justice.

"These outrageous allegations are, of course, totally unfounded . . . But first let us make it quite clear that it *was The News Of The World* that passed information to the police. It was our plain duty to do so . . ."

And the charge of planting Schneiderman?
"(It) was made without a shred of evidence. It was made within the privilege of a court of law which denied us the opportunity of answering back. These outrageous allegations are of course totally unfounded. We have had no connection whatsoever with Mr Schneidermann [*sic*] directly or indirectly, before, during or after this case.

"We shall never be deterred from doing what we conceive to be our duty. We believe that unauthorised drug taking is a menace in Britain today and that we are right to bring any suspicion of this to public attention."

But, as John Gordon in the Sunday Express *confirms, if the case was brought in a bid to punish those troublesome Rolling Stones, then it was in danger of backfiring.*
"Was Jagger convicted of taking one of the evil drugs like heroin or cocaine? Or LSD with which some of the Beatles confess that they have been experimenting? Not at all. Did he smoke marijuana which some experts say is evil, but others, equally expert, say is not so evil? That wasn't

alleged against him. He merely had four benzedrine tablets, legally purchased abroad, which, with the knowledge and approval of his doctor, he took to keep him awake while he worked . . . I repeat, have we lost our sense of proportion?"

THURSDAY, 6 JULY 1967

The New Law Journal weighs in with a leader claiming that "two disturbing features" of the case were the jailing of Jagger for a first offence, and the use of the nude girl in a fur rug cited as evidence.
"If so disproportionate a sentence is defended on the ground that drug-taking is a grave social problem, particularly among young people, then the imposition of this sentence upon this particular offender is certain to be ineffective as a deterrent to others, and may well have precisely the opposite effect.

"Since the sentence is indefensible in relation to the particular offence and the particular offender, and since it is not justifiable in terms of the social problem of drug-taking, then it can only be explained as marking disapproval of the general habits and way of life of a section of the community of whom the community generally apparently disapprove. The section of the community in question was not on trial and incurring public disapproval is not, happily, a criminal offence."

In London for the Poetry International event at the Royal Festival Hall, visiting Beat poet Allen Ginsberg, expresses his own idiosyncratic view on the episode.
"The Rolling Stones are one of Britain's major cultural assets, who should be honoured by the kingdom instead of jailed."

MONDAY, 31 JULY 1967

"APPEALS COURT LIFTS SENTENCES"

Lord Chief Justice Parker: "The Court quashes the conviction of Keith Richards for permitting, as an occupier, his house at West Wittering to be used for the purpose of smoking cannabis resin, contrary to section 5 (1) of the Dangerous Drugs Act, 1965, because the Chairman of West Sussex Quarter Sessions (Judge Block), did not warn the jury that there was only tenuous evidence which would make them sure that a girl at the house, dressed only in a rug, smoked cannabis resin and that Mr Richards must have known about it."

136

Mick's three-month prison sentence is also nullified.
Lord Chief Justice Parker: "You are, whether you like it or not, the idol of a large number of the young in this country. Being in that position, you have very grave responsibilities. . . If you keep out of trouble for the next 12 months, what has happened will not be on your record as a conviction. If you do commit another offence, you will not only be punished for that but brought back and punished for this one."
Brian: "Thank God, justice has prevailed."
Paul McCartney: "I am always pleased about the idea of people not going to jail."

Later that day, Mick holds a press conference in Soho.
Q: "The judge remarked that as an idol of many young people in this country today, you have a very grave responsibility. How do you propose to exercise it?"
Mick: "That's very difficult. One perhaps doesn't ask for responsibilities. Perhaps one is given responsibilities when one is pushed into the limelight in this particular sphere. My responsibilities as far as my private life goes are only to myself. In the public sector – with my work, my records, etc. – I have a responsibility, but the amount of baths I take or my personal habits are of no consequence to anyone else."
Q: "Do you think you've been picked upon because you are who you are."
Mick: "I don't think we were picked upon in that way . . . I have never come out in any sort of argument for or against drugs. I don't propagate religious views as some pop stars do, and I don't propagate views on drugs as some pop stars do. This whole thing has been pushed upon me."
Q: "By whom?"
Mick: "By the mere fact of being prosecuted."
Q: "How does it feel to be free?"
Mick: "I had prepared myself mentally, physically and business-wise for the possibility of going to jail. It felt lovely to be sure of freedom . . . I'll be recording and travelling around. I shall not be making any public appearance for the next few months. I'm not celebrating tonight. Just grooving on, the same as usual."

The Times *journalist Stephen Jessel paints a flattering portrait of the man of the moment.*
"He is so unlike the cartoon stereotype as to be almost unrecognisable in reality. He is a slighter figure than you expect, and thin to the point of skinniness. He is quieter and has much more grace of manner than one

would have expected. He is articulate, and the philosophy he outlines is obviously the product of sustained consideration. But the quality that impresses most on first meeting him is his overwhelming self-possession. He is so self-assured that it is hard to think of anything that would upset him."

Mick: "I was very cynical. We were all cynical people. We just grew up and learnt a bit and thought a bit and talked a bit, and became less cynical. If people continually push this generation by pushing the people who are its leaders, they will really alienate them."

Mick on drugs . . .
"My purpose isn't to build a socialist state. It is to reach a state at which I'm one with myself and the world . . . I think pot's more respectable than ten years ago, much more chi-chi. I don't see what's wrong with going on trips. I don't see what's wrong with not going on trips either. It's up to me to pick the things I want to do and I will. What I do with my conscience is my business.

"The maximum sentence is longer than you would serve for man-slaughter, which is absurd; it's ludicrous. You can take any case 50 years ago, like Oscar Wilde, and see what they thought about it in ten years' time."

On religion . . .
"I believe in God but I'm not religious. One uses the term God when one gets to the end, to the 'don't know' part. All right is just pointing in the same direction: right is a light on the path, the path to Nirvana if you like. The difficulty is to articulate your experience."

On politics . . .
"I'm very political, but against all sorts of politicians. I got very interested in political thought and form and the more I learnt about it the less I liked it. When they give the vote to the under-21s, I don't think they will vote."

But would he encourage them?
"I might well do. They won't achieve anything. Of course, they don't want to go to Transport House and I'm very glad they don't. The earlier one realises most things are not important the better."

On the older generation . . .
"They've been on a bigger trip than any of us. (With the war) they've had the opportunity for danger and excitement."

That evening, the unelected spokesman of the younger generation is invited to take part in a special edition of World In Action, *broadcast by Granada Television. Also on the programme are* Times *editor Mr William Rees-Mogg, Father Thomas Corbishley, a leading Jesuit priest, Lord Stowe Hill and the Bishop of Woolwich Dr John Robinson. The subject is the great moral and cultural divide between the generations, and the programme begins with a startling statistic – that in a new poll, 85% of young people say that Jagger deserved the prison sentence.*

William Rees-Mogg: "You've had a difficult day and a difficult three months. Perhaps I could begin by asking you this. You are often taken as a symbol of rebellion, and mothers deplore the influence of The Rolling Stones because they think that The Rolling Stones are rebels. Do you think that the society you live in is one you ought to rebel against, or do you think you're rebelling against it?"

Mick: "Yes, definitely rebelling against it. Obviously we feel there are things wrong with society. Society more or less has pushed oneself into this position. Lord Parker today said I had a great responsibility, but the influence we have has been pushed upon us, especially during this drug thing when one's been asked to make certain pronouncements on it, when really it's part of one's private life. Before this, I really didn't have to talk about it."

Lord Stowe Hill: "You appeal to millions of young people. You give them pleasure. They enjoy your 'art'. What is the way in which you'd like yourself to be understood amongst young people particularly?"

Mick: "The very way I started myself when I was young, which was just to have as good a time as possible, which is what most young people try to do without regard to responsibilities of any sort."

Lord Stowe Hill: "Is it really freedom that you seek to promote, or is it just intensity of living? Is it an appeal to develop themselves, to live fully, freely, without trespassing on other people's freedoms?"

Mick: "They should never trespass on other people's freedom. But quite often the law seems to work by protecting a minority of interests or interests which one would regard as kind of empty, for example the law against committing suicide or homosexuality. In the same way as those two things, one would think that someone who takes a bad drug, such as heroin, commits a crime against himself. I can't see how it can be a crime against society any more than jumping out of a window is. For one to say that society wants these people to be put away – I can't see the point."

William Rees-Mogg: "Do you feel that your protests have got anywhere?"

Mick: "I'm not a keen protester at all. I don't go marching, or anything like that. But I do feel that there are certain things, the outlets for protesting about them are just not enough . . . These normal channels don't interest me at all. By and large politics and politicians throughout history seem to get bogged down, drawn into the whole system . . . They seem to achieve very little."

W.H. Auden was less convinced that the Stones and their entourage were now enjoying a stimulant-free existence. According to flamboyant Labour MP Tom Driberg, the writer sidled up to Marianne Faithfull and blurted: "When you're smuggling drugs, d'you pack them up your arse?"

FRIDAY, 18 AUGUST 1967

'We Love You' is released. Although work on the song was begun in May before the outcome of the case, it is widely interpreted as a 'thank you' to fans for their continued support.
Mick: "It's just a bit of fun. You're not meant to think about it – it's very funny, I think. I'm not involved in this 'Love and Flowers' scene, but it is something to bring people together for the summer – something to latch on to. In the winter we'll probably latch on to snow!"

Despite its title, the song threatens to spill over into musical anarchy, thanks in part to a dramatic mellotron part played by Brian Jones.
George Chkiantz (engineer): "It was a big old mellotron, and though there was a delay between the moment you pressed a note and achieving a sound, Brian managed to get an extremely tight rhythmic punch for that record. The instrument actually belonged to Keith Richard."

Top Of The Pops *producer Johnny Stewart refuses to show a four-minute promotional film made by Peter Whitehead that – topically – parodies the trial of Oscar Wilde.*
A BBC spokesman: "The producer has seen the film, and he does not think it is suitable for the type of audience that watches the programme. This is in no sense a 'ban' by the BBC – it was entirely the producer's decision."

FRIDAY, 25 AUGUST 1967

Mick Jagger and Marianne Faithfull travel with the Beatles to a weekend Transcendental Meditation study school in Bangor, North Wales.

Mick: "I know (TM guru Maharishi Mahesh Yogi) can teach me the direction in which I should go . . . I am just seeking to be at one with the universe and myself – it's the same thing, really. We have pushed everything as far as we can by study and thought, but this is different. We are not doing it because we are unhappy. In fact, we are very happy. But we are trying to find even greater spiritual happiness to balance up our active lives. This kind of thing doesn't deny worldly activity. We are not going to drop out of life. It will help us balance the material and spiritual sides of life in perfect happiness."

THURSDAY, 14 SEPTEMBER 1967

Allen Klein confirms that Andrew Oldham is no longer connected with The Rolling Stones. Jo Bergman is hired as the group's PA and is soon installed in a new office in Maddox Street, Mayfair.
Mick: "I just felt we were doing practically everything ourselves anyway. And we just didn't think along the same lines. But I don't want to have a go at Andrew. We'll really be managing ourselves."

SUNDAY, 17 SEPTEMBER 1967

Evidence that Mick has been radicalised by his recent troubles comes in a frank interview with Jack Bentley in the Sunday Mirror.
Mick: "The Commandments say 'Thou Shalt Not Kill' and half the world is training to annihilate the other half. Nobody would get me in uniform and off to Aden to kill a lot of people I've never met and have nothing against anyway . . .

"Anarchy is the only slight glimmer of hope. Not the popular conception of it – men in black cloaks lurking around with hidden bombs – but a freedom of every man being personally responsible for himself. There should be no such thing as private property. Anybody should be able to go where he likes and do what he likes. Politics, like the legal system, is dominated by old men. Old men who are also bugged by religion. And the law – the law's outdated and doesn't cater enough for individual cases."

MONDAY, 16 OCTOBER 1967

A Beatles spokesman leaks a story that the Beatles and the Rolling Stones are discussing "possible business projects".

"These might include the acquisition of a recording studio and equipment, which would be shared and which might be used to produce not only records by the groups separately but recorded work by other artists."

Rolling Stones press officer Leslie Perrin moves quickly to deny the rumours.
"In view of statements made over the weekend, but not emanating from The Rolling Stones, that a business merger between them and the Beatles is imminent, it is felt that the position should be clarified. Mr Mick Jagger states that preparatory conversations of a purely exploratory nature were held between him and Mr Paul McCartney.

"Discussed was the possibility, or advisability, of opening a recording studio at some unspecified future date. These conversations have not been resolved and any assumption to the contrary should be considered premature."

MONDAY, 30 OCTOBER 1967

"'A GROWING CANKER', CHAIRMAN SAYS"

Brian is found guilty on charges of unauthorised possession of cannabis resin and allowing his home to be used for cannabis consumption. He is found not guilty of a further charge of possessing cocaine and methedrine.
James Comyn, QC (defence lawyer): "(Drugs) have never solved any problems for him, but have created problems, and he is very anxious to see that no others take this example of his conduct in the past, but that they should take example from his present plight. He has never taken hard drugs and never will, and will not take soft drugs in the future.

"Jones is a man of considerable attainment as an entertainer. He has never peddled or pushed drugs, never bought drugs, and never circulated them or carried them around. He has had many people coming to his flat, and some of them have smoked cannabis sometimes. On his own shoulder, he has now taken the responsibility for that. There are degrees in possessing hemp and permitting its use, and this is a case which, I admit, is in a minor category.

"He has never been to prison and it is my urgent plea that it is not now necessary for him to go to prison. People in the public eye who offend are sometimes inflicted with a higher penalty, which sometimes can be harsh and even cruel.

"It is a great ordeal for someone in the public eye to come up on these matters, and he has suffered very greatly."

142

Dr Leonard Henry (psychiatrist): "(Brian) has a sensible and sane approach to his problem and had ceased smoking marijuana . . . I have given this matter a great deal of thought and have reached the conclusion that any confinement in prison would completely destroy his mental health, and he would go into psychotic depression as he could not possibly stand the stigma of a prison sentence. He might well attempt to injure himself."

Court Chairman R.E. Seaton: "Although no blame attaches to you for that phial of cocaine, it shows what happens at that sort of party. People who go there are smokers of cannabis. Others take hard drugs and that is how the rot starts . . . You occupy a position by which you have a large following of youth, and therefore it behoves you to set an example, and you have broken down on that. Although I am moved with everything I have heard, I am quite satisfied that I should be failing in my duty if I did not indicate the seriousness of this offence by passing a sentence of imprisonment."

Brian receives a prison sentence of nine months and is taken to Wormwood Scrubs. He is released from jail the following day on £750 bail, pending an appeal.

MONDAY, 13 NOVEMBER 1967

Judge Block, who presided over the Jagger/Richards court case in the summer, talks out of turn at The Horsham Ploughing And Agricultural Society's annual dinner at Rudgwick, Sussex.

Judge Block: "I refer to certain objects of no use to farmers. I may say they are of no use to man or beast, unless they are otherwise dealt with by being ground very small to surface roads or being cut down in size for other uses. I refer to the stones.

"I looked up in my book the other day to see what Shakespeare had to say about these things, and in Julius Caesar I found, 'You blocks, you stones, you worse than senseless things.'

"Be that as it may, we did our best, your fellow countrymen and I, and my fellow magistrates to cut these stones down to size, but alas, it was not to be because the Court of Criminal Appeal let them roll free."

The Stones publicist Les Perrin calls the speech "deplorable . . . the judge seems to have forgotten that one of the Stones, Brian Jones, is on bail pending his appeal in a drugs case – so the matter is *sub judice*."

FRIDAY, 8 DECEMBER 1967

Their Satanic Majesties Request, *the Stones' belated contribution to the psychedelic summer, is released.*

Brian: "It's too much, man. Far out. Really far out! Hey, Robert (Fraser), that's you there, man. Banging that pot! This album's gonna knock everybody out. How can anyone *not* be knocked out *completely?*"

Charlie: "I think our new album is our most progressive yet."

Mick: "I'm fed up with arrangers and people. We've done all the music ourselves . . . I didn't want to come on and say, 'We're progressing.' We're just changing, that's all. There's no forwards, no backwards. It's just the sounds we do one night in a studio. I don't know if it's progressing or not. People talk a lot of rubbish and get so pretentious about records. They talk about them as conscious patterns of development rather than spontaneous feeling."

Brian: "Yes, of course the album is a very personal thing. But the Beatles are just as introspective. You have to remember that our entire lives have been affected lately by socio-political influences. You have to expect these things to come out in our work."

Mick: "We don't write commercial music. We write what we want – and if that happens to be commercial, that's fine. We're not trying to inflict our kind of music on fans. They either buy it or they don't. We're not asking them to."

Jon Landau (*Rolling Stone* critic): "They have been for too long influenced by their musical inferiors, and the result is an insecure album in which they try too hard to prove that they too are innovators."

Keith: "It ended up as a real patchwork. Half of it was, 'Let's give the people what we think they want.' The other half was, 'Let's get out of here as quickly as possible.'"

Bill (on 'In Another Land'): "Mick said that as I'd written it I could damn well sing it!"

Candy Darling (Andy Warhol acolyte): "Listen! This is the song Mick wrote for me and my girlfriend Taffy . . . Here it comes now! Listen! 'Candy and Taffy/Hope you both are well/Please come see me/In the Citadel.' Did you *hear* it? We met them in the Hotel Albert. We were on the floor above them and we dangled a bunch of grapes down on a string outside their window. You see, the Citadel is New York and the song is a message to *us* – Taffy and me."

The 3D cover, which cost $50,000 to produce, provides another talking point.

Mick: "It's not really meant to be a nice picture at all – look at the expressions on our faces. It's a Grimm's fairy tale, one of those stories that used to frighten as a child."

With the court case and the record's difficult birth behind him Mick outlines his hopes for a "great world tour. We want to do something really different, visiting everywhere we can, not even a concert tour in the real sense of the word, something far more exciting."

But, he adds, Brian Jones cannot leave the country until his appeal is heard . . .

TUESDAY, 12 DECEMBER 1967

"THE TORMENTED MIND OF BRIAN JONES"

Brian attends the Court of Appeal where several important professionals speak up on his behalf.

James Comyn, QC (defence lawyer): "An important point is that he has said in clear terms he has cut out drugs, soft, hard or what you will, for the future . . . The sentence hanging over him has placed extra strain upon 'an already fragile mental make-up' . . . It is in that sense that the time which has passed since the offence has meant more suffering for him than perhaps it would for 99 out of 100 people. It may sound trite, but Jones has suffered every single day since sentence was passed upon him – a suffering which cannot be removed and may be regarded as penalty enough . . . It has been a troublesome summer for the whole group . . . This man is at the very crossroads of life and if you uphold the sentence it is liable to break him and his career. Brian Jones is at your mercy and it is mercy that he seeks. His medical advisers are saying that if he receives that mercy he will turn it into good account.

"There is a lot of talent in this young man. He is not only a pop singer but has a versatility of talents that he can turn to good account and so forget this troubled year of 1967 and get down to something worthwhile."

Dr Anthony Flood (psychiatrist): "My concern since his last appearance in court has been trying to calm his apprehensions as well as treat his underlying illness. He has been an extremely frightened young man . . . anxious, considerably depressed, perhaps even suicidal . . . He is easily depressed and easily thwarted. He cannot sort out his problems satisfactorily because he becomes so anxious and depressed . . . He has not a great deal of confidence in himself as a person. He is not sure of his identity as a person. He is still trying to grow up in many ways . . . I think if one put a reefer within half a mile of Brian Jones he would start running."

A second psychiatrist, Dr Walter Lindsey Neustatter, found Brian "quiet and courteous despite his attire . . . He came in the most extraordinary clothes which one could only describe as flamboyant. I think he had gold trousers and something which looked like a fur rug."

The nine-month jail sentence for drugs offences is set aside and Brian is placed on probation for three years and fined £1,000 with £250 costs. It is a condition of the probation order that he continues to receive the psychiatric treatment he has undergone since his arrest.

Lord Parker, the Lord Chief Justice: "Remember, this is a degree of mercy which the court has shown. It is not a let-off. You cannot go boasting about saying you have been let off. You are still under the control of the court. If you fail to co-operate with the probation officer or Dr Flood, or you commit another offence of any sort, you will be brought back and punished afresh for this offence. You know the sort of punishment you will get."

As the most traumatic year in the group's career comes to a close, Mick is asked for his views on the contemporary music scene.

Mick: "There were lots of new sounds – I can't even remember what they are – but there was no one particular thing that I thought was the start of some really big movement. They're all just little things going on, and then they just fade away."

Q: "Is there anything you particularly like that came out from it?"

Mick: "I can't think of anybody that I didn't already know existed in 1965, when people like Hendrix and others were already happening. All the people that were happening in 1967 we already knew about. The ones that I liked anyway."

Q: "Do you think The Rolling Stones progressed as a group?"

Mick: "Not particularly. We did a lot but we didn't progress. I don't think progression exists. Forwards or backwards don't really exist because you don't know if you're going forwards or backwards or sideways. You can go backwards right to where you began."

SATURDAY, 9 MARCH 1968

After a quiet, recuperative start to the New Year, Mick reveals that the group have been working on new material.

Mick: "We're rehearsing because we've forgotten how to do it. We've forgotten how to put the plugs in the amplifier. We're just having a good time."

146

Inevitably, he has a view on the latest Beatles 45, 'Lady Madonna'.
"It could have been groovier if Paul had done it like 'Long Tall Sally', but the words are very nice. In fact, the words are the best part. But I feel it is too relaxed, with not enough excitement."

FRIDAY, 15 MARCH 1968

The Stones enter Olympic Studios in Barnes, West London to begin sessions for a new album. With them is a new producer, Jimmy Miller.
Jimmy Miller: "Mick found it too much of a strain producing *Their Satanic Majesties Request* and playing as well. So he contacted me. He told me that he'd liked what I'd done with Traffic. We met and discussed ideas and later began the sessions. The Stones are easy to work with. They know what they're after, but it sometimes takes days to get it right. Mick Jagger sees just what he wants and won't settle for anything less."
Mick: "It doesn't mean we do everything we are told in the studio . . . We chose Jimmy Miller because unlike so many other record producers he does not have an ego problem. He will do what we want and not just what he wants. Besides, I liked his work on the early Spencer Davis hits."

SUNDAY, 17 MARCH 1968

Mick joins a huge demonstration outside the American Embassy in Grosvenor Square, central London, to protest against the continuing Vietnam War. He is asked about the role of violence and revolution as forces of social change.
Mick: "There's far better ways of doing it. I mean, what are you aiming for? To have a proper revolution. To have a change. There is no alternative society. There is none. There are lots, but they're not alternatives. They're not – really! You can have a left-wing revolution . . . but they're just the same. It's all the same. I can't see it as an alternative society. The only thing I can see, looking at it a lot, is that you're in a fantastic change period, though. Everyone keeps saying so, and probably we are."

MONDAY, 6 MAY 1968

The Byrds' hit London and play the Middle Earth club. The tour sparks one of rock's great friendships.
Keith: "I went out to visit The Byrds when they came to England. I was really going to see Roger (McGuinn). Gram (Parsons) was with him and we just hit it off right away."

When the Byrds return later that summer for a charity concert at the Royal Albert Hall, prior to a tour of South Africa, Gram resigns and stays on with Keith.

While Keith is undergoing a conversion to Gram's beloved country music, the rest of the music scene appears to be in the grip of a rock'n'roll revival.

Mick: "If you are a groover and all you've got is these ballads in the charts, I can understand you wanting to go back to rock'n'roll. But this is just living in the past. I suppose somebody will start saying our single is rock because it has a blues basis."

TUESDAY, 17 MAY 1968

Underground Bible International Times *publishes an extensive interview with Mick in conversation with editor Miles. It's probably his most stoned – and uncharacteristically woolly – conversation ever published.*

Mick: "When there's no songs, it nearly always means I'm very contented and I can't be bothered to write about it. I'm too busy to be worried about writing about it. It doesn't worry me. I don't want it, I don't want to write about it. Don't want to work, don't want to do anything, just want to . . . just carry on. But then someone phones up and says, 'Mmm, got to make a record . . .'"

Q: "How much are you into that scene?"

Mick: "I've cut myself off from that now, really have. I'm just trying to forget it . . . just living, just not working, just being very spiritual, being very religious or being very . . . enthused with one . . . into my own head . . . just getting into all that . . . My soul just keeps telling me what's right and what isn't right for me to do at the present time and I just follow it."

The conversation drifts to alternative societies . . .

Mick: "There's no doubt that there's a *vast* cyclic change on top of a lot of smaller ones. I can imagine America becoming just ablaze, just being ruined, but this country's so weird, you know. It always does things slightly differently, always more moderately and more boringly. The changes are so suppressed. The people suppress them. Everyone knew about the white backlash in England . . . It even cuts across class, which shows how strong it is, because there's very few things in England that do transcend class . . . It's amusing, though, because all these freaks, these people, it's their great grandfathers that broke up a civilisation, a tribal grouping, which had been going on for perhaps 30 million years . . . And, you know, you get five million black people in it (can) really change things, because they just are different and they do act differently . . . I mean, why should they?"

And, invariably, religion . . .

Mick: "The Christian thing is that man is inherently evil. Now that's where you've got your education scene coming in, your religion, your western world and all that because when you're really young, 'You're a naughty little boy, aren't you?', and when you go to school, you're evil and some weird scene in the Garden of Eden, and 'You're so awful that God gave his only son and suffered for you because you're so rotten.' Thank you, well, wow! You, know, am I really that bad? I mean, it's absolute rubbish."

Q: "You've been reading quite a lot about Buddhism . . ."

Mick: "Yeah, I've been swept along the river."

Q: "The river of fashion?"

Mick: "Yes, it's fashion, but it's a realisation of a need for some sort of spirituality which is living, which doesn't look like a corpse . . . The Buddhist approach is easier to compare with higher physics than the Christian approach to the same thing."

Q: "How do you feel when students riot when you're on stage? Do you pick up on the energy?"

Mick: "Yes, wow! Tingle with it! The energy's great. I mean, they give you *so* much energy I just don't know what to do with it, man. And it lasts, too. Every performer has felt that . . . I never went on stage with the idea of keeping everything cool. I never wanted it to be peaceful. Even if I did before I went on stage . . . I mean, they were totally in control, as much as I was."

Q: "Which direction do you think you're going in?"

Mick: "I dunno! I never know till we get in there. It's really how you feel. It's like a reflection of what you feel, which is why it's so groovy. Last year, we felt so freaky and so uptight and 'orrible, we just made very freaky records, half of which we never released, they were so strange. They just weren't any good. But now it's much more together . . . Our last disc wasn't a unit because one never knew if you were going to be in jail, so we never knew whether to book sessions. You didn't know who was going to be there. It was done over such a long period . . . But you see this album's been done in a space like a month and a half. We should finish off by the end of next month, so it's all in two months, you see. It's much more of a unit because all of the songs all sound the same. It's much more together. It's very basic, but it isn't backwards, it doesn't sound like Rolling Stones or anything like that."

Q: "Much of your work is descriptive of people."

Mick: "Yeah. The single's called 'Jumpin' Jack Flash' and he's a person. And the other side is called 'Child Of The Moon' and she's a person. There's one called 'Mr Gorilla Man' (*possibly a working title for 'Monkey Man', off* Let It Bleed), he's a person, and there's one called 'Parachute Man' (*actually 'Parachute Woman'!*)."

Q: "Are you aiming at technical improvement?"

Mick: "Yes, but I don't really think I will. Brian will get into electronics. I'm more interested in writing. I'd like to be a very good writer of songs."

Q: "A lot of people think that modern pop lyrics are the only solid form of poetry these days."

Mick: "But that's not true, you know . . . Some of it is probably very good."

Q: "Dylan stands up very well . . ."

Mick: "Oh, yeah, Dylan stands up. There's very few modern poets I like . . . I mean, most of them aren't even as good as The Byrds' songs. It's not very good and it's not very modern. It always reminds me of 1950 rather than now. It always makes me feel like a child because it reminds me of rationing or something."

Elsewhere, Mick reckons the new LP will be ready by June, enclosed in a David Bailey cover . . .

Mick: "The only person so far on the album, apart from the Stones, is Dave Mason. There's one song, a ballad, that I think we will use an orchestra on, but most of the tracks are uptempo things, all our own stuff. We rehearsed quite a long time before we started recording, in a studio in Surrey (*R.G. Jones, in Morden*)."

TUESDAY, 21 MAY 1968

"ROLLING STONE HAS 'A COMPLETE ANSWER'."

Brian Jones is busted at 7.20 a.m. in his flat in Royal Avenue House, King's Road, Chelsea. He is subsequently charged with illegal possession of cannabis and released on £1,000 bail.

Brian: "Oh no! This can't happen again, just when we were getting on our feet . . . Why do you have to pick on me?"

Mr Clive Nicholls (defence): "I would like to say at this stage that Jones has a complete answer to this which will be disclosed in due course."

FRIDAY, 24 MAY 1968

'Jumpin' Jack Flash' is released. Mick and Brian discuss the record with BBC Radio's Brian Matthew.

Mick: "A nice, uptempo groover is how I'd describe it."

Brian: "It's got a nice riff pattern like 'Satisfaction'. I dig it in the same way as I dig 'Satisfaction'. It's very different but it has the same basic funky quality."

Brian Matthew: "It's a very basic, simple sound compared with your *Satanic Majesties* LP . . ."

Mick: "*Satanic Majesties* was an album, which might have been very complex. This is a single. This is one track of what we're doing at the moment. We're not making an LP like this. Some of the LP will be in a way as complicated, in a way totally different. This is one track and it happens to be very basic."

Mick: "We didn't say, 'Right, we'll go backwards.' All you are really saying is that it has a good beat – it's not weird and full of electric sounds. We could do it on stage. In fact we have done – for a film for *Top Of The Pops*. We did it live, with no backing track or anything.

"We didn't do it as a single. We are over halfway through the new album and it was difficult picking which track should be the single because they are all quite good for singles . . . We did some of the single on a cassette tape recorder, which is a pretty mad way of making a record. We were all round at my house and we were recording everything. We got such weird sounds on drums and guitar with the cassette that we decided to use it. Charlie was just playing toy drums but we liked it and thought, 'So why not use it.' We recorded again over the top of it."

The flipside, 'Child Of The Moon', proves a bit more troublesome.

Mick: "We did it with country piano and acoustic guitar. I rather liked it, but Keith didn't dig it. We did it another way, all more electric, and I must admit it turned out better."

The single's remarkable success takes the Stones by surprise. Cue another opportunity to thank the fans for their loyalty.

"Dear readers of *NME*. 'Jumpin' Jack Flash' is really gassed that he made number one. So are the Rolling Stones. Thank you. We are slaving over a hot album which is coming out next month. Until then . . ."

Mick has his own reasons why the song returns the band to the top of the British singles chart after an absence of two years.

Mick: "The visual impact of The Rolling Stones is one of the most important parts. 'Jumpin' Jack Flash' was made a hit by the film. We did not promote it. Straight performance, nothing else, no freakin' about on the heath and the whole trip. That was what really helped the record, made it commercial . . . and it was shown all over the world."

TUESDAY, 4 JUNE 1968

French new wave film auteur *Jean-Luc Godard begins filming the Stones at work in Olympic Studios for his new movie.*

Mick: "I have no idea (what it's about). I know he's shooting with colour film used by astronauts when re-entering the earth's atmosphere. I mean, he's completely freaky. I think the idea for the movie is great but I don't think it will be the same when it's finished . . . It's his wife who plays the lead chick. She comes to London and gets totally destroyed with some spade cat. Gets involved with drugs or something. Anyway, while she is getting destroyed, we find the Rolling Stones freaking out at the recording studio making these sounds.

"Godard happened to catch us on two very good nights . . . One night he got us going over and over this song called 'Sympathy For The Devil'. It started out as a folky thing like 'Jigsaw Puzzle' but that didn't make it so we kept going over it and changing it until finally it comes out as a samba. So Godard has the whole thing from beginning to end . . . When he's finished cutting it, it will be great."

Jean-Luc Godard: "I just wanted to show something in construction. To show that democracy was nowhere, not even constructive."

Mick: "It's not a movie really . . . just a lot of footage of the Stones playing in some improvised scenes. I was very turned on by Godard; he's very quiet and very good. I like his work very much, very unobtrusive and pleasant. I think it will be ready in about two months."

Roger Greenspun (*New York Times* critic): ". . . *1 + 1* is a heavily didactic, even instructional, film, like much recent Godard, and it builds upon repetition, or, if you will, addition. The Rolling Stones' repeated assays upon 'Sympathy For The Devil' in their recording studio, the rote repetitions of passages and slogans passed back and forth among Black Power revolutionaries . . . all suggest a concern with ways of putting things together."

Mick: "Movies are kind of interesting. I'm going to learn a lot from movies, not just from acting but about making a movie."

152

SATURDAY, 22 JUNE 1968

It is announced that Mick will make his acting début in The Performers. *The title is eventually changed to* Performance.
Mick: "I'm going to play a kind of drop-out. I've been working quite hard on it because I have to understand the person before I play him. Shooting is due to start in July."

SATURDAY, 10 AUGUST 1968

"ROLLING STONES COMEBACK"

Rolling Stone *editor Jann Wenner gets a sneak preview of the forthcoming Rolling Stones album and announces:* "The Stones make the great comeback of their career." *It is, Wenner insists,* "the best record they have yet done . . . a great rock'n'roll album, without pretence, an achievement of significance in both lyrics and music."

The Who's Pete Townshend agrees.
"I've heard some of The Rolling Stones tracks . . . incredible, delicious and wonderful rock'n'roll and well overdue from them. The Rolling Stones should always be a non-progressive group. That's what I dig about them."

SATURDAY, 31 AUGUST 1968

'Street Fighting Man' is released on 45 in America. Fearing that the song may incite violence during the forthcoming National Democratic Convention in September, Chicago radio stations refuse to play the song.
Mick: "I'm rather pleased to hear they have banned 'Street Fighting Man' as long as it's still available in the shops. The last time they banned one of our records in America, it sold a million."
Keith: "The fact that a couple of American radio stations in Chicago banned the record just goes to show how paranoid they are. Yet they want us to make live appearances. If you really want us to cause trouble, we could do a few stage appearances. We are more subversive when we go on stage."
Mick: "They told me that 'Street Fighting Man' was subversive. Of course it's subversive. It's stupid to think you can start a revolution with a record. I wish you could."

MONDAY, 2 SEPTEMBER 1968

Mick, who is cast as a reclusive ex-rock star Turner, begins work on Performance.
Mick: "It's very much me. I'm going to make it – if I can – different to me. He's supposed to be a great writer, like Dylan. But he's completely immersed in himself. He's a horrible person, really."

Another key character in the film is played by Keith's girlfriend, Anita Pallenberg.
Donald Cammell (co-director): "Anita didn't help Keith's insecurity. She seemed to be teasing him about wanting Mick the way she used to tease Brian about wanting Keith. While we were filming, Keith never came near the set. He'd sit in the car outside and send in messages."

Upon completion of shooting, Mick changes his mind about his character.
Mick: "I think Turner is a projection of Donald's fantasy or idea of what I imagine how I am. The thing is that it's very easy for people to believe that's what I'm like. It was easy to do in a way because it's just another facet of me if I felt inclined to go that way. But now when I look at it there's so many things I could have done to make it stranger or to make it more real, to my mind, of how Turner would be and how he would live. I think it was a bit too much like me in a few ways. But he's not quite hopeless enough . . . It isn't me really. You just get into the part – that's acting, isn't it?"

When Warner Brothers head Ted Ashley demands radical edits before sanctioning the film's release, Mick and Donald Cammell argue their case via letter.
"Re: *Performance*. This film is about the perverted love affair between *Homo sapiens* and Lady Violence. It is necessarily horrifying, paradoxical and absurd. To make such a film means accepting that the subject is loaded with every taboo in the book.

"You seem to want to emasculate (1) the most savage and (2) the most affectionate scenes in our movie. If *Performance* does not upset audiences, it is nothing. If this fact upsets you, the alternative is to sell it fast and no more bullshit. Your misguided censorship will ultimately diminish said audiences in quality and quantity.

"Cordially, Mick Jagger, Donald Cammell."

THURSDAY, 5 SEPTEMBER 1968

Production of the Stones' forthcoming LP, Beggars Banquet, *has been held up. Decca Records insist that the projected sleeve – which depicts a lavatory wall bearing graffiti such as "God rolls his own" and "Music from Big Brown" – "is in poor taste".*

154

Mick: "We have tried to keep it within the bounds of good taste. I mean, we haven't shown the whole lavatory. That would have been rude. We've only shown the top half. I don't know when it will be released now. I don't think it's offensive. And I haven't met anyone, apart from two people at the record company, who finds it offensive. I even suggested that they put it out in a brown paper bag with 'Unfit For Children' and the title of the album on the outside if they felt that bad about it . . . I don't find it at all offensive. Decca has put out a sleeve showing an atom bomb exploding (*A-tom-ic Jones*). I find that more upsetting."

Keith: "The job of the record company is to distribute. All they've got to do is put it in the shops, not dictate to people what they should or should not have."

Mick: "What it all comes down to is that we design the sleeves and make the records – just like we have been doing for the last five years. We'll get this album distributed somehow even if I have to go down the end of Greek Street and Carlisle Street at two o'clock on Saturday morning and sell them myself."

The Stones take out an advert in Melody Maker *that shows the offending sleeve.* "This is the front of our new album which we finished two months ago. Due to religious disagreements, no release date has been set."

Mick: "No, we did not deliberately go out to produce a cover of this kind for sensationalism or to offend 'them'. It was simply an idea that had not been done before and we chose to put the writing on a lavatory wall because that's where you see most writing on walls."

Arguing his case in Rave *magazine, Mick insists:* "I am opposed to all forms of censorship. The only censorship you should impose is that imposed by the artists themselves. There is nothing dirty about the sleeve except in the minds of those that find it so."

Eventually, the band is forced to back down.

Mick: "I've lost interest in that situation. It's been a complete waste of energy. We agreed to them using a different sleeve in the end and it still hasn't been realised yet."

THURSDAY, 26 SEPTEMBER 1968

Brian's drug trial takes place at Inner London Sessions.

Mr Roger Frisbee (prosecutor): "The (police) search (of Brian's flat) bore fruit when a top drawer in a bureau was opened. It contained a

Rolling Stones record. On top of the record there was an innocent-looking ball of wool."

Brian: "The first thing I heard was a loud banging at the door. I did not immediately become aware of what it was. A minute might have passed before I knew it was something very intent on entering the flat. I put on a kaftan – kimono sort of thing – went to the door and looked through the spy hole."

Q: "What did you see?"

Brian: "Three large men."

Q: "Who did you think they were?"

Brian: "Police, perhaps, or agents."

Q: "Of the police?"

Brian: "Yes. Since last year I seem to have had an inborn fear of the police . . . When the ball of wool was shown to me I was absolutely shattered. I felt everything swim. I don't knit. I don't darn socks. I don't have a girlfriend who darns socks. I did not have the slightest knowledge that the ball of wool was in the flat."

Brian is found guilty of possessing cannabis resin at Inner London Sessions. He narrowly escapes a jail sentence.

R.E. Seaton (court chairman): "Mr Jones, you have been found guilty. I am going to fine you fifty pounds, and one hundred guineas costs. You really must watch your step and keep clear of this stuff. For goodness' sake, don't get into trouble again. If you do, there will be some real trouble."

Brian: "I still protest my innocence. I had no idea the cannabis resin was in the ball of wool. I didn't even know the wool was there.

"It's great not to be in jail. I was sure I was going to jail for at least a year. I never expected that I would be going home. It was such a wonderful relief when I heard I was only going to be fined. I'm happy to be free. It's wonderful. This summer has been a long worry for me. I knew I was innocent, but everything seems to happen to me."

Mick: "We are very pleased that Brian didn't have to go to jail. Money doesn't matter."

Mr Lewis Jones: "It's not for me to criticise the workings of officialdom. But I am absolutely convinced and I shall always remain convinced that Brian was unjustly convicted on the second of his drug charges. I pass no comment on the first, but on the second one I shall remain convinced for the rest of my life that Brian was innocent of that charge. And I base this mainly on the fact that the very night it happened he rang in a state of great distress because he was deeply concerned how his affairs were affecting his family, and he swore to me that he was innocent of it and he hoped that I would always believe him. I promised him on that occasion that I believed him and nothing has ever or will ever change my mind."

Tom Keylock (Rolling Stones employee): "The one time in his life Brian tells the truth, the poor bastard gets done for it."

Brian's paranoia is such at this stage in his life that he often answers the telephone with the following words:
"If you want to know if I use drugs – yes, I do."

FRIDAY, 4 OCTOBER 1968

" 'I'M PROUD', SAYS MICK"

Live-in lovers Mick and Marianne announce they are going to have a baby. It reopens the great marriage debate.
Marianne Faithfull: "Why should we marry? We are not the marrying sort of people. We've got along fine together so far. The baby is not going to change the way we feel about each other. Neither of us really cares what people say."
Mick: "I don't care for convention. I am very proud . . . It's real groovy. I'm very happy about Marianne having our baby. We'll probably have another three. But marriage? Can't see it happening. We just don't believe in it."

Less than two months later came a second announcement.
Mick: "Marianne has lost the baby following pregnancy complications. She is all right but we are both very upset."

SATURDAY, 12 OCTOBER 1968

Films, drug busts, banned records. Would the Stones ever tour again?
Mick: "I'd like to do them (tours) but the thought of going onstage and playing 'Satisfaction', 'Paint It Black', 'Jumpin' Jack Flash' and six others just doesn't appeal to me. I certainly don't want to go on stage and just stand there like Scott Walker and be ever so pretentious. I can't hardly sing, you know what I mean. I'm no Tom Jones and I couldn't give a fuck."
Keith: "The Beatles at the moment are dying to get on the stage again. Whether they actually make it is another thing. We do, too, and we're gonna start tearing the place to pieces starting January/February in South America, which I think is a very good revolutionary stamping ground."

MONDAY, 28 OCTOBER 1968

In a television interview given the day after a second huge demonstration in Grosvenor Square, Mick's patience with radical politics appears to have wilted.
Mick (to interviewer): "Did you go yesterday to the demonstration? It was very boring. It was a very large public school scrum. There's no politeness in anarchy. There's no room for *politesse* in anarchy! Everyone shakes hands at the end."
Q: "It was supposed to be a revolution?"
Mick: "Yeah!"

The European press seems more interested in Jagger's politics than those at home.
Q: "You sing of politics, protest and revolution."
Mick: "Oh, no, I don't sing of revolution."
Q: "In your song, 'Street Fighting Man', it says, 'The time is right for fighting in the street'."
Mick: "But it then says, 'But what can a poor boy do, except sing in a rock'n'roll band' – what else can I do besides sing?"
Q: "Do you really think it's appropriate *not* to sing about the revolution?"
Mick: "We don't do that. In America, the rock'n'roll bands have gotten very political. They express themselves very directly about the Vietnam war. But when I come home to England, everything is completely different, so quiet and peaceful. If one lives in such an atmosphere, one has a great detachment from politics and writes completely different about them.

"I have given money for large concerts that were for the benefit of conscientious objectors and the anti-Vietnam war movement. Nonetheless, I am no Marxist-Leninist, and I also don't wish to live under a Communist government. In America, many young people think Marxism is the only alternative to the present society. But Americans don't have any of their own personal experience about the practice of a Marxist system. That makes it easy for them to be members of such left-wing movements."

THURSDAY, 5 DECEMBER

The Beggars Banquet *album is launched with a bawdy banquet at the Kensington Gore Hotel in London. After announcing to the guests that "We didn't invite you here just to eat and drink", Mick lets battle commence by thrusting a custard pie into the face of Brian Jones.*
Lord Harlech: "Not quite the sort of party I'm accustomed to, but thoroughly enjoyable."

The album is universally well received, which comes as no surprise to Keith.
"After *Satanic Majesties*, we wanted to make a Stones album."

Mick is asked whether the Stones have been influenced by recent, country-tinged albums by The Byrds and Bob Dylan.
Mick: "Yeah, but Keith has always been country. That's what his scene was. We still think of country songs as a bit of a joke, I'm afraid. We don't really know anything about country music, really. We're just playing games."

Keith reveals the true secret behind the band's new sound – using a five-stringed guitar and an open G tuning.
Keith: "I was disenchanted with my own playing to standard tuning and, after playing around with these slide tunings in E and D as well as G, I realised that you could use them for rhythm guitar as well. It was like learning guitar all over again."

TUESDAY, 10 DECEMBER 1968

The Stones begin shooting their television spectacular The Rolling Stones' Rock'n'Roll Circus *at a studio in Wembley, Middlesex. According to the official press release, the Circus will feature a number of British and American recording acts, as well as "animals, clowns and dwarfs" . . .*

. . . and Jethro Tull.
Keith: "I really liked the band on *Rock'n'Roll Circus*. I hope Ian Anderson doesn't get into a cliché thing with his leg routine."
Mick: "You've heard of Oxford Circus, you've heard of Piccadilly Circus, and this is *The Rolling Stones' Rock'n'Roll Circus* . . . If we aren't pleased with the result, we will scrap it."

He wasn't, and he did – until eventually sanctioning the film's release on video in 1996.

WEDNESDAY, 18 DECEMBER

On Keith's 25th birthday, he and Mick leave for a winter trip to South America.
Keith: "We have become very interested in magic and we are very serious about this trip. We are hoping to see this magician who practises both white and black magic. He has a very long and difficult name which we cannot pronounce – we just call him Banana for short."

EARLY 1969

His Satanic Majesty Mick writes to artist M.C. Escher with an enthusiastic request.
"Dear Maurits,

For quite some time now I have had in my possession your book and it never ceases to amaze me . . . In fact I think your work is quite incredible and it would make me very happy for a lot more people to see and know and understand exactly what you are doing. In March or April we have scheduled our next LP record for release, and I am most eager to reproduce one of your works on the cover-sleeve. Would you please consider either designing a 'picture' for it, or have you any unpublished works which you might think suitable?"

The painter's response is curt, and considerably less familiar.
"Some days ago I received a letter from Mr Jagger asking me either to design a picture or to place at his disposal unpublished work to reproduce on the cover-sleeve for a record. My answer to both questions must be no . . . By the way, please tell Mr Jagger I am not Maurits to him, but very sincerely, M.C. Escher."

A second option proves no less fruitful.
Mick (in a letter to business manager Allen Klein): "Your inefficiency is a drag. What the fuck did you do with all the photographs? They were supposed to be delivered to Andy Warhol. We await your reply."

FRIDAY, 21 FEBRUARY 1969

Marianne Faithfull's new single, 'Sister Morphine', co-written with Mick and Keith, is withdrawn on orders from Decca boss Sir Edward Lewis. However, her relationship with Mick keeps her in the public eye.
Marianne Faithfull: "I am still happily sinning away with Mick. We won't get married for several reasons, one of which is the divorce law in this country. I am not committing adultery because I'm in love. It's the law that makes our relationship seem sordid and disgusting . . . I would never marry again. If I liked someone, I would live with him and have children. One hopes that society will change and stop being so stupid about these things."

EARLY MARCH, 1969

Increasingly ostracised from the band, Brian hands in a request to Stones' office manager, Jo Bergman.

"Dear Jo,

I need the following dates to do my recording thing in Morocco: 22nd–25th or 26th March. This is the only time I can get it done, and I honestly believe I can get something really worthwhile from this venture for us. If this means I have to miss a session or two, I can dub my scenes on after, while vocals are being done or whatever. Incidentally, the Morocco thing is only part of my venture. I am confident I can come up with something really groovy. I will talk to you later about financing the thing, if that be possible. I don't need that much. Hope it happens!

Love Brian"

No one objects to Brian's trip, so with engineer George Chkiantz and a Uher tape-recorder, he sets off to capture the music of the Master Musicians of Joujouka. While there, Brian bumps into an old friend.

Brion Gysin: "We were sitting on the ground with Brian, under the very low eaves of this thatched farm house, and the musicians were working just four or five feet away, ahead of us in the courtyard where the animals usually are. It was getting to be time to eat, and suddenly two of the musicians came along with a snow-white goat. The goat disappeared off in the shadows with the two musicians, one of whom was holding a long knife which Brian suddenly caught the glitter of, and he started to get up, making a sort of funny noise, and he said, 'That's me!' And everybody picked up on it right at once and said, 'Yeah right, it looks just like you.' It was perfectly true, he had this fringe of blond hair hanging right down in front of his eyes, and we said, 'Of course that's you.' Then about twenty minutes later, we were eating this goat's liver on shish-kebab sticks."

Brian: "I don't know if I possess the stamina to endure the incredible constant strain of the festival, such psychic weaklings has Western civilisation made of so many of us."

Back in London, confusion reigns in the Stones camp, as Jo Bergman makes clear in a private letter to Mick Jagger.

"What's happening to the group? Is there any real interest in doing public appearances. Or do you want to just record and make movies?"

She also expresses her misgivings about business manager Allen Klein.

"The Klein problem is more than a drag. We're puppets. How can you work, or run the office, if we have to spend so much time pleading for bread . . .?"

SATURDAY, 8 MARCH 1969

His recent troubles with record sleeves alert Mick to the importance of adopting an increasing professionalism in matters of business – and morality.
Leo Perrin (PR): "Jagger is an original brain. He's quietly outspoken, has strong convictions and debates them. Things like the question of whether he should marry Marianne were discussed sanely to me but not without a lot of soul searching by him. It is wrong to presume that his attitudes are rushed into wildly . . . Joe Public in general views him as a man who wears his hair long, creating music which a lot of them don't understand and don't want to understand. This is not Jagger at all. He takes a meticulous attitude to the way things are handled."

He also begins to think about his own mortality.
Mick: "I don't think I shall live to a very old age, anyway. I've always had that feeling. But if you can stop your body falling apart you've won half the battle. Degeneration of a physical nature is half the problem."

LATE APRIL, 1969

When Brian returns, the band are in the middle of sessions for their forthcoming album.
Brian: "What can *I* play?"
Mick: "I don't know. What *can* you play?"
By early May, even the Daily Express *was muttering . . .*
"Things look bad for the Rolling Stones."

WEDNESDAY, 28 MAY 1969

"JAGGER AND MARIANNE CHARGED BY DRUG SQUAD"

After police raid Mick's Cheyne Walk home in Chelsea, he and Marianne are charged with unlawful possession of cannabis and released on £50 bail. Mick later appears on his doorstep, dressed in a pink velvet suit, to make a brief statement.
Mick: "The police – about six or seven of them – arrived just after Marianne and I had finished our tea. They took us down to the police station. We went in my own car, not a police car . . . I am going to work now. We are going to the recording studios."

162

FRIDAY, 30 MAY 1969

21-year-old guitarist Mick Taylor joins the Stones at Olympic Studios, during sessions for the next single, 'Honky Tonk Women'.

Mick Taylor: "I was invited to do a session with the Stones. It puzzled me. I had never met Mick Jagger in my life and here he was phoning me. I went down and played on some tracks and thought little more about it. Then they asked me if I wanted to be a Stone. I was amazed. Brian Jones was leaving, I was told. I said I'd love to be a Stone and that was that."

Mick Taylor: "I was a bit nervous at the session obviously; I hadn't met them or even seen them play before. But after a couple of minutes, I felt really comfortable and at ease. After all, with Mayall I'd been playing blues, the Stones play heavy rock and really there's not that much difference."

SUNDAY, 8 JUNE 1969

"BRIAN JONES QUITS STONES AS GROUP CLASH OVER SONGS."

Mick and Keith visit Brian Jones at Cotchford Farm, his 16th century home in Hartfield, Sussex – where A.A. Milne penned his Winnie The Pooh *children's stories some 40 years earlier – and make it clear that The Rolling Stones no longer require his services.*

Mick: "We'd known for a few months that Brian wasn't keen. He wasn't enjoying himself and it got to the stage where we had to sit down and talk about it. So we did and decided the best thing was for him to leave . . . He's gotta do his own thing, man, and he hasn't said anything to us about it."

Brian: "I no longer see eye-to-eye with the others over the discs we are cutting . . . I have a desire to play my own brand of music . . . We have agreed that an amicable termination of our relationship is the only answer."

Mick: "Brian wants to play music which is more his own rather than always playing ours. We have decided he is best to be free to follow his own inclinations. But we part on the best of terms. We will continue to be friends. Obviously you cannot break up a friendship after so long."

Brian: "The Stones' music is not to my taste anymore. I want to play my own kind of music. The music Mick and Keith have been writing has progressed at a tangent to my own musical tastes."

MONDAY, 9 JUNE 1969

Brian sends a telegram to Janie Perrin, wife of the band's publicist Les Perrin.
Brian: "I'm very unhappy. So unhappy, I've done things. But I've sorted out things financially and morally. I've done the best I can for the people I love. I love you and Les very much."

Several friends and musicians visit Brian in the aftermath of his sacking, including Alexis Korner.
"I was in touch with Brian again because he needed to speak to someone who could help him to reorganise his musical thinking so he could start playing again. He said, 'I'm sorry I haven't seen you for all these years.' I said, 'That's all right,' and that's all we said about it.

"He talked a lot about the old days, as if I wanted to hear about getting back to the old days . . . I dug some of his ideas – the things he wanted to do with Creedence Clearwater bits and the James Cleveland gospel bits. But I didn't dig going back to the Muddy Waters and Elmore James thing, didn't dig his ideas about using the Mezzrow-Bechet with soprano either. Those are some of the things Brian was talking about, the kind of band he had in mind. It seemed like a retrogression . . .

"What we decided was that I would help Brian get the proper musicians together, he would play his part in the band, and I would act as a sort of musical director to see that all the parts fitted together . . . He began talking very excitedly about the things he wanted to do, the music he wanted to play. And he was getting happy again, really enthusiastic about the band."

MID JUNE, 1969

Brian also receives an unprecedented visit from his parents.
Mr Lewis Jones: "Typical of Brian, we had a call in the early hours of the morning, full of bubbling enthusiasm about the beauties of his new house, the loveliness of the particular summer we were having at that time. He said, 'Come down in the morning.' We said that was easier said than done. It was a Tuesday . . . We did in fact go down the following weekend and spent the weekend with him – an intensely happy weekend with him, the happiest and closest weekend we had spent with him since he was a child. It was the last time we ever saw him . . . He had proved us wrong, and I'll always say to his credit that he never came home and said, 'I told you so.' He only said with a rather wry smile, 'Well, I haven't done so bad, dad, have I?'"

FRIDAY, 13 JUNE

The Stones call a press conference in Hyde Park, London, to unveil Mick Taylor as their replacement for Brian Jones. They also announce that Taylor will make his début with the Rolling Stones at a free concert in the park on 5 July.

Mick: "He's been through the John Mayall school of guitarists – people like Peter Green and Clapton. I didn't want to go through the whole bit of auditioning guitarists, so I spoke to Mayall, a man whose judgment I respect in these matters. John just sort of grunted when I told him we'd like to see Mick, so I took it as a 'yes' . . . I'd never heard him live before – only on records, but he got on well with Keith and he picked things up quickly, so we got the track done more quickly. He doesn't play anything like Brian. He's a bluesman and he wants to play rock'n'roll, so that's okay."

Mick Taylor: "Now I can write numbers that will have a better chance of being used. Since I am a lead guitarist, both Keith and I will be playing lead, more or less."

Mick: "I don't think we'll have any trouble."

SATURDAY, 28 JUNE 1969

"STONES WON'T ROLL THE SAME WITHOUT BRIAN"

Not everyone welcomes the changes, as this Disc & Music Echo *reader confirms . . .*

"After hearing such disturbing news that Brian Jones has left the Stones, I must complain. How can Stones fans accept someone else after being Brian Jones fans for nearly six years? I have always loved and admired Brian very much and Mick Taylor and the Stones are just not going to roll the same.

Stones fan, Bracklesham Bay, Sussex."

THURSDAY, 3 JULY 1969

"3.30 a.m. LATEST: BRIAN JONES OF THE 'STONES' FOUND DEAD."

"Pop guitarist Brian Jones, who quit The Rolling Stones last month, was found dead early today.

"His body was discovered by friends who called at his £30,000 home at Hartfield, Sussex . . .

"The Rolling Stones tour manager, Tom Keylock, phoned me early today and said: 'I got a call from Brian's house, and the voice said there was trouble at the house. But when I rang Brian back there was no reply, and I am extremely worried.'

"When I broke the news, Keylock said: 'This is a terrible shock. I spoke to Brian yesterday morning and he was full of spirits and raring to go. I can't say what his plans were. But he was full of enthusiasm about them.'"

The news spread quickly . . .

"BRIAN JONES DIES IN POOL TRAGEDY"

Keith: "We were at a session that night and we weren't expecting Brian to come along. He'd officially left the band . . . And someone called us up at midnight and said, 'Brian's dead.' Well, what the fuck's going on? We had these chauffeurs working for us and we tried to find out . . . some of them had a weird hold over Brian. There were a lot of chicks there and there was a whole thing going on, they were having a party. I don't know, man, I just don't know what happened to Brian that night."

Police spokesman: "There was no question of a party being held at the house at the time. Mr Jones was staying there with just the three friends."

Tom Keylock: "Brian had suffered from asthma for some years and it was particularly bad when there was a lot of pollen about. There was an asthma inhaler, which Brian used to help him breathe, by the side of the swimming-pool and there was a very high pollen count yesterday."

Mick: "I am just so unhappy. I am so shocked and wordless and so sad. Something has gone. I have really lost something. We were like a pack, one family in a way. I just say my prayers for him. I hope he becomes blessed, I hope he is finding peace . . . and I really want him to."

Charlie: "I can't really say anything about Brian – it's such a personal thing and it's impossible to sum up a friend cold-bloodedly. It's a great personal loss that leaves me at a loss for words. No matter what I were to say, it would not be enough."

George Harrison: "When I met him I liked him quite a lot. I got to know him very well, I think, and I felt very close to him. You know how it is with some people, you feel for them, feel near to them. He was born on 28 February 1943 [*sic*], and I was born on 25 February 1943, and he was with Mick and Keith and I was with John and Paul in the groups, so there was a sort of understanding between the two of us. There was nothing the matter with him that a little extra love wouldn't have cured. I don't think he had enough love or understanding. He was very nice and sincere and sensitive, and we must remember him like that because that's what he was."

Les Perrin: "I think it was a terrible mistake. I felt I'd lost a very good friend. I liked him tremendously, I make no apologies at all. I found him a great conversationalist, a rather remarkable monster, a lovely man."

Jimmy Miller: "He was entirely a musician. He never quite adapted to the commercial and image aspects of the Stones. As a musician, he should be remembered for the brilliant bottleneck guitar work on *Beggars Banquet*, for his interpretation of blues – played honestly as a white man. And he composed a brilliant score for the German film *Mort Und Totschlag*."

Derek Taylor (Apple Records): "It isn't for any of us to tapdance with our typewriters to pay tribute to Brian Jones or to involve our own egos with the sadness of his passing. But it's as well to answer the slimy Sunday papers, and a few of their daily colleagues, who have suggested that Brian was a 'victim' of pop music.

"It's as well to remember that we all have to die – pop stars, tennis players, poets, peasants, pearl fishermen, and swines who sell their stories to pigsty newspapers.

"Those of us who live in or by, or on, this cheerful and joyous pop music industry are sick of having it held up as a danger to our health, our morals or our lifestyle. Most of us are happy, temperate, free-living souls who have come a little closer than some others to a way of living which is of our own choosing.

"Let us pray that those who for whatever reason have axes to grind against grass or acid, music or freedom, or youth and peace, or any of the other bogeymen of contemporary life will, instead of spewing into the grave of Brian Jones, turn their pens instead (if they must) against the living, who are better equipped to reply.

"Brian suffered enough pain in his chest while he was alive. For Christ's sake now let him rest in peace."

Mick: "I suppose there was a kind of feeling that I knew that if anyone was gonna die, Brian was gonna die. I always knew that Brian wouldn't really live that long. He just lived his life very fast. He was like a butterfly."

John Lennon: "He disintegrated. He ended up the kind of guy that you dread when he would come on the phone, because you knew it was trouble. He was really in a lot of pain. He wasn't sort of brilliant or anything, he was just a nice guy."

The Who's Pete Townshend pays tribute in verse form in a song – 'A Normal Day For Brian, A Man Who Died Every Day' – written on the day he died.

I used to play my guitar as a kid
Wishing that I could be like him
But today I changed my mind I
Decided that I don't want to die
But it was a normal day for Brian
Rock and Roll's that way
It was a normal day for Brian
A man who died every day.

Alexis Korner: "In a way, for Brian it was a good thing. He really was happy at the time that he died, because he was getting this new band together. We were going to rehearse it. I wasn't going to play with him but I was going to act as his rehearsal director. He was talking very excitedly and we'd laid some tracks down of things we wanted to do. I'm not sure that he would have made it. At the time that he died he was sure that he would have made it and that's all that was important."

FRIDAY, 4 JULY 1969

The Times . . .
"Obituary

MR BRIAN JONES
Former guitarist with The Rolling Stones
". . . Brian Jones' wide grey-green eyes fringed by his long blond hair became an important part of the group's public image. In Europe he was almost as quickly identified as Mick Jagger . . . Brian Jones' personal life was less settled over the past year and tensions within The Rolling Stones were growing . . . (He) does not feature on their new record released last week, for early last month he finally left to be replaced by another guitarist.
    "In the group's six years of success, Brian Jones was a constant source of musical invention and ability within the group. He was also the most co-operative and talkative of the group, but over the past two years, he has suffered from feelings of persecution and unhappiness. He felt that his relationship with his personal brand of music was threatened and he was about to form a new group."

'Honky Tonk Women', the first Stones record to feature Mick Taylor, is released.
Keith: "Last Christmas, Mick and I went to Brazil and spent some time on a ranch. I suddenly got into cowboy songs. I wrote 'Honky Tonk

Women' as a straight Hank Williams sort of number. Later, when we were fooling around with it, trying to make it sound funkier, we hit on the sound we had on the single. We all thought, 'Wow, this has got to be a hit single.' And it was, probably because it's the sort of song which transcends all tastes."

SATURDAY, 5 JULY 1969

The Stones' free show at Hyde Park goes ahead.
Mick: "We will do the concert – for Brian. We have thought about it and feel he would have wanted it to go on. I hope people will understand that it is because of our love for him that we are still doing it."
Mick (to crowd): "Aw-right . . . Now listen . . . Will you just cool it for a minute, 'cos I would really like to say something about (for) Brian . . . and what we feel about him just goin' when we didn't expect him to."

In tribute, Mick reads a poem by Percy B. Shelley:

> Peace, peace! He is not dead, he doth not sleep –
> He hath awakened from the dream of life –
> 'Tis we who, lost in stormy visions, keep
> With phantoms an unprofitable strife,
> And in mad trance strike with our spirit's knife
> Invulnerable nothings. We decay
> Like corpses in a charnel; fear and grief
> Convulse us and consume us day by day,
> And cold hopes swarm like worms within our living clay.
> The One remains, the many change and pass
> Heaven's light forever shines, Earth's shadows fly;
> Life, like a dome of many coloured glass,
> Stains the white radiance of Eternity,
> Until Death tramples it to fragments – Die,
> If thou wouldst be with that which thou dost seek
> Follow where all is fled!

Thousands of white butterflies are then released as a tribute to the deceased Stone.
Mick: "Hyde Park? Yeah, I can't stop dreaming about it. It had to be the biggest crowd I've ever seen. They were the stars of the show, like some massive religious gathering on the shores of the Ganges. I was a bit shaky at first but then I started enjoying myself."

The event is primarily a wake for Brian, and a chance to introduce the world to Mick Taylor, but Mick Jagger's Mr Fish-designed "little girl's white party frock" became the talking point in the press the next day.

Barry Sainsbury (Mr Fish's business partner): "It's very masculine. They cost 85 guineas and we've sold several. One went to a lady from South Africa . . . Sammy Davis, Jnr. liked the outfit very much and he's just ordered three – in black, brown and champagne."

A few days later, Thomas Frankland, Chairman of the British Butterfly Conservation Society writes to The Times to complain about "the wanton releasing of thousands of butterflies in a park without food plants in the centre of a large city . . . a trivial gimmick in terms of entertainment and for such a meaningless purpose in terms of conservation. I trust Mr Jagger will redeem himself by offering to buy as many again and entrust them to my society so that they can be released throughout Britain . . . to give pleasure to many who are saddened by the disappearance of butterflies . . ."

MONDAY, 7 JULY 1969

"BRIAN JONES HAD TAKEN SPIRITS AND DRUGS"

A verdict of 'death by misadventure' is recorded by Dr Angus Sommerville, the East Sussex coroner, at Brian's inquest held at East Grinstead, East Sussex.

Janet Lawson (nurse): "He had been drinking. He was a bit unsteady on his feet. I attempted conversation but it was a little garbled. Brian said it was because he had had his sleepers."

Frank Thorogood (builder): "He had some difficulty on the springboard, but he swam quite normally."

Janet Lawson: "Both Frank and Brian were in no fit condition to swim. They had been drinking. I mentioned it to the men, but they disregarded the warning. Despite Brian's condition he was able to swim. However, he was rather sluggish."

Anna Wohlin (girlfriend): "I dived in and Frank came to help pull him out while Janet telephoned for help. Then all three of us applied artificial respiration. While doing this I felt Brian's hand grip mine, but there was no other movement."

Dr Albert Sachs (pathologist): "For a man of his age his heart was a bit larger than it should have been. It was fatty and flabby. His liver was twice the normal weight. It was in an advanced state of fatty degeneration and not functioning properly. I could find no evidence microscopically that he had had an attack of asthma."

TUESDAY, 8 JULY 1969

"COLLAPSE! DRUG SQUAD AT HOSPITAL"

While accompanying Mick Jagger to Australia, as he begins work on a new film,
Ned Kelly, *Marianne Faithfull is found in a coma after taking 150 sleeping tablets, in the couple's suite at the Chevron Hotel, Sydney.*
Mick: "I don't think she's overdosed. Marianne's very delicate and the air journey has exhausted her. Her condition doesn't seem serious, but they are checking her up to see if she will be all right."

Marianne is taken to St Vincent's Hospital and does not regain consciousness for five days.
Mick: "Marianne recognised me – that's very important. She told me she loved me. The hospital allowed me to be with her for fifteen minutes – any longer may well have tired her, they told me . . . Marianne is going to be okay. She's on her own now and doesn't need help any more."
Q: "What does she mean to you, Mick?"
Mick: "She turns me on to lots of good things. She has led me into music, drama and literature which I haven't read before . . . I turn her on to things more basic."
Marianne: "I was virtually dead. They saved my life. I expect it will be two months before I recover fully. I will spend a week riding horses, relaxing and watching Mick on the set of his film."

THURSDAY, 10 JULY 1969

Brian Jones' funeral service takes place in his home town of Cheltenham.
Canon Hugh Evan Hopkin: "I hold in my hand a telegram which Brian's parents treasure more than they can say. He sent it to them some little while ago, after he had come into conflict with the law. I read this with the parents' permission: 'Please don't judge me too harshly.'

"Here I believe Brian speaks not only for himself, but also for all his generation, and I pass his words on to any who will hear of this service today . . .

"Brian had little patience with authority, convention and tradition. In this, he was typical of many of his generation who have come to see in The Rolling Stones an expression of their whole attitude to life."
Pat Andrews: "He was the hardest boy in the world to understand and I think we all believed we could understand him if we tried long enough . . . But really no one ever could."

Doors' vocalist Jim Morrison pays tribute to Brian in his 'Ode To LA While Thinking Of Brian Jones, Deceased, 1969'

> I hope you went out
> Smiling
> Like a child
> Into the cool remnant
> Of a dream.

Lewis Jones: "We had our violent disagreements, but we never stopped loving him."
Graveside tribute from fan: "It will never be the same without the boy we used to adore."

SUNDAY, 13 JULY 1969

Mick begins filming Ned Kelly *outside Canberra, Australia. Between shoots, he finds time to talk to the local press – and to Patrick McCarville, his dialogue coach.*
Mick: "This is the first big challenge I've ever had as an actor. I've got to live the part if I'm to get the best of me. I'm sympathetic with this Kelly character. He reminds me a bit of me. One of the reasons I accepted the part was because I knew what Ned Kelly was like and I liked him.

"Everything's so serious in this world. I'd love to be able to think of something to do about the mess. I've got lots of negative answers, but nothing positive. John Lennon has found some kind of answer. He uses a simple formula – absolute integrity. I respect him for it.

"We British are a weird race. A hundred years ago we ruled the world. Our so-called moral standards were the greatest hypocrisy in history. At home we couldn't walk down the street and say 'bum' without getting arrested. But in our colonies, we plundered, murdered, raped, thieved and generally ravaged every black, brown or yellow poor chump unfortunate enough to be 'discovered' by us.

"A hundred years ago, all over the world, anybody who got in the way of the British was just stepped on. Now what's the result? World wars won? Two. World wars lost. Nil. And what are we? Bloody skint. That's what.

"These Australian women amaze me. I was cruising in Sydney Harbour and we moved in close to the beach to look at the people. I had binoculars and was looking at the birds in their bikinis. The Aussie birds look fantastic in bikinis. Sexiest things you'll see anywhere in the world. They've got this sexy bronzed skin and their bodies are fantastic. But when they get

172

dressed up in their gear they look shocking. Terrible! They don't know how to wear clothes at all. They don't know how to walk. They don't know how to talk. The only time they look any good is when they're practically naked on the beach."

WEDNESDAY, 16 JULY 1969

"JAGGER GIVES HIS VIEWS ON GOD"

Mick tells a radio station in Melbourne, Australia that he believes in God but that does not necessarily make him a Christian. He adds that he also believes in "crazy forces like good and evil".
Mick: "Jesus Christ was fantastic and something to base life on but I don't like the church. The church does more harm than good. I think if you read what Jesus Christ says you needn't bother about church. Jesus Christ didn't like church. He used to kick people out of temples. I think they all ought to be kicked out of temples."

He then turns to matters more corporeal.
"My ears – I don't like them. My feet are too big and I'd like to be two inches taller. If I had my life over again I'd change what I look like."

And that old chestnut . . .
"Marriage used to mean something religious – now it's just a gesture. I might change (my views) when I'm 55. It might depend, too, on the woman I'm going with. I don't want to have children. I'm not ready. You don't have to be married to have a secure background for children."

It's obvious that Ned Kelly *has put some strain on the Stones' 'marriage' . . .*
Keith: "That whole film thing in Australia was a bit of a drag. I mean, it sounds dangerous to me. He's had his hand blown off, and he had to get his hair cut short. But Mick thinks he needs to do those things. We've often talked about it and I've asked him why the hell he wants to be a film star. But he says, 'Keith, you're a musician. But I don't play anything.'"

SUNDAY, 10 AUGUST 1969

Keith and Anita's son, Marlon, is born.
Keith: "I'm very happy but this makes no difference to my marriage plans. There aren't any. I'm not saying marriage is out, but it's not in, either. Neither of us is talking about that at the moment.

Anita Pallenberg: "I agree entirely with Keith."

Keith is then asked to hold the baby . . .
Keith: "I don't dare − it's a woman's job."

Legend has it that the first words that Marlon learns are 'Room Service'.

FRIDAY, 12 SEPTEMBER 1969

The band's new hits collection, Through The Past, Darkly (Big Hits Vol. 2), *carries a self-penned epitaph by Brian Jones.*

> "When this you see, remember me
> And bear me in your mind
> Let all the world say what they may
> Speak of me as you find."

As the group line up a late autumn tour of America, Keith discusses the competition with journalist Ritchie Yorke at the band's central London office in Maddox Street.

Creedence Clearwater Revival . . .
"When I first heard them, I was really knocked out, but I became bored with them very quickly."

Blood Sweat & Tears . . .
"I don't really like them . . . The only brass that ever knocked me out was a few soul bands."

Led Zeppelin . . .
"I played their album quite a few times when I first got it, but then the guy's voice started to get on my nerves . . . Maybe he's just a little too acrobatic."

Blind Faith
"I don't think Stevie (Winwood) has got himself together. He's an incredible singer, guitarist and organist, but he never does the things I want to hear him do."

The Band
"I saw them at the Isle of Wight and I was disappointed . . . They were just a little too perfect for me."

The Bee Gees
"They're in their own little fantasy world . . . how many suits they've got and that kind of crap. It's all kids' stuff."

Crosby Stills & Nash
"I thought the album was nice, really pretty."

And the old adversaries . . .
"Mick has said it before but it's worth repeating: the Beatles are primarily a recording group. I think the Beatles had passed their performing peak before they were famous."

And Mick had a little more to say . . .
Mick: "I don't like the Beatles' new stuff much. I mean, I don't think the Beatles should get back . . . I wish they'd gone on. I think they were really going the right way, you know, *Sgt. Pepper* was really 'whoo!'"

John Lennon: "I was always very respectful about Mick and the Stones, but he said a lot of tarty things about the Beatles, which I am hurt by, because you know, I can knock the Beatles but don't let Mick Jagger knock them. I would just like to list what we did and what the Stones did two months after on every fuckin' album. Every fuckin' thing we did, Mick does exactly the same – he imitates us . . . You know, *Satanic Majesties* is *Pepper*, 'We Love You', it's the most fuckin' bullshit, that's 'All You Need Is Love'.

"I resent the implications that the Stones are like revolutionaries and that the Beatles weren't. If the Stones were, or are, the Beatles really were too. But they are not in the same class, music-wise or power-wise, never were."

It wasn't all one-way traffic, though, as the Stones' long-term business manager Allen Klein takes over the Beatles' business affairs.
John Lennon: "It was Mick who got us together. I had heard all these dreadful rumours about him but I could never co-ordinate it with the fact that the Stones seemed to be going on and on with him and nobody ever said a word. Mick's not the type to just clam up, so I started thinking he must be all right."

FRIDAY, 17 OCTOBER 1969

The Stones fly out to Los Angeles for their first American tour in over three years.
Keith: "We really need to do a tour because we haven't played live for so long. A tour's the only thing that knocks you into shape. Especially now that we've got Mick Taylor in the band, we really need to go through the paces again to get back together. After you've been doing gigs every night for four or five years, it's strange to suddenly stop. It's exactly three years

since we quit now. What decided us to get back into it was Hyde Park. It was such a unique feeling."

Q: "Why did you stop touring in the first place? It's been three years, hasn't it?"

Keith: "Yeah, something like that. One of the reasons we stopped is we just couldn't get back out there, on the road. There were a lot of people coming in '66 and '67 with a lot more energy than we had back then. Don't forget we'd been on the road, touring steadily since '63, so we were just wasted, you know."

Keith: "It's always been the Stones thing to get up on stage and kick the crap out of everything. We had three years of that before we made it, and were only just getting it together when we became famous. We still had plenty to do on stage, and I think we still have. That's why the tour should be such a groove for us."

MONDAY, 27 OCTOBER 1969

At a press conference held at the Beverly Wilshire in Los Angeles, to announce an extensive 18-show US tour, the Stones are asked about rumours that they intend to play a free concert.

Mick: "There has been talk of that. I should think towards the end. We'll have to see how things go. I don't want to plan that right now . . . I don't want to say that's what we want to do or not do. I'm leaving it rather blurry. I'm not committing myself."

And those much-hiked ticket prices?

Mick: "We were offered a lot of money to do some very good dates in Europe before we left, really a lot of bread. We didn't accept because we thought the tickets would be too expensive on the basis of the money we'd get. We didn't say that unless we walk out of America with x dollars, we ain't gonna come. We're really not into that sort of economic scene. Either you're gonna sing and all that crap, or you're gonna be a fucking economist. I really don't know whether this is more expensive than recent tours by local bands. I don't know how much people can afford. I've no idea. Is that a lot? You'll have to tell me."

Q: "What do you think of Timothy Leary running for Governor (of California)?"

Mick: "Isn't it a bit late for California to have a psychedelic governor?"

Q: "Charlie, do you plan another book?"

Charlie: "No." (laughs all round)

Q: "Do The Rolling Stones plan to go independent once the contract with London Records (the band's US label) expires in 1970?"
Mick: "No, I don't want to become a weirdo, pseudo-capitalist."
On that theme, Mick explains elsewhere that "I never expanded the Rolling Stones into an Apple because I'm just not interested in being a business-man. I wouldn't get any satisfaction out of creating a Mary Hopkin."
However, the issue of ticket prices continues to dog the band. Respected Rolling Stone *co-founder Ralph Gleason weighs in and asks:* "Can the Rolling Stones actually need all that money? If they really dig the black musicians as much as every note they play and every syllable they utter indicate, is it possible to take out a show with Ike & Tina Turner and not let them share in the loot? How much can the Stones take back to Merrie England after taxes, anyway? . . . Paying six and seven dollars for an hour of the Stones a quarter of a mile away because the artists demand such outrageous fees says a very bad thing to me about the artists' attitude to the public. It says they despise their audience."

NOVEMBER, 1969

Meanwhile, tucked away on the property pages of The Times:
"Cotchford Farm, near Hartfield, Sussex, is a fine old farmhouse which was once the home of A.A. Milne and later of Brian Jones, of The Rolling Stones group, and it is for sale through Bernard Walsh and Co. Although the home is built of brick, partly hung with tiles, parts are thought to be a good deal older and may date back to the 13th century. Latterly, a good deal of money was spent on the property, which has two reception rooms, a breakfast room and six bedrooms. The garage block has a staff flat over it, and there are ornamental gardens, a paddock and woodland extending to about 112 acres. Asking price is £32,500."

SUNDAY, 9 NOVEMBER 1969

Some radical groups saw no contradiction between the high ticket prices and the Stones' role as rock agitators, as a manifesto distributed at the band's shows in Oakland, California reveals.
"Greetings and welcome Rolling Stones, our comrades in the desperate battle against the maniacs who hold power. The revolutionary youth of the world hears your music and is inspired to even more deadly acts . . . We will play your music in rock'n'roll marching bands as we tear down the jails and free the prisoners, as we tear down the State schools and free

the students, as we tear down the military bases and arm the poor, as we tattoo BURN BABY BURN! on the bellies of the wardens and the generals and create a new society from the ashes of our fires.

"Comrades, you will return to this country when it is free from the tyranny of the State and you will play your splendid music in factories run by the workers, in the domes of emptied city halls, on the rubble of police stations, under the hanging corpses of priests, under a million red flags waving over a million anarchist communities. In the words of Breton, THE ROLLING STONES ARE THAT WHICH SHALL BE! LYNDON JOHNSON – THE YOUTH OF CALIFORNIA DEDICATES ITSELF TO YOUR DESTRUCTION! ROLLING STONES – THE YOUTH OF CALIFORNIA HEARS YOUR MESSAGE! LONG LIVE THE REVOLUTION!!!"

THURSDAY, 20 NOVEMBER 1969

Writer Albert Goldman catches the show at the LA Forum and observes a different pattern of politics at play. Describing the Stones' style as "sado-homosexual-junkie-diabolical-sarcastic-nigger-evil", and certain that he sees the audience 'Seig Heil!' in unison, Goldman concludes:

"What a climax! What a gesture! What pure Nuremberg! . . . Ja wohl, mein friends, dat's right! Dat good old rock'n'roll could warm the cockles of a storm trooper's heart . . . Der Fuhrer would have been gassed out of his kugel by the scene at the Forum . . . Actually, the idea that rock is Fascism spelled Fashion is as familiar as the fact that smoking causes cancer."

WEDNESDAY, 26 NOVEMBER 1969

At a press conference held in the Rainbow Grill, New York City, Mick announces that the Stones will play a free show in San Francisco ("at Golden Gate Park or nearby") on 6 December.

Q: "What are your impressions of the United States?"
Mick: "It's great. It changes."
Q: "What are your views on the war in Vietnam?"
Mick: "Just leave and get it over with as soon as you can."
Q: "What about Ed Sullivan blocking some of your vocals out?"
Mick: "It doesn't matter. It's all a joke."
Q: "How do you feel about a press conference like this?"
Mick: "It's like being in the front row of a concert in Philadelphia."

Q: "What do you think about the worldwide revolutionary movement of young people?"

Mick: "How long do I have? You can't ask a question like that at a thing like this."

Q: "You sang you couldn't get no satisfaction. Are you any more satisfied now than when you last came over here?"

Mick: "Do you mean financially, sexually or philosophically?"

Q: "Financially and philosophically satisfied . . ."

Mick: "Financially satisfied, sexually satisfied, philosophically trying."

Q: "Why don't you do a free concert in New York?"

Mick: "New York is too cold. You can't do it outside. San Francisco is into that sort of thing."

Q: "How did you like your Hyde Park concert this summer?"

Mick: "It was very weird. I've never played to that many people before."

Q: "What do you think about Lennon returning the MBE?"

Mick: "At last. He should have done it sooner."

Q: "Would you have done it?"

Mick: "We would never have gotten it in the first place."

Q: "What do you think about the new sexual morality as reflected in all the sex newspapers? Is it catching up with you?"

Mick: "No."

Away from the spotlight, Mick is already thinking about life after the tour . . .

Mick: "Touring's all right, but there's so many other things to do in life. I don't have to go on stage to get that buzz, that ego fulfilment. To tour and to perform, you have to get your ego way up there. And I don't need that all the time. I'd like to lose that now, just do something else. Sit home maybe, travel about, for six months before I start to think about any more tours."

THURSDAY, 27 NOVEMBER 1969

The Stones play the first of three shows at Madison Square Garden, New York, which provide the bulk of the material for the Get Yer Ya-Ya's Out! *album, issued in 1970. The shows also yielded one of Mick's most infamous on-stage quips, printed here in full.*

Mick: "Oh yeah, thank you kindly. I think I bust a button on mah trousers, hope they don't fall down. It's that jumping around, man. I have to do it up again . . . Whoo! You don't want my trousers to fall down now, do ya?"

179

Elsewhere, Mick expresses his pleasure at how well the new line-up is gelling.
Mick: "It's more of a band now. It's definitely a different band. It's fucking incredibly hard now. I mean, we haven't got a lot of the things Brian could do. Like none of us play dulcimer and those things . . . But we're so hard now as a band . . . And with Mick – Mick's really good – and it means Keith can sort of lay out and tune up in the middle of a tune. There's more time to think. And sometimes they'll get to tossing solos back and forth between the guitars, like on 'Sympathy For The Devil'. And it's great, beautiful to hear. It's something we've never gotten into before."

FRIDAY, 5 DECEMBER 1969

"FREE ROLLING STONES: IT'S GOING TO HAPPEN!"

The Californian airwaves are hot with the on-off saga of The Rolling Stones' end of tour freebie. "This is KFRC, and let me repeat, the Rolling Stones free concert is going to be on tomorrow at the Altamont Speedway."
Jo Bergman (Stones office): "It's going to happen. Don't worry. We've always done everything at the end, at the last minute, and it works."
Chip Monck (production stage manager): "This is going to be like a little Woodstock, y'know!"

Let It Bleed is released. Keith has plenty more to tell Ritchie Yorke.
Keith: "I think this will be the best album we've ever done. There's a blues thing called 'Midnight Rambler', which goes through a lot of changes, a very basic Chicago sound. The biggest production number is 'You Can't Always Get What You Want', which runs about seven minutes. But most of the album is fairly simple. There's an awful lot of bottleneck guitar playing, probably too much. There's three really hard blues tracks, and one funky rock thing. *Let It Bleed* will also have the original Hank Williams-like version of 'Honky Tonk Women' ('Country Honk'), which was one of my songs."
Gram Parsons: "That's the way they originally wrote it, and they recorded it and they didn't think it was a single. I think Keith did. He sort of compromised and let them put the horns on it and put the screaming guitars and everything to show them it was a really good song, that it could be number one."
Q: "Why didn't you get an arrangement credit on 'Country Honk', Gram?"

Gram Parsons: "I didn't ask. It was an honour bestowed on me."

Merry Clayton: "Bonnie (Bramlett) was going to do the second voice on the Stones record of 'Gimme Shelter', but when it came time, she had a sore throat or something. So Jack Nitzsche called me at home – I was half asleep – and asked me to come down to the studio. I'd never worked with the Stones before but it was quite easy. Mick and Keith just stood in front of me and told me where they wanted me to sing. Any way that I felt it . . . Everything was written out for me. I managed it and we got it second take."

Ry Cooder: "My participation was limited to sitting around. The Stones kept getting bogged down and puzzled. Keith Richard didn't like me. He left the room when I walked in. But I tried to be invisible and just blend in . . . (Nicky Hopkins and I) would pick up an instrument, Mick'd dance around and we had a good time. I did a mandolin thing (on 'Love In Vain') and played some jams; just got spaced out and played every note I could think of. Then all of a sudden, Mick said: 'That's it. We've got it. Let's go home.'"

SATURDAY, 6 DECEMBER 1969

"BIRTHS AND DEATHS AS STONES SING"

300,000 people attend the Stones' free concert at Altamont Speedway, California. Four are born, and four die – one person drowns in a canal, two more are run over by a car in the dark, and Meredith Hunter dies of a stab wound after a scuffle at the front of the stage during the Stones' set. The Stones arrive on site at around 3 p.m.

Mick Taylor: "About five minutes after we arrived, just after we got out of the helicopter, a guy broke through and punched Mick in the face. That put me off a bit."

Carlos Santana: "There was bad vibes from the beginning. The fights started because the Hell's Angels pushed people around. It all happened so fast, it just went right on before us and we didn't know what was going on. There were lots of people just fucking freaking out. During our set I could see a guy from the stage who had a knife and just wanted to stab somebody. I mean, he really wanted a fight. There were kids being stabbed and heads cracking the whole time."

After numerous scuffles and assaults throughout the day, the Stones take the stage at nightfall.

181

A Hell's Angel to Jagger: "Hey, you know what? You got a half million fuckin' people out there that made you what you are, and here you are, stalling!"

Mick: "Well, my make-up looks better at night."

A fan: "We are all going to die. Right here! We've been tricked."

Violence erupts in front of the stage during 'Sympathy For The Devil'.

Mick: "Brothers and sisters, come on now. That means everybody just cool OUT! We can cool out. Everybody. Everybody be cool now. Come *on.*

"How are we doin' over there? Everybody all right? Can we still collect ourselves? I don't know what happened, I couldn't see, I hope you're all right. Are you all right? Okay, let's just give ourselves another half a minute before we get our breath back. Everyone just cool down. Is there anyone there who's hurt? Okay, I think we're cool, we can groove. We always have something very funny happen when we start that number."

The show is halted again during 'Under My Thumb'. Unknown to the band, Meredith Hunter is dying just yards away from the stage.

Mick: "I cannot see what's going on. I just know that every time we get to a number, something happens . . . (*more scuffles*). Who's fighting and what for? Why are we fighting? Why are we fighting? We don't want to fight, *come on!* Every other scene has been cool . . ."

Keith: "Either those cats cool it, man, or we don't play."

Mick: "All I can ask you, San Francisco is like, the whole thing. This could be the most beautiful evening we've had this winter. I can't do any more than just ask you, to beg you to keep it together. You can do it. It's within your power – everyone, Hell's Angels, everybody. Let's just keep ourselves together. Y'know, if we are all one, let's show we're all one." (*more fighting erupts*)

Keith: "Look, we're splitting man if those cats don't stop beating everybody up in sight. I want 'em out of the way, man!"

Unnamed Hell's Angel: "Fuck you!"

SUNDAY, 7 DECEMBER 1969

"THE LET IT BLEED FESTIVAL OF ANGELS AND DEATH"

Within 24 hours of the show, San Francisco rock radio station KSAN-FM holds its own inquest. Rolling Stones road manager and festival organiser Sam Cutler is asked whether he regrets hiring the Hell's Angels, whom he reportedly hired in exchange for $500 worth of free beer.

Sam Cutler: "I feel that the Hell's Angels were as helpful as they could be in a situation which most people found very confusing, including the Hell's Angels . . . If you're asking me to issue a general put-down of the Angels, which I imagine a lot of people would be only to happy to do, I'm not prepared to do that. The Angels did as they saw best in a difficult situation. Now 50% of the people will dig what they did and 50% will not dig what they did. As far as I was concerned, they were people who tried to help in their own way . . . These people didn't dig it? I'm sorry. I didn't dig what a lot of people did yesterday."

The Hell's Angels certainly didn't dig their bikes being tampered with . . .
Sonny Barger (President, Oakland Hell's Angels): "I didn't go there to police nuthin', man . . . They used us for dupes. I ain't no peace creep, man . . . Ain't nobody gonna get on my bike, man. Anyone tries that, they gonna get got. And they got got."

Keith: "I thought the show would have been stopped, but hardly anybody seemed to want to take any notice. The violence just in front of the stage was incredible. I don't think it was a good idea to have Hell's Angels there. But we had them at the suggestion of The Grateful Dead who've organised these shows before, and they thought they were the best people to organise the concert. Last week was my first experience of American Hell's Angels. I believe the alternative would have been the Black Panthers. I wouldn't like to say whether they would have been any more vicious. Out of the whole 300 Angels working as stewards, the vast majority did what they were supposed to do, which was to regulate the crowds without causing any trouble. But there were about 10 or 20 who were completely out of their minds and trying to drive their motorcycles through the middle of the crowds. In Hyde Park, everybody had a good time and there was no trouble. You can put half a million young English people together and they won't start killing each other. That's the difference . . ."

Mick Taylor: "I was really scared. I was frightened for all of us, particularly for Mick because he had to be very careful what he said all the time. He had to pick and choose his words. I saw violence all the time. I've always heard about the incredible violence in America, but I'd never actually seen it. It was completely barbaric. It was impossible to enjoy the music, because most of the violence was going on in front of the stage, right in front of our eyes. I've never seen anything like it before."

KFRC News correspondent Ron Naso is rather more relaxed about the event.
"We think it was beautiful. Things went smoothly and people were happy. When you have a big amount of people together, a couple of

things happen, unfortunately. It's nothing anybody can do about. After all, look what happens in Vietnam every day."

One festivalgoer, Leo H. from Los Angeles, puts forward his own theory.
"To those who know, it's been obvious that the Stones, or at least some of them, have been involved in the practice of Magick ever since the *Satanic Majesties* album. But there, at least, the colour was more white than black. Since then the hue has gone steadily darker and darker.

"At Altamont he (Jagger) appeared in his full majesty with his full consort of demons, the Hell's Angels. It was just a few days before the Winter Solstice when the forces of darkness are at their most powerful. The moon was in Scorpio, which is the time of the month when the universal vibration is at its most unstable. It was held in a place dedicated to destruction through motion. Then Mick comes on only after it is dark enough for the red lights to work their Magick.

"I don't know if they were truly aware of what they were doing or not. I feel that they are sadder and wiser from the experience. But an agonising price was paid for the lesson. And we were all guilty because we have all eaten of the cake the Stones baked."

To David Crosby, the Stones are guilty of naivety rather than anything more sinister.
"The Rolling Stones are still a little bit in 1965. They didn't really know that security isn't a part of anyone's concert anymore . . . We didn't need the Angels. I'm not downgrading the Angels, because it's not healthy and because they only did what they were expected to do . . . The Stones don't know about Angels. To them an Angel is something in between Peter Fonda and Dennis Hopper. That's not real. But I don't think the Angels were the major mistake. They were just the obvious mistake. I think the major mistake was taking what was essentially a party and turning it into an ego game and a star trip . . . I think (the Stones) have an exaggerated view of their own importance. They're on a grotesque ego trip, negative trips, essentially, especially the two leaders."

Bill Graham (US concert promoter): "I'll ask you what right you had, Mr Jagger, to walk out on stage every night with your Uncle Sam hat, throw it down with complete disdain, and leave this country with $1.2 million? And what right did you have in going through with this free festival? And you couldn't tell me you didn't know the way it would have come off. What right did you have to leave the way you did, thanking everybody for a wonderful time and the Angels for helping out? He's now in his home country somewhere – what did he leave behind throughout the country? Every gig he was late. Every fucking gig he made the pro-moter and the people bleed. What right does this god have to descend on this country this way? But you know what is the greatest tragedy to me? That cunt is a great entertainer."

Gwen Hunter (Meredith Hunter's 17-year-old sister): "No one has con-tacted us. The Stones should have, but I didn't expect them to because I know they didn't care. The Stones should have called my mother, but they didn't because it doesn't matter to them. They'll just go off some-where and have another rock festival . . . He (Meredith) had (the gun) for his own protection. He pulled it out and showed it to them, but only to make them stop and think when they were beating him. I don't know if their being a mixed couple had anything to do with it (Meredith was with a white girl, Patty Bredahoff); it may have had a lot to do with it. The Hell's Angels are just white men with badges on their backs . . . He was a very educated boy. He almost never raised his voice; he talked very quietly. That would make people mad when they wanted to fight . . . The Rolling Stones are responsible because they hired the Hell's Angels as police and paid them. But they don't care."

Sonny Barger: "The crowd was waiting all day to see the Stones, and they were sitting in their trailers acting like prima donnas. They got the crowd worked up and they used us to keep the whole thing going. All that shit about Altamont being the end of an era was a bunch of intellectual crap. It was the end of nothing."

Mick: "Seems like the only ones who didn't have a good time were me and the guy that got killed . . ."

3

Respectable

"DOG LED TO DRUG AT JAGGER HOME"

Mick is fined £200 at Marlborough Street Magistrates' Court for cannabis possession. At the hearing, allegations are made against Detective Sergeant Robin Constable who – with intrepid Labrador Yogi in tow – claims he found some white powder during the search.

Mick: "I got very excited at this and said, 'You bastard, you have planted me with heroin.' I thought it was some kind of hard drug."

It was then alleged that Mick shouted, "Marianne, Marianne, don't open the door. It's the law: they are after the weed."

Mick: "I would not have been able to shout because someone had a hand over my mouth. I would not use the word 'weed' anyway. It is an archaic word. I had no knowledge there was any cannabis in the house."

According to Mick, the conversation continues when Constable asks, "Where is all your LSD then?"

Mick: "I have not got any."

Constable: "We can do something about it . . . Well, a man can be guilty and plead 'Not Guilty' and in that way he will get off. Well, how much is it worth to you?"

Mick: "I had only heard about this going on and it was very difficult to take in. I did not want to incriminate myself, and I wanted him to name the figure. He named one and said, '£1,000' so I just shrugged my shoulders . . . He suggested I should not mention it to anyone and not to Marianne. He said, 'Don't worry, you can have the money back if it doesn't work.'"

Mick then alleges that he was given a Kensington phone number by the Detective Sergeant which he was told to ring after 5 p.m.

Mick: "I did not ask him for a telephone number. By this time I told the lawyers about being asked about money. They had given certain instructions what to do. I telephoned about five o'clock and spoke to Constable. He said, 'Don't worry, it's all going to be sorted out. Someone will be in touch with you.' Nobody got in touch with me and I did not ring him again."

Unsurprisingly, Constable categorically denies all of these actions: "These allegations are totally malicious."

Later in the month, Scotland Yard announces that "An investigating officer has been appointed to investigate a complaint under Section 49 of the Police Act, and his inquiries are continuing."

Although Constable subsequently sues for libel, neither matter comes to court and the Detective Sergeant is subsequently transferred from Chelsea Police Station.

FEBRUARY, 1970

It emerges that Meredith Hunter's death has been captured on film by the Maysles brothers, while the pair were making their documentary on the Stones' American tour.

Porter Bibb (Executive Producer): "This film is not going to exploit the killing. We had decided before Altamont to do a film, before we had seen any film of the killing. It doesn't hinge on the murder. We don't want to exploit the sensationalism of the thing.

"We want to make it clear that this film is going to be about violence – about the relationship between the Stones and their American audience, and about the relationship of both to violence."

As the debate surrounding Altamont continues, John Lennon attempts to hold a free 'peace concert' in Toronto, Canada.

John Lennon: "The Stones one was bad. It won't be like that here. The kind of image the Stones want, and the sort of thing they create around them . . . I think they created that either subconsciously or whatever. That is the result of the image and the mood they create."

The Maysles continue to shoot footage while Mick and Keith mix the forthcoming US concert album at Trident Studios.

David Maysles: "We've got to think of a title for the film."

Keith: "I have no idea."

Al Maysles: "The slogan we could use might be: Peter Fonda went looking for America. The Stones found it."

Mick: "Call the film *Old Glory*. I don't know anything about America. It's just the title of a song we wrote a year ago . . . 'Love In Vain'. Maybe we should call it that. Pictures of nude chicks. They loved in vain. Naked as they came."

Keith: "Naughty ladies."

Mick: "Call it *Naughty Ladies '70*."

APRIL, 1970

With Jethro Tull becoming the latest band to turn their back on releasing singles, the new decade is being proclaimed as the era of progressive music. Mick isn't convinced.

Mick: "People talk about progressive music and that. They just talk without considering. A band that can play rock and make it swing is still a good progressive band. Even now, we get the best reaction from the old rockers. I hate getting into an argument with other musicians because it makes us no better than those grey men who think they know everything. But if you look back on our career, I don't think you'll find that we've deliberately repeated ourselves on any of the records . . . It could well be progressive to have the Stones suddenly play a country song, or bring an old rock song to new life. You don't have to get hidden away in your own music to be regarded as progressive."

FRIDAY, 29 MAY 1970

The Flying Burrito Brothers, featuring Gram Parsons, release their version of a new Jagger/Richard song, 'Wild Horses', on their second album, Burrito Deluxe.

Gram Parsons: "It's a logical combination between our music and their music. It's something that Mick Jagger can accept and it's something that I can accept . . . The rock'n'roll I picked up from Keith Richard and Mick knows an awful lot about country music. I learned a lot about singing from Mick. When the three of us sing together it sounds like Gaelic music, like The Incredible String Band. We were doing Hank Williams songs – Mick's southern accent and my English accent. What does it tell you? It's the same."

SUNDAY, 28 JUNE 1970

Jefferson Airplane, who shared the stage with the Stones at Altamont, perform at the Bath Festival. While they're in the country, Paul Kantner and Grace Slick visit Mick at his London home to discuss the group's appearance in the forthcoming Stones film.

Paul Kantner: "(Mick's) a nice warm, honest cat. And he said it was no hassle about the bread because they didn't particularly want any money from the movie, but they did definitely want it to be shown . . . Mick has integrity, no problem with that."

TUESDAY, 28 JULY 1970

Ned Kelly premieres in Melbourne, Australia.

Mick: "That was a load of shit. I only made it because I had nothing else to do. I knew Tony Richardson was a reasonable director and I thought he'd make a reasonable film. The thing is, you never know until you do it whether a film will turn out to be a load of shit, and if it does, all you can say is, 'Well that was a load of shit,' and try to make sure you don't do anything like it again."

A Warner Brothers studio executive agrees.

"We can't understand a word Jagger is saying – the picture is a disaster. We're going to kill it off."

WEDNESDAY, 29 JULY 1970

Two days before the group's contract with Decca Records expires, The Rolling Stones break their ties with business manager, Allen Klein.

A press release states that "Neither Allen Klein nor ABKCO Industries Inc, nor any other company have any authority to negotiate recording contracts on their behalf in the future."

Allen Klein: "This development will not alter the rights of ABKCO Industries under existing agreements including the right to manufacture Rolling Stones records in the future."

SATURDAY, 15 AUGUST 1970

It is announced that The Rolling Stones intend to form their own record label.

Mick: "We want to release the odd blues record and Charlie Watts wants to do some jazz. What we're not interested in is bubblegum material. We want to control prices to stop the price of records going up. I'd like to find new ways of distribution. I don't want to do any production. We haven't a name yet."

The changes prompt some of the first 'Stones To Split?' rumours since the mid-Sixties. One suggests that Mick Jagger is off to front Eric Clapton's new band, Derek & The Dominoes. Clapton rather likes the idea . . .

Eric Clapton: "Well, he asked me to play with the Stones last year before he found Mick Taylor. But I was into the Blind Faith thing. Since then, we've seen a hell of a lot of one another, but he's never suggested anything. Maybe he's too shy to say it, because he's as shy as I am. I know that he likes the group and he'd probably like to use us on some sessions. But I think he's got a good band himself."

Mick's response is rather more curt.
Mick: "As long as the band swings, we won't split."

SUNDAY, 30 AUGUST 1970

During the quietest year in their career, the Stones kick off their first European tour in three years with a concert in Malmo, Sweden. The group hold a press conference in Copenhagen, Denmark.
Q: "Do you like Simon & Garfunkel?"
Mick: "Oh, come on!"
Q: "Who is the greatest person in showbiz today?"
Keith: "Shirley Bassey."
Q: "Mr Jagger, are you satisfied with your performance in *Ned Kelly*?"
Mick: "No, it's not worth seeing."
Q: "Your opinion on dope?"
Mick: "Oh, come on . . . Foolish questions. Let me out of here."

Jagger is nevertheless keen to pay lip service to proletarian sympathies . . .
Mick: "We are not making any money out of this. It has only been arranged as a friendly gesture for our European fans. The contact with the audience makes us feel happy. There's nothing to replace it . . . I want to earn money on our new records, both for the sake of the money but to invest it in other things, such as the Black Panther breakfast programme for ghetto children. We have already set money aside for that."

THURSDAY, 3 SEPTEMBER 1970

Marianne Faithfull's husband John Dunbar files for divorce, citing Mick Jagger as the third party. Ironically, by this time, the couple's relationship has itself broken down.

Marianne Faithfull: "The worst thing about being with Mick was this rule he laid down that you must never show emotion in case people realised you weren't cool."

Meanwhile, Mick remains mistrustful of long-term relationships.
"I don't envisage a time when I shall ever get married and settle down. I might have kids and I might get married, but I'll never settle down. I'm not the type."

FRIDAY, 4 SEPTEMBER 1970

Get Yer Ya-Ya's Out!, *recorded live on the 1969 US tour, is released.*
Mick: "The album's better than the (*Liver Than You'll Ever Be*) bootleg. It doesn't sound as if it's recorded right up close as it usually does when you make a live recording. And it doesn't sound as if it's coming through the PA either, the way you hear it at the concert. What we have done is mix the voice and put a bit of echo on it."

FRIDAY, 18 SEPTEMBER 1970

As Performance *premieres in the States, the soundtrack gets a release in the UK. Advertising slogan: "Somewhere in your head there's a wild electric dream. Come see it in* PERFORMANCE.*"*
Turner (played by Mick Jagger): "The only performance that makes it, that really makes it, that makes it all the way, is the one that achieves madness."
Donald Cammell (co-producer): "It is a movie that gets into an allegorical area and it moves from a definition of what violence is to an explanation of a way of being. It is an attempt to use a film for exploring the nature of violence as seen from the point of view of an artist. It says that this crook leads this fading pop star to realise that violence is a facet of creative art, that his energy is derived from the same sources as those of the crook. And that energy is always dangerous, sometimes fatal."
Mick: "I don't understand the connection between music and violence. Donald's always trying to explain it to me . . . I just know that I get very aroused by music, but it doesn't arouse me violently. I feel more sexual than physically violent."

Donald Cammell: "You'll have to understand that youth is still attracted to violence. The Woodstock Nation is attracted to violence. It's attractive. Otherwise Mick would not be where he is today. Mick will probably be annoyed at this. But his dilemma is that he knows about the violence. This movie was finished before Altamont and Altamont actualised it."

Performance Trims, a ten-minute short of out-takes from the bedroom scenes featuring Jagger, Anita Pallenberg and Michele Breton, is subsequently premiered at the first Wet Dream Festival in Amsterdam, Holland.
The Frij Nederlands *newspaper:* "The revealed apparatus of the king of The Rolling Stones got much applause, but also disappointed people because Jagger's cock, of course, isn't any different from other cocks."

A single, 'Memo From Turner', is lifted from the soundtrack.
Mick: "They didn't ask me if I wanted it out – it's just out. It was recorded two years ago. It's all right, the thing is the backing track was cut after the voice . . . The next Rolling Stones record is going to be fantastic. A single should be out before Christmas. We've cut eight tracks since we've come back – eight exciting gassers. And we're going to have the album out in the New Year, I think. We've got a cover made out of old socks – sewn together by hand. We've got them all working on it at the office. That's why it's been held up."

TUESDAY, 22 SEPTEMBER 1970

Donald Cammell accompanies a young Nicaraguan woman named Bianca Perez Morena De Macias to the Stones' Paris Olympia show. Later that night, at the George V Hotel, he introduces her to Mick with the words, "You were made for each other."

Despite the instant karma, Mick maintains that he's not the marrying kind.
"I think marriage is a lovely initiation into adulthood, for which I'm not ready or willing or able. Nah, it doesn't exist in this country. Marriage is a pagan ceremony taken over by the church. Unfortunately, it's been totally destroyed by that same church because you can't be married and conse-crate your union to God and be divorced and all that. I think some marriage initiation rites are beautiful. I don't particularly like the English one . . . If I lived in Japan or something, I might get married. I'm talking about that part of it, as opposed to the legal part of it which I deem totally unnecessary. If you're a religious person, you shouldn't need a contract; your word should be enough."

WEDNESDAY, 23 SEPTEMBER 1970

When the tour plays two shows at the Paris Palais des Sports, fans arrive with banners bearing a variety of revolutionary slogans – Liberté Pour Les Peuples ("Power To The People"), Palestine Vaincra ("Palestine Will Win"), Ce N'est Qu'un Début, Continuons Le Combat ("It's Only A Beginning, Let's Continue The Fight"). A handful of ancien régime dignitaries feel uncomfortable enough to vacate their front row seats.

Princess de Polignac: "There was no use resisting. Those disgusting young hairy people would have torn us to pieces."

Unnamed fan: "We're fed up with having our music appropriated by the bourgeois."

OCTOBER 1970

As Led Zeppelin's third album tops the charts on both sides of the Atlantic, and with recent albums by Santana, Crosby, Stills, Nash & Young and Creedence Clearwater Revival all hitting the two million sales mark, the Stones' status appears to be under threat. Nevertheless, the bidding war to sign the band – and their planned new label – continues, with an apparent $6 million, six-LP deal on the table . . .

Ahmet Ertegun (President, Atlantic Records): "We have not signed The Rolling Stones. I hope that I'm going to sign them, because I think they're a great group and I'd love to have them if we can work out a deal."

Marsha Hunt gives birth to a daughter, Karis, in Paddington, London. She initially refuses to acknowledge that Mick is the father.

Marsha Hunt: "We had a child on purpose. He said he wanted a child and I said I wanted one as well. So we had a baby together and now he is no longer involved with us. At first I thought he was a person I cared for a lot, but I found out afterwards I didn't really know him at all. I mean, when people said he was no good I didn't believe them because I saw goodness in him, and I do forgive him, because I don't think he understands what he's doing."

WEDNESDAY, 25 NOVEMBER 1970

"MYSTERY OF THE NEW GIRL IN MICK'S LIFE"

Mick is cornered by press as he travels through Heathrow Airport with a friend in tow.

Q: "What's your name?"

Bianca: "I have no name. I do not speak English."
Mick: "We're just good friends."

Shortly afterwards, Bianca breaks her silence and the relationship goes public.
Bianca Jagger: "So shy, so sweet, so vulnerable, so unlike how I imagined Mick Jagger would be."

SATURDAY, 5 DECEMBER 1970

Gimme Shelter *premieres at the Plaza Theater in New York. The film is marketed by a slogan that reads "The music that thrilled the world . . . and the killing that stunned it!"*
David Maysles: "The film is not a shocker, but a very heavy film, full of lots of meanings . . . It's consistent with what The Rolling Stones represent, in two words, 'No bullshit', the honest feeling you get from all their songs . . . The Stones will be respected for this rather than criticised the way they were."

On the same day, it is announced that an album of Moroccan music, recorded by Brian Jones, is likely to become one of the first releases on The Rolling Stones' label, due to be launched in 1971.
A Rolling Stones spokesman: "It's the music which accompanies the rites of Pan ceremony in Moroccan mythology. The festival goes on for days and all the master musicians there played specially so Brian could record them."

MONDAY, 14 DECEMBER 1970

The trial of Hell's Angel Alan David Passaro, in conjunction with the death of Meredith Hunter at Altamont, begins.
Alan Passaro: "At Altamont that day, I was just doing what I had to do. I did what I thought was right. For me and my people . . . By the time the Stones came on, everybody was wired up. And the Stones blew it. They just kicked back and didn't do shit. When that dude (Meredith Hunter) pulled out a piece and somebody says, 'He's going to do Jagger,' being closest I jump up and almost get my head blown off and get my face blasted from coast to coast – which I don't dig. Well, I figure Jagger could have said something instead of blaming it all on the Angels. I don't know Jagger, but I think he's a punk. A brat. I mean, maybe the Stones are all right, but they used us. They used the (Hell's Angels) club for publicity, for this movie of theirs. And they been using me since."

Passaro, who reportedly turns down a $10,000 fee from the Maysles for his 'superstar' role in Gimme Shelter, *was acquitted in February 1971.*

TUESDAY, 2 MARCH 1971

A BBC Radio 4 documentary, Brian Jones, The Rolling Stone – A Story Of Our Time, *written and narrated by Michael Wale, is broadcast. It presents a sober look at the life of the man the Stones left behind.*

Mick: "Brian was so sensitive. At the beginning, it was a good-natured joke. Seven years ago, when people used to get uptight because they thought you were dirty, Brian used to get upset by it all. Everyone else used to laugh it off, but it really used to hurt him to think that people actually thought he didn't wash his hair when he did."

Q: "It's been said that he would have rather had some of his tunes played . . ."

Mick: "Well, I didn't really understand quite what Brian wanted to do, really. He kept a lot of things to himself like that. He never played me a song he'd written, so it was really quite hard to know if he really wanted to do songs with us that he'd written. I think he did, but he was very shy and I think he found it rather hard to lay it down to us that this was a song and it went like this. Because he didn't do it, we didn't try to bring it out, probably. I mean, it wasn't a question of forcefully stifling him."

Q: "Did the wild, uncouth image overtake Brian at any time?"

Mick: "No, a lot of people put it in a nutshell that Brian Jones lived up to be a Rolling Stone more than anybody, whatever that means. It means vaguely that he freaked out more than anybody, which is probably true! I mean, he did it in a very nice way, and he was very funny."

Among those seeking to draw insight from the late Stone's life is the band's PR man, Les Perrin.

"I think Brian suffered from pressures which were not necessarily of being a Stone. I think Brian had private problems like he wanted to be loved tremendously. He needed to have the kind of almost maternal love more than any other kind of love. I know he found a shoulder to cry on in my wife. He used to phone at odd intervals and talk to her at great length about his problems."

THURSDAY, 4 MARCH 1971

"ROLLING STONES TO QUIT BRITAIN"

Hours before the start of the Stones' nine-city British tour, Mick confirms that the Stones are leaving Britain.

Mick: "It's only for the change of scenery and temperature. I love Britain. I just want a change. We will probably be back more often than we have in the past."

Les Perrin: "The move to the south of France has been in the air for some time. Now it is definite. I shouldn't be surprised if they leave within the next couple of months. It has taken the boys months to arrange to emigrate. They have had long and complicated talks with lawyers and financial advisers. This is a big step for them. The real reason they are leaving this country is that they like France – and the climate is so much better . . . They will not be resident in Britain for some long, long time. But they will all stick together. They are tremendously popular in France. In some way, the French people have come to regard them as their own group. It was the first country on the Continent where they really made an impact. There is no question of them being disillusioned with Britain or anything like that. And it certainly does not mean this is the start of a break-up."

Mick: "The band is not retiring just because we're going away. We'll remain a functioning group, a touring group, and a happy group. We're not going to stay in the South of France for a whole year. We're going on the road. I couldn't live in France for a whole year."

Some time later, 'Honest' Bill Wyman comes clean.

Bill: "After eight years working with one of the world's top bands, you would have thought I was set up for life, but I finished up almost broke. We must have sold over 100 million records, but I have never seen a million dollars. I have just a couple of grand in the bank, a car and two houses, but I owed the Inland Revenue a fortune. There was no way I could remain in Britain. I had to go and live in France anyway – you can't earn money in England any more. You can earn just as much from one record in England as if you made six records a year. The trouble is they don't encourage the ambitious people in England. All the ambitious people leave."

SATURDAY, 13 MARCH 1971

After the Daily Telegraph *makes extravagant claims concerning the buoyant state of the Stones' finances, Mick is sufficiently piqued to take out an advert in the music press, denying the claims.*

"Comment, I feel, on behalf of The Rolling Stones should be made on reports which estimate that The Rolling Stones' fortune from recordings alone is reckoned to be £83,000,000 . . . The sum mentioned is ludicrous; in our opinion it most probably exceeds the collective recording earnings of the Beatles, Elvis Presley, ourselves and others."

FRIDAY, 26 MARCH 1971

"STONES TV SHOW ROLLS INTO TROUBLE"

A projected TV show, filmed at London's Marquee Club for American television, is abandoned after an hour when around 150 invited guests are told to leave for not providing the right atmosphere. The filming subsequently continues with a much sparser audience.

Les Perrin (PR): "I gather one of the sound crew tried to remove the Marquee sign from the back of the stage and that [Marquee owner] Mr Pendleton objected. Compared to the reports, it was all rather tame."

Keith Richard apparently swings his guitar at Harold Pendleton's head in disgust. He had not forgotten Pendleton's jazz-based distaste for the Stones back in 1962/63.

SATURDAY, 3 APRIL 1971

As the Stones quit Britain on the eve of the new financial year, ex-Beatles publicist Derek Taylor is employed to fire a shot on the band's behalf.
"We love you Rolling Stones and if you are now not the best living band in the world, then who is?"

Certainly not the Beatles, whose dirty laundry is currently being dragged through the High Courts.
Q: "John Lennon . . . said that The Rolling Stones always did things after the Beatles did them. Are you then too planning to break up?"
Mick: "Charlie, are we gonna break up then? Are ya gettin' tired of all this? Naw, we're not breakin' up. And if we did, we wouldn't be as bitchy as them."

Not everyone feels automatically compelled to uncritically laud and applaud.
John Peel (DJ): "(Kids) feel resentful, as I do myself, at going along to see The Rolling Stones when they're charging 20 bob a head for a three quarters of an hour set which they've just about got themselves together to rehearse. Groups charge appalling prices for gigs. So many rock musicians have lost sight of the people."

Inevitably, the talk turns from tax to endurance.

Mick: "Ugh, it's 'orrible, to be the Grand Old Men. If all this talk gets any worse I'll be getting another band. I dunno why, but it's not nice to be asked that question. It makes us sound like survivors from a holocaust. I suppose I should be grateful that I survived the Swinging Blue Jeans era, but that was the era before us, I always believed. I never felt I was part of it, The Swinging Blue Jeans and that, doing me Top 20 hits every evening on stage. Whenever I used to see them play they were just all them, standing in line together, doing their hits. I think they were something else. We played in a different way."

Elton John, one of a new breed of brightly dressed Seventies stars, weighs in for the defence.

"Mick Jagger is the perfect pop star. There's nobody more perfect than Jagger. He's rude, he's ugly-attractive, he's brilliant. The Rolling Stones are the perfect pop group. The Beatles were a bit showbiz, but the Stones – they don't give a shit."

Mick senses a change at the heart of rock culture, telling Melody Maker*:*

"I think a lot of young people have started something and we're never going to finish it. I think maybe they went too far in their faith in (rock music). They expected it to be everything, to express all they feel and do."

Keith continues to let nothing affect him.

"How can you worry about world population? Whose problem is that? You tell me. Everybody feels they ought to do something about it . . . I mean, what about that tidal wave in Pakistan, man? Quarter of a million in one night. I'll just keep on rocking and hope for the best. I mean, that's really what in all honesty it comes down to. I mean, why do people want to be entertainers or want to listen to music or come and watch people make music? Is it just a distraction, or is it a vision or God knows what? It's everything to all kinds of people."

As further evidence that cultural politics is giving way to pop gossip, another Stones-related story returns to the headlines.

Q: "We've been seeing a lot of pictures of you and a beautiful lady called Bianca. Have you anything to say about all these rumours?"

Mick: "No, in a word! What can I say but rumours bring mischief. She's quite pretty. I can't imagine bein' married now either. I tell ya, I mean my old lady, I don't know what she'd say. She'd probably scream at me in Spanish or something. But I wouldn't recommend it. I don't think it's necessary. I feel the same about it. I carry on the same and I find it works.

You might find that contradictory but everyone's life's contradictory, innit?"

Bianca: "There's not going to be a wedding this week, next week or ever. Mick and I are very happy together. We don't need to get married. Why should we?"

WEDNESDAY, 7 APRIL 1971

After months of rumour and meticulous negotiation, a press release confirms that the Rolling Stones' future is assured.

"ROLLING STONES SIGN WITH KINNEY"

Ahmet Ertegun announced this week on behalf of Kinney Services Inc that Kinney has obtained worldwide rights to recordings by the ROLLING STONES . . .

"These recordings will be released worldwide on a newly created label called ROLLING STONES RECORDS."

Mick: "By signing this contract we are guaranteeing to produce six new albums over the next four years – this includes (new album) *Sticky Fingers*. Additionally, perhaps, there may be some solo albums projecting the Stones individually over this period."

Mick outlined the ethos of the new label to renowned US journalist Tom Donahue.
"I always looked at Apple Records, and the whole thing about Apple was you got the feeling that it was a new company with new ideas, right? Running through the old structure by signing up all these artists that everyone liked – or didn't like or whatever. It was gonna be an important record label. They ran ads every week saying, 'You can be a millionaire like Paul McCartney if you come over to Apple with your songs.' But this isn't like that. It's just our records. Like instead of putting Atlantic on it, we'd just put 'Rolling Stone Record Number 2' on it, or something. We're not gonna try and make some big corporate image and build a sky-scraper in the corner of Savile Row. We just wanna keep it a very small thing, a small operation which we can handle."

FRIDAY, 16 APRIL 1971

The first release on Rolling Stones Records is a three-track maxi-single, with 'Brown Sugar' as the A-side. Bobby Keys plays the gritty sax solo.
Bobby Keys: "It was a one-time thing. It was as unrehearsed as a hiccup. I didn't even know they were recording . . ."

199

The Who's Pete Townshend questions the Stones' apparent spontaneity.

Pete Townshend: "I think that on 'Brown Sugar', they copied us a bit. But Keith Richard is one of my favourite guitarists and I tend to pick up on what he does a lot. That thing I do on 'Won't Get Fooled Again' is actually a straight nick from . . . is it 'Gimme Shelter'? There's a lot we've pinched from the Stones – absolutely nothing from the Beatles, funnily enough."

FRIDAY, 23 APRIL 1971

Sticky Fingers *becomes the Stones' first new studio album of the Seventies. The old 'bad boy' imagery hasn't gone away, though . . .*

Keith: "I don't think *Sticky Fingers* is a heavy drug album . . . There are songs with heavy drug references, as people have pointed out to me. They're all actually quite old, which maybe indicates that we were into those things a couple of years ago. I mean, you can't take a fucking record like other people take a Bible. It's only a fucking record, man."

Mick: "Sometimes we get an idea for a song from, say, a rhythm that Charlie and Keith have played together, or like 'Bitch' that Charlie and Bobby and me played. Quite often, we go into it without the song being written – which annoys me intensely. But that's the way we record sometimes . . .

"The music quite often comes ahead of the words. That annoys me. It's very hard to write lyrics to the track . . . I always try to write the lyrics to the songs. Like that thing with strings on, 'Moonlight Mile', the lyrics weren't written to that before we cut the track. That was very extemporised. We didn't think of having strings or anything. It just comes. Whereas 'Dead Flowers' was all written before. I'd played it a hundred times at home."

The Andy Warhol-designed crotch shot sleeve pays homage to the sexual prowess that lies at the heart of the Stones' appeal. It leaves one letter-writer disappointed . . .
"Sigh. When I unzipped the zipper on my new copy of *Sticky Fingers*, nothing popped out." *Deborah Hunt, Viola, Illinois.*

On the same day, and by no coincidence, Decca release a spoiler album, Stone Age, *a hotchpotch of largely second-rate material from the band's Sixties catalogue. The Stones place full-page advertisements in the music press.*
"BEWARE!
"We didn't know this record was going to be released.

"It is, in our opinion, below the standard we try to keep up, both in choice of content and cover design.

"Signed Mick Jagger, Keith Richard, Charlie Watts, Bill Wyman, Mick Taylor."

And back again to those other rumours . . .

The Earl Of Lichfield: "He has changed his mind lots of times. The wedding was to have been two weeks ago, but it was called off. The tip is Wednesday, but who knows . . .?"

WEDNESDAY, 12 MAY 1971

"MICK WEDS IN HIPPIE CHAOS"

In the presence of a chartered plane's worth of guests, Mick performs a volte-face on his earlier marriage comments by marrying Bianca Perez Morena De Macias in San Tropez, in the south of France.

Abbé Baud (clergyman): "You have told me that youth seeks happiness and a certain ideal and faith. I think you are seeking it, too, and I hope it arrives today with your marriage."

Richard Neville (*Oz* magazine): "The wedding was stark public confirmation of the growing suspicion that Mick Jagger has firmly repudiated the possibilities of a counterculture of which his music is a part . . . The Jagger myth, epitomising multi-level protest for nearly a decade, finally exploded with the champagne corks."

Q: "Did you ever imagine a church wedding for your son?"

Mrs Eva Jagger: "I don't know. I never thought a lot about it. I wouldn't say that I didn't really expect it. I half expected it one day but not quite so soon . . . I hope my other son doesn't become a superstar."

Q: "Let me put it this way. Did you ever expect a wedding at all of any sort, church or otherwise?"

Mr Joe Jagger: "Yes, I thought he would get married because there's quite a serious side to him which perhaps doesn't always fit in with his public image. But the serious side I'm sure would have come out in his desire to get married, and to have a family, and he's spoken about this on many occasions."

JULY, 1971

The Stones convene for recording sessions at Nellcote, Keith Richard's expansive, Roman-style villa on a hill above Villefranche-sur-Mer, in the south of France.

The sessions are captured on the Rolling Stones' Mobile 16-track studio.

Keith: "It's a pretty good house. We're doing our best to fill it with kids and A&R."

Mick: "We've not finished the album. We've just cut 20 tracks, plus we've got about 28 others . . . The studios aren't that great. Okay, but not really good. It's terrible. I don't like it. It's too hot in the summer. I can't hear anything down there. We cut some nice things, but we'll mix it at Island or someplace . . . We can't record in America. They've sent us warning letters. Legally, English bands aren't supposed to record there, but they all do."

Keith: "It just got a little hectic in the house, what with playing all night in the blazing heat . . . but with the 16-track truck always outside and ready, we'd go downstairs whenever we felt like it and work on a riff."

Jimmy Miller: "*Exile* wasn't recorded in very good conditions. The studio was technically restricted and a lot of the ideas we had had to be scrapped."

Mick Taylor: "We tried to convert Keith's basement into a studio and it was quite successful. But I don't think you can beat using a proper studio."

Among the houseguests is Gram Parsons, who continues to provide an inspiring sparring partner for Keith.

Gram: "(Keith) knew some of the old-time stuff, but I was the one who really turned him on to Merle Haggard, George Jones and Waylon Jennings."

TUESDAY, 31 AUGUST 1971

"STONES SUE KLEIN"

The Rolling Stones sue Allen Klein, ABKCO Industries and ABKCO Klein Corp for a reputed £12 million. Referring to deals struck in 1965 and 1966, the High Court writ alleges "false or fraudulent" representations with intent to "deceive and defraud" the group.

Allen Klein: "ABKCO . . . denied any impropriety in their dealings with The Rolling Stones and further declared that they believed The Rolling Stones' lawsuits to be without merit. Speaking only for myself, however, I believe the allegations are at best ludicrous, and at worst, malicious."

The Stones are also suing Andrew Oldham and Eric Easton who allegedly "failed to advise" that Decca would have upped their royalty rate to 14 per cent, far and above the agreed 6 per cent.

Mick: "We tried to be nice about it for about 18 months. I mean, I really hate lawsuits, but he won't . . . Eventually, we had to do it like this. It's not big business, it's just that I don't have much money. Really. He just got us into a terrific mess and he's not a very nice person. I don't think he's genuine . . . Allen Klein can jump in the East River for all I care."

SATURDAY, 11 SEPTEMBER 1971

The Stones clean up in Sounds *magazine's 1971 Readers' Poll awards.*
Band – 1. Rolling Stones; Bass guitarist – 10. Bill Wyman; Male Vocalist –
1. Mick Jagger; Album – 2. Sticky Fingers; Composer – 4. Jagger/Richard; Keyboard – 8. Nicky Hopkins; Record Producer – 1. Jimmy Miller; Album Design –
1. Sticky Fingers.

FRIDAY, 8 OCTOBER 1971

Brian Jones Presents The Pipes Of Pan At Joujouka *is the first non-Stones release on the band's new label. Advertised as "The 4,000 Year Old Rock'n'Roll Band", it features music Jones recorded in the mountains of Morocco.*
Mick: "(It's) really strange – it was recorded in the mountains and all you can hear are women's voices, drums and panpipes. We offered it to a number of companies, but they dithered about releasing it, and eventually we decided to put it out ourselves."

THURSDAY, 21 OCTOBER 1971

Mick and Bianca's first child, a daughter Jade, is born in Paris.
Mick: "She's very precious and quite, quite perfect."

While awaiting the birth, Mick discusses life in exile . . .
"France is all right as long as you can get out. There's fuck-all live music here, there's Jacques Brel and electronic music. Even the accordion players are dead."

Jagger's absence from Nellcote is duly noted.
Nicky Hopkins: "(Sessions) took so long because we were only working four nights a week. Then there would be another week off for some reason or another, and then another break for something else. There was a four-week break at one stage when Mick had to go to Paris because of Bianca's baby. When Mick was away, we carried on doing some things, and these were Keith's songs, but they weren't really finished properly. Mick came back and added more to them."

TUESDAY, 26 OCTOBER 1971

Mick is interviewed for Beaton By Bailey, *a television documentary uniting two old friends.*

Q: "You give the impression that you're a really shrewd professional performer."

Mick: "Nah, it's not true. It's just instinctive really. I mean, all rock'n'roll performers are more or less instinctive."

Q: "Does a part of your mind always think that you've left the bathwater running?"

Mick: "Yeah, part of my mind is always wondering what the next number's gonna be. Or where shall we go and eat tonight. Did I leave that girl in my hotel room or not – I hope she hasn't stolen everything!"

Q: "Do you worry about time passing?"

Mick: "Not really, no."

Q: "There's a line in *Performance* when James Fox says to you, 'You'll be a funny little fellow when you're 50.' I was terribly intrigued to know what you thought of that?"

Mick: "I hope I will be funny! I don't think I'll really get there, unfortunately."

SATURDAY, 30 OCTOBER 1971

It is reported that the Stones hope to release a new album in February and tour the States in April. Twenty songs have been recorded for the new, as yet untitled LP.

Mick: "This new album is fucking mad. There's so many different tracks. It's very rock'n'roll. I didn't want it to be like that. I'm the more experimental person in the group . . . not go over the same thing over and over. I'm not against rock'n'roll, but I really want to experiment. The new album's very rock'n'roll and it's good. I think rock'n'roll is getting a bit . . . I mean, I'm bored with rock'n'roll. The revival. Everyone knows what their roots are, but you've got to explore everywhere."

Trevor Churchill (RSR accountant): "It's more basic rock'n'roll than the last one. Perhaps you could say the emphasis is back on straightforward rock. There's a lot more of Keith's influence on these tracks."

Sounds magazine subsequently reports that "Eat It is the tentative title of the Stones LP due out in February. One of the cover concepts for the LP might be candy which you'd be able to pick off and eat . . ."

In Los Angeles to complete and mix what will become Exile On Main Street, *Mick tells* Rolling Stone *writer Robert Greenfield:*
"The anonymity here is pretty good. It's not like England, where it's so crowded one has to buy 1,000 acres to have any privacy, where they line up outside your house to find out who you fucked the night before. I hate that place . . . Really, it's such a pathetic little village sometimes."

Mick is not particularly impressed by English audiences, either . . .
"When we played at the Roundhouse the last time we were here (14/3/71), it was good. I think they're all right, everyone accuses them of this, that and the other. There are not a lot of places to play in London. That's the trouble with England all round. In America, they're more spoiled. You can't really beat playing in Madison Square Garden with all those people and all that energy. There's nowhere like that here that's a regular gig. It's not the same country. It's England, they've got their own way of doing it."

FRIDAY, 7 JANUARY 1972

Jamming With Edward, *a collection of jams featuring Ry Cooder recorded during the sessions for* Let It Bleed, *is released on Rolling Stones Records. The Stones' office issues a statement: "This is really a Nicky Hopkins album, because he has done most of the work for it."*
Mick: "It was just a jam that we held on to. Then we put it out for a laugh because Nicky (Hopkins) and Ry (Cooder) wanted to put it out. I guess they wanted it out because they wanted the bread or something, so we said, 'Okay, put it out.' I mean, I didn't dig it that much."

'Sixth Stone' Nicky Hopkins explains the record's background to Melody Maker *writer Chris Charlesworth.*
Nicky Hopkins: "This was done in May 1969 at Olympic one night in the middle of some Stones sessions. We were halfway through a track when Keith had to leave early, and so we were sitting around with nothing to do. Ry Cooder was hanging around at the time, and I played piano, so we started playing. Mick plays harmonica, but everything happened on the spur of the moment, really. We jammed around for about two hours together and Glyn taped it all."
Mick: "I hope you spend longer listening to this record than we did making it."

205

Engineer Glyn Johns tells Vox Pop *author Michael Wale that 'hanging around' is intrinsic to Rolling Stones recording sessions.*

Glyn Johns: "The process of recording them is no different from anyone else, except that they take much longer than most people – between six and nine months to make an album, which is an awful long time. I don't know (why). For a start, there's absolutely no pressure on them at any time to get an album finished. There's no pressure from the money point of view either; they can spend what they want. So I think this must result in a lackadaisical attitude about it, don't give a shit, which is the Stones anyway. I find it very frustrating. There's no doubt they're an incredible group, but I don't understand why they have to sit and play one number over and over again for nine hours or two days in order to get it right.

"It's Keith Richard more than anyone else, the way he's formulated getting the feel he wants. He doesn't communicate tremendously with the others, I mean, they just go along with it. It seems to have got worse over the years. If they record two tracks in one night, I mean, history's made. But you can't knock the results."

SATURDAY, 19 FEBRUARY 1972

Allen Klein declares in Melody Maker *that "I have the ability to think like a thief."*

SATURDAY, 15 APRIL 1972

It is reported that Mick Jagger has accepted the part of Billy The Kid in a film version of Michael McLure's controversial stage play, The Beard – *based on an imaginary meeting between Billy The Kid and Jean Harlow.*
Asked about the project by Radio Luxemburg DJ Kid Jensen, Mick says, "Maybe I'm going to do that, nothing's been signed or anything. *The Beard* was a play that was on in London. It's a fantasy, Billy The Kid and Jean Harlow in eternity having a conversation. That's what it's about."

TUESDAY, 25 APRIL 1972

In the run-up to the release of the Stones' new album, Mick is grilled by Richard Williams for BBC-TV's The Old Grey Whistle Test.
Q: "Where did you make the album?"
Mick: "Everywhere. The South of France, then we did the mixing in Los Angeles. It's hard work doing a double album."

yde Park photo-call to announce Brian Jones' replacement, 21-year old Mick Taylor, June 13, 1969. "He doesn't
ay anything like Brian," said Mick. "He's a bluesman and he wants to play rock 'n' roll, so that's okay." (*Rex*)

On With The Show. The Stones backstage at *Top Of The Pops*, with new guitarist, Mick Taylor, on July, 1969 – the day the news broke of Brian Jones' death. (*Harry Goodwin*)

Mick Taylor's baptism of fire at the Stones' free Hyde Park concert, July 5, 1969. Standing stage left is Stones gofer, Tom Keylock, with Ian Stewart (arms folded on speaker cabinet) while Jagger's lover, Marsha Hunt (with Afro, standing on scaffolding) looks on.
(*Barrie Wentzell/Star File*)

"Something always happens when we start that number." Altamont Speedway, California, December 6, 1969. The free event was marred by the fatal stabbing of 18-year old Meredith Hunter by Hell's Angels. (*Associated Press*)

Mick and Keith check the competition out in the *NME*, while mixing *Get Yer Ya-Ya's Out!* at Trident Studios, summer 1970. (*Redferns/Michael Ochs*)

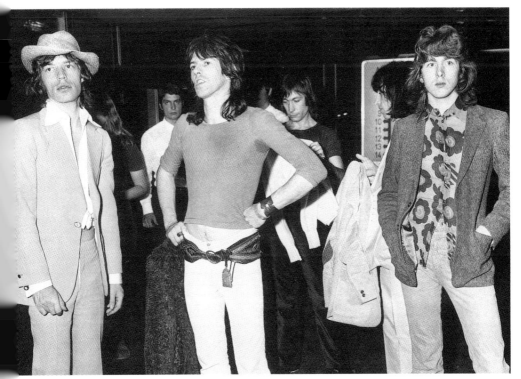

he Stones backstage at the Palazzo dello Sport, Rome, Italy, September 29, 1970. (*Popperfoto*)

Opposite ends of decorum: Jagger with socialite (and future wife) Bianca Perez Morena de Macias (*Jim Wheeler/Redferns*) and the elegantly wasted Richards and partner Anita Pallenberg. (*Graham Wiltshire/Redferns*)

Back to the clubs, March 26, 1971 where the Stones were videotaping a television special for American television at the Marquee. An altercation between Keith and club owner Harold Pendleton turned nasty when Richards' swung his guitar at Pendleton's head. (*Associated Press*)

e Stones onstage at the Empire Pool, Wembley, September 1973. "In England, a lot of people that came to see band certainly weren't around ten years ago," claimed Jagger. "If you continue touring, then hopefully you get enewed audience. You keep a large part of your old audience, and you pick up new ones along the way." *raham Wiltshire/Camera Press*)

1 Wood and Keith Richards onstage at the Kilburn 1mont, July 1974, to promote Wood's album *I've My Own Album To Do*. "The gas about playing 1 Keith is how smoothly our styles meshed" said od. "I'd always thought we had that street feel in 1mon." (*LFI*)

Mick Taylor quits the Stones, December 1974. When asked about a replacement, Jagger quipped "No doubt we can find a brilliant 6'3" blond guitarist who can do his own make-up." (*Barrie Wentzell/Star File*)

Takin' it to the streets, May 1 1975. The Stones announce their 1975 Tour Of The Americas by playing 'Brown Sugar' from the back of a flatbed truck. On far left is guest keyboardist, Billy Preston and 'fill-in' guitarist, Ron Wood who became a permanent Stone the following year. (*Waring Abbott/Pictorial Press*)

Star, Star – an inflatable penis aka 'the tired grandfather' - rises to the occasion during the Stones performance Madison Square Garden, June 1975. Such gimmicks left the Stones open to charges of self-parody. (*Ron Pownall/Star File*)

'Everything alright in the critics section?" The Stones perform two low-key gigs at the El Mocambo Club, Toronto, March 1977. A week before, Keith was arrested for possessing heroin for the purposes of trafficking and faced a life sentence. (*Camera Press*)

ick checks his assets, US tour, 1978. "It's very nice
be just a body. I feel like a stripper when I go on
age. I have a great sympathy for girls that are sex
jects. There's nothing more sleazy than an old
ripper!" (*Graham Wiltshire*)

Ronnie and Keith, The New Barbarians tour, 1979.
"When I see (Keith) up there it's a great feeling," said
Doris Richards. "I feel like shouting to everybody,
'That's my son up there!' I'm so proud. To me he's
still my Keith." (*Richard E. Aaron/Star File*)

Keith and Mick in 1980 promoting *Emotional Rescue*. "Mick is more involved with what's happening at this moment - and fashion," said Richards. "He has to go backwards and compare himself with who's hitting the Top Ten at that moment." (*Rolling Stones Records/EMI*)

Q: "Any particular reason why you did a double?"

Mick: "I dunno. After a while we realised we'd got enough to do a double album. It was very hard mixing it, for us anyway because we get very perfectionist about it."

Q: "Is it difficult to keep the roughness and spontaneity with all that mixing?"

Mick: "Well, as long as it's on the tape. We recorded it on the (Rolling Stones) Mobile but in the studio you wanna mess around with it a lot more because you don't have all the echo that you have in the studio. Especially when you've got 18 songs; you wanna make one sound different to the other."

Q: "Does it mark a change in direction?"

Mick: "I dunno. It's difficult for me to analyse it. It's pretty fast, very danceable. One side is very uptempo, really, really fast. The next side is a bit more relaxed. The other two are just a mixture. It's pretty straight Stones to me. Good mixture of different kinds of styles that we like to do. I'm glad it's over, though, and we can get on with the next one."

Q: "Most people get more sophisticated as they get older musically. You seem to be getting rougher . . ."

Mick: "I know what you mean. You mean, people get soft as they get older. This album just turned out the way it did. After you start something it kind of has a mind of its own. I would like to do something, not softer or sophisticated, but different. But we just weren't in that mood at the time. We just wanted to play quick songs, very rock'n'roll, dancey, commercially memorable tunes. I do like to do things that are a bit stranger sometimes."

Q: "In the last couple of years it's become a lot more apparent that Keith has had a lot to do with the musical direction of the band. What's your relationship like with him when you're working?"

Mick: "We work very much together; we always have done. Keith's always written a lot of the songs. Sometimes we write on our own and when we come to the studio we change them around, we might change the words. If I have to sing one of the songs that he's written I obviously change it to the way I think that the melody should go – and vice versa. You try every combination. But basically we work pretty much together. I write more of the lyrics and the melodies."

Q: "Do you differ greatly in your attitudes?"

Mick: "Yeah. I always accuse him of being an out and out rocker, which he is, you know. That's not completely justified! It balances out because he's always rocking and I always want to make it a bit different. That's the point of two people writing. You've got to have someone to sound off your ideas against. The best songs we've ever written are the songs we wrote together."

Q: "What are they?"

Mick: "The ones that everyone knows, 'Satisfaction' and all that. I think that applies to John Lennon and Paul McCartney, too."

Q: "You're setting up a tour of the States at the moment. Is it gonna be a big one?"

Mick: "Yeah, it's long enough. About 27 towns in about eight weeks."

Q: "Is there anything you can do to avoid another Altamont?"

Mick: "Not do another one! Not do another free concert in Altamont! That's basically all you can do. I hope it's not gonna happen again."

Q: "If you found yourself in the same situation again, is there anything you'd do differently?"

Mick: "Well, yeah, but you can't ever relive any moment. That's a real Hughie Green question! I've no idea. You learn from what you do."

Q: "Are you playing Britain?"

Mick: "There's this gig, the Lincolnshire Express or something, we might do that but it coincides with the beginning of the American tour. If we can get back for it we might do it."

Q: "You've been living in France for a while for various reasons. Are you thinking of coming back here?"

Mick: "It's a nice place to live . . . better than France is!"

Q: "While you've been out of the country, I suppose you've been watching the T. Rex phenomenon growing . . ."

Mick: "I saw Marc Bolan play in LA when he played his so-called début, which was about the fourth time he's played there. He played in a ballroom. He looked nice and went down well. I thought he was best when he played his acoustic numbers sitting on his podium. Yeah, he was good."

Q: "For the first time there's something growing up underneath your generation. And you're in a way being displaced as involuntary leader of the youngest generation."

Mick: "Well, I'm not 19 and neither's Marc Bolan. Musically speaking, I don't think you'll really have a new thing until you get a new music. While you're still basing your music on Chuck Berry, music's still the same, unfortunately. I want something else. I don't want Chuck Berry until we die! But I like Marc Bolan. He's all right."

Q: "Finally, is there anything you'd like to do outside the context of the Stones?"

Mick: "Yeah, there are. You can't do everything with the same people forever. There are things that I'd like to do but at the moment, I'm happy here. I'm all right."

SATURDAY, 29 APRIL 1972

Melody Maker writer Michael Watts puts a similar set of questions to Keith Richard, who compares the forthcoming album to Aftermath.
Keith: "It's not the same, of course, but it has the same feeling of a band that's been working and feels together."

Songwriting with Mick . . .
Keith: "I can't sit around on a song for too long. I like to get in the studio and write it there. Mick, on the other hand, likes to have it all worked out and rehearsed before he goes in. That's the basic difference between us. I get bored quicker."

That imminent, six-week tour of the States – and the band's fear of another Altamont . . .
Keith: "It's rare that we do an American tour when someone doesn't die. That thing on film just made it more obvious. . . . We're just gonna try and make sure it doesn't happen this time."

Those new Glam gods, T. Rex and Slade . . .
Keith: "We all know where those riffs come from."

Too old to rock'n'roll?
Keith: "Oh, c'mon! We're not exactly old! Muddy Waters and Howlin' Wolf are still getting it on. Just because we got a few kids these days!"

And that Keith Richard solo album . . .
Keith: "I can't see it happening. I want to do it with the rest of the Stones around me. I only hear it with Jagger singing anyway. I can force it, make it happen, but as it is I spend all my fucking time writing for the Stones."

The following week, T. Rex mainman Marc Bolan bites back.
Marc Bolan: "They're just not that important anymore. I think they're finding it difficult to live within the context of 16-year-old kids. That's who they were important to, that's what they were about, and that's what Mick still wants . . . The beginning of 'Tumbling Dice' is a bit like (T. Rex's) 'Get It On'. In fact, they played it to me and watched my reaction. But maybe they've left it a little late . . ."

Also musing on the state of contemporary pop is Faces guitarist Ron Wood, who can't help revealing where his loyalties lie.

Ron Wood: "The Stones are still there, which makes the whole thing kind of unreal. The whole thing is getting stranger, what with Ringo endorsing Marc. Yeah, there is that same sort of feel with (The Faces) and the Stones. But we never actually sat down and thought this is how we are going to sound."

Mick, meanwhile, occasionally lets the veil of diplomacy slip.

Mick: "I don't listen to rock'n'roll music nowadays. There's nothing much I listen to, except for gospel music, maybe . . . There's nothing happening here. The music is negligible. There's a lack of originality, and that's why I don't care about it. I'm not interested in going back to small English towns and turning on all the ten-year-olds. I've been and done all that."

WEDNESDAY, 10 MAY 1972

Rolling Stones publicist Les Perrin issues a press statement.

"The Rolling Stones and ABKCO Industries Incorporated and Allen Klein jointly announce the settlement of all outstanding differences to the satisfaction of all parties . . . Both Allen Klein and The Rolling Stones wish it to be made clear that ABKCO no longer act as business managers for The Rolling Stones."

Mick: "The settlement is that Allen Klein never has anything else to do with us."

Allen Klein: "Law suits are like wars – no one wins."

Mick: "Allen Klein would probably sue me if I told you my opinion of him. He's a person to be avoided as far as I'm concerned. He's just interested in himself!"

FRIDAY, 12 MAY 1972

The Stones 2-LP tour de force, Exile On Main Street, *is released.*

Mick: "It's raunchier and earthier than *Sticky Fingers*. The words are simple; it's less . . . pretentious."

Keith: "Double albums come once every ten years, like Dylan's *Blonde On Blonde*. It's very rare that you come up with that much material. Last year in France, we had nothing else to do and we just worked every night. It's a big hassle to put out a double album. Record companies don't like it.

It's more difficult to promote and for people to identify with. There's also so much on it, you can't immediately put it into perspective, and it takes people twice as long to get into."

It was also a hassle to put together, as producer Jimmy Miller tells Caroline Boucher in Disc.

Jimmy Miller: "Seven weeks went by and we hadn't cut the first track. Every night, I would say, 'Has somebody got a song?' There were a lot of problems with that album, it was the one I was least happy with. I would have been happier had it been a single album. I think that's the case with most double albums, but even so we chose the material out of almost twice as much stuff."

Mick Taylor: "We suddenly found we had some new songs that were all good. I think *Exile On Main Street* is more forceful than *Sticky Fingers* but it's not as imaginative or as adventurous. That's purely a personal opinion. No, there isn't any dissent within the band, surprisingly enough."

In a Melody Maker *review titled "The Stones: quite simply the best", Richard Williams defies contemporary scepticism and insists that the band's latest is a classic.*

Richard Williams: "*Exile On Main Street* is definitely going to take its place in history. It is, I think, the best album they've made, which is pretty remarkable because it's a double album and consistency has never been the Stones' forte . . . This is an album which utterly repulses the sneers and arrows of outraged put-down artists. Once and for all, it answers any questions about their ability as rock'n'rollers."

The obligatory pre-album trailer is 'Tumbling Dice'.

Mick: "I think they used the wrong mix with that. I'm sure they did. With the fast ones, I really like me voice to be part of the band, but with the slow ones I generally like it upfront a bit."

Keith: "I wanted to release 'Sweet Virginia' as a kind of easy listening single."

With the album behind them, the two Micks fantasise about doing something else beyond the confines of the band.

Mick: "I'd like to do something completely different. There's too much pressure being in a group: if I don't wanna do something, they do and vice versa. I'd like to take a year off and study . . . Naah. I've got a few projects. I think it's all talk."

Mick Taylor: "I'm very happy with the band – but there are a lot of other things I'd like to do. Possibly I could make a solo album, writing my own songs and participating with other musicians. I couldn't tell you who yet but there are a lot of people I like on the Atlantic label. All these ideas are vague and nebulous and I couldn't do it yet. I think everybody in the group has decided to explore other areas and directions. Everybody has different ideas in the Stones and the freedom to express them."

Taylor's evident frustration extends to the relative inactivity of the band's label.
Mick Taylor: "It would be nice to expand the Rolling Stones label and sign up some other groups. After all, that's the whole point of having your own label – to have complete artistic control."

Both express relief that the obligatory year in France is over.
Mick: "France? I didn't enjoy it at all, fucking drag it was."
Mick Taylor: "No problem at all. I don't speak French. So there was no language problem."

But before any band member has the opportunity to realise their extracurricular desires, there is some urgent Rolling Stones business to attend to, namely . . .

SATURDAY, 3 JUNE 1972

"THE HEAVIEST ROCK AND ROLL TOUR EVER"

The Stones' North American tour begins with a show in Vancouver, Canada.
Robert Greenfield: "Will it be the last tour?"
Keith: "I doubt it. We need the money."
Mick: "A pretty wild tour. Girls. Drink. You name it. Rock'n'roll, even."
Peter Rudge (tour manager): "This one is a military campaign. Truly. It's more than rock'n'roll. It's an event. People know the Beatles are gone and that Dylan will never tour again, so the Stones are the only one of that triumvirate they'll ever get a chance to see."
Bill Graham (promoter): "One of the most important things is the Stones' position as the only gods of rock music that an audience can see in person. The rock audience can't see the Beatles, they can't see Dylan, and Presley is no longer part of their world. So all that attention is focused on the Stones . . . They always have been able to hold on to their audience as it got older, and then able to capture the new rock audience. They've never lost momentum, their audience keeps growing and growing."

The 'military campaign' begins with the circulation of a neatly itemised rider.
"Dear Promoter
"We know it doesn't happen in America, but in the rather barbarous

outlands (sic) of Europe we have encountered many dressing rooms which lacked towels and soap . . . It would be nice to know we do not have to worry about the same problem. A clean group is a happy group.

Amenities to be provided in backstage changing area:

Two bottles per show of Chivas Regal, Dewar's or Teachers scotch.

Two bottles per show Jack Daniel's Black Label.

Two bottles per show tequila (lemon quarters and salt to accompany).

Three bottles iced Liebfraumilch.

One bottle per show Courvoisier or Hine brandy.

Fresh fruit, cheese (preferably not plastic), brown bread, butter, chicken legs, roast beef, tomatoes, pickles, etc.

Alka Seltzer.

Yours sincerely, the Rolling Stones."

As Peter Rudge asserts, the organisation owes very little to rock'n'roll . . .

Peter Rudge: "I feel a bit like Montgomery before Alamein – it's not like a rock'n'roll tour, more like the Normandy landings. Security for this tour will be unbelievable. We're having people wear coded badges made by this machine that will get them backstage – and if they lose them they're fined $50. This tour is incredible, just incredible. I keep having to pinch myself to realise it *is* a rock'n'roll tour. To me, it's such a vast administrative task that it's hard to absorb the fact that what we're trying to put on is a rock'n'roll band playing some good music.

"The basic problem is that the Stones tour so infrequently and haven't any machine going for them: no agent or manager. So you have to start from scratch. And because they are The Rolling Stones, you have to make doubly sure that you hire the right people to work on the tour, people who won't take liberties or lose us money. The Stones aim to make money this time, so they've been very careful about expenses. Before, everyone seemed to have *carte blanche* to buy what they wanted – the biggest, the most expensive. This has been planned as a 'roots' tour of eight weeks, and though we've chartered an aeroplane to get from town to town, we're staying in Holiday Inns, trying to hold it all back from the big-time thing that a Stones tour could easily become . . .

"The trouble is that so many people are in awe of them, especially in America which is a crazy country – you know, a country that's seen an attempt to assassinate (politician George) Wallace and the Charles Manson thing – it's just a crazy country where people behave strangely. So we've been especially careful in hiring security people. This group seems to still have the tag of the bad boys of rock, and even the police in some places seem to regard The Rolling Stones as criminals who will be trying to incite the children of their city to commit crimes."

A pressure group calling itself Men Struggling To Smash Sexism joins the long tradition of distributing a manifesto at Stones shows.

"THE STONES AND COCK ROCK"

"If you are male, this concert is yours. The music you will hear tonight is written for your head. It will talk to you about *your* woman, how good it is to have her under your thumb, so that she talks when she's spoken to. Men will play hard, driving music for you that will turn you on, hype you up, get you ready for action . . . like the action at Altamont, San Diego, Vancouver. This is your night, if you are male . . .

"The Stones are tough men – hard and powerful. They're the kind of men we're supposed to imitate: never crying, always strong, keeping women in their place (under our thumbs). In Vietnam, to save honour (which means preserving our manhood), our brothers have killed and raped millions of people in the name of this ideal: the masculine man. Is this the kind of person you want to be?

"We resent the image the Stones present to males as examples we should imitate . . .

"If you are female, you don't need this leaflet to tell you where to fit in. You will get enough of that tonight. If you choose to be angry, to fight, to unite with other women to smash the sexist society that has been constructed to oppress you, tonight, here – and every day, throughout America – we, the men who wrote this leaflet, will attempt, to the extent we can successfully smash our own sexism, to support your struggle."

SUNDAY, 4 JUNE 1972

As the Stones prepare to play 'Sweet Black Angel' during a show at the Seattle Coliseum, Mick makes a final gesture towards radical politics.
Mick: "Who got free today? Angela Davis got free today. Fuckin' great . . ."

More characteristic of the tour are the parasitic socialites that become part of the group's entourage.
Keith: "It's a difficult thing to handle, because it starts with things like – 'Oh, Truman Capote is going to come along and write something on the Stones' – and he comes along and brings along Princess Lee Radziwill and some other socialites from New York and you're surrounded by those people. It just takes one guy like Capote to trigger it off."

214

Sounds *report that the atmosphere at the shows is decidedly frivolous.*
"The most frequent question before the show is, 'What do you think he'll be wearing?' The answer is: a silver lamé jacket, violet panne velvet jacket trimmed with silver studs, scarf round his neck, a silver studded belt, jewelled bracelet and a glittering silver star at the corner of his right eye."

Truman Capote's verdict is hardly flattering.
Mick Taylor, he says, is "Pretty, a Jean Harlow blond-type, but dumb and totally uninteresting." *And the rest?* "Complete idiots."

TUESDAY, 25 JULY 1972

Before the Stones' afternoon show at Madison Square Garden, US TV host Dick Cavett probes Mick and Bill.
Q: "How did you sleep after the opening night last night?"
Mick: "Not very well. Didn't sleep at all."
Q: "I don't know if I was supposed to see this, but there was a plate or something going round, people offering these little pills."
Mick: "Vitamins A, B, C and salt."
Q: "Do you do any kind of exercise?"
Mick: "Yeah, but last night I forgot and pulled a muscle."
Q: "The kids outside are very upset about scalping, having to pay $75 dollars for a ticket. They say that has ruined the atmosphere for them."
Mick: "That's just the free enterprise system. Tickets aren't set at $75. And they are arresting the scalpers."
Q: "When you were at the LSE, were you keen to be an economist?"
Mick: "That was what I was told I was gonna be. A Keynesian."
Q: "Do they get as upset in England as they do here about drugs in the lyrics?"
Mick: "Yeah. And if they hear an advertised brand they won't play the record either."
Q: "What's running through your nervous system right now, Bill? Are you worried or scared?"
Bill: "Nah."
Q: "Would you ever do 30 cities again?"
Bill: "Yeah, as long as you get holidays. There's never been so much energy as on this tour. It always used to be screamers who didn't seem to worry much about the music. Now you hear everything and see everything and there's so much tension."

Q: "Can you tell if it's the same audience as before or are you hitting a younger group that hadn't seen the Stones before?"

Bill: "It used to be 15 to 20, now it's 15 to 30. It's great. You're not getting the mums and dads."

Q: "Are you a chain smoker?"

Bill: "No."

Q: "Can you picture yourself at 50?"

Bill: "I have no idea what I'm doing next year. I dunno. Retired."

Q: "If the Stones broke up what would you do?"

Bill: "I'd just get together and make some more music. I wouldn't form a group."

Q: "What will you do when you finish this tour?"

Bill: "I'm going to Bermuda for a week. I've got family there."

Q: "Has there been anything on this trip that's scared you?"

Bill: "When the cops beat the kids up that scares me a bit sometimes."

Q: "Has there been much of that?"

Bill: "Not too much, not as much as usual. But we have seen a bit of that. You do see them grab guys out of the audience and take them out . . . They often cause more trouble than there is."

Q: "Do you still talk about Altamont and what happened there?"

Bill: "We talk about it, but I'd sooner forget about it. It was the last show of the tour and we weren't gonna do it. There were 200,000 people there. There were only 300 fighting."

Q: "Do you ever notice if it's a bad night and the audience isn't with you?"

Bill: "It hasn't happened on this tour. You get more hung up on whether your amplifier blows up. But the audiences have been fantastic, very receptive."

As Mick limbers up ready for the show . . .

Q: "Mick, how do you move around in public?"

Mick: "The Twist, I think!"

Q: "Can security affect the audience?"

Mick: "Yes, it does. You have to find a happy medium. In a lot of these towns, the police don't allow dancing. You try and talk to them and some are reasonable and some aren't."

Q: "Can you walk out and tell what it's gonna be like each night?"

Mick: "You know what the audience is like as soon as you get on there."

Q: What's going through you now? Are you nervous?"

Mick: "Yeah, I'm nervous."

Q: "Would you ever do 30 cities again?"

Mick: "Yeah. Just give me a week off."

Q: "Can you picture yourself at 60 doing what it is you do now?"

Mick: "Yeah, easily."

Q: "Really? Going on stage with a cane, moving the way you do?"

Mick: "There's a lot of people doing it at 60 and I think it's a bit weird but they still seem to get their rocks off. Marlene Dietrich still does it and she's more than 60."

Mick tells it differently elsewhere.

Mick: "When I'm 33, I quit. That's the time when a man has to do something else. I don't want to be a rock'n'roll singer all my life. I couldn't bear to end up as an Elvis Presley and sing in Las Vegas with all those housewives and old ladies coming in with their handbags. It's really sick."

Soon afterwards, a rough cut of Robert Frank's tour documentary, provisionally titled Cocksucker Blues, *hits the underground circuit. Inevitably, perhaps,* The News Of The World *obtains a copy.*

"THE TRUTH ABOUT THE REVOLTING STONES"

"Sex and drug scenes in the movie that Jagger banned.

- A sky-high gang bang, in which members of the tour entourage strip and make love to two 'groupie' girls 30,000 feet up in a jet taking the Stones between US cities. Jagger and other members of the group play tambourines and maracas as they watch.
- A naked girl lying on a hotel bed and talking about the joys of drugs and sex while she rubs her breasts and private parts.
- Stone Keith Richard apparently being injected by a beautiful blonde girl, who later appears to inject herself.
- Women in the Stones' dressing rooms sniffing powder from a long spoon held by a man. One woman says, "I guess it's just great. I never knew how great it was."
- Jagger taking a knife with a powdery substance on the blade, and inhaling it through one nostril.
- A girl fan queuing to see her heroes saying: "I just love acid. They took my child away because I love acid. Sure, the Stones are acid to me."

Mick: "Why can't (Robert Frank) go and do something else? It was my idea of making that stupid movie. He was just paid to film what I told him to do . . . It's *our* movie. And if I want to go and shred it in the shredder, or if I want to show it to my friends, or if I want to put it in general release, it's up to me."

The film is duly shelved.

SATURDAY, 5 AUGUST 1972

Despite his apparent disinterest in rock's past, Mick turns up at The London Rock'n'Roll Show, a day-long feast of Fifties music held at Wembley Stadium, London.

Mick: "You wouldn't have thought this was possible even ten years ago. I wouldn't have thought anyone would have wanted to come. It's really strange. I dunno what to make of it. It's a fossilised scene, 'cos all the audience wants to hear are certain numbers, and if they don't hear 'em they ain't gonna feel very happy!"

SEPTEMBER 1972

Mick sings backing vocals on Carly Simon's 'You're So Vain', a British hit single for the singer three months later.

Carly Simon: "I was putting the vocals on when Mick Jagger phoned. He'd just come into London and I hadn't seen him since LA. Ostensibly, he just phoned to say hello, but during the call I advised him to come along to the session. Harry Nilsson came along too . . . As far as I'm concerned, Mick and the strings really made that track for me."

Mick: "People say she wrote that song about me, but that's not true. She didn't know me. I did the session because she asked me to. I do know who the song's about, but I'm not going to tell you. All I can say is it's about this very rich actor cat who's a friend of mine."

Carly Simon: "It certainly is not about Mick Jagger. I would never ever have done that. I mean, that really takes a lot of slyness and I'm just not that sly. I really like Mick. He's a friend of mine and in no way would I ever do anything like that to a person that I really cared for . . . I guess it would be very interesting if it were about Mick Jagger. I mean, let them think that it's about him. It's just not at all. It is about a lot of people. The actual examples that I've used in the song are from my imagination, but the stimulus is directly from a couple of different sources. It's not just one particular person."

NOVEMBER 1972

Mick also puts in an appearance at sessions in New York for Yoko Ono's third solo album, Approximately Infinite Universe.

Mick: "I just went in there and disrupted it, really. I started playing the guitar very loudly with John. Actually, it was Yoko's record they were doing. She's doing very straight things and trying to sing properly. She's not screaming, she's really trying to sing."

SATURDAY, 25 NOVEMBER 1972

The Stones begin a month-long stretch in Byron Lee's Dynamic Sounds Studios in Kingston, Jamaica.

Byron Lee: "The group came over to Kingston to check out the studios and the accommodation. They told how much they had heard of our sound over the last three years, and they specified exactly what additional equipment they would need – a Yamaha piano, limiters, mikes and echo units. I have gone out and bought everything because I figure that their requirements are the best criteria of what anyone else would want. They will be the first to use our new 16-track installation which is the only one in Jamaica."

Keith: "There's a lot of music in Jamaica and they play it loud, which is nice. Although it's reggae, once you've been living there you begin to actually turn on to it because it's Jamaica's whole rhythm of life. To them it isn't just a new record on the radio or something, it's the way they walk, it's everything they do in that rhythm."

Andy Johns (engineer): "It was a really primitive old place. They'd just got a 16-track. The mixer and recording equipment were very basic. No limiters or anything. It didn't matter. The room was so good and it was that which really affected the music."

Keith: "I really don't think Jamaica has influenced the music we've been recording, because when we're in a studio we could be anywhere. It's always a shock to me to walk out of Dynamic Sounds every night and suddenly realise I'm in Jamaica. Studios are like airports – you could be anywhere, because they're basically the same."

Jimmy Miller (producer): "The sessions for this album have gone really well. This is probably the easiest I can remember with the Stones. The studio in Jamaica was just right. The sound in the room was perfect."

Nicky Hopkins: "The tracks are certainly nice, but I hated Jamaica, detested it. Kingston has to be one of the dirtiest, poorest places in the world. It really depressed me. We worked at Dynamic right through every night and it wasn't brilliant but it was all right, considering. We were there two and a half weeks and I was really glad to get out. They stayed on for another week and Billy Preston went down to work with them."

Keith: "It was a very good studio, and it'll be very simple in a way this album. We haven't done a lot of overdubs or anything. We've tried to leave it and get as much of the studio sound as possible because it was a very strong sound."

Mick Taylor: "The backing tracks were all done in Jamaica. We started off with 'Winter', which was just Mick strumming on a guitar in the studio, and everything fell in together from there. 'Angie' and 'Dancing With Mr. D' were recorded in the middle of the sessions and 'Starfucker' was about the last. Some of the songs used were pretty old. '100 Years Ago' was one that Mick had written two years ago and which we hadn't really got around to using before."

Mick: "The album will be less freaky, more melodic than the last one."

WEDNESDAY, 6 DECEMBER 1972

Arrest warrants are issued for Keith Richard and Anita Pallenberg in Nice, France. The other Stones had already been wrongly implicated in the drug-related charges.

Mick: "Charlie Watts, Bill Wyman, Mick Taylor and myself deny categorically that we have been charged by the French police with the buying and use of heroin. It has never been suggested that we used or bought heroin. The four of us were not freed on 'provisional liberty' because we had never been arrested on any charge . . . At no time did we hold drug parties in our homes."

MONDAY, 1 JANUARY 1973

Mick begins the year by explaining the real problem with rock'n'roll to television inquisitor, David Dimbleby.

Mick: "Rock'n'roll's got into such a weird thing now because so many people are analysing it, they're reviewing one song taking six columns – the sociological meaning, the religious meaning, political meaning, and then what they personally think. There seems to be a bit much appreciation from the older generation as far as I can make out. You can't get rid of them at concerts!"

SUNDAY, 11 FEBRUARY 1973

As the Stones' Australasian tour kicks off in Auckland, New Zealand, Mick explains his ideas for a new type of rock show to Sounds *staffer Steve Peacock.*

Mick: "That tour was quite funny because it was all outside. I've never really played outside and enjoyed it before, but I had a really great time and the sound was fantastic. The band was really tight. But it was still circusy – fireworks and all that – because in big places what can you see? You can't just come to see a band on stage – it's not fun if you're 89 rows back. The only way round that is visual amplification – video – which I'd like to do but it's so expensive. Also, I don't know if people like it. I do – quite. The first time I saw it used was when I was watching Ike and Tina Turner at one of our gigs. It was nice because you could see her in real close-up!"

SATURDAY, 16 JUNE 1973

"STONES TOUR HERE! – And Richards Denies Split"

Keith reveals the band's plans for a European tour later in the year, says that the working title for the new album is Goat's Head Soup, *and dismisses the latest wave of 'Stones To Split' rumours, as well as a counter story claiming Ronnie Wood, of the Faces, was to replace Keith . . .*

Keith: "I haven't actually seen the story, but the peculiar thing was it was supposed to come from Nicky (Hopkins), which I find pretty incredible because I haven't seen Nicky since the end of February when we finished touring Australia . . . Jokingly over dinner, Ronnie (Wood) and I were larking about and saying, 'Why don't we all change places,' and I think that's how that one grew. Maybe through two or three people. I mean, rumours usually do. But it was a complete shock to me."

Mick: "It's just one of those trade press rumours. There's obviously frictions, bound to be, but we haven't had a real fight for a long time. Just sort of, 'I might not like a mix' or something, that's as far as it gets . . . We don't all go out to the same restaurant or anything. I see quite a lot of Mick Taylor, and when Charlie's in town on his own, I see quite a lot of him, go round all those places he likes to go, buying all that militaristic rubbish he likes – 1908 airmen in boxes, no, 1914 airmen in glass cases. I don't see much of Bill when we're not on the road, but I see Keith quite a lot because we're usually working together. But I don't just hang around with the group . . . I think one's got to try to do other things, to be some other person as well, because I don't think just being a singer with The Rolling Stones is enough."

Keith: "Nobody's ever really thought about splitting and also there's no indication from the public that they're fed up with us. I'm sure Mick would like to try his hand at other things and do another movie but they've never interfered with Stones stuff in the past. I wouldn't mind doing a movie, too, just for a laugh!"

Rod Stewart: "I didn't think twice about it. It takes a lot more than that to upset me."

Ron Wood: "Remember when I was supposed to join the Stones? I didn't even know about that one till we were coming off stage one night and I said, 'Well then, what's wrong with you lot tonight?' And they looked at me and said, 'You didn't tell us you were gonna leave and join the Stones.' Well, it's only rock'n'roll, but . . .'"

MONDAY, 18 JUNE 1973

Marsha Hunt files a paternity suit against Mick alleging that he is the father of her daughter Karis.

Marsha: "Mick was involved with Karis for the first couple of years of her life, so to have him turn round and suddenly say, 'I'm not the father,' was a shock. Suddenly the onus was on me to prove paternity and proving paternity is extraordinarily difficult."

MONDAY, 25 JUNE 1973

Mick Taylor guests on guitar during a live performance of Mike Oldfield's epic Tubular Bells.

Mick Taylor: "It was a total departure in the sense that I'd never done anything like that in public before. But I have a very varied number of musical influences. I like classical music and jazz and that's why I wanted to do the Mike Oldfield thing, because there's so many different textures going on in *Tubular Bells* . . . I didn't play too much anyway – I just played carefully worked out parts for the electric guitar."

Inevitably, there is renewed speculation about solo Stones projects.

Mick: "It's always in the air, innit, Keith."

Mick Taylor: "A spokesman for Mick Jagger says that he intends to make a solo album in the near future."

Keith: "I'm not interested in solo albums. All these bands splintering up for individual members to record their own stuff seems pointless . . . You come up against the problem of whether to hold back your best material for your album or the band's next effort."

Mick Taylor: "I have a very strong desire to do things with other people, but as far as doing a purely solo album goes I don't think I'm ready to do that, and until I'm ready I won't do it. I get much more satisfaction out of playing with other people anyway. I can't see the point of getting any grandiose solo plans because I'm not a particularly strong singer and I haven't written enough songs. I'm not really at a stage when I can call myself a songwriter. I just have random choruses and catchphrases. Nothing really substantial."

TUESDAY, 26 JUNE 1973

"ROLLING STONE RICHARD – GUN, DRUGS CHARGES"

He's not quitting the Stones. Neither, it seems, has Keith quit his nasty habits, according to the police who raid his house in Cheyne Walk, Chelsea.
Keith: "Actually it was a very nice gun, the new model revolver with a hammer guard. It'd been sent to me by a bodyguard on our '72 tour of America who felt I should never be without one. You're never alone with a Smith and Wesson."

TUESDAY, 3 JULY 1973

Mick attends the post-show party following David Bowie's 'retirement' concert at the Hammersmith Odeon.
Mick: "People bandy that word decadence about and don't know what it means. They haven't seen decadence because they can't see it in our society. They're too involved in what they are doing to see it. What do they mean by decadence? Bisexuality? That's not decadence, but people think there is some mystique about it . . . I think David (Bowie) is sincere and I like what he does. It would be a lie to say his image is a hype. I think he is very talented. I don't think in three years we'll be laughing at what he does, because he's done it better than anybody else."

Meanwhile, in New Musical Express, *Nick Kent asks Keith for his view on Stones clones, The New York Dolls . . .*
Keith: "I've never heard 'em – seen pictures of 'em though and they look very pretty. Bands have always been into copying us. Really, I mean what were bands like The Pretty Things and Them with Van Morrison doing back then? It's not a piss-off and it's not particularly flattering either."

Mick is more scathing, telling Roy Carr of the same paper:
"I don't think they're very good. They're all right if you want a good laugh, but they're so very camp and silly. I mean, one of them is quite pretty in a funny sort of way, but they're not very good players and that bloke can't sing. They're all right for a laugh, and for all I fucking know

they might be the biggest thing to emerge this year, but I don't really care either way."

Keith: "I only know that they sound like the Stones 'cos people tell me that they do. I've never actually seen them working. I've seen the photos and it's obvious that guy (David Johansen) mimics Mick, and he does look incredibly like him . . . I'm sure they'd be happier if they were making it on the strength of something a little less tenuous than having a guy in the band who happens to look like somebody that's rather more famous."

The ersatz Stones frontman David Johansen sums things up. . . .

David Johansen: "People are desperate for comparisons. That'll blow over, just like when Jim Morrison came out he was the new Mick Jagger of the mid-Sixties. And when Iggy was the Mick Jagger of the late Sixties. It's just crap. The Dolls are the Dolls. They're better than all of 'em."

TUESDAY, 31 JULY 1973

More problems for Keith. Redlands, his 12th century farmhouse in West Wittering, Sussex, is badly damaged by fire.

Keith: "It may have been due to an electrical fault. We don't know for certain. It's a terrible thing to have happened to such a beautiful place. The place is probably worth £50,000 now . . . I will probably build a new one on the site, or use the existing framework and build it up again . . ."

MONDAY, 20 AUGUST 1973

'Angie' is the surprising choice of single from the forthcoming Stones album.

Jimmy Miller: "When Mick came up with 'Angie', I was really satisfied. I was hoping he'd come up with something that was a real song."

Keith: "I had the whole chord sequence down maybe a year ago with just the title, 'Angie'. It could have been 'Randy' or 'Mangy' or anything, y'know, but Mick just picked up on the title and wrote a song around it. He added the strings – all the strings on the album are his idea. I don't know who chose it as a single. I think somebody said that it would make a change and that it would get a heavy reaction on AM stations. I'm not really interested in picking singles."

Mick: "I didn't pick it, because I'd picked 'Tumbling Dice' and that didn't do particularly well. I really fancied 'Dancing With Mr. D', but I didn't put my foot down. A ballad once every four years is okay."

Mick explains to Roy Carr from New Musical Express *that 'Angie'* ". . . is a throwback to the 'Back Street Girl', 'Lady Jane', 'You Better Move On' ballads we used to do. We've always done that and they've always come off . . . I don't always want to come off with a rocker. It's important to try and do something else, so that's why we did 'Angie'."

It is widely – and incorrectly – rumoured that the song was written for David Bowie's wife.

Angie Bowie: "I think Mick Jagger would be astounded and amazed if he realised to how many people he is not a sex symbol . . ."

David Bowie: ". . . but a mother image!"

FRIDAY, 31 AUGUST 1973

Goat's Head Soup *is released.*

Mick: "We were pleased with *Goat's Head Soup* as an album. The title was the name of a national dish in Jamaica, where we cut it. When we were recording, instead of getting hamburgers or fish and chips, we got things like goat pâté, which we find a bit distasteful but which no doubt they love."

Mick Taylor: "Goat patties . . . are some kind of Jamaican delicacy. Some natives find a goat that's been run down on the highway, scrape it off the road and then serve it as a main course. It's quite a tradition out there."

Mick: "To me it sounds radically different from *Exile On Main Street* I think it's better, I think the songs are better, with a few exceptions. And it's more compact though it's quite long . . . Definitive? If we made the definitive album, we wouldn't bother to make any more. Who has made a definitive album? Ah, I know, the Beatles' *Sgt. Pepper*. Well, s'pose it was definitive. They didn't make as good a one afterwards. This might be, you haven't heard it yet!"

John Peel (on 'Silver Train'): "I've always thought that one of the main reasons for the success of Rolling Stones' records lies in the way Mick's voice is always kept down in the mix. Here it disappears completely at times . . ."

Mick: "A lot of people don't like it. Too bad . . ."

Keith: " 'Coming Down Again' is my song . . . 'Starfucker' is all Mick's. 'Dancing With Mr. D' is my riff and Mick's lyrics. I tend to work more on riffs while Mick has finished songs."

Mick: "I really felt close to this album and I really put all I had into it . . .

but whatever you do it's always wrong. If you do it rocky, people say, 'Oh it's like the same old rock'n'roll,' and if you do slow ballads, they say it's too pretty."

Mick: "It was delayed for two months because they're having all this trouble in America with these anti-pornography laws and Atlantic were incredibly uptight. They wanted to exclude 'Starfucker' altogether. They got the complete horrors and screamed we're gonna be sued. I said, I don't mind if I'm sued. I just fought and fought and fought . . . that finished me."

Keith: "They've given us a lot of trouble over 'Starfucker' for all the wrong reasons – I mean, they even got down to saying that Steve McQueen would pass an injunction against the song because of the line about him. So we just sent a tape of the song to him and of course he okayed it. It was just a hustle, though. Obstacles put in our way."

Mick: "I suppose we ask for it if we record things like that. Christ, I don't do these things intentionally. I just wrote it. If I'd written it with other words that were just as good, I'm sure it could be a hit."

Mick: "I'm not saying all women are starfuckers, but I see an awful lot of them."

'Starfucker' is retitled 'Star Star' prior to the record's release.

The album is the first with a discernible vocal presence from the 'Quiet Stone' . . .
Mick: "Mick Taylor's started to sing, he's singing on a couple of tracks – shyly, but he's there."

. . . and the last with their regular producer.
Jimmy Miller: "They're very difficult to work with. I feel quite often that I'm not necessarily the only person who could work with them, but there are very few people who could. Looking back, I never realised I had so much patience, and at times you have to eat humble pie."

Even a much respected journalist such as New Musical Express *stalwart Keith Altham (then reporting for* Record & Radio Mirror, *and who later became the Rolling Stones' press officer) encounters difficulties with the band.*
Mick: "Go and await my presence in the next office. You're not dealing with a new boy, y'know . . . I thought about ending (interviews). Then I thought, 'Why not do them?' I only do them with people I know and when we've got something to say as a group, such as a new album or a tour. I wouldn't do it with someone who was going to put me through it . . . I'd just walk out."

SATURDAY, 1 SEPTEMBER 1973

"WILL THIS BE THE LAST TIME?"

The Stones' European tour opens at the Stadthalle in Vienna, Austria.

Mick: "We spent a long period off the road in the early Seventies and somehow it had changed when we got back. There was much more importance placed on lights, equipment and theatrics and I was always into that . . . I'd always wanted to make our shows theatre, and with improved equipment it was possible to do a lot of good things. A lot of people have done the theatre thing – some very well, and some quite appallingly."

Peter Rudge: "Hopefully, the Stones are about the best group in the world, or at least the best known, so we have to spend money to make them appear the best. We can afford to spend money on lighting and sound, and we can afford the services of the best road crew available. We're having sound and lighting men flown in from all over the world to make up the crew on this tour. Also we can afford to have someone like Billy Preston on the tour as a supporting act whereas in most cases Billy Preston would be topping the bill himself."

The demands become even more extravagant as each promoter receives a 20-page tour contract that includes the following stipulations (among countless others).
"A promoter must
   – provide at least 50 security men at each concert
   – provide a make-up room with at least 12 towels and bars of soap
   – there must be no discrimination on grounds of sex, religion, race or age when it comes to selling tickets
   – there must be a doctor available 24 hours a day
   – there must be five limousines provided for the benefit of the group
   – the promoter must provide ten dozen red roses for the group
   – and supply a complete list of first-class restaurants in the town with details of which restaurant provides a private room."

Peter Rudge (tour manager): "If things are not right, Mick gets absolutely hysterical. If his salt water in his dressing-room isn't there, he gets hysterical. He phoned me at six the other morning to tell me the colour of the shadow on Charlie Watts' eyes was wrong."

Support on the tour is Billy Preston and a new band, Kracker, the first signing to the Stones label.
Keith: "Everyone agreed to signing Kracker and Jimmy Miller was recording them so it seemed natural. As to why they're the first – well, there's no hurry. We're not interested in becoming another Apple. Sure

there have been other bands we've had our eye on – Stone The Crows were one but they've broken up. Rory Gallagher is another artist I've thought about, just because he's good and he seems to have had a raw deal from his record company."

Mick: "They already had a single out that had done quite well in America. They're quite a good band, they write good songs. I thought, let's sign them and see what happens."

There is a conspicuous absence of vintage songs at the shows.

Keith: "Actually, we were doing a bunch of old numbers when we were touring Australia . . . 'Route 66', 'Bye Bye Johnny', 'It's All Over Now'. One thing about working up the old songs is that Mick (Taylor) doesn't know 'em . . . Another reason is that Decca have stopped us releasing new live versions of material recorded on their label. A whole live album with Stevie Wonder on it, recorded on the American tour, has been scrapped because they've ballsed that up."

SUNDAY, 9 SEPTEMBER 1973

A group of ex-servicemen walk out during the last of four shows given by the Stones at the Empire Pool, Wembley.

Mick: "Hey, Sergeant, we don't need any of that. Mister Commission-aire, we're here to have a good time. We don't want any security."

Sgt Major Charles Dawson: "He (Mick) called us pigs. Just think, we fought for the likes of him. We are very incensed. Our job had been to take people to their seats on the arena floor. We had to make sure that the gangways were clear as per regulations. One of our men moved a person from the gangway, and Mick Jagger shouted: 'Xxxx off, sergeants. We don't need you.' Then he sang to the audience: 'The sergeants are pigs, the sergeants are pigs.' We have never been treated like this. We are not pigs. He made no attempt at all to apologise. It's the last time we help Mr Jagger."

Keith: "Jobsworths are just the lowest as far as I'm concerned. I mean, the guy on Sunday who was causing that disturbance, was just looking for a chance to get into some violence. He must have been frustrated or something. Anyway, after the show he had all his commissionaire chums standing on some scaffolding going like this (grimaces). So Mick and I threw some Coke bottles at 'em."

WEDNESDAY, 19 SEPTEMBER 1973

Gram Parsons is found dead in Joshua Tree, California.

Keith: "I hadn't seen Gram for some time. He had a band together and made an album with Glen Hardin and James Burton. He was into a very purist country trip – stuff like 'Streets Of Baltimore'."

There had been rumours that the pair had recorded an album together.

Keith: "Gram and I didn't cut anything together in the studio. There's a lotta cassettes laying around featuring the both of us, and I did a couple of studio songs by myself that he'd shown me, but we never did get around to making an album . . . Gram was one of my closest friends. Unfortunately, many of my closest friends have died suddenly . . . Once he'd moved back to LA or whatever to form his own band, I started hearing stories. Hollywood is the end of the line for so many people. It's a killer and if you're weak you can be sure it'll get you."

FRIDAY, 28 SEPTEMBER 1973

Mick entertains Old Grey Whistle Test *presenter Bob Harris in Munich. 'Whispering' Bob begins with the hardware question, a favourite of the early Seventies rock interviewer.*

Q: "How much machinery is needed these days to get the Stones on the road?"

Mick: "Since '69 we've had a large crew. The crew's smaller in Europe. We don't have the money to spend on the production that we do in America. Everything's done by road and you can always get stopped at customs which can hold things up. But I guess there's about 25 people that aren't musicians."

Q: "Do you still get motivated to go out on the road?"

Mick: "Yeah, or else we wouldn't be out here. The simple answer to that is that's what I do. That's why we tour. I like to sing live."

Q: "Last year's projected album with Stevie Wonder wasn't released."

Mick: "Well, it's the great old enemy, our old record company, Decca and our old manager, Allen Klein. They didn't want the live album to come out because they had certain rights on re-recordings of material that's already been out. We offered them money, a percentage per track. Everyone has something to gain. I don't understand their attitudes."

Q: "None of you have gone off and done solo albums. Have you felt that you've wanted to?"

Mick: "Yeah, we've all wanted to but we're all so lazy that none of us have ever done it. You've got this problem that unless you're really prolific as a writer, I'd feel that if I did an album on my own, what would I

229

choose to put on my album or a Stones album? You've been in this position of holding back songs. I'd like to do an album. I think Keith could do a nice album."

Q: "People who were into the Stones in 1963 have not necessarily been replaced by younger people. A true theory?"

Mick: "Not really. I know that in certain places there is a new audience because we've never played there before. In England, a lot of people that came to see the band certainly weren't around ten years ago. If you continue touring, then hopefully you get a renewed audience. You keep a large part of your old audience, and you pick up new ones along the way."

Q: "How does the energy level compare in Los Angeles and London?"

Mick: "LA has probably got a higher energy level, but a lot of great things have come out of both towns. London's got a very bad reputation with bands as a quiet and difficult place to play. But I really enjoyed it this time."

Q: "There's been a lot of talk about this being the last tour. Is that true?"

Mick: "Wishful thinking! I don't think so, otherwise I would have made an announcement from the stage at Wembley. No, I don't think so. We've got a bit more to go yet."

FRIDAY, 5 OCTOBER 1973

Decca release No Stone Unturned, *a collection of largely forgotten Rolling Stones B-sides. 'Sad Day', the flip of the US edition of 'Paint It Black', is lifted off the album and issued on 45.*

Keith: "I don't really mind them repackaging old stuff if they use a little bit of imagination, but putting out old flipsides as singles is shit. Decca are supposed to be making records but they might just as easily be making baked beans . . . I think they're the biggest bunch of shits in the world."

FRIDAY, 12 OCTOBER 1973

As the Stones prepare for the final leg of the European tour, Mick, Keith and Mick Taylor sit down for a press conference at the American Hotel in Amsterdam, Holland.

Q: "Do the Stones need to tour?"

Keith: "Yeah, every band needs to tour."

Q: "Do you need it financially?"

Keith: "No, it's not a financial situation."
Mick: "It helps financially."
Keith: "Not the way I spend money."
Mick: "It 'elps me."
Q: "Do you think playing large halls like you do now gives you contact with the audiences that you had in the beginning in the clubs?"
Keith: "A small hall is obviously better to play."
Mick: "I don't like playing in concert halls where people are sitting down in plush velvet seats. I like to play in small ballrooms 'cos people can dance."
Q: "In England there was an underground Top 10 about rock people that are expected to die soon."
Keith: "Am I on the list?"
Q: "Yes, you take the Number One position."
Keith: "Great, okay. I'll let you know."
Mick: "It's a bit morbid. I don't think you should answer that."
Q: "Lou Reed's in second place and he's very proud of it."
Keith: "I think he can beat me, actually."
Mick: "He is destructive. I don't think Keith's that kind of person."
Q: "Nik Cohn . . ."
Mick: "Don't like him . . ."
Q: ". . . wrote it would be better if they (the Stones) would all die in an airplane crash before they were 30."
Mick: "Yeah, he's thick. Maybe *he* should die . . . I think it was a very rude thing, and if Nik Cohn was here now, I'd punch him in the mouth."
Q: "Keith, in the *New Musical Express*, you stated about Eric Clapton that there was a difference between a musician and a performer, and that he was a musician. What do you think you are?"
Keith: "Oh, I'm a performer, baby!"
Q: "What's the difference?"
Keith: "Let's say some people are more showmen than others. It's not a matter of good or bad."
Mick: "If Eric did more shows, he might become a performer, 'cos he only recently started singing."
Q: "Mick, there are strong rumours that you have a certain relationship with David Bowie. What's true about that?"
Mick: "I've just met him a few times, that's all. We're just good friends."
Q: "Well, he's very attractive . . ."
Mick: "You might find him attractive. In the morning he doesn't look that good."

Q: "Truman Capote. Did you read what he wrote in *Rolling Stone*?"
Mick: "I didn't read it."
Keith: "It's very interesting to know what some old queen from New York thinks of things, you know?!"
Q: "Are the Rolling Stones still the biggest rock'n'roll group in the world?"
Keith: "You tell me, baby."

While in Holland, Mick takes time out from a boisterous music industry party to answer some questions regarding . . .

Future plans?
Mick: "I'd like to do another album, a quick album. I don't wanna spend six months on it. I'd like to put out some live things. We recorded some of the concerts on this tour, but unfortunately the old record company won't let us re-record the songs that are already out. So we're gonna make one side of the album live. Then we're gonna record some more songs in November and a new single. It should come out at the end of January.

"After that, Mick Taylor's gonna do some recording in Los Angeles, I'm gonna do a bit of work with Billy Preston, help him write some new songs. Maybe I'll make an album on my own."

But with whom?
Mick: "I haven't contacted them yet. Mostly Americans. Maybe Mick Taylor, maybe Eric Clapton. Billy will play on some of it. I've got a lot of songs that I've never done with the Stones that I don't think we will do. I'd like to do them at some point."

Elsewhere, Mick confirms that he's "written a lot of songs for a solo album, but I don't know what the format will be, because I'm just not sure myself."

Bill Wyman is also seriously considering a solo record.
Bill: "I've been thinking of doing an album for at least nine months. I seriously sat down a year ago and started trying to write some songs and I got a lot of songs together. It's just a matter of finding some people and having the time to go to America and record it . . . I'd like to use a lot of people in America like Roy Buchanan, Ry Cooder, Jim Keltner and Dallas Taylor."

Mick also tells the tabloids that he plans to relocate to New York.
Mick: "France is quiet; there's no music in France. You can't call up a session, so that's why New York is better for me. We don't like it. It's unsettling, but on the other hand we did get into a bit of a rut in England

and I've changed completely since I left. There's only a few things you need: books and clothes. I've got it down to one suitcase and one guitar now, and a few cassette machines."

Bill agrees that France is not where it's at.
Bill: "It's a dead music scene there. There's nowhere to go out most of the time, no clubs to go to really. Not many people to meet and get to know who are into the same sort of thing as you are. It's difficult to communicate because I don't speak much French, but the weather is certainly okay and I do like the food."
Q: "So are you there for tax reasons?"
Bill (grinning): "No, I just love France. I just wanted a change."

Keith's only real concern is that the Stones keep him busy.
Keith: "Any time I'm not touring or making a record I feel redundant. I turn to all kinds of weird chemicals to make up for it, and that's not good for me. People are always saying about me they can't understand how I've survived so long – they've got this image of me – but that's because so many of them are weak in their nervous systems and imagine everyone else is too. The worst damage you can see around is alcohol . . . People's idea about junk is equivalent to what people think about meths drinkers and winos, who are greedy, who are the dregs, who just go over the top. You should take the trouble to know what the stuff does, how it works, and decide physically and mentally whether you're capable of handling it."

SATURDAY, 8 DECEMBER 1973

It is reported that the Stones have recorded five cuts in ten days at a new studio in Munich. Faces guitarist Ron Wood joined them for a night, but more importantly, a new song featuring Mick and Ron on guitars, Willie Weeks on bass, Kenny Jones on drums, and David Bowie on backing vocals has been recorded at Wood's Richmond home in his eight-track basement studio.
Mick: "It was all done in three takes. I just wrote it very quickly one day . . . I suppose it does sound as though it could have come off any one of our first three albums, 'cept that the chorus, it's a bit rock'n'roll revival in parts, don't you think? But that was done quite unconsciously."

Keith later explained the genesis of the song – 'It's Only Rock'n'Roll' – to Nick Kent in ZigZag *magazine.*
Keith: "The track itself was originally recorded at Ronnie Wood's place with Mick, Ronnie and Kenny Jones. (Bowie was) only handclappin'.

And we even wiped 'em off and overdubbed new ones! Mick took the track down to Munich, and when I heard it I thought, 'Great.' It said what it had to say very well, what with everybody running around trying to write the definitive rock'n'roll song. It was put very simply and directly.

"We immediately set about re-recording it but the problem was that Kenny Jones had done a great take-off of Charlie's drumming which, for that number, even surpassed Charlie himself. So Charlie had to do a take-off of Kenny Jones doing a take-off of him and ended up so paranoid about it that I decided to leave the original track on. Mick Taylor's not on it at all. Mick Jagger's playing one guitar and I think Ronnie's playing an acoustic."

SATURDAY, 5 JANUARY 1974

After the highs of 1971–73, the Stones' showing in recent British music press polls reaches a new low. Sounds *readers virtually ignore the band in the UK categories, while the Stones merit just three mentions in the International Section:*
Best Band – 8. Rolling Stones; Best Song – 7. 'Angie'; Best Wind Instrument – 8. Bobby Keys.

Worse still, that same American establishment which, not too long ago, was banning Rolling Stones records now seems oblivious to them.
Gerald Ford (US Vice President): "Mick Jagger? Never heard of him."

SATURDAY, 2 FEBRUARY 1974

Marianne Faithfull gives an infamous, blow-by-blow account of her life and times with the Stones to Andrew Tyler in New Musical Express.
Marianne Faithfull: "My first move was to get a Rolling Stone as a boy-friend. I slept with three and then I decided the lead singer would be the best bet . . . I don't know if he was the most important because I had always understood that, in the Stones, Keith was the most important – and I think, in the beginning, I was always really in love with Keith much more than anyone else, as a fan. He's the epitome of the Romantic Hero and, if you're a middle-class girl and you've read your Byron, that's Keith Richard . . . He's turned into Count Dracula now, but he's still an injured, tortured, damned youth . . . (Mick's) cleaner. That's the thing about the Stones. That they're dirty and awful and arrogant, and Keith is still like that."

234

SUNDAY, 14 APRIL 1974

Ladies And Gentlemen: The Rolling Stones, *a concert film shot during the 1972 US tour, is premiered in New York. It disappears shortly afterwards.*
Mick: "The sound's good, the playing's good, but I think that as a film it's very boring. In fact, it's 'orrible and it's got absolutely nothing to do with me. You'll have to ask Keith about it."

FRIDAY, 10 MAY 1974

Bill Wyman becomes the first Stone to find both time and inspiration to record a solo album, Monkey Grip. *He writes and arranges everything, and plays acoustic and electric guitar, and harmonica.*
Bill: "When I first mentioned I was going to do my own album, they assumed it was going to be instrumental. When I said, 'No,' they asked, 'But who's going to sing on it?' When I told them I was, they said, 'But you can't sing!' . . . I wish they would just see it as something I need to do outside the Stones, just another project like Mick's two films or Mick Taylor's involvement with *Tubular Bells*."
Mick: "Great – he's got it off his chest at last. No one was stopping him. Mick (Taylor) wants to do one and I'd like to do one. I've never actually started one, but we could all do bits of recording in between working with the Stones. And not everything we record with the Stones comes out. Maybe now we'll have time to think and do what we want."
Bill: "If you come up with something Keith doesn't want, he'll ask you to change it – 'I'd rather you did it this way.' They were making the decisions and I wasn't strong enough to get them to do it my way because I wasn't sure. After all these years, I managed to pick up enough courage and do it my way . . . I feel like a big cloud has been lifted off my head now. Or like an aching tooth has been taken out of my head."

TUESDAY, 28 MAY 1974

Mick and Keith attend sessions for Ronnie Wood's début solo album, which continue through June, at the guitarist's home studio at The Wick in Richmond. Keith contributes two songs, 'Act Together' and 'Sure The One You Need', and plays on more than half of the album.
Ron Wood: "Yeah, (Mick and I) have been recording together. We did an old Curtis Mayfield number the other night, just making up the words.

But there's nothing that could come out of it. We're just having fun. I see a lot of Mick, but we're all working – sometimes we don't meet for months on end."

Ron: "When Keith and I first got together, I didn't know if we would hit it off, but he turned out to be the good fella I thought he was."

Keith: "I was hanging around with nothing to do. One night, Ronnie called me up and said, 'Come down, I've got this fantastic rhythm section – (bassist) Willie Weeks, (drummer) Andy Newmark.' I went down one night to see what was happening and got roped in to do a guitar overdub."

Ron: "He knew I was recording, came round to the house for a drink and ended up staying a month. Wore the ass out of all me pants, and tore me jacket, too. We had been working with rhythms, but once Keith arrived and got well into it, we had two guitars going all the time . . . The gas about playing with Keith is how smoothly our styles meshed. I'd always thought we had that street feel in common."

Keith: "Woody's album was a relief because I had no responsibility. By the time I arrived, Ron didn't know what to do next. They had lots of songs but on a first album like that it's a mistake to do only original material so I suggested doing some oldies.

". . . We rummaged around the old singles pile and we found 'Am I Grooving You', a Freddie Scott oldie that Bert Berns wrote. And the old James Ray number, 'If You Gotta Make A Fool Of Somebody', which was made famous by an English leaping gentleman (Freddie & The Dreamers). It turned out very well and to play with that rhythm section was enough of a turn-on to do those (Ronnie solo) gigs at Kilburn (13/14 July)."

Ron: "I didn't really know what I was going to do with the vocals. I didn't even know if I could sing . . . Keith's vocals sounded so good. Sometimes our voices would blend so closely that you couldn't tell the difference, same as the guitars. Then Mick would sing along and blend in with Keith, and suddenly the whole thing came together."

Keith: "The two songs I wrote were done right there at Ronnie's house early one morning. We were rather intoxicated, so we had Andy Newmark and Willie Weeks take a taxi out to Richmond. When they arrived they said, 'What are we going to play?', so I hastily ripped off 'Sure The One You Need'. It's one of those songs you like immediately. Mick later cursed me for not saving it for the Stones . . ."

A chance comment from Mick provides the inspiration for the album title.
"Hurry up – I've got me own album to do!"

Mick explains to Roy Carr in New Musical Express *why he's still not bitten the bullet.*

Mick: "Any solo album I do has gotta be good otherwise I'm not gonna put it out. Also, it's gotta be different. And it will be. I'd like to do one because I happen to be in the mood to be in the studio, and we have no plans to do any more shows this year . . . The time could be right because I'd wanna do it quickly, but most probably I'll end up doing the next Stones album."

WEDNESDAY, 3 JULY 1974

The fifth anniversary of the death of Brian Jones prompts a gathering of fans by his graveside at Cheltenham.

"We were so saddened when went up to Cheltenham to take flowers on the anniversary of the death of a close friend, Brian Jones. Although his grave was covered with flowers, which had been brought by fans from all over Europe with their hard-earned money, the founder of the greatest rock'n'roll band in the world had been forgotten not only by Mick Jagger, Bill Wyman, Charlie Watts, Keith Richard and Anita, but by all the people he trusted and called his friends, (with the exception of Shirley [Watts]). Nicholas, Chelsea."

The letter, published in New Musical Express, *prompts a response from Stones PR man, Les Perrin.*

"While understanding the sense of hurt which caused an open letter to be written by Nicholas of Chelsea (I wish he had appended his full name and address because a personal note would be in place), I think I should elucidate concerning the attitudes of other members of The Rolling Stones in connection with the anniversary of the death of Brian Jones.

"Brian is not forgotten by Mick, Bill, Charlie, Keith or Anita – the reverse is the case and considerable thought was given to sending a floral tribute.

"After much heart-searching it was decided that – rather than the ephemeral salutation of flowers – a donation to charity should be made.

"Knowing as the boys did of Brian's personal contributions to children's funds, it was decided to donate money to the United Nations Children's Fund for relief to refugee children of Bangladesh. Normally, this matter would not be mentioned, but it is because it is felt, in this case, that an explanation is needed.

"Cordially, Leslie Perrin (Public Relations Officer For The Rolling Stones)."

FRIDAY, 26 JULY 1974

Each passing Mick Jagger birthday – he's 31 today – is now deemed worthy of comment.
Mick: "I could go on forever, ya know. I don't know about the rest of the Stones but I'll never retire. I like it. Touring is great fun. It's not something you feel like doing every day. Or even every year. But I'm never going to give it up completely."

The same day sees the release of the new single, 'It's Only Rock'n'Roll'.
Mick: "It's me anti-intellectual record."
Mick: "As soon as I'd written it, I knew it was a single. And I haven't felt that about a song for years . . . It's my answer to everybody who takes what I do, or what the band does, too seriously. It's only rock'n'roll, man, so what the hell."

The single goes Top 10 – just.

Keith is unrepentant, telling (future biographer) Barbara Charone . . .
Keith: "Everybody kept saying, 'Oh, that shouldn't be the single,' but to me that song is classic even if it isn't a Top 10. The title alone is classic and that's the whole thing about it. I mean, that had to be a single. So what if it didn't sell fantastic amounts? Singles are no longer our main thing anyway; it was just a taster for the album . . . Besides, rock'n'roll is such a hip word again. I remember when The Rolling Stones would leap up and tear their hair out if anyone called us a rock'n'roll band. We played rhythm and blues . . ."
Mick: "I like the new record – and the next album – because it's more upfront. It's a grower . . . it only takes a couple of listens to get into it. It's definitely much more instant than 'Angie'. That really did get bum reviews."

Not everyone is convinced by the song. Suzanne Vickery of Eastcote, Ruislip, is moved to express her disapproval in a letter to Melody Maker.
"How the mighty are fallen! It had to happen of course. I have just heard the Stones' new single and they commit the ultimate sin by including 'Rock And Roll' in the title. Not content with that the incessantly repeated lyrics sound more like a Gary Glitter song. It trudges along with a boring, plodding beat. Surely now, there can be no hope left?"

The accompanying promo video proves equally frothy . . .

Mick: "Oh, that was detergent. Most unpleasant and it took such a long time to do. We couldn't have the lights and cameras inside the tent in case we all got electrocuted and we had to be insured for quite a lot of money just to shoot the scene."

Keith: "Oh, those suits, they came up right at the last moment, simply because nobody wanted to get their own clothes messed up in all that foam. Poor old Charlie nearly drowned – he was the first to get it because we forgot he was sitting down."

During this time, two lurid biographies on Mick Jagger are published; one by J. Marks (author of Rock . . . And Other Four Letter Words*), the other by American writer, Anthony Scaduto, who had previously published an equally controversial tome on Bob Dylan. Predictably, Mick is scathing about both, telling the NME's Roy Carr . . .*

Mick: "They were mostly fictional, written by people that had never met me, and wrote them based on rumours or their imagination. J. Marks' book you've got to read. It's pretty bad . . . I don't want to see another book about me again . . . Anthony Scaduto wrote about me and Brian Jones having a swordfight. It sounds very romantic, me and Brian jumping about, fighting with swords, but it didn't occur . . . It's all pretty sick really. I expect he'll be writing a book on John Lennon next."

The source for some of the more outrageous fiction is an estranged flame . . .

Mick: "Most of it is the stoned ramblings of Marianne Faithfull's nostalgic fantasies. It's all pure fiction. Even Scaduto knows that she made most of it up. Now if (the knife fight) had happened, I'd say, 'Yeah,' and admit it, but the truth is that it just didn't happen . . . What you have is Marianne Faithfull just repeating herself over and over and over again. Scaduto just buys her all the right things she needs to make her talk."

Keith: "I've only read excerpts, though Mick's told me about it. I can't bring myself to listen to somebody verbally raping Marianne Faithfull because she'll say anything. I mean, the guy writes about Jagger and doesn't even approach me, who has known him longer than anybody else apart from his mother and father."

Mick explains to Disc *magazine that he's far more interested in playing roles other than Mick Jagger.*

Mick: "I can't think of anything more dull than my life. I've been approached by people who want to film my life story – I'd like to do more films, but they'll probably wait until I'm dead for that one. I get a lot of offers, usually strange roles. Demon parts. Evil parts. I don't want to be typecast in that way. I'm working on a screenplay at the moment – about my impressions as a child and as an adult."

Perhaps this renewed enthusiasm for film reflects the malaise that, he explains to Disc magazine's Lon Goddard, lies at the heart of the contemporary music scene.
Mick: "I hate to intellectualise about songs, but the face of rock'n'roll is due for a change. I predict this is the last year for the Glitters and the Stardusts – that phase is ending. These here-today, gone-tomorrow people are just clichés who have been around before. We've got to have different artists all the time; people are ready for something new. Look at Sweet. They know they have to do something different. Don't ask me where music is going – I always go my own way, anyway – but only some people will survive the next five years. A lot of black artists will: Stevie Wonder, Marvin Gaye and so on. Not the Rubettes or Showaddywaddy. The ones who will survive are surviving already. Apart from that, people are buying sounds. How many hits will George McRae have? That's what it's all about . . . records from nowhere."

Roy Carr wonders whether rich rock stars are part of the problem.
Mick: "Getting rich quick is all part of the rock'n'roll fantasy. For most people, the fantasy is driving around in a big car, having all the chicks you want and being able to pay for it all. It always has been and it still is. Anyone who says it isn't is talking bullshit. I'll tell you, I could never have gotten as rich as I am through any other means . . . If I wanted to get as rich as I possibly could then I'd play Las Vegas as a soloist."

SATURDAY, 17 AUGUST 1974

Keith Richard's biggest fantasy is getting back on the road and deciding what drink he and Bobby Keys will nominate for that particular tour.
Keith: "We started off on Rusty Nails, that's Drambuie and scotch, then it was Tequila and the last one was champagne and orange juice, which was a nice drink to get down before the eggs arrived in the morning after a show."

SATURDAY, 31 AUGUST 1974

However, as Pete Erskine understands, it's what Keith gets up to when he's not on the road that readers really want to know about.

240

Keith: "I've been in the Swiss mountains for months ever since the last tour . . ."

And undergoing a blood transfusion in a bid to beat off the demon drug habits?
Keith: "That's beautiful. I'd love to do it just because I'm sure that eating motorway food for ten years has done my blood no good at all. The only time I've ever been to Switzerland is to ski . . . I gave up drugs when the doctor told me I had six months to live. If you're gonna get wasted, get wasted elegantly."

Shortly afterwards, Keith teases . . .
Keith: "I'm changing my image. I've arranged for a whole series of dental appointments in Switzerland. I only get ill when I give up drugs."

MONDAY, 23 SEPTEMBER 1974

Ron Wood's début solo album, I've Got My Own Album To Do, *is released.*
Keith: "The success of the album's got nothing to do with me. It's all to Ron's credit. If you've got a good rhythm section, you're 75 per cent there. It just goes to show that you don't need huge professional studios and 24-track monster machines to make a good album. It was a real pleasure to go back a few years in technology . . .

"Most of the magic moments of rock'n'roll have come about through sheer overloading of the meters. And that gets harder and harder each year with all the sophisticated equipment."

TUESDAY, 1 OCTOBER 1974

A visibly stoned Keith Richard sits down with Bob Harris to preview the forthcoming Stones album on BBC-TV's Old Grey Whistle Test.
Q: "When did you record the album? And when did you finish?"
Keith: "We started before Xmas, about three weeks after we finished the European tour. We had Billy Preston . . . We recorded in Munich, a very good studio. The band was very hot, and we cut half the album in two weeks. Then everybody split for Xmas, and in February we came back to Munich with Nicky Hopkins on keyboards for another two weeks. That was basically it. We left it till April when we came to London and Mick and I started doing the vocals. The mixing took about six weeks . . . two months."
Q: "The team is very much the same . . . plus Nicky and Billy Preston."
Keith: "And of course Stu, our favourite pianist."

Q: "How does the production of a Stones album work, Keith? Is it basically you and Mick?"

Keith: "This was the first one without Jimmy Miller. We decided we'd like to have a go again ourselves. The last time, *Satanic Majesties* received mixed reviews. It was quite easy to do, maybe because the band had just come off the road and everyone was into playing."

Q: "Are all the band involved all the time, Keith?"

Keith: "Basically, everybody's together to cut the tracks. After that everybody leaves it to Mick and I because they get confused sitting in the studio saying, 'This should be louder.' Mick and I struggle along by ourselves."

Q: "Has working with Ronnie Wood motivated you to think about doing more things outside the Stones, Keith?"

Keith: "Well, I've got one little thing I want to do, in Jamaica with some Rastafarians. They're very heavy, happy dudes, they play with drums, they chant and they've got some amazing songs. They roped me in to play guitar because they've never had a guitar around before, so I got my reggae chopsticks out. When I get back there, I'd like to get it down on tape properly."

Q: "Do you see many bands you'd like to record? Are you thinking of making the Rolling Stones label more active?"

Keith: "I'd love to, but by the time we've done our things, there never seems to be time to go out and find a band that nobody's heard. There's a lot of bands I'd love to record, like The Meters, and Little Feat. It'd be a gas to do that."

Q: "What's happening with the Stones? Are you planning a tour?"

Keith: "I think we're going to the States in the spring. We were supposed to be going this year, but we finished the record instead. Maybe a few gigs around Xmas would be nice. I'd like to get on stage again."

Q: "Do you want to play smaller venues?"

Keith: "It's kind of selfish to go into a city where 60,000 people want to see you and say, 'We wanna play a 3,000 seater hall,' because the other 57,000 just have to lump it. The thing is to do the big ballpark and then do the small theatre as well, so 63,000 people get to see us."

Q: "How many people are involved now in getting a Stones tour on the road?"

Keith: "Forty or fifty people get carried about on an American tour, slightly less on a European tour. It takes such a long time to set the tour up."

Q: "Do you enjoy touring?"

Keith: "I love it. It's lifeblood for me. Any band that doesn't play live is only half a band as far as I'm concerned, because that is where it all comes from. I think with this new album you can feel that we'd come off stage three weeks before."

Q: "Are you thinking of touring Britain?

Keith: "I'd like to play Britain. I wouldn't mind doing a few gigs!"

Elsewhere, Keith sings the praises of his Rolling Stones sidekick, Mick Taylor.

Keith: "Since the first night he came along, it's been a turn-on to play with him. Looking back now, we weren't half as good two years ago as we are now, and we're improving all the time. Live, we swap roles all the time. It's more than just rhythm and lead, and it's really liberated me having Mick there . . . Obviously he could go out and do the whole solo blues guitar virtuoso trip, but he's not into that on any level. Like me, he's more interested in creating something with the band."

Mick Taylor appears to be satisfied with his role within the Stones . . .

Mick Taylor: "I don't know how long we'll go on but there's still so many things we can do as long as we keep progressing onstage. There's nothing more pathetic than rock stars living on past glories and nostalgia. Nothing."

. . . even when Barbara Charone quizzes him about a solo album.

Mick Taylor: "I wouldn't do a solo album as such, because I don't think of myself as a solo artist. I think of myself as a musician who likes to accompany other people. If I did an album it wouldn't be a solo album but a group album by a bunch of musicians."

But then, Keith, who is asked the same question, is seated next to him.

Keith: "Strangely, I've hardly thought about it. Every once in a while it crosses my mind, but I know that if I really wanted to do one there'd be no stopping me. Right now, it doesn't seem terribly important that I do one. I manage to keep pretty busy with the Stones.

"My own album? Naw, I've never wanted to front a band . . . too much responsibility. If I was to do a solo album, I'd see it happening track by track over a couple of years. But it won't be for a while especially as I've only got one track and it's not completed."

FRIDAY, 18 OCTOBER 1974

It's Only Rock'n'Roll – *the band's final collaboration with producer Jimmy Miller – is released.*

Keith: "We'd come to a point with Jimmy where it'd got to be a habit, a way of life, for Jimmy to do one Stones album a year. He'd got over the initial excitement which you can feel on *Beggars Banquet* and *Let It Bleed*. Mick and I also wanted to try and do it ourselves because we really felt we knew much more about techniques and recording and had our own ideas of how we wanted things to go."

The pair adopt the production name, The Glimmer Twins.

Keith: "It's extraordinary how that name came about. Back in '68, Mick, Marianne Faithfull, Anita Pallenberg and me took a boat to Rio which was full of these upper-class English people, all drinking like mad, pink gins and pink champagne, crowding the bar. I was dressed in a diaphanous djellaba, Mexican shoes and a tropical army hat. After a while they discovered who we were and became very perturbed. They started asking us questions: 'What are you really trying to do?' and 'Do try and explain to us what this whole thing is about!' We never answered them and after a few days, one woman stepped forward from the group and said: 'Can't you give us just a glimmer?' Mick turned to me and said: 'We're the Glimmer Twins.'"

Mick: "They're just another of our pseudonyms, because our motto has always been 'Give Us A Glimmer!'"

Keith: "Rock'n'roll can't be planned or prepared. You can have a few basic structures, though. I wrote maybe three of the songs in the studio just warming up before the rest of the guys arrived and Mick had a couple that he had ready. That's the way it goes. I'm not the sort of person who sits down at home with a guitar, writes a whole song and says, 'That's how I hear it,' because I play in a band and leave it up to them to tell me how it should go for them."

Mick: "The album is a very mixed bag. There's even a bossa nova, a couple of slow ones, some ballads, a Caribbean tune. It's a lot different from the last one anyway."

Keith: "*Goat's Head Soup*, to me, was a marking time album. I like it in many ways but I don't think it has the freshness that this one has."

The Jamaican influence, surprisingly absent on Goat's Head Soup, *finally filters through on one song, 'Luxury', as Keith tells ZigZag.*

Keith: "That is a bona fide reggae on-beat being played there, no matter what anyone may tell you. The song's mine, basically. It all came about while I was driving from the Munich Hilton to the studios, fucked right out of my head and the radio was playing this soul number – I still don't know the title of it. But it had this chord sequence . . . which turned out later as 'Luxury'. I just played it as a straight rock'n'roll thing until Charlie turned the beat around and it all fell spontaneously into place with Mick getting into that whole West Indian bit. That really is a prime typical Stones track in the way that it fell together by accident."

Keith: "People have such preconceived ideas about what they want from The Rolling Stones that on first hearing, our albums don't come up to those expectations. It's only afterwards when they've heard it a few times that they end up liking it. That's especially true with our last couple of albums. Even though this new one seems to have lots of long tracks, the feel is quite immediate."

But is it the definitive Stones album?
Keith: "We haven't made it yet. It's definitely still to come."

Mick Taylor is absolutely certain it's not.
Mick Taylor: "The new album has some interesting songs, like the synthesizer part I did on 'Time Waits For No One'. Even though Mick and Keith write most of the songs, we all contribute. Sure, I've got the freedom to play when and what I want. The guitar on 'Time Waits . . .' isn't your standard lead guitar . . . Some of the songs I like and some of them I don't like but the album is well balanced. Mick and Keith have the final say in the end about what songs are left out, but five people at a mixing session is no good. With five opinions it takes forever."

The sleeve – designed by Rock Dreams *artist Guy Peellaert – provides a major talking point. Though unlike his sleeve for David Bowie's* Diamond Dogs*, it manages to avoid being altered.*
Keith: "Ours is cherubic and naïve by comparison – not a genital in sight."
Keith: "It looks as though all of those women are adoring The Rolling Stones, but then you notice that the people on the top left are into these chicks on the right and there are other chicks who're completely into a different bag, the ones who've seen it all. I mean, I see Bill Wyman in drag all over the place."

The irony of the Stones following Bowie's example by using Peellaert for the sleeve design is completely lost on Mick.
Mick: "I do admire David in a way because he's doing something which a part of me would really like to do – I don't know if I can be more explicit about that but I hope you know what I mean, right? I mean, 'Knock On Wood' was awful, right, and that *David Live* . . . Christ, I mean, if I'd got the kind of reviews that he got for that album, I would honestly never record again. Never. But at the same time . . . and Christ, it's got to a

point where I daren't even wear a new pair of shoes in front of David now because he'd probably nick the idea."

With the album out, Keith restates his desire to get back on the road.
Keith: "I like playing live because it helps everything else. It helps me write songs, it helps me improve my playing, it gives me ideas and it stimulates me. But I have to respect the fact that there are other members of the band, say Bill and Charlie, who have a need for a really stable home life in one place. They need that anchor, whereas my old lady and myself are very nomadic sort of people."

Mick has other plans . . .
Mick: "On December 7, we are going to the Munich studios where we made *It's Only Rock'n'Roll*. We will record half of the album in Germany and the other half in either Canada or America."

But before they get there, Mick Taylor has an announcement to make.
"MICK TAYLOR LEAVES"

The official statement, issued on Thursday, 12 December, states that:
"After five and a half years, Mick wishes a change of scene and wants the chance to try out new ventures, new endeavours. While we are all sorry that he is going, we wish him great success and much happiness."
Mick Taylor: "The last five and a half years with the Stones have been very exciting, and proved to be a most inspiring period. And as far as my attitude to the other four members is concerned, it is one of respect for them, both as musicians and as people. I have nothing but admiration for the group, but I feel now is the time to move on and do something new."

With a bit of journalistic coaxing, Taylor opened up a little . . .
Mick Taylor: "I'd worked with them in such a way and for so long, that I didn't think I could go much further without some different musicians. So when this chance with Jack Bruce came up, well, I wanted to be with him. I'd known for several months that he wanted to put together a new band. We'd played a lot together lately and we'd really hit it off. It was all purely musical reasons. There was no personal animosity in the split – no row, no quibbling or squabbling."

Temporarily – and uncharacteristically – wrong-footed, Mick Jagger saves face by announcing that the Stones are heading to the States in 1975 for some 'new-concept' live shows.
Mick: "We'll be touring extensively from next May. We shall be playing

very few old numbers and the act will mainly be a showcase for new material."

But what about your second guitarist?
Mick: "No doubt we can find a brilliant 6′ 3″ blond guitarist who can do his own make-up. Mick's departure doesn't really affect the plans. By then, we'll probably have a new man."

It takes New Musical Express *writer Nick Kent to get closer to the real story.*
Mick: "What pisses me off is not that he wanted to leave. It's the way he left. We all met in Geneva three weeks ago to talk about the album, we booked time at Musicland (Munich), discussed our upcoming tour of the States. Never once did he voice any doubts about continuing with the group. He obviously had a lot of 'troubles' – personal problems that are nothing to do with us or the press. I don't honestly know the true nature of them . . .

"I was in Managua, Nicaragua, when I received a call from the office to say that Mick Taylor wasn't coming to the Munich sessions. Then I received a call saying Mick Taylor wasn't going anywhere anymore with the Stones. I flew back to London, we went to the Clapton concert together and then had a heart-to-heart at a party at Robert Stigwood's. He said, 'I'd like to leave the group,' and I said 'Fine.' He seemed a bit unsure. I mean, he obviously wanted to do something else, but then again it's a bit of a gamble. I am, however, very, *very* disappointed that he's leaving because he's such a great musician."

Soon enough, adversity was being transformed into bravado.
Mick: "Personally, if you want to know my opinion, I think the split's a very good thing . . . I don't think it could have come at a better time. I mean, the Stones have used him and got what they wanted out of him . . . I mean, I think Mick is a great musician and I liked him as a bloke but he wasn't one of The Rolling Stones. His sound was different. I mean, Keith's guitar sound *is* the Stones sound, right."

Despite the blond's bombshell, the remaining four Stones continue their plans to begin work on a new album in Munich.
Mick: "It would have been nice if Ron (Wood) had come down for the sessions, but he's touring at the moment. I don't know about permanently finding someone. It's going to take a little while. In the meantime, I want to play with a lot of people . . . There's a lot of people I could dig working with. I've played with Ron a lot. I had one very good night playing with

247

Jeff Beck recently. There's Eric (Clapton), too. They're all great friends of mine."

Melody Maker *celebrates the arrival of 1975 with further speculation concerning the Stones' vacancy.*

"STONES' SHOPPING LIST"

They put forward ten names, with star ratings, among them . . .

Jeff Beck
★★★★

"Prone to problems of temperament, due to basic shyness and an occasional crisis of confidence . . . Might be induced to wear the odd sparkle or backcomb his hair if Jagger insists."

Mick Ronson
★★★★★

"Mick's guitar work, with flowing, angular lines, could nicely complement Keith's . . . He would be a useful addition to the Stones in many capacities and perhaps inject new vitality and direction to their music."

Andy Somers (alias Summers)
★

"Would love to work with the Stones and is an old friend of Mick Taylor."

Peter Frampton
★★★★

"With a well-defined style, he could bring guts and imagination to the Stones guitar section."

Ry Cooder
★

"Could lead the band back to a more serious role in rock, and inject a fresh strain of authenticity to their music."

Steve Hillage
★★★★

"Gong's music, Steve has often said, is essentially feminine and far removed from the macho Stones stance."

Also on the list is the band's mentor, Alexis Korner, who shares his disbelief with the paper's Karl Dallas.
Alexis Korner: "Oh, no way! Image-wise I should think I'm totally

wrong for them. It never entered my mind. I just thought it was high time that someone went over to Keith Richard and said, 'Hey, let's play, man,' because I knew he would appreciate it. I went over because Keith's done some recording for me and he's worked on my latest album. I did a version of 'Get Off Of My Cloud'. He played some really nice guitar and sang beautifully on it.

"In fact we sat and looked over the list of prospective players that was published in the *Melody Maker* and we laughed, I must say, to a certain extent because Mick had not heard of half the people suggested. Steve Marriott had come over with me 'cos he wanted to talk to Keith about various things. Steve would have been a better bet than me, but I don't think that would have been a practical proposition either."

The likeliest lad, Ron Wood, apparently counts himself out of the running.
Ron Wood: "The Stones probably have influenced me more than any other band. Under different circumstances, I suppose, it could have happened. I get along really well with Mick Jagger and Keith Richard. I guess they know I could do the job – we play together quite a bit. But I am a member of the Faces and that's what's really important to me. Sure, it was tempting, and it was an enormous compliment to be considered. But, deep down, we all knew it could never happen."
Rod Stewart: "Ronnie's my best mate. There's never been anyone closer to me than Woody. I'm taking bets that it won't happen. I know him too well."

The Stones' office insists, "They are not in any hurry to find a permanent replacement for Mick Taylor, and they intend to use various guest guitarists on the new album."

WEDNESDAY, 22 JANUARY 1975

The four Stones regroup for sessions in Rotterdam, where they operate a revolving door policy of guitarists. Among those invited are Leslie West, Peter Frampton, Shuggie Otis, Wayne Perkins, and Rory Gallagher, who spends two days with the band.
David Oddy (Gallagher's manager): "Rory has been friendly with Keith Richard for some time, and it was at Keith's invitation that he joined the Stones in Holland. Of course, this was only a guest appearance, and there is no question of Rory joining the Stones on a permanent basis."

Towards the end of the three week session, Jeff Beck drops by for a weekend.

Among the covers he cuts with the group are Max Middleton's 'Freeway Jam' and the Martha & The Vandellas' classic, 'Heatwave'.

Jeff Beck: "I went over there and I found out they wanted me to join. I couldn't believe that. I mean, the money was tempting. I could have made a fortune and never had to work again, but I would have been half-dead and my reputation would have been shot."

While the speculation continues, Mick Taylor re-emerges with some advice for anyone with their eye on the job.

Mick Taylor: "I knew it would be difficult. It's not that there aren't any good guitarists, there's loads of guitarists that could probably join the Stones and fit perfectly on a musical level. But . . . you've got to have that something extra. It's a question of your personality. It's necessary to blend in with Mick and Keith's lifestyle in a natural way. And I had the time to do it . . . It was different for me because when I joined it was like the rebirth of the band, not just because I joined but because up until then they hadn't played together for years."

Sounds' Barbara Charone finally tempts Mick Taylor to talk frankly about the split.

Mick Taylor: "For a long time I felt that I wasn't developing musically and that began affecting me as a person. My musical potential was wasting away. I had already decided to leave the Stones before I met Jack . . . The Stones' music is the same now as it was five years ago, just more refined. Sure I added a lot in terms of musical ideas. But we never went far enough on record, never did enough of what we were capable of . . . My playing tended to get very mechanical. There just wasn't enough depth for me to feel satisfied after playing the same material every night. I used to come off stage feeling bored."

Keith: "I admire somebody who can walk out on a situation like that. Walk out on the fucking Rolling Stones . . . Mick came in the band as a guitar player and he went out, in his own mind, as a composer who could play piano, bass, drums as well as being a better guitar player. As far as he was concerned, he developed so much musically from 1969 to '75 that he couldn't do whatever he wanted to do within the Stones. Personally, I think he was wrong . . ."

Meanwhile, a Munich bartender dispenses some advice.

Barman: "Doing some German TV?"
Mick: "We don't do TV."
Barman: "A record?"

Mick: "Yeah, a record."

Barman: "You should retire. Buy a farm, milk the cows, plenty of fresh air, have your whisky."

Mick: "At 31? I've tried all that. It's boring. Maybe at 61, not 31 . . . Asshole."

Keith: "The Rolling Stones ain't gonna end just because a guitar player dies or leaves. It just ain't so.

"At the moment I'm only interested in a guitar player who's gonna come in and be totally committed to what the band's all about even if it means learning his history, getting it down, listening to what Taylor's done, what Brian's done, then deciding what he wants to do. Which all comes back to the band's inherent ability to adapt, a personality trait integral to survival."

SATURDAY, 22 MARCH 1975

Guitarists Harvey Mandel and Wayne Perkins are invited to the latest round of recording sessions at Musicland in Munich.

Mick: "Harvey Mandel was recommended through a friend of a friend. He was very nice, but he's a kind of strange guitar player. I think you can hear it on that track ('Hand Of Fate'). He plays really strange effects which he has permanently on. Wayne Perkins was recommended by Eric Clapton. He's done a lot of session work, but he hasn't done a lot of work on the road, which put me off him a bit. They were all very nice, so it was difficult. The more I hear it, he sounds very much like Mick Taylor in places."

MONDAY, 31 MARCH 1975

Both guitarists sit in on the session for a new song, 'Memory Motel'.

Mick: "They both played very nicely on this one 'cos Keith and I don't play any guitars on it. It's quite a strange line-up in a way, 'cos there are no overdubs – it was all done live, two pianos, two guitars . . . We were trying them out, really. We had these sessions booked and we wanted to cut some tracks, 'cos we had some songs to do. It was one way of doing it. It made the recording rather long and laborious, though."

By early spring, Keith's mind is made up.

Keith: "I'm pretty certain that when we go onstage on 3 June, it will be Wayne with us. I'd be happy with the man we've got here. In the first few sessions, he's shown more promise in a much shorter amount of time than Mick Taylor did. Still, everybody says we're an English rock'n'roll band. I personally don't give a shit. I mean, The Faces got a Japanese bass player."

Then has second thoughts . . .
Keith: "I thought Wayne Perkins was great. He's a lovely guitar player but he's too much like Mick Taylor in one respect. It would have been lovely to have him but he was American and we had to own up that we were an English rock band. That became so obvious when Ronnie walked into the studio."

WEDNESDAY, 2 APRIL 1975

Ron Wood gets his invite.
Ron: "I received a phone call from Mick while I was in LA. He said, 'Do you remember what we said? That I wouldn't ring you unless we really needed you. Well, we really need you! So could you possibly come?' I said, 'Great, I was planning to come over and see you anyway.'

"The first track that I cut was 'Hey Negrita'. Keith and me had got that riff together back at the hotel. I arrived a bit late, and he said, 'What was that lick again?' I started playing it, and we did about two run-throughs then cut the track live. There were no overdubs on that except for Billy Preston's piano."

MONDAY, 14 APRIL 1975

The Rolling Stones' office issues a press statement.
"It is confirmed today by Mick Jagger that Ronnie Wood, lead guitarist with the British group, The Faces will be accompanying the Rolling Stones when they undertake a tour of North and South America which is due to start in June . . . This arrangement is in no way permanent . . ."
Ron Wood: "What am I doing?! I'm with these blokes till 14 August, then I go straight out with The Faces, then with these guys again. Then I have a decision to make! It changed when they finally said, 'Look, we aren't gonna do the tour if you don't do it.' So I said, 'It's serious then?' I'd known all along that I'd like to do it, but I hadn't dared to think about it too long. Same as they hadn't, because they like our band as much as we like theirs. And I always think of The Faces before I do anything. But I thought, 'Well, they can't blame me, really.'"
Mick: "He had to please me and Keith. I can tell a good guitar player

but Keith can tell better than me. Remember, Keith used to be the lead guitarist for The Rolling Stones. Woody seems a natural in the respect that both he and Keith are brilliant rhythm guitarists. It allows a certain cross-trading of riffs not previously possible. They can both play solos; maybe Keith's going to have to play more solos.

"I wanted someone that was easy to get on with, that was a good player and was used to playing on stage. It's quite a lot to ask someone to come and do a big American tour with a band like the Stones. Not that I think the Stones are any big deal, but it tends to be a bit of a paralysing experience for people. Woody can sing a little, his personality seems to fit the bill and onstage he's got a lot of style. And it's *got* to be fun on the road. That's what it's all about, isn't it?"

Ian Stewart, the genuine 'sixth Stone', gives a rare interview and explains to Lisa Robinson in New Musical Express *just how central Mick is to the Stones' organisation.*
Stu: "You've got to admire Mick because of what he takes on. Most groups just get onstage and play and everything else is left to managers, record producers, accountants and other staff members. Mick literally supervises everything. He has most of the original ideas and he usually wins his arguments with advisers who tell him what he can and can't do . . . Mick is always on top of everything, more or less on behalf of the other three. He could probably make a lot more money doing movies. He could do a single album with other people and he could probably do a tour with Billy Preston and some other people if he wanted to. I sometimes wonder why he takes all the responsibility for the Rolling Stones. I know he loves doing it, but it really means that he has to work 365 days a year."

And Keith?
Stu: "Keith plays and that's the end of it. He doesn't want to know about anything else."

THURSDAY, 1 MAY 1975

The Stones announce their forthcoming 'Tour of The Americas' from a flatbed truck on Fifth Avenue, New York City. The shows will be augmented by various theatrical devices – a dragon, a lotus stage, a rope and a giant phallus, apparently.
Mick: "I enjoy all those things. Some people say, 'Why do you use these gimmicks?', others say they wish we used more. I think it's nice to use those things. All the halls hold 18,000 or 19,000 people; they're very large.

Those things, like the dragon or the big phallic symbol, get people involved. They can be seen from the back, so I think those things are worthwhile. Also, they're funny. The swinging is my favourite part of the show."

One man's amusement is, of course, another man's lifeline.
Keith: "I can't live without being on the road. Every minute spent off the road, I either turn into an alcoholic or a junkie 'cause I've got nothing else to do. It's just a waste of time. I can turn into anything: a Dr Jekyll and Mr Hyde, a psychedelic treat, a Jehovah's Witness, a junkie – anything can happen 'cause I'm not doing *that*."

Or another man's burden . . .
Charlie: "I hate touring. It's a love/hate relationship for me. I love playing live, although after a while it gets at you, you know. I love the playing, I hate the fact that many people have turned up to see you, and they expect something. And I hate living in hotel rooms, always have done. Nothing annoys me more than unpacking them bloody suitcases! You know, financially, mentally, in every respect, I like being this close to friends, you know, Mick and Keith and (percussionist) Ollie (Brown). But getting on a plane, as good as the one we've got, and packing the suitcase, as good as the one I've got, is a drag. It's no life. I mean, I hate leaving my family and all that, but I've done it for 12 years or longer and I don't know what I'd do if I didn't do it."

America's reactionary moral forces wouldn't know where to turn if the Stones weren't there to abuse. Over to Steve Dunleavy from the National Star *. . .*
"IT'S TIME WE EXORCISED THIS DEMONIC INFLUENCE OVER OUR CHILDREN"
"Mick Jagger should come to America more often. I say that because it does us good, really good to look at ourselves squarely in the eye and see where we have failed. Where have we failed that this pimple-faced disciple of dirt is a hero, a rootin' tootin' hero to our teenage kids? We have this pale-faced foreigner, this Englishman, getting $10 a seat from our kids to see him perform. And what do they see? They are blitzkrieged by a tightly packaged excess of four-letter words and tacky smut.

"Okay, squares like me can live with that outrage. But what I can't tolerate, and won't, damn it, is seeing him come to our shores and bombard our kids with filth. No it's not our kids' faults. It's our fault. Somewhere between telling ourselves that we must 'be modern', must 'keep up with the changing world' – we forgot to tell them a few things –

like the timeless values that have made us great people. Things that have a lot to do with God, a flag and a country."

SATURDAY, 5 JULY 1975

Bang on cue, Keith and Ronnie are arrested in Fordyce, Arkansas. Keith is charged with possessing an offensive weapon.
Keith: "I bent down to change the waveband on the radio, and the car swerved slightly. A police patrol vehicle then pulled out from a lay-by and stopped us. I was also questioned about having a concealed weapon – which turned out to be a penknife complete with tin-opener and a device for removing stones from horses' hooves."

The law appears to show a forgiving face.
Judge Tom Wynne: "The boys are okay. Although this looks bad for them, I'm a cool judge. I'm seeing what I can do. I will see they get off, don't you worry about that. I love the English."

One hour later, Wynne was off the case.
Judge Tom Wynne: "The police chief decided to take it to a higher court."

The tour may be dogged by potential bans and busts, but Mick remains remarkably cool.
Mick: "They say, 'You are married and all that, got money and settled down and all that, betcha don't feel rebellious any more.' The answer is no more and no less. I am not writing overt political songs. But I'm not complacent."

SATURDAY, 2 AUGUST 1975

Back on his favourite dependency – the concert stage – Keith, speaking on BBC Radio, from Jacksonville, midway through the tour – savours the moment.
Keith: "With Mick Taylor, the role of the guitar player was very fixed because Mick plays lead solos and I play rhythm. Because Mick is that kind of guitar player, you'll never get the kind of thing you get with Ronnie, which is throwing it around between us. It's not that one is better but this is more fun. I prefer it his way because I don't like rigidly defined rules for playing. I don't agree that so and so is a lead guitar and so and so is a rhythm guitar. We're all just guitar players. Playing with Ronnie is a lot more how Brian and I started in '62–'63."

Mick, meanwhile, gets quizzed about loneliness . . .
Mick: "Lonely? No, not lonely at all. Why should I be? I have my dearest friends with me, Keith, Charlie . . . Most of the band are my friends, and a lot of other people who have been my friends for years. It's not like I'm on tour and I'm the Lonely Rock Star. I mean, forget it . . ."

. . . and that perennial ageing question.
Mick: "There is a perpetual adolescent influence, because of what I was doing when I was 18. I mean, the room I had at the Olympic Hotel in Seattle is the same room I had in 1964. Instead of travelling on commercial planes we've got our own, but it's still the same thing . . . Obviously being in a rock band makes you more adolescent than if you worked for IBM and really had to worry about your future. I don't worry about the future. I'm living out my adolescent dreams perpetually."

"Who The Fuck Is Mick Jagger?" (*from a T-shirt worn on tour by Keith*)

FRIDAY, 8 AUGUST 1975

The US tour concludes at the Rich Stadium in Buffalo, New York. Keith bows out on a high.
Keith: "This band is less slick and sophisticated sounding than the other one at its best when everybody was in tune and could hear each other. This is a lot funkier, dirtier and rougher and a lot more exciting."

Back home, it is reported that Mick Taylor has quit the Jack Bruce Band after a "personality conflict".
A spokesman for the band says, "Jack was very upset because Mick walked out 90 minutes before recording sessions were due to begin."

The Stones office suggests that a reunion between Taylor and the Rolling Stones was "highly unlikely".

FRIDAY, 14 NOVEMBER 1975

A double album collection, Rolled Gold, *is released by the Stones' old label, Decca. The advertisements claim:*
"Seven years of the Rolling Stones . . . They could be the best years of your life."

MONDAY, 8 DECEMBER 1975

Rod Stewart quits the Faces.

Tony Toon (spokesman): "Rod feels he can no longer work in a situation where the group's lead guitarist, Ron Wood, seems to be permanently on loan to The Rolling Stones . . . Rod doesn't think Ron Wood can do two jobs at once."

THURSDAY, 26 FEBRUARY 1976

Bill Wyman's second solo album, Stone Alone, *is released. So alone, in fact, that some public service workers thought he'd disappeared completely.*

Airport security guard: " 'Ere, didn't you used to be one of the Rolling Stones?"

Bill: "I still am."

Bill: "The album was going to be called *Don't Hold It, Eat It* but the night before I had to phone the credits through, I dreamt I saw the album in the shop with a different title. It said *Stone Alone.* I woke up and thought *Stone Alone* fits perfectly. It sums everything up . . ."

And just why is that, wonders Roy Carr.

Bill: "Over the years, Mick and Keith have written so many excellent songs that there's really no room for anyone else in the band to write. They know precisely what they're doing. Truthfully, I have no desire to do my own music within the context of the Stones. Even if we were on the road and my album went gold, I'd never perform one of my songs on a Rolling Stones show. It's got absolutely nothing to do with the group . . . The Rolling Stones are The Rolling Stones.

"I was getting to the point where I was starting to dislike recording. I started to wish they weren't happening, wishing I didn't have to record . . . It was messing me up so much inside. The solo thing has given me a chance to air my creative abilities. And it's given me more confidence to contribute to the Stones . . . I hope the album goes. It's more important than 13 years in The Rolling Stones."

So is the end in sight?

Bill: "I've never seen the band going on for a long time. I've always seen the band going on for another couple of albums and another year or two since 1962!"

The Daily Mail *comes looking for a juicier story – and gets one.*

Bill: "In an awful lot of ways Mick is a hypocrite. He will say one thing

257

and mean another. He will contradict himself every minute of the day sometimes. It's amazing the way he gets things resolved in ways I don't agree with. He has a disregard at times for other people's feelings if it interferes with something he wants to get done. I like Mick. I respect him at a certain level. But I wouldn't say he was a close friend.

"I always have a feeling Mick and Keith are not sure where I'm at, so they always put up some kind of front. They never know what I'm thinking about them. It's possible they think I don't approve of them. They think I might see through them, through their guises and little devious methods of producing records and getting results . . . I've more or less given up making suggestions at Stones sessions now."

Mick: "Bill was very upset recently. He talked to a reporter and then this piece appeared and he was quoted as saying all these things about me – like I was a hypocrite who said one thing and meant another and that we weren't close friends, all that kind of thing. I tell you, if I worried about everything I read about myself, I'd be in a mental home."

SATURDAY, 28 FEBRUARY 1976

Ron Wood is officially confirmed as a full-time member of The Rolling Stones.

Ron: "We didn't really want to make a big fanfare announcement where we invite all the press and say, 'Ronnie is now officially a member.' I've found that, just biding my time, I've come to the decision that I really enjoy being amongst the boys and slotting in as a permanent member. And as we tour around and do more things together, everyone just accepted that way."

Bill: "Ron Wood was a fresh shot in the arm. He added something new, different and exciting. We're not quite so pretty, but we're much funkier now, much raunchier. New blood is good for the band. We're kickin' more now."

FRIDAY, 12 MARCH 1976

"STONES TO TOUR – BUT THIS COULD BE THE LAST TIME!" (Record Mirror & Disc) *The band announce details of their forthcoming European tour.*

Mick: "It does get boring people asking me, 'Is this the last Stones tour?' They have been askin' that since 1964."

Keith: "Thank God there wasn't a two year lay-off this time. I couldn't survive another lay-off."

Mick: "It's not as important for me to be on the road as it is for Keith. It's the main thing I do in life but it's not the only thing. I'm quite happy off-stage and onstage. I don't think Keith would *really* like to be on the road all the time. I don't think the band would have lasted this long if we'd been on the road the whole time. I think we would have gone mad. You've got to have some other interests."

Keith begs to differ, as he tells his favourite writer of the moment, Barbara Charone.

Keith: "I don't know whether he knows it's as important to him as me. I think he knows how important it is although perhaps he's more reluctant to admit it than I am. But there ain't a band in the world that can survive without going on the road."

TUESDAY, 20 APRIL 1976

The Stones' new single is a ballad, 'Fool To Cry'.

Mick: "I always think the Rolling Stones are a rock'n'roll band and every time they say a ballad should be a single it worries me. But I don't mind. The song is quite catchy. And it will do reasonably well. I didn't think there *was* a single on the album. I guess I still care about hit records. If people didn't tell me the chart positions, I'd still look."

The same day sees the release of the long-awaited Black And Blue *album, "the audition album" as Keith calls it.*

Mick: "It's a different band. It's a whole bunch of different bands. It's a bit like *Let It Bleed*, though, in the sense that it was just the four of us. A lot of people have said we're trying to be commercial with the disco tracks but I don't think that's true. 'Hot Stuff' is just a good dance tune. I've always thought of the band as just a good dance band. There's always got to be something on each album to dance to."

The album finds Mick branching out, playing piano, electric piano and, on 'Crazy Mama', electric guitar.

Keith: "In the last five or six years it's been a big thing for Mick to be accepted as a musician, not just as a lead singer who has nothing to do until his tracks are cut. It's a closed shop thing – you're either a musician or you're not. He's a lead vocalist and most lead vocalists aren't musicians. Most of 'em are fairies!"

Mick: 'Melody' is very different, but I really like playing that because we don't often play that kind of rhythm. That's just the way Billy started knocking it out, and we all dropped in. It grabbed a bit of nostalgia for me, and I really liked doing it."

Ron: "('Cherry Oh Baby') developed through this growing interest that Keith and I had in local reggae music. We got tremendous enjoyment from being able to play two guitars off against each other. And Charlie, I think, plays incredibly native-style drums."

DJ John Peel, on the cusp of a conversion to the emergent punk rock, gives the record an enthusiastic thumbs-up.

John Peel: "Until this morning, my favourite Stones LP has been, I reckon, *Get Yer Ya-Ya's Out!* Not everyone's fave, I grant you, but I like the energy and, besides, I've always had a soft spot for live recordings. Today all of this changed with the arrival of *Black And Blue* . . . The first three tracks on side two, 'Hey Negrita', 'Melody' and the single 'Fool To Cry', make for the strongest sequence of just plain good old songs that I can recall on any Rolling Stones record. . . . So there you are. It's a new Rolling Stones LP. Maybe their best ever."

The album is advertised with a bondage photograph of a woman tied up.

Mick: "What does it matter if the Stones get off on tying girls up and beating them black and blue? Funny isn't it: a women's group get that cover banned. I've seen far worse things but they just decided to single out the Stones, probably because they wanted the publicity."

WEDNESDAY, 28 APRIL 1976

The tour kicks off at the Festhalle in Frankfurt, Germany.

Bill: "It's nice playing in those smaller halls, four or five thousand instead of those 85,000 stadiums in America. You can't have that much contact with the fans out there, where all you can see are pinheads out there."

SUNDAY, 2 MAY 1976

Speaking only weeks after Ronnie's wife Krissie is cleared of cocaine possession, Keith begins to feel uncomfortable back in his home country.

Keith: "I think it was me and Anita the police were after. Before they went into Woody's house, they broke into a little cottage at the end of his garden where I sometimes stay when I'm in Britain. I was out of the country at the time, but it looks as though they were hoping to pin something on Woody and me in one go."

Less experienced in matters of the law, Ronnie is more anxious still.

Ron: "I love Britain but I haven't been there since last year mainly because I wouldn't feel safe sleeping in my own bed. That whole thing was really disgusting. It makes me feel sick to think about it. I looked at houses out there (California) and I think it would be a good place to live. I'll rent out my home and become a tax exile like the rest of the Stones. It's really sad. But how would you feel about a place where the police break in and drag your wife out of bed? And where you are only allowed to keep about two per cent of what you earn?"

WEDNESDAY, 19 MAY 1976

After writing off his Bentley on the M1 in Buckinghamshire, Keith Richard is arrested after police find "substances" in the vehicle.

Mick: "We're always worried about being busted. Not, of course, that we have anything to do with drugs. But I'm always afraid some of the people around us might be carrying them."

The incident hardly endears Keith to his own country, as Sounds *writer Chris Ingham discovers.*

Keith: "Britain's going down the tubes. They've driven out anybody who was any good, even those staunch Britishers Reg (Elton John) and Rod (Stewart), who, two years ago, swore they would never leave Britain. The minute their mansions were threatened they were in LA like a shot. You go to LA these days and it's a colony of English rock stars. I don't know why they want to go to LA. I like to go there for two weeks and then get the fuck out."

In light of recent developments, Mick takes extra care to protect himself.

Mick: "I don't have people hanging around. It upsets me to see Rolling Stones casualties but it's not The Rolling Stones that destroy people, it's themselves. They shouldn't hang out. I don't have anyone hanging out in *my* room, nobody except the band."

There are suggestions that one of those adversely affected by The Rolling Stones' lifestyle is ex-guitarist Mick Taylor.

Keith: "All Mick did was pick up bad habits, which is a shame. I'm not trying to knock the guy, but what's he done but skyrocket to oblivion. It's sad 'cos in a way he's another Stones casualty in the same way that Brian was . . . That won't happen to Ron. He's got the strength to survive."

FRIDAY, 21 MAY 1976

The band begin a week-long residency at Earls Court, London.
Mick: "This is the worst toilet I've played in, and I've seen toilets. There just aren't any places to play in London. It really is a problem that we have nowhere else."

Critics maul the poor sound at the shows; some accuse the Stones of turning into parodies of themselves.
Mick: "Those people who say I'm a self-parody don't know what they're talking about. I always feel pretty loose. I don't do the same thing every night. I never behave the same way. I know some rock bands that go through the same thing every night, y'know. They even tell the same jokes. I doubt whether these people who say the Stones are a self-parody ever saw us ten years ago anyway."

Nevertheless, there is a familiar ring to some of the opinions expressed in interviews around the time of the tour . . .
Keith: "I only really listen to black music these days. I ain't too interested in white bands who rip off white bands who ripped off black bands."
Ron: "When we're on the road, Keith reckons on sleeping about one night in four. The trouble is he's such an interesting guy. You can sit down to talk with him, and by the time the conversation has finished, 13 hours have gone by."

In conversation with Sun *writer Bob Hart, Mick strikes a customary pose, too.*
Mick: "What I do now is a bit limiting. Writing and singing a song like 'Brown Sugar' is a good thing to do. But it doesn't actually tax the intellect. One day there has to be something else."

Then comes the headline-grabber . . .
Mick: "And the thing that attracts me most at the moment is the idea of becoming an academic. I would like to study things that interest me, like history, maybe even music."

He was soon backtracking.
Mick: "Load of crap. It was six in the morning and I had to tell them something. The guy was asking about what happens if I get fed up with rock'n'roll. I just said I could go back to college or become a farmer, which is true. People automatically think you have to carry on in some kind of show business."

There was another distraction from the business of rock'n'roll – his new diamond-studded tooth. But why?

Mick: "To look pretty. It hurt a bit when it was being done. I tried an emerald first, but it didn't look nice – it looked like a piece of spinach. And then a ruby, but that looked like a spot of blood. So it came down to a diamond."

Ron: "Trouble is, you never know whose mouth it's been in!"

SATURDAY, 22 MAY 1976

Jerry Hall (with partner Bryan Ferry) meets Mick backstage at Earls Court.

Jerry: "He was so much smaller than I'd imagined . . . After we went out to dinner, we all got in the limousine and that's when Mick really got to me. He pressed his knee next to mine and I could feel the electricity."

FRIDAY, 11 JUNE 1976

The Stones play their first gig in Barcelona, Spain, just months after the death of dictator General Franco. The locals are keen to know why the change of heart, and so is James Fox from The Sunday Times.

Mick: "They asked, 'Have you ever played in Spain before?' And Charlie said, 'No, you're just a bunch of fascists,' which wasn't exactly the reason. The reason why we're going to play in Barcelona is because we say we're going . . . I don't see why we shouldn't play anywhere as long as there are no hassles. Somebody said to me, 'Why do you go on holiday to Brazil which is a fascist country?' I don't think in music you should worry about the politics of a country. I mean, the Russians like American country music. So does George Wallace. The Chinese like Nixon. The fascist view and the Marxist view coincide in the result; in the interpretation they don't.

"Charlie and I had a big argument over dinner about playing in South Africa. I went to the Apollo Theatre in Harlem to a jazz concert and all the white people sat on one side and all the black people on the other."

SUNDAY, 1 AUGUST 1976

Mick is collared by a Canadian film crew while attending the Olympic Games in Montreal.

Q: "I don't think that I've seen anything in the world that seems to be more of a draining physical experience than what you do on stage."

Mick: "It's not so trained as what I've seen this past week. Nobody really trains for rock'n'roll, only one or two people. Most people stand there scratching their beards and getting stoned! That's not what athletics is about. It helps you if you wanna stay together. If you're working on stage and you wanna do things, you gotta keep fit."

SATURDAY, 21 AUGUST 1976

The Stones headline the annual Knebworth Festival in Hertfordshire. Typically, they amble on stage almost two hours late. Sounds *magazine isn't impressed, and runs a cover story emblazoned with the words "It's nearly midnight, it's cold and you've waited 12 hours to see these men. Was it worth it?" Thanks to a two-hour set that included numerous dives into the band's history, the answer is resoundingly affirmative.*
Mick: "I'm sorry. We've had a lot of hassles."

The Stones take a break after the tour, but Ron can't wait to get stuck into the next studio album, as he tells NME *writer Steve Clarke.*
Ron: "I wasn't involved with *Black And Blue* from the beginning and I'd just like to see how an album would turn out if I was involved from the start . . . Recording with the Stones is a long, drawn out process. You've got to track everybody down and get everyone in the same country at the same time, in the same studio, and that takes a hell of a lot of doing."

MONDAY, 20 SEPTEMBER 1976

But first there's the contract-fulfilling live album, which Ron helps Mick mix in New York, after Mick and Keith had sifted through the raw tapes.
Mick: "We must have listened to about 100 hours of tape for the live album. It took about three months to get through them all."

MONDAY, 25 OCTOBER 1976

Mick tells Woman's Own: *"I got married for something to do. I've never been madly, deeply in love. I wouldn't know what that feels like. I'm not an emotional person."*
Bianca Jagger: "Perhaps Mick isn't attracted to me anymore. When I first met him I knew who he was. But I don't know now. He has changed."

MONDAY, 10 JANUARY 1977

Keith Richard ("a composer of popular music of variable income") attends a three-day trial at Aylesbury Crown Court for alleged possession of cocaine and LSD, from the previous May.

Sir Peter Rawlinson, QC (defence): "What does it mean by you being lead guitarist?"

Keith: "It means I make the most noise."

The outcome of the case hinges on ownership of a silver necklace chain. When quizzed about the object at the time of his arrest, Keith claimed:

"It's not mine. It must belong to someone else in the car. The car is used by so many members of the group."

Mr Bruce Laughland (prosecuting): "I suggest the reason you denied knowledge of the chain is because you knew it would contain traces of cocaine . . . His denying all knowledge of it, or ownership of it, is an indication of guilt."

Keith: "If I had known such things were in the car I would not have had them on me."

Q: "You mean you'd have ditched them?"

Keith: "Yes . . . I always expect to be searched when I come across the police. If I had known the necklace and the paper were in the car I would have ditched them."

The prosecution alleges that the chain is the same one as in newspaper photos taken at a show in Leicester four days prior to his arrest.

Keith: "There is a pretty high turnover on our costume jewellery. It gets thrown off and left lying around and all sorts of people help themselves to it."

Judge Lawrence Verney: "Keith Richard, while in this country you must obey the laws of this country. The possession of a Class A drug is regarded in this country as a sufficiently serious offence to merit both a substantial period of imprisonment and a fine . . . but in the circumstances of this case, we do not consider that a period of imprisonment is appropriate at all. This is, however, the second conviction for the possession of drugs, and it would be as well for you to bear in mind that should there be a third, a court is not by any means likely to take the same view.

"In assessing a fine upon you, we had to take account of both the quantity of the drug and the fact that it was, as it appears, intended for personal consumption, and your means . . . and bearing both matters in mind, we impose upon you the fine of £750 . . . and £250 towards costs."

After the verdict, Keith attends a press conference.

Q: "Hey, Keef, watcha gonna do with the chain?"

Keith: "It ain't mine, so they can do what they like with it. I don't want it."

Q: "How's this going to affect the Stones touring America?"

Keith: "It's too early to say."

Q: "Will there be an appeal?"

Keith: "I'll have to discuss that with my solicitors."

Q: "What have fans thrown at you?"

Keith: "You name it . . ."

Q: "What's going to be the consequences?"

Keith: "I might get a song out of it."

Keith: "What was on trial was the same old thing that's always been on trial. Dear old them and us. I just wish they'd pick on The Sex Pistols. I've done my stint in the dock.

"It was ridiculous not to argue the case because of the small amount of drugs involved. I knew these things weren't mine and I was hoping to be able to make the court see that not everyone lives exactly like they do. Cornflakes at 8.30, work by 9.15.

"Basically, I think the general attitude of the jury was, 'Let's be fair, but he is a druggie.' I was a suspect public image. They can't differentiate between the public image and what you actually are."

The conviction raises doubts over the band's future intentions to tour America.

Keith: "Nothing is the end of this band. We'll always be able to play somewhere. The State Department takes a more adult point of view . . . It's gonna take a lot more to put this lot out of business. We're a determined group of lads. Nothing short of nuclear weapons is gonna put this lot out of action."

It also propels the Daily Mirror *into moral panic mode.*

"The craze – which is sweeping the pop world – is cocaine sniffing. Earlier this week, Rolling Stone Keith Richard was fined £750 for having cocaine."

Measured Mick is having none of it.

Mick: "If you came to me and said you were taking drugs because you were a fan of mine, I'd feel sorry for you, sorry that you copied someone else. But I might also ask why you're taking drugs. Are you desperately unhappy? But I wouldn't feel to blame. It's up to you to decide what's best for you."

Keith: "I'd rather carry on being elegantly wasted without being busted anymore. I just don't need it."

WEDNESDAY, 16 FEBRUARY 1977

The Stones announce that they have signed a new, four-album deal with EMI for a rumoured £2 million (though they remain with Atlantic in America).

Prince Rupert Lowenstein (Stones' business manager): "Before signing, Mick Jagger read every one of the 46 clauses in the contract very carefully indeed. Then he visited the head office to see if the A&R people and the marketing men were bright and swinging, and if they'd get along together."

Mick: "In this Jubilee year, I think it only fitting that we sign with a British company . . . EMI are very alive. I was amazed. I thought they'd be like Decca, but they seem to be jumping. It'll be interesting to work with new people. That's one of the reasons we signed with them. Well, there is quite a lot of money (too), but we've got to sell a lot of records. If we don't then there's not a lot of money."

Ron: "If you've got it, flaunt it. Charlie goes and buys French shoes and French suits. Mick is always globetrotting. Keith's trying to bed down in any country that will have him."

Mick: "We hope to go on the road and do an American tour in the spring. After that, Australia, Japan and England."

SUNDAY, 20 FEBRUARY 1977

The band telegram Keith from Toronto where they are rehearsing for a couple of low-key club shows.

"WE WANT TO PLAY. YOU WANT TO PLAY. WHERE ARE YOU?"

SUNDAY, 27 FEBRUARY 1977

"ROLLING STONE FACES DRUG LIFE SENTENCE"

Keith faces possible life imprisonment after being charged by Canadian police with possessing an ounce of heroin "for the purpose of trafficking". Earlier in the day, at 4.30 p.m., four drug squad officers swooped on his room in Toronto's £50-a-day Harbour Castle Hotel.

Mick: "Knock, knock knock. I said, 'Who is it?' 'Security.' I said, 'What do you want? I've just come out of the bath.' He said, 'There's something wrong with your toilet.' I said, 'Why don't you send a plumber? I don't need security men to mend my toilet!' I said, 'Go away.' They said, 'We gotta come in.' I said, 'You ain't coming in.' I locked the door. And then they went off to bust Keith. They were cops, you know."

Keith: "What disappointed me was that not one of them was wearing a proper Mounties uniform when they burst into my hotel room. They were all in anoraks with droopy moustaches and bald heads. Real weeds, the lot of 'em, all after their picture in the paper. Fifteen of 'em round me bed trying to wake me up. I'd have woken up a lot quicker if I'd seen the red tunic and Smokey the Bear hat. I was taken down to the jail and I asked them to give me a couple of grammes back just to tide me over."

Ron Belanger (Drug Squad chief): "There was no difficulty at all in finding the drug. Richard didn't say much. Nor did Miss Pallenberg. He wasn't angry, but he wasn't exactly calm. I suppose you could say he took it in his stride. We also found a syringe which is now being analysed. In Toronto an ounce of heroin is a substantial amount. It is a very serious, grave charge and carries a life sentence, although that is not normally imposed. The courts here take a very serious view of heroin and Keith Richard could face a substantial sentence in prison. But if he could convince the judge through medical evidence that he is an addict, it might be a different scene. In that case, the judge might be sympathetic and order medical rehabilitation."

Paul Wasserman (Stones PR): "Keith thinks the charge is very strange. There seems to be a discrepancy between bail of £650 and a charge like drug trafficking."

Mick: "You mean, did I know it was going to happen? Yeah, of course. Christ, Keith fuckin' gets busted every year."

FRIDAY, 4 MARCH 1977

Despite the bust, and its potentially catastrophic consequences for the band's future, the Stones play the first of two nights at the tiny El Mocambo club in Toronto.

Keith: "We haven't played in a place that small since '62, but it felt very natural. It's been a long time since I've had my legs stroked while playing. Mind you, first night the band sounded like it was playing for something in New Delhi. There were all these weird quarter tones, out of tune, very frantic. It was all the adrenaline."

Mick: "It was fun on stage last night but all these girls were grabbing my balls. Once they started they didn't stop. It was great up to a point, then it got very difficult to sing."

Keith: "If we done a couple more nights, things would have got even better."

The shows are taped for inclusion on the forthcoming live album.
Keith: "All live albums are the same; they all have different versions of songs already released on album. We wanted to do something different – add some new numbers, add some old numbers. That way the kids get something extra."

The Stones get a new song out of the venture.
Mick: "I wrote 'Miss You' during rehearsals for the El Mocambo gig. I remember that because I was waiting with Billy Preston for everyone in the band to turn up. Billy was playing the kick drum and I was playing the guitar and I wrote 'Miss You'."

The tabloids strike lucky, too, when Margaret Trudeau, wife of the Canadian Prime Minister, parties with the Stones after the shows.
Margaret Trudeau: "It's quite a buzz. I've always been a Rolling Stones fan."
Bill: "She's helping to improve English-Canadian relations."
Charlie: "I wouldn't want my wife associating with us."
Mick: "Margaret Trudeau is a very attractive and nice person, but we are not having an affair. I never met her before and haven't seen her since I got to New York. In fact I haven't seen her since Sunday. What can I say? I'm in New York with my wife and daughter."
Margaret Trudeau: "I'm very fond of him. I'd like to think he is a friend. But look, I'm a married lady, the wife of the Canadian Prime Minister. I love my husband and I love music."
Margaret Trudeau: "I happen to love the Stones' music and I had a chance to photograph them while performing. It seemed like a good idea at the time. What I didn't know was that their press agent was calling journalists and telling everybody I was going to be there. The one mistake that I made – and it was a bad one – was taking the press agent up on his offer to have a complimentary room at the hotel where the group were staying. The Stones had taken over an entire floor of the hotel and they gave me one of those rooms. But a romance? Not true. All-night parties? Just not true. I was at the concert because I love their music and saw a wonderful opportunity to launch my career as a photographer."
Les Perrin (Stones PR man): "They didn't invite her to their hotel – she simply booked herself in and then set about attaching herself to the entourage. As far as I know, no member of the group was having an affair

with her. Mick certainly wasn't. He described her to me as a pain in the neck."

Pierre Trudeau (Canadian Prime Minister): "I think that if she goes to rock concerts she has to expect to be noticed and written about. I have no complaints about that, but I believe that my wife's private life is her affair and mine."

Ron: "She was a bit mixed up, but I think she's got her family problems sorted out now. It was all very innocent. She just came along and had a boogie with us for two days. She travelled with us and we became good friends. But it was a very short-lived friendship."

JUNE 1977

As The Sex Pistols' 'God Save The Queen' prompts renewed debate about punk rock, Mick weighs in with a few thoughts on the subject – as he does on several occasions during the year. Sounds writer Sandy Robertson gets an earful . . .

Mick: "I think it's crap. I think (Patti Smith's) awful. She's full of rubbish, full of words and crap. I mean, she's a poseur of the worst kind, intellectual bullshit, trying to be a street girl when she doesn't seem to me to be one. I mean . . . a useless guitar player, a bad singer, not attractive. I was always very attractive, a much better singer, much better with words, and I wasn't an intellectual poseur. She's got her heart in the right place – but she's such a poseur.

"Keith Richard is the original punk rocker. You can't really out-punk Keith. It's a useless gesture.

"People have compared us and Andrew Oldham to Malcolm McLaren and The Sex Pistols. But it was too obvious to work and it didn't. I'm sure Johnny Rotten realised that it was all a set-up, and went along with it, while the others in the group couldn't think of enough swear words to keep it going! We never did anything consciously to shock people in the days when the Stones were always in the paper. It was only other people who were shocked when we did things that had to be done."

One rumour that writer Nick Kent brings to Mick's attention is the one that has Rotten slamming the door in Jagger's face outside McLaren's Sex shop.

Mick: "Now this is all total fantasy, complete and utter fantasy. I don't even know where the Sex shop is . . . Hold on, I vaguely recall, where Let It Rock used to be. There's a lot of clothes shops in the King's Road, dear, and I've seen 'em all come and go. Nobody ever slams the door on me in the King's Road. They all know I'm the only one who's got any money to spend on their crappy cloth, though even I would draw the line on spending money on torn T-shirts!"

Kent also discovers that the Stones were closet Velvet Underground fans – back in 1968.

Mick: "Lou Reed started everything about that style of music, the whole sound and the way you play it. I mean, even we've been influenced by The Velvet Underground. No, really. I'll tell you exactly what we pinched from him. Y'know 'Stray Cat Blues'? The whole sound and the way it's paced, we pinched from the first Velvet Underground album. Y'know, the sound on 'Heroin'. Honest to God, we did!"

But that was a decade ago. American critic Chet Flippo throws another quote in Mick's direction.

Q: "Johnny Rotten says you should have retired in 1965."

Mick: "I don't care what Johnny Rotten says. Everything Johnny Rotten says about me is only 'cause he loves me 'cause I'm so good. It's true."

Mick: "Don't you think the Stranglers are the worst thing you've ever fuckin' heard? I do. They're hideous, rubbishy . . . so bloody stupid. Fuckin' nauseatin', they are."

And his conclusion?

Mick: "I don't think new wave's going to last. I've been watching it closely in the States. The bands aren't getting widespread popularity there and after the initial reaction in Britain, I reckon it's going to fade. No British new wave bands are getting into the charts over there – even Marc Bolan managed that."

TUESDAY, 28 JUNE 1977

Mick meets Jerry Hall again at a dinner party at the 21 in New York.

Andy Warhol: "I thought things were fishy with Mick and Jerry, then the plot started to thicken. Mick was so out of it that I could tell the waiters were scared he'd pass out. His head was so far back he was singing to himself. The top part of his body was like jelly and the bottom half was tapping 3,000 taps a minute. He was putting his sunglasses on and off . . . I found out later from Fred (Hughes) that he's really passionately in love with Jerry, and it looks like there's trouble for Bianca."

The liaison soon becomes public knowledge, though Mick denies the rumours and insists all is well at home with Bianca.

Mick: "Absolute rubbish. We are still living together and in love with each other. I haven't got the seven-year itch. In fact I didn't know we had been married for seven years until I read it in the newspapers. We have no intention of splitting up. Yesterday I was told that I was supposed to be getting a divorce on 15 December in Nevada. It's not true . . ."

TUESDAY, 16 AUGUST 1977

Elvis Presley dies. Mick remembers the moment with Gordon Burn in Men Only.
Mick: "I was sitting on a bench in Turkey listening to the news in Turkish and heard the name Elvis Presley. They started playing his records. I figured he'd snuffed it . . . He couldn't help getting fat; he was ill. And he had another American disease, eating ice-cream, which Muhammad Ali also has. Eating all this junk food, it's real addiction, y'know. Like heroin. They go on binges of it. It's from childhood. They never stop. Elvis hadn't made any good records for a long time. He was great when he first came out, but he never wrote . . . He was a totally interpretative artist, and a lot of his later interpretations of other people's songs were really not very good. He did some really rotten versions.

"It's pathetic the way he's being remembered. I was watching American TV and all they were showing were films of him in Las Vegas in a glittery suit. They should be using the old stuff when he had something to say and people really listened to his voice."

WEDNESDAY, 14 SEPTEMBER 1977

While Keith Richard awaits his trial, Mick gives The Daily Express *a progress report.*
Mick: "(Keith) has been having treatment in a New York hospital and has now finished it. At present he is living in the country outside New York. We all know Keith could get nothing or life imprisonment. If he got life, I would carry on with the band but I don't know what I'd do. I'd be very upset. I'm sure Keith could write in prison. He'd have nothing else to do. I think the law's out to get us. Once you get any notoriety it seems to happen."

Chris Welch at Melody Maker *elicits a more detailed account.*
Mick: "He can leave the States, go back and forward. They seem to be very sweet about it. The trial is on 2 December unless they put it back again. This seems to be a tough one. I've been worrying about it, but it's much more worrying for Keith. I can't make plans because anything can

272

happen. They might put him on probation, he might have to report to Canada every week. They could make him live in Toronto or go into hospital. They can do anything they want. We just hope they are going to be fair about it . . . Of course I want the band to continue. We're supposed to be touring next year. I just keep thinking about it very positively. We want to make a new album. A single. Go on the road in the spring, so I'm just going ahead and planning it . . . They keep asking me if Jimmy Page is going to join the Stones."

That evening, Mick and Ron attend a Crickets show, organised by Paul McCartney at the Kilburn Gaumont, London, to mark the 41st anniversary of Buddy Holly's birth.

Mick: "Rock'n'roll music is for adolescents. It's a dead end. I think the whole history of rock'n'roll has proved that. There is nothing wrong with it, but it's just for kids. My whole life isn't rock'n'roll. It's an absurd idea that it should be."

To that end, he continues to cultivate the notion of "multi-faceted Mick".

Mick: "I just enjoy changing personalities. I feel I've got to be very chameleon-like just to preserve my own identity. I don't want to have just one front. I feel like I need at least two just to carry on doing what I'm doing comfortably. It's acting, sure it is. It just gives me the facility to do practically anything I want . . . It's all part of being a rock'n'roll star."

FRIDAY, 16 SEPTEMBER 1977

T. Rex frontman Marc Bolan dies.

Mick: "It was a shame about Marc. His death upset me. The last time I saw him was at Earl's Court. He came up to me and tried to grab me. We had to hit him and that's not a very nice way to remember someone."

On the same day, the Stones release a two-LP concert set, Love You Live, *advertised as "The Greatest Rock'n'Roll the Greatest Rock'n'Roll Band ever made." Unlike previous projected live albums, it does at least include material from the Decca era.*

Mick: "We had a live album ready to go in 1973 – a double live album with Stevie Wonder on one album and us on the other but Decca and Allen Klein, our loveable ex-manager, didn't want it out. They managed to stop it because of all kinds of restrictions they had in their contracts. We had to wait until those restrictions passed before we could release live versions of songs like 'Honky Tonk Women' and 'You Can't Always Get What You Want'."

It also boasts a side of material taped at the El Mocambo, including a version of Bo Diddley's 'Crackin' Up'.

Mick: "John Lennon suggested it to me. We did a lot of songs that night . . . and we recorded new songs that I wrote that didn't come out too well because we didn't have long enough rehearsal. So we just picked those four."

TUESDAY, 20 SEPTEMBER 1977

Mick, Charlie and Ron talk to host Bob Harris as part of an hour-long BBC Old Grey Whistle Test *special on the Stones.*

Q: "How did you go about the selection process for the tracks?"

Mick: "Oh, gawd. Well, I listened to every show that we recorded and picked the best ones."

Q: "How many hours did you have, Mick?"

Mick: "I listened to every show that we recorded – 54 shows at roughly two hours a show. Well, I didn't actually listen to them all because I knew half of them were rubbish. We also wanted to do something different."

Ron: "Side three is pulled from two nights at the El Mocambo, at that 300-seater club in Toronto. That's my favourite side."

Q: "Do you prefer the atmosphere and the energy from small places?"

Charlie: "I do (looks towards Mick), 'e doesn't."

Mick: "It doesn't matter. The energy can be very low if there's 100,000 people there, amazingly enough."

Q: "What are your plans over the next three or four months?"

Charlie: (*grumbling*) "We're gonna go out on the road again . . ."

Ron: "Because none of us have got any houses!"

MONDAY, 10 OCTOBER 1977

The Stones regroup in Paris at the Pathé-Marconi Studios for a lengthy recording stint.

Bill: "We had such a great time in the studio that we never stopped really. We were going to be there for four or five weeks originally – middle of October till early December – and we were still there in February. We were enjoying ourselves, we were getting things done and getting off on new songs. We probably finished 12 or 13 songs, and then there's a whole mass of demos and jams. We finished up with 96 reels of tape, where a normal band might use six for an album."

Roy Carr digs deeper for ZigZag.
Keith: "The big decision we made when cutting tracks for *Some Girls* was . . ."
Mick: "Only one slow number . . ."
Keith: ". . . that we were not gonna touch the tracks more than necessary."
Mick: "Hardly any overdubs . . ."
Keith: "Only a little bit of extra rhythm here and there . . ."
Mick: "When we did 'Respectable' we'd been up for about 12 hours and had gotten fed up with the number we were doing, so we were all feeling very up when we did it first take . . ."
Keith: " 'Beast Of Burden' is also a first take."
Mick: "We had so many songs that if we got fed up, we'd say, 'Fuck it,' and immediately try something else."

SATURDAY, 31 DECEMBER 1977

Mick sees in the New Year from inside a 'magic ring' of lit candles in a flower-covered cottage in Barbados. With him is Jerry Hall. Bianca Jagger is alone in New York.
Mick: "What do you want me to say about it all? People always ask me whether my marriage is over."
A friend: "Although they've gone their own ways before, this is the first time that Mick has publicly produced another woman. The marriage is clearly over and there won't be a reconciliation."
Another friend: "I don't think this affair with Jerry will be lasting, but that's not the point. She told me she has been on the point of leaving Bryan (Ferry) several times. It's unfortunate that it was Mick. He and Bryan were good mates."

FRIDAY, 3 FEBRUARY 1978

Bianca insists there is no disagreement between her and Mick.
Bianca Jagger: "I deny categorically and consider it absurd to think there is any link, other than friendship, between Mr Rod Stewart and myself. My marriage is very important to me and I am very much in love with my husband. I am departing today to join him in the States."

SATURDAY, 8 APRIL 1978

Mick and Jerry dine out with Andy Warhol in New York.

Mick: "If you're with a woman and the sexual relationship is working like a Rolls-Royce or a Mercedes Benz, everything smooths out. The other things aren't important."

Andy Warhol: "I think it's really a shame that Mick and Bianca have drifted apart. Bianca really is the girl of Mick's dreams because she's the female Mick Jagger. Having her over is just like having him over. That's why I was so embarrassed one day when Victor Hugo, a young fashion artist everyone knows, told Mick: 'All your gestures are like Bianca's. Every year you look more and more like her.' Mick snapped back: 'I'm glad I'm as beautiful as my beautiful fucking wife. But she looks like me.'"

WEDNESDAY, 10 MAY 1978

The Stones begin rehearsals for the tour at Woodstock, outside New York. Geraldo Rivera for the Today *show pays them a visit, and has a question for Keith.*

Q: "Are you looking forward to going out?"

Keith: "Sure, it's all I do. It's all I'm good at. What else am I gonna do?"

He finds the rest of the band in boisterous form.

Mick: "We all compete: to play the best, sing the best, be the most together, or the most untogether, see who can get the most girls, or a particular girl first. It's like a really dumb baseball team!"

Ron: "What we have going is the old corny thing – the family. It's a bit like having four other brothers."

Bill: "I enjoy being at the back observing as well as playing. That's why I don't jump about. If I do, I can't see what's happening in the audience, and I can't see what Jagger's doing."

Q: "What do you think of him as a performer?"

Bill: "Oh he's fantastic, one of the best."

Q: "What makes him that way?"

Bill: "Ego!"

Q: "How have you managed to do the same Mick Jagger act over the past 16 years?"

Mick: "It's a very English approach. We were brought up to believe that everything you do is a joke, that you're only an amateur and you don't ever claim to be any good at it. And that if you do get success, it's only by luck."

Q: "Did you think it might last 16 years?"

Bill: "No, two or three. Nobody lasts 16 years."

And the retirement question?

Mick: "No, there are a million things you can do. You could be an actor. That would be very nice. There are a lot of job opportunities about."

Q: "What keeps you together as a band?"

Mick: "I really don't know. The only answer I can give you is that the band enjoys themselves very much being together, and is also very successful. And if any one of those things were missing, they wouldn't be together."

Q: "Are your tax problems over?"

Mick: "Everyone has to pay taxes. I was broke because they taxed me so highly in the UK. I owed them so much money that I had to leave to pay what I owed. Now I pay taxes everywhere. I really have to work. I come from that generation of western people that spend all the money it can get."

Q: "So unlike the Beatles, you are not endowed with great wealth."

Mick: "No, I spent it all. I had it and it went just like that."

Q: "Does that limit your freedom?"

Mick: "In one way, because you haven't got all the money in the world to buy the most beautiful yacht, or the most beautiful girls to put in that yacht. On the other hand, you've seen money come and go and so you don't need it."

Q: "Do you feel any sense of disappointment that most people don't view you as an intellectual person?"

Mick: "It's very nice to be just a body. I feel like a stripper when I go on stage. I have a great sympathy for girls that are sex objects. There's nothing more sleazy than an old stripper!"

Q: "Do you take yourself seriously?"

Mick: "Nah, definitely not. That's the worst thing you can do. I think being serious is carrying it much too far."

Q: "So what do you think about your life?"

Mick: "It's meaningless."

SATURDAY, 13 MAY 1978

Despite the fact that Keith Richards' (the guitarist has recently reverted back to the original spelling of his name) court case still hangs over them, the Stones announce details of their summer American tour.

Mick: "It would be stupid to wait, say, five years. I mean, in five years' time the Stones will be almost through with touring."

SUNDAY, 14 MAY 1978

Bianca Jagger files for divorce citing "irreconcilable differences".
Mick: "Bianca is divorcing me. I'm just an innocent bystander. But we still talk to each other every other day . . . If she wants to divorce me, then there's nothing I can do about it. If Bianca wants to get divorced I'm only too happy to go along with whatever she wants. The thing one has to be sensible about is Jade."

She subsequently withdraws the lawsuit.
Bianca Jagger: "I couldn't go along with what the lawyers wanted me to say. Mick knows I don't want to live with him again. The fact is I've discovered that I like living on my own. Now I find I like seeing my own friends and making my own decisions. And there's nobody around to destroy my confidence . . . I finally know something. I'm going to make it as an actress."

FRIDAY, 19 MAY 1978

The new single is 'Miss You'.
Mick: " 'Miss You' is an emotion. It's not really about a girl. To me, the feeling of longing is what the song is about. I don't like to interpret my own fucking songs, but that's what it is."
Charlie: " 'Miss You' is really very easy, it's just four in a bar. It's even easier to play than a triplet. But it's a good song, so it works."

A 12" edition, featuring a fashionably extended disco mix, follows a couple of weeks later.
Keith: "The amount of thump from Bill and Charlie is quite amazing . . . It's the first time we've done it this way. We just sent the tape to (Bob Clearmountain), whom I've never met at all, but who is experienced in mixing disco cuts. It worked really well."
Mick: "The extended 12-inch disco cut is, in some ways, a kinda Stonesy dub – where the voice comes in and where the guitars are all cut up. It's just our way of doing it."

The flipside, 'Faraway Eyes', becomes a big hit on the country music stations.
Mick: "It's not a put-down. It's the truth. I'm not making fun of country music. It was a real story as it happened."

FRIDAY, 9 JUNE 1978

Some Girls, *the Stones' first new studio album in two years, is released.*

Q: "Why call the album *Some Girls?*"

Keith: "Because we couldn't remember their fucking names."

Keith: "Personally I don't want to milk this album for singles, but potentially there are at least three strong singles on it."

Bill: "Woody's come along and, especially in the last year, he's pulled both sides together. I think he was the main reason for the band being so close and super-friendly in, say, the last nine months, more than we've been since '66 maybe. I'd had great difficulty being able to communicate with Mick and Keith . . . Woody's fabulous! He's made this band come back to life again."

Ron: "I'll tell you where my influence really paid off on *Some Girls* – giving Mick guitar lessons. I encouraged him to play things like 'Respectable', 'Lies', 'When The Whip Comes Down', all that upbeat, punky stuff. Mick felt very punky at the time."

Keith: "The real difference for us was cutting *Some Girls* without having any other musicians present. This album was purely our own affair. We overdubbed a couple of things later, but the actual record and the overall feel depended entirely on the five of us. And that kinda made us work harder."

Mick: "If you go to LA to record, you've got dozens of musicians crowding around waiting for the gig, but in Paris, nobody wants the fuckin' gig . . . We brought 'Mac' (ex-Faces keyboardist Ian McLagan) in for a couple of numbers, and then when we needed a harmonica player, Sugar Blue turned up."

Bill: "(Engineer) Chris Kimsey got the best bass sound I've ever had apart from an occasional track here and there, so immediately when you're listening back to something, a rough even, you get turned on because it sounds great anyway. He got beautiful sounds for me and Charlie, and that inspires you."

Mick: "I think that this album sounds particularly good because the studio had a high ceiling, which is what you need when making a rock album. That's how you get that particular drum sound on 'When The Whip Comes Down'."

No Stones album comes without controversy, as Australian TV host Norman Gunston reminds Mick.

Mick: "Raquel Welch! She should be so lucky to have her picture on the cover. She phones up and says, 'I like the fact that I'm on the cover but can you change the picture?' Well, we've already made two million of 'em, right? So she said, 'When you make some more, I'll send you my picture.' I said, 'You've had it, we're gonna get Carrie Fisher in.'"

But that's nothing to the furore that surrounds the title track, which includes the line, "Black girls just want to get fucked all night, I just don't have that much jam."

Rev. Jesse Jackson: "It is an insult to our race and degrading to our women."

Press release: "It never occurred to us that our parody of certain stereotypical attitudes would be taken seriously by anyone who has heard the entire lyrics of the song in question. No insult was intended, and if any was taken, we sincerely apologise."

Ahmet Ertegun (chairman, Atlantic Records): "Mick Jagger is certainly not a racist. He is consciously anti-racist. He owes his whole being to black people and black music."

Keith: "We write our songs from personal experiences. Okay, so over the last 15 years we've happened to meet extra horny black chicks. Well, I'm sorry but I don't think I'm wrong and neither does Mick, I'm quite sure of that."

Q: "Some say the record is sexist and possibly racist. What do you think about that?"

Mick: "The next one's gonna be more sexist and more racist and it's gonna be a whole bunch better."

As the furore dies down, the Stones bask in the knowledge that their commercial and critical standing is once again on a high.

Charlie: "We're bloody lucky. We've signed a record deal three or four times, and each time we've had a fucking good single and a good album. We did it with Atlantic with 'Brown Sugar' and *Sticky Fingers* and we've done it again this time."

Hungry again, and with their ears to the ground, Mick and Keith debate the emergence of a new black street sound in ZigZag.

Mick: "In my opinion, most black bands are real corny, simply because there's big money in disco."

Keith: "It's now all down to a very basic and predictable formula. But, at street level, there's much more going on than people realise."

Mick: "But that kinda music that you're talkin' about ain't making much money, not nearly as much as disco, and as a result not too many people are interested in recording it."

Keith: "So what! Half of what's happenin' on the streets right now is gonna be what's happenin' in a big way later."

Mick: "That's true, and when it does come, it's gonna come right through the underground and finally surface in New York City. That's where it's gonna happen."

While Mick and Keith feel the earliest stirrings of rap and hip hop, Anita turns instead to the New York punk rock scene. A rumour spreads that Keith bans her from going to punk clubs.

Keith: "I didn't actually ban her. I said, 'If you're gonna drop by some clubs to hear bands, there's much better music to listen to than that.' Through Anita, I met a few young musicians who proved quite interesting to hang out with . . . but it was all typical New York."

As the Stones geared up for the American tour, Keith's intimate knowledge of the streets of New York, acquired through contacts in the drugs trade, would be worth nothing if he was handed a hefty jail sentence when his case comes to trial in the autumn.

Q: "Keith Richards is in a bit of a problem at the moment."

Mick: "He does have a problem."

Q: "Does he have a problem with heavy drugs?"

Mick: "I think it's a very personal question."

By now, Keith had reason to be less coy on the subject. He'd taken the "electro-acupuncture" cure with a British doctor, Margaret Patterson, who'd already success-fully treated Eric Clapton.

Keith: "It's so simple, but whether they'll ever let people know about it is another thing. I can't even tell you how it works because they don't even know for sure. All they know is that it does work. It's a little metal box with leads that clip on to your ears, and in two or three days – which is the worst period for kickin' junk – it leaves your system. You should be incredibly sick, but for some reason you're not. It is a very simple electronic nine-volt battery-run operation."

SATURDAY, 10 JUNE 1978

The tour opens at the Civic Centre in Florida, Miami.

Mick: "I have noticed on the Southern dates that the audiences seem to be very young . . . Lotsa 15- and 16-year-old boppers, the kinda kids you'd imagine would be following the newer bands. Which reminds me of that great quote by Johnny Rotten . . . no, it was the Clash – 'No Stones in '77'. And no Sex Pistols in '78, eh!"

The favourable reception of both album and tour restores the group's self-image . . .

Keith: "From what I can see, a lotta good bands have come up in the last couple of years but the movement started to hit its demise when it tried to get out of England . . . A lot of what happened in '77 was more theatre than music."

Mick: "Yeah, but we didn't really make any gas-out records in early '77 either. We were just fuckin' around."

. . . the camaraderie is good . . .

Q: "Ronnie Wood was saying that even after three years, he still feels like an outsider."

Mick: "Yeah, that's how we'd like to keep it, cunt that he is! Keep him in his place."

. . . and Mick's been handling even more guitar on stage.

Mick: "I enjoyed it very much. Keith keeps adjusting my settings while I'm singing, of course! If I did that with him, he'd probably go bananas. Having the cordless mike made a lot of difference because three people tripping over each other's leads is not much fun. I did get a bit nervous the first night, and made a lot of clangers, but I got into it. It made a change from leaping about without a guitar. Now I can leap about with it."

TUESDAY, 18 JULY 1978

But, battle-hardened after winning their fight against punk's 'Old Farts' assaults, the Stones go on the offensive against their critics. At the after-show party in Fort Worth, Texas, Rolling Stone *writer Chet Flippo is ejected.*

Mick: "I'm fucking pissed off . . . I get real mad at this vicious shit . . . This is the end. No more interviews. I don't mind criticism – real criticism – but I don't expect the kind of bitchiness in these reviews."

A little later, he softens his tone.

Mick: "Journalists like to stereotype people. I like to change the stereotype. Today, I think I'm funny, nice and warm, enjoyable, fun and not too violent."

Q: "If you had a chance to write the truth, what would you say?"

Mick: "I'd have to write a book. It's not that interesting. I don't wanna understand anything. I just wanna go out there and play. I don't consider what I stand for. You'll go mad if you do that. Singers and actors don't have to worry about what they stand for. Just do what you do."

But there are plenty, particularly Evangelist preachers in the American South, who worry a lot about what Mick and the Stones stand for.

"You love the Rolling Stones more than you love God. You love liquor more than you love God. You love that harlot you're running around with more than you love God!"

Mick reacts by adopting an even more flippant tone in interviews.
Q: "You touch a lot of people's lives. How does that make you feel?"
Mick: "Useless."
Q: "Do you have any regrets?"
Mick: "No, except when I was about 13, I couldn't get any girls. But that problem's over now."

WEDNESDAY, 26 JULY 1978

The tour ends with a show at the Oakland Coliseum in California. Anne Nightingale asks Mick for his verdict.
Mick: "It was good fun. The gigs I really dug were the small ones, and that really big indoor one where they had the Ali fight (New Orleans). It was like playing an outdoor gig inside and the acoustics were good too."
Q: "You pulled in a record number of people, too . . ."
Mick: "Yeah, not so much money as (Muhammad) Ali but more people!"
Q: "You were very apprehensive when I saw you last about coming back here."
Mick: "When I was going, 'I'm not coming back to England'? That one? I was only joking. Did that go out on the radio?"
Q: "Yeah. So why haven't you come back to play?"
Mick: "We thought we'd get Keith's trial out of the way first. Then we thought we'd go to Australia and then come back to England next year."

Elsewhere, he confirms that itinerancy is his natural state.
Mick: "I don't have a home. I have nowhere to go. I've been carrying the same two suitcases around since last October. Two suitcases and a guitar. I don't see what's wrong with that. The less possessions you have, the less you have hanging round your neck . . . I'm really only interested in working. And therefore it's better to be free to travel. When we made our last album in Paris, I had an apartment there for three and a half months. It was the longest I'd stayed anywhere!"
Mick: "It's impossible for me to settle down and still do what I want. I've tried it. That was the great myth about being a rock singer. You went out and worked very hard for three or four years, then bought a house in the country. That wasn't for me. It makes you not want to work. I had the house ('Stargroves', in Berkshire) ten years and lived in it ten days."

SEPTEMBER 1978

Keith's domestic situation is hardly any more secure when the Hollywood house he has been renting in Laurel Canyon burns down.

Keith: "I'm in the bedroom with the flavour of the month, my girlfriend of the hour. I wake up and the room's full of smoke. I open the door to the bedroom and I'm looking at a fireball rushing down the corridor towards the oxygen . . . and me! There's the two of us stark naked. Half the house is already destroyed, the roof is falling in on us but we've managed to get through – with a few burns here and there – to the swimming pool . . . Stark fucking bollock naked with this blonde, bless her heart, good girl, solid gold, saying to me, 'Do something.' And I said, 'What d'you want me to do? Piss on it?' Suddenly this car stops and it's Anita's cousin! And I never know how she recognised me because she could only see my cock! And she goes, 'Get in!' and she just scooped us up and whisked me off so nobody could find me for a couple of days."

FRIDAY, 29 SEPTEMBER 1978

Peter Tosh's first single for the Stones' label, '(You Gotta Walk) Don't Look Back', features Mick Jagger as secondary vocalist.

Mick: "It's more of a duet. I get as much as I can in. Keith and Woody played some licks, too. It was Peter's idea to do this particular number . . . No, he's not a protégé of mine. He doesn't need introducing by me. I mean, he's not a young kid. He's older than me, which is quite an achievement these days.

"Peter first cut the song in the early Sixties, or whenever it was that The Temptations came out with it. I think (that version) was only released in Jamaica. Back then, he was a ska man with a black suit and a tie."

SATURDAY, 7 OCTOBER 1978

The Stones make their first live appearance on American television since the days of The Ed Sullivan Show *when they perform three songs for* Saturday Night Live.

Ron: "There we were on stage . . . I had my eyes closed for a few seconds and suddenly I felt this wet warm thing slurping on my face. It was Mick's tongue. I tried to kick him but he was too fast. He loves putting people on the spot."

Mick: "There's very little live television now. Most of it's taped. It was good fun; the sound was good. We just did three numbers straight. Four days' rehearsal. A lot of people watched it so we're very 'appy, though we didn't get paid of course, like all television programmes. They're all charity. I think we got $300 for the band, and as I'm the leader, I got an extra bit. $50 extra!"

Days before Keith's court case, Mick is interviewed by Anne Nightingale for BBC-TV's Old Grey Whistle Test.

Q: "If the worst should happen, does that mean that the Stones wouldn't be able to tour?"

Mick: "There are so many variables. What happens if they cut his head off, you know what I mean? I just wanna wait and see what happens. Obviously it's a bit difficult planning long expensive tours when we don't know what we're doing."

Q: "Would you go on stage without him?"

Mick: "I'd be on stage without him. I went on a stage with Peter Tosh. But the Stones wouldn't go on stage if Keith was unavailable for a month. I dunno . . . We'll just have to wait and see."

Q: "How is he?"

Mick: "He's very well. He's in Los Angeles sunning up. He's in very good spirits."

Q: "What have you been doing since the tour finished?"

Mick: "I've done a bit of writing, a bit of rehearsing, and we've written a lot of songs for the new album. I dunno when it'll be out. A lot of it depends on what happens to Keith. I suppose I'll have to go and finish it off myself. Keith'll get out on appeal, there's no problem, and we'll go straight into the studio. He'll be out by early spring."

Q: "Are you thinking of keeping (keyboard player) Ian McLagan with you? He was on the last album and did the American tour with you."

Mick: "I dunno. I mean, he hasn't asked me. I do like to keep some elements of the band free, so we've never really kept a piano player, though they've worked with us for years. I mean, it's bad enough playing with Charlie all the time, let alone having to work with six other people!"

Q: "When I last saw you, you seemed very disillusioned about music generally."

Mick: "Not as much as Pete Townshend! I was saying I was fed up with all those LA bands. I don't like LA music. It's got its place but you're very much aware it's a music industry town and no one wants to step out of line 'cos they're selling so many millions of Linda Ronstadt albums, who's very sweet but . . . No one likes new wave bands or new music there. They like the same old thing. There's very little live entertainment. It's more or less your old-fashioned establishment West Coast groups. You know the ones – The Eagles, Linda Ronstadt!"

Q: "Do you think England's got a more healthy music scene?"

Mick: "Yeah, I think so. New York and London are much healthier because they've got more people who really wanna get out there and do something. In LA, it's more, 'I've just bought my $750,000 dollar house, man, and my car's in the yard.' It's not for me, I'm afraid."

Q: "Assuming everything's all right, will you be coming back to play England soon?"

Mick: "Oh, yeah! Soon . . . soon."

MONDAY, 23 OCTOBER 1978

Keith appears in court in Toronto.

Austin Cooper (defence lawyer) describes the guitarist's long journey to the dock:
"It was after a very gruelling schedule (in 1967) with the group, and he was exhausted after all the playing and touring, he experimented with drugs. In 1969, he started with heroin and it got to the state where he was taking such quantities of the drug and getting no euphoria from it. He was taking such powerful amounts – as much as two and a half grams a day – just to feel normal."

Cooper adds that his client has tried two cures, in 1973 and 1974, "but again he fell off the wagon, so to speak".
"He should not be dealt with as a special person, but I ask your honour to understand him as a tortured creative person, as a major contributor to an art form. He turned to heroin to prop up a sagging existence. I ask you to understand the whole man. He has fought a tremendous personal battle to rid himself of this terrible problem."

Keith confirms that the arrest has prompted him to rethink his entire attitude towards drugs.
Keith: "If you want to get off it, you will, and this time I really wanted it to work. I've got to stay on the treatment if I want to stay off it for good."

TUESDAY, 24 OCTOBER 1978

Keith pleads guilty to possession of 22 grams of heroin, a considerably lesser charge than the original one of 'trafficking with a narcotic'. He is sentenced to one year's probation, is ordered to continue his treatment and, bizarrely, to play a benefit concert.

Judge Lloyd Graburn: "It may be that The Rolling Stones have, in their music, glorified and sanctioned the use of drugs – something that should be roundly condemned. Nevertheless, Richards' efforts in removing himself from the drug subculture can only have a salutary effect on the thousands of young people who admire and respect him . . . The Crown seeks a jail term, but I will not incarcerate him for addiction and wealth . . . You will give a benefit performance yourself, or with a group of musicians of your own choice, to the blind young people of the Canadian Institute for the Blind."

Keith: "I'm feeling good about it, obviously, I think it's fair, slightly strange . . . I'm elated and grateful. Now I'll have to find some sidemen for the concert."

Keith Altham (Stones PR): "Mick says he's very pleased, and he thinks Keith will be excellent on his own."

At a press conference held within an hour of the verdict, Keith is asked how he'd been affected by the entire affair.
Keith: "Oh, it's all show business. Every day of my life is show business. I didn't give it much thought until the last few days. I mean, it wasn't as if I was waking up each day thinking the trial is coming."

Had he made any contingency plans for a lengthy jail sentence?
Keith: "I just wondered if the uniform was with stripes or arrows."

How does he view heroin now?
Keith: "It's boring. You lose your respect and confidence. Once you get to the stage of addiction, it is just where you get to ask, 'Where is the dope?' You wonder what you are doing sitting in an apartment with four men who are dribbling. I'm happy to be off it . . . I have become a lush."

And the reaction of the rest of the band?
Keith: "They were very ticked off I didn't get put away for 30 years. I'm going to use the bail money to bribe the rest of the band to do the benefit."

And the Stones' role in glorifying drug use?
Keith: "I think that is a misconception. There are drug overtones in about 1 per cent of the band's songs, and Mick wrote them, not me."

Keith's mother strikes a surprisingly confident tone . . .
Mrs Doris Richards: "I never worried that they'd send him to prison. How could they? The kids would have rioted."

. . . others, such as the Toronto Sun, *feign outrage.*
"Imagine the laughter among Rolling Stones fans throughout the world . . . Their hero got busted and got off."

While, unexpectedly, Keith emerges as the true voice of reason.
Keith: "The only point of sending someone on a drug bust to jail is to rehabilitate them. As I've done that myself, there shouldn't be any need for jail."

WEDNESDAY, 22 NOVEMBER 1978

The Federal Crown Prosecutor is granted an extension to appeal against Keith Richards' sentence.
Keith: "They've put in an appeal in Canada, so we're back to square one. I don't have to go through the whole case again, but if the appeal judge says the trial judge was wrong, then I'm back where I started . . . They've turned it into a stupid internal squabble. It's 'Canada v The Rolling Stones'. The trial judge did his best to please everybody. I don't have to make any more appearances, only in concert in front of the blind. How can you appear in front of the blind?"

TUESDAY, 12 DECEMBER 1978

A Keith Richards solo single, 'Run Rudolph Run', is released in the States. It revives rumours of a solo album.
Keith: "I've met a few people during the past year or so, and we've got together and put some stuff on tape. That's as far as it goes. Whether it comes out or not is another thing. They've put out a single in the States and no one likes it. It was cut at Island in Hammersmith two years ago. It hasn't been released here (in Britain). We're letting the Americans suffer first."
Q: "But are you hoping to get a solo album out?"
Keith: "No . . . certain executives are. I don't give a shit. I've got some stuff but I don't know if roots reggae is what people want to hear from me. That's most of the stuff I've done while playing with (Peter) Tosh's band in Kingston. Either I cut some more to make enough for an album or I leave it in the warehouse."

It's been over three years since Bill Wyman's last solo album . . .
Bill: "If I write a song, there's no way the band's gonna do it because I can't sing the bloody thing to the rest of them or play the guitar, as Keith might, to show them what it could sound like. I've got to pick up a bass to try to get a song across, or an acoustic guitar which I can't play − I can't play chords . . ."

And, as Bill knows, despite sell-out tours and successful recordings, it's in songwriting where the real money lies.
Bill: "If the band brings in a million dollars in a year, there's obviously a vast difference in what Keith gets and what I get. He probably gets five times more than me. I don't feel bad about that because he writes the songs, but what does get me sometimes is *if* I had an idea for a song, I would like to be equally considered."

Keith might now be free, but during a fractious interview with Chris Welch at London's Ritz Hotel in January 1979, he and Anita's tensions show through.
Keith: "I don't want no tea, or coffee. I just want this bottle (of vodka) . . . All right, leave me to it, you've heard it all before."
Anita Pallenberg: "I haven't heard it all before."
Q: "Can we turn the music down a little bit?"
Keith: "Sure!"

Anita begins to answer on Keith's behalf.
Keith: "Look, darling, will you please shut up! . . . Back to my train of thought."

A little later . . .

Keith looks angrily towards Anita, who is on a couch giggling conspiratorially with Barbara Charone.
Keith: "You know, there's nothing more disturbing than two chicks whispering to each other."
Anita: "Oh, just throw me out. Don't mind it. I mean . . . y'know . . . all that about the Palladium, that's *old* stuff."

A little later . . .
Anita: "Mumble, mumble."
Keith: "Look darling, who's doing this interview?"
Anita: "I am!"
Keith: "The problem is if two people talk at once, you don't hear anything."

Later still . . .
Keith: "Five years ago there were people who said they could never get behind reggae."
Anita: "Like Keith Richard."
Keith: "Thank *you,* darling . . . okay, fuck off."
Anita: "You baam claat man."
Q: "What does *that* mean?"
Keith: "It was a cloth that they used to mop up the blood after whipping a slave."

The interview grinds to an unsatisfactory halt.

SATURDAY, 13 JANUARY 1979

Keith: "I'm probably a little out of touch with the music here, but most of the stuff that's happening here has lost touch with itself anyway. It's back to fads. One minute it's Bay City Rollers, then it's punk rock, then it's power pop or new wave, then that's finished. People are back to sticking labels on things . . . Where they went wrong with the punk thing was they were trying to make four-track records on 32-track. We were trying to do the same thing in a way. We tried to make 1964 sound like 1956, which wasn't possible either. But we did end up with something that was our own."

Out of touch, but not that out of touch . . .
Keith: "Who's that band who sound like The Doors (The Stranglers)? I hate them. What's Public Image about? Johnny Rotten or Lydon or whatever you call him . . . I like him, but that single's just a Byrds guitar sound, innit?"

TUESDAY, 23 JANUARY 1979

Mick is ordered to pay $1,500 per week towards the upkeep of his daughter, Karis Hunt.
Marsha Hunt: "He knew we were having hard times and he made no offer of contribution, which I found stunning. He knew I wasn't being heavy, I wasn't demanding. I said, 'Look, we're in trouble. I haven't been working. Can you help me?' And he didn't come through. You don't come through when you're on a tour grossing millions of dollars?!

"Over the years I've made incredible excuses for Mick. He was my friend and I don't dump on friends. But automatically his reaction was – 'She's making the charge, well, I deny it.'

"I knew I was walking into a den of lions, but I was strong. I said, if I get 15 cents and a declaration of paternity, then I'll be happy . . . I WON! Winning turned everything negative into positive. Now I've got this wonderful daughter and there are no longer any financial problems about providing her with the things she needs."

Curiously, Mick maintains a traditional line on parenting.
Mick: "I don't think girls should have kids without there being some sort of father figure around, however little he might be there. I don't go along with single women just getting pregnant and bringing up a baby alone because I think that's bad for the child. The child needs both. If I've got strong views, it's mostly from experience."

THURSDAY, 5 APRIL 1979

After several months of trying, lawyers acting for Bianca Jagger finally serve divorce papers on Mick.
Marvin Mitchelson (lawyer): "Bianca would have preferred to have kept the marriage going because they have a beautiful child. But Mick has made his choice – another woman."
Bianca Jagger: "Despite all the things you have read about me, I am really a very moral person. I had just one lapse during the whole time I was with Mick – a romance with Ryan O'Neal. I told Mick all about that."
Bianca Jagger: "Mick has bragged that he has never given any woman anything and never would."
Jerry Hall: "I love the Stones. They're great and they make a lot of money. Why should I try to ruin such a good thing? . . . Even if he loses all his money I've got enough for both of us."

SUNDAY, 22 APRIL 1979

Keith plays two benefit shows in Ontario, Canada with a specially assembled band, The New Barbarians, featuring Ron Wood in the line-up. The group continue to tour throughout April and May, and bow out with a show at Knebworth, where Keith's mum caught up with him.
Mrs Doris Richards: "When I see him up there it's a great feeling. I feel like shouting to everybody, 'That's my son up there!' I'm so proud. To me he's still my Keith. He's still my baby. I do worry about the trouble he gets

in but people always make it out to be much worse than it is. He always comes through all right . . . The drugs did upset me for a time but now it's all finished he looks so much better. I think he knows what he's doing."

Keith reckons that one of his heroes ought to take a leaf out of his book.
Keith: "Chuck Berry is the biggest cunt I've ever met. That's on the record by the way! He's also the most charming cunt and I've got to like him for it all the same even if he's so tight he'll never get a halfway decent band together."

FRIDAY, 11 MAY 1979

Ron Wood's third solo album, Gimme Some Neck, *includes a new song by Bob Dylan titled 'Seven Days'.*
Ron: "I've always had a lot of front with Bob ever since he came to the party for my first solo album in New York. He was the first to arrive, and no one recognised him at all. He sidled up to me and said, 'Heeeeey, man, I really dig your album.' Since then, he's always been really nice. If I call his office, he calls me back in five minutes. I've got more front than Harrods, I have!"

THURSDAY, 21 JUNE 1979

The Stones return to the Pathé-Marconi Studios in Paris for sessions for their forthcoming album. The sessions continue intermittently until late October.
Keith: "A really successful album makes you wanna do better the next time. When we first recorded there, we had no previous success to go on. It worked out fine, we got a good sound, and we enjoyed the studio."
Mick: "We recorded the last one there. It's a good studio, has a real high ceiling, and French people don't record after eight o'clock at night so we've got the place to ourselves. And Paris is very quiet for us. People don't bother us much there."

WEDNESDAY, 27 JUNE 1979

The appeal against Keith's sentence is heard in Toronto. He files an affidavit that is read out in court.
Keith: "I have grimly determined to change my life and abstain from any drug use. I can truthfully say that the prospect of ever using drugs again in the future is totally alien to my thinking. My experience has also had an

important effect not only on my happiness, but on my happiness at home in which my young son is brought up."

The appeal is unsuccessful.

WEDNESDAY, 20 JULY 1979

"STONE'S WIFE IN GUN DRAMA"

Seventeen-year-old Scott Cantrell is found dying in Frog Hollow, Keith and Anita's country house in South Salem, Westchester County, Connecticut. He has a single gunshot wound to the head. Anita is charged with possessing stolen property and having the gun without a licence and is freed on £250 bail.

Police spokesman: "He apparently committed suicide. Miss Pallenberg was in the master bedroom with him . . . Keith Richards was not at the house at the time."

Anita Pallenberg: "Scott and I had been lying in bed watching *The Odd Couple* on TV. I got out of bed to tidy up. Then I heard a shot. I saw him lying there with blood coming from the side of his head . . . I picked up the revolver and put it on the chest of drawers just to get rid of it. I hate the awful things."

Jim Cantrell (brother): "The police have told me that Scott had so much alcohol in his blood it was incredible. I am not sure about their relationship, but he was just a mixed-up kid and she is supposed to be a mature woman and a mother. She should have known better than to allow someone who was under age to get himself drunk all day and then play around with a loaded gun. She may not have pulled the trigger, but we blame her for what happened."

Sue Cantrell (sister-in-law): "There are a lot of questions to be answered. The police seem to think it's going to be an open and shut case. But we are determined to try to make sure the whole story comes out."

Jeffrey Sessler (friend): "Anita invited him to come and live at the place about a month ago. She wanted to let him work for the family as an odd-job man, but quite honestly I don't think he could adapt to the warmth and love he was being shown. Although Anita cared for him, it was not a sex-type relationship."

MONDAY, 19 NOVEMBER 1979

Anita Pallenberg is cleared of any involvement in the death of Scott Cantrell by a grand jury in Westchester County, Connecticut.

Mr Cantrell (father): "I think they were lovers and she had supplied him with drugs. A 37-year-old woman should have known better than to associate with a 17-year-old boy in her bedroom. I feel she is fully responsible for the death of my son, no matter how they wrap it up."

Detective Douglas Lamanna: "From the angle of the bullet we know it was self-inflicted. He held the gun to his temple and pulled the trigger. But what made the poor, mixed-up kid do it we will never know . . . I would not like to open wounds and make a statement about the relationship between Miss Pallenberg and the dead man. But I will say that the facts speak for themselves."

Keith and Anita separate shortly afterwards.

Anita Pallenberg: "That boy of 17 who shot himself in my house really ended it for us. And although we occasionally saw each other for the sake of the children, it was the end of our personal relationship."

4

Dirty Work

MONDAY, 18 FEBRUARY 1980

With the next Stones album having been completed the previous autumn, Bill Wyman hints that he's ready to move on.
Bill: "That's it for me. I want to do other things. I only got into rock'n' roll for a bit of fun and to see the world for a couple of years. It ended up becoming such a part of me, but I refuse to let it dominate my life."

Mick shrugs his shoulders at the news.
Mick: "I don't think it was (a joke). He seems to be quite serious about it, which is all right with me. I don't mind . . . I don't think Charlie Watts is going to leave, but if Bill wants to leave the band, I mean, what can I do?"

SATURDAY, 1 MARCH 1980

Mick visits Beat writer William Burroughs at his 'bunker' on the Bowery, New York. The dinner has been organised to provide raw material for an article Burroughs has been commissioned to write. According to his biographer Victor Bockris, Burroughs opens the conversation with some thoughts about the role of rock music in the wider cultural revolution.
Mick: "What is this cultural revolution you're talking about?"
William Burroughs: "Do you realise that 30 or 40 years ago, a four-letter word could not appear on a printed page? You're asking *what* cultural revolution? Holy shit, man, what'd you think we've been doing all these years?"
Andy Warhol: "He's young enough that he doesn't think about it. A lot of people don't think about it."
William Burroughs: "Pop music was one of the key things in the whole cultural revolution. Every time they got busted for drugs, we got that

much closer to decriminalisation of pot all over the world because it was becoming a household word."

Mick: "Is there a phone in this joint?"

The summit meeting lasts just 15 minutes.

SPRING 1980

Mick and Keith are interviewed for a Jamaican television show, Earl Chin's Rockers. *Inevitably, the conversation swings round to the country's biggest musical export, Bob Marley.*

Mick: "I like his music very much. I like his songs, which is basically the reason for a lot of the success he's had . . . apart from being pushed so hard."

Keith: "He's put up as reggae music when there's lots of different types of reggae music. Bob's good, but there are others just as good. It just so happens that Bob's out front with the image and all that."

Mick: "Someone has to do that. He's come in for a lot of criticism for that, talk about compromise and all that. But you do have to compromise. I'm not saying that Bob Marley's compromised his music, but you have to compromise your way of living a bit. You can't be touring America and all that and expect to be exactly the same person that you were when you were living in Trenchtown."

Q: "How do you see reggae developing in the Eighties?"

Keith: "A lot of people have been trying to make reggae the next big thing for years. But reggae music works from the roots. It's gonna grab 'em from the ground up."

Mick: "Reggae music is evolving because in England, and now in America, you get white kids who are brought up on it – like The Police, for example. So instead of being music from Jamaica, it's actually made universal. It's not alien, ethnic or territorial . . . (It's like) the ska thing that the new wave people like and The Specials had a hit with."

Keith: "They were real small kids when ska was big, so for them it's like going back to the music that they heard when they were kids."

Q: "What is the formula for The Rolling Stones' success?"

Keith: "Positive vibration!"

Q: "How do you see Rastafari? Positively?"

Keith: "Definitely, especially the 'erb! The basic thing is that they're mainly great guys to hang out with. You can communicate easily, there's no bullshit. That is the main thing. Without getting into the philosophy,

296

Rastas are the easiest guys to get along with and the most turned on to what's going on. It's a lifestyle."

Mick: "I like it 'cos they don't really proselytise you. On the other hand, they do! Maybe they think we're completely beyond saving. I think I'm right in saying that Rastafarians are quite free personally. There's a lot of scope to make your own rules."

Q: "Any other favourite reggae artists?"

Keith: "Jacob Miller, Black Uhuru, Dillinger, Big Youth. I can go on."

Q: "Will you ever perform in Jamaica?"

Keith: "When we get good enough."

Q: "Will reggae eventually become an accepted art form?"

Mick: "Two years ago, in countries like France, you wouldn't hear reggae on the radio. This year, they're recording it in French. It will become accepted. You've got people who are trying to bend it for their own commercial ends, like in France, and you've got the people back in Jamaica still recording roots. I guess it'll always be like that."

Keith: "It's a matter of time. There's no need to hurry . . ."

FRIDAY, 20 JUNE 1980

A new single, 'Emotional Rescue', is released.

Mick: "It's a bit of a strange track. I wrote that on the electric piano and I sang it in that falsetto from the beginning. So I kept that. It started off with me playing the piano, Ronnie on bass and Charlie on drums. After that, we added saxophone, so it's not actually the band playing. That's maybe why it turned out a bit strange . . . It's just about some girl who's in some sort of manhood problems. I don't mean she's going crazy, she's just a little bit screwed up. And he wants to be the one that helps her out."

MONDAY, 23 JUNE 1980

Emotional Rescue is released.

Mick: "I don't think anyone can expect a new album necessarily to be as good as the last one. You can't expect them to be all of the same standard and to please the same people."

In Melody Maker, *Ray Bonici suggests that the Stones might be running out of songs.*

Mick: "On the contrary. Instead of going in with ten songs and recording those, we recorded about 40 songs and finished about 25 of them. And then we had to pick 10 out of the 25 for the album . . . We just continued recording and forgot to put the record out. All I know is, the later it got, the more mad I got. It didn't seem to get me anywhere and everyone just slowed down."

Mick: "When we first started, we used to be very separate and I just used to write the words. Now we mix it up a lot and I write quite a lot of the music and Keith writes some words here and there. He always did write a lot of the words but now it's more mixed up than ever. It's mixed up but in some senses it's separate. So some songs I wrote on my own and some songs he wrote on his own."

Mick: "Nearly all the songs are about girls on this album. I think every single one is."

Mick, who handles much of the promotion work for the record, also feels moved to deny the overriding critical feeling.

"We didn't rework any of the *Some Girls* leftovers."

WEDNESDAY, 25 JUNE 1980

Mick appears on Dutch television show Countdown *to promote the new album. Invariably, the interviewer is more interested in other matters.*

Q: "You must have a lot of songs left over from previous albums. Will we ever hear them?"

Mick: "When I'm run under a bus you might."

Q: "Did you ever feel like making a solo album?"

Mick: "Yeah, I did, actually. I might well do one – this year maybe. Maybe I'll rework some of the old songs. It depends on whether we go into the studio or not. If we don't, then maybe I'll do one."

Q: "What kind of music turns you on these days?"

Mick: "I listen to everything. I like most kinds of music."

Q: "You play more guitar on the new album."

Mick: "Yeah, I play on most tracks. I play piano too."

Q: "Do you have any plans for acting in films again?"

Mick: "No."

Q: "How do you keep yourself in shape?"

Mick: "By a bike. I don't like jogging . . ."

SUMMER 1980

Mick is rumoured to be working on a new film, Hot.

Mick: "They should be telling me soon if they have all the money. It's quite an interesting story . . . I'm the good boy. I'm not really the hero. There's two actually and one of them is an anti-hero. It's not just a bullshit film. It's interesting and could be something out of the ordinary and very scary."

And rumours of a solo album persist in the wake of the group's relative inactivity.
Mick: "Yeah, I'll do one. If no one wants to go in the studios in a couple of months, I'll go and give it a try. I've got a lot of stupid songs which the others will never like, so I'll put those out. It'll be an opportunity to do certain things which I couldn't do with the Stones. There are endless possibilities."

MONDAY, 4 AUGUST 1980

John Lennon breaks his five-year retirement and begins work on a new album at the Hit Factory Studios in New York City.
Mick: "I don't think anyone gives a fuck what he does anymore. I don't. He's a cunt! He's right over there – you can see the fucking apartment from my window. Does he ever call me? Does he ever go out? No! Changes his phone number every five minutes. And that Dakota building. Have you ever tried to get in? It's like a jail. I've given up . . . What is all this crap? Hiding behind all this kindergarten stuff. You can bring up children and work at the same time. He's just kow-towing to his fucking wife, probably. She's probably trying to screen him off. I know, mate. I've seen it all before."

John Lennon: "When Mick Jagger or David Bowie or Elton John came to town, I wouldn't respond because they'd always want me to go down to the studio or to the clubs and I didn't want to get in there again. Mick did this whole spiel, 'Come on John, get out of there' . . . You know, what's it got to do with Mick? He was going on about hiding behind your kid, you know. He was trying to be nice about it – he wasn't attacking me but there was a little sort of edge to it."

Lennon proves that he can still get a little edgy, too . . .
John Lennon: "You know they're congratulating the Stones on being together 112 years. Whoopee! At least Charlie's still got his family. In the Eighties, they'll be asking, 'Why are these guys still together? Can't they hack it on their own? Why do they have to be surrounded by a gang? Is the little leader frightened somebody's gonna knife him in the back?' That's gonna be the question. They're gonna look at the Beatles and

Stones and all those guys as relics. They'll be showing pictures of the guy with lipstick wriggling his ass and the four guys with the evil black make-up on their eyes trying to look raunchy. That's gonna be the joke of the future."

SATURDAY, 27 SEPTEMBER 1980

The Police's 'Don't Stand So Close To Me' enters the British chart. It becomes the band's third consecutive number one single.
Mick: "The Police? It's hardly new, is it. The music isn't new. It sounds very old. I quite like The Clash, though, but they really sound old-fashioned. It's fine. I'm very old-fashioned, too. The Clash remind me a bit of the early Stones albums. I think Elvis Costello is a really good song-writer. I like The Specials but I thought their album was very badly recorded. But I've got this tape of them live at this club, which they sent me, and it sounds great."

MONDAY, 1 DECEMBER 1980

Jerry Hall gives Mick a big thumbs up for his off-stage performances.
Jerry Hall: "I can't believe how weird and dirty Mick Jagger is. When I have to be sexy in front of the camera, I think of Mick Jagger and it always does the trick. Mick is one of the sexiest men in the world and the best lover I've ever had. He's a genius."

Bill confines his enthusiasm to professional matters.
Bill: "Mick Jagger is a fantastic performer. No other band has a Mick Jagger. He's no good without the band and the band would be a little dull without him. However, we could go on stage without him, while he couldn't go on stage without us."

MONDAY, 8 DECEMBER 1980

When John Lennon is murdered outside his residence at the Dakota, New York, Mark Chapman's bullets send shivers through the world of celebrity.
Mick: "I think the John Lennon thing was an isolated incident. There were always nuts prowling the streets out there but they're not necessarily going to shoot you. I liked John Lennon. He was a great bloke. What can you say when a friend of yours is shot dead in the street right outside the apartment next to your own?"

TUESDAY, 27 JANUARY 1981

Ian Stewart produces and plays on Rocket 88's eponymous album, recorded live in 1979 with an all-star cast including Charlie Watts, Jack Bruce and Alexis Korner. The self-styled "sixth Stone" also breaks a lengthy silence to talk about the record to Bill German, editor of the respected Stones fanzine Beggars Banquet.

Ian Stewart: "The Stones are basically one thing, and this is another. (Boogie-woogie) has always been my favourite music, and instead of waiting around and wishing that people would play the bloody stuff, I actually did something about it. All I ever do with the Stones is play boogie-woogie anyway. I mean, Chuck Berry's guitar playing is purely boogie-woogie piano transcribed to a guitar."

FEBRUARY 1981

Work stops on Werner Herzog's Fitzcarraldo *as – characteristic of many of the German director's projects – it is beset by various production problems.*

Mick: "It was a drag because I did two months' filming and they'd got all my major scenes. Now they can't use any of it . . . Production stopped because the leading actor, Jason Robards, got ill and left. I sat around in Lima waiting and nothing happened. By that time my contract was up and I couldn't sit around for another three months while they re-shot the whole thing. So I said, 'Goodbye, I'm going back to the record business.' "

But there is another project, Kalki *– scripted by Gore Vidal – waiting in the wings.*

Mick: "The guy starts a new religion. It's very black comedy, a piss-take of America, religion, the CIA, a lot of things. We hope to make it next summer. David Bowie and I have also been knocking a few film scripts around together."

MONDAY, 13 APRIL 1981

A compilation of material from the previous decade, Sucking In The Seventies, *is released.*

Q: "Do you ever listen to old Rolling Stones albums?"

Mick: "No. Never. Never. Never. Not even one. I don't think any of us listen to them. Perhaps Keith does a little bit."

SATURDAY, 25 JULY 1981

Bill Wyman's solo single, '(Si Si) Je Suis Un Rock Star', enters the British chart. It becomes the most successful single released thus far by a solo Stone.

Bill: "It began as a demo I did for Ian Dury. I thought the song had a strong potential but I wasn't prepared to do it because I didn't want to make solo records anymore. But nobody would play it to Ian, and nobody would play it to other artists because they all thought I should do it."

But is Bill surprised by its extraordinary success?
Bill: "I didn't know so many people in the world spoke Cockney French!"

WEDNESDAY, 26 AUGUST 1981

The group hold a press conference at the JFK Stadium, Philadelphia, where they unveil plans for an extensive, four-month tour of America.
Q: "Is this going to be the last Stones tour?"
Mick: "No, this is not a farewell tour."
Q: "Are you looking forward to the tour, Charlie?"
Charlie: "No comment."
Keith: "He always says he doesn't want to go on tour, but he always does. He's one of these guys who appear over the poop deck after it's all over and says, 'I quite enjoyed that.' He just pretends he doesn't want to do it. Why else would he still be here?"

In light of Keith's difficulties, the tour contract for staff includes a new clause.
"If anyone is found in possession of drugs in any part of the backstage area, that person will be immediately banished from the vicinity, whatever their capacity."

THURSDAY, 27 AUGUST 1981

Tattoo You *is released.*
Mick: "Dare I say it, this album seems to be selling better. But to me the last three are all the same. *Some Girls*, *Emotional Rescue* and this one don't have any quality difference. Sometimes people say we are pretentious, but this new one is quite cool and relaxed. It's not a great step forward or backwards . . . When we did *Some Girls*, we were feeling very vicious and snarling. But I got that out of my system and there are a few ballads coming now. I'm not straining so much."
Mick: "Usually we have lots of half-finished songs left over and then we decide whether to keep them for the next album or not. But this time we actually have finished ones and I think they're good."
Mick: " 'Heaven' is a nice song. It started out with just me and Charlie

playing in the studio, then we added Keith. I was just fooling around singing on my own. Keith said it sounded really good, and that we should leave it alone, but we added some harmonies and guitar. There's not much of a lyric – just a sound and a mood."

Mick: "People always sniff their noses when we play a blues, but 'Black Limousine' has turned out to be the one that everyone likes."

And, as usual, the artwork is a talking point – but this time more among the band than for anyone else.

Mick: "I don't think it came off too well. I like the picture of Keith but not of me. Covers don't mean much, do they? If the record is good and the cover is shit, people don't blame you, I hope."

MONDAY, 14 DECEMBER 1981

Mick Taylor joins the Stones on stage at the Kemper Arena in Kansas City.
Ron: "He shocked us with how loud he was blasting it, bulldozing through parts of songs that should have been subtle, ignoring breaks and taking uninvited solos."

APRIL 1982

Britain sends its armed forces across the other side of the globe in a bid to liberate the Falkland Islands from invasion by Argentina.
Mick: "It's really none of my business."

MAY 1982

Keith is reconciled with his father Bert after a 20-year hiatus.
Keith: "It was a long time coming. I haven't seen my father since I left home when I was 18. I realised that I'd been away from him longer than I'd been with him. When I left home, my parents separated. Every good boy's natural inclination is to take care of mummy, and that means taking sides. It's been fantastic."

Also on the domestic front, despite a seemingly settled relationship with Jerry Hall, Mick insists that he's no longer the marrying kind.
Mick: "I won't marry again. If you're not successful at it, it isn't a case of try, try again . . . Since the divorce we're not even friends. She's been so difficult and devious that I'll never be friends with her again."

Meanwhile, the Stones begin rehearsals for their forthcoming European tour at Shepperton Studios. Fifteen years after he last worked with the band, photographer Gered Mankowitz gets the call to drop by and shoot the Stones at work. After an initial meeting, Mankowitz is instructed to return a couple of nights later.

Keith: "Ah, you're back again."

Gered Mankowitz: "Yeah, we're going to do this session."

Keith: "I don't think we are."

Gered: "Why?"

Keith: "Well, you remind us of really bad times. Whenever we look at you we think of $1.5 million."

Gered: "Well, that was nothing to do with me."

A drunken Mick finally arrives at 3.30 in the morning to rescue the situation. Kind of . . .

Mick: "Yeah, all right, let's do it. Don't take too long about it!"

WEDNESDAY, 26 MAY 1982

The Stones begin their British tour at the Capitol Theatre in Aberdeen.

Q: "Why do you think so many people still come?"

Mick: "I dunno. I'm sure some come 'cos they like the Stones or they've seen them before. Perhaps they've heard it's a good show."

MONDAY, 31 MAY 1982

The Rolling Stones return to their London roots with a secret show at the 400-capacity 100 Club in central London. Radio 1's Andy Peebles wonders what it feels like.

Mick: "Club gigs are so hot compared with a stadium with lots of fresh air and oxygen. I just get out of breath in places like the 100 Club. You get more wiped out playing there than Wembley Stadium. We'd played some clubs in America but this one was much more unannounced and last minute. I enjoyed it; it's just a very different atmosphere. You can relax in between numbers, and it doesn't matter if you want to do a different number. You tend to get locked into a certain show in stadiums."

Q: "Is it difficult trying to communicate to stadium audiences?"

Mick: "It's impossible! You try to, but hopefully they're hearing you at the back if you've got a good enough sound system. And that's the way of communicating. Also, everyone these days in stadiums uses video. That's one of the reasons why we try to build ramps into the audience, and I think that works really well."

TUESDAY, 1 JUNE 1982

Still Life, a live document recorded during the 1981 American tour, is released. A cover of Smokey Robinson's 'Going To A Go-Go' is lifted off as the album's first single – and promoted with a video featuring animation.
Keith: "I've never seen it. That's something to look forward to, Ronnie!"
Q: "Obviously you weren't involved in the final production . . ."
Keith: "The animation was added to footage we'd already shot."

Does Keith really believe in the power of the new video medium?
Keith: "Television's never really been set up for music, but now with videos you can plug them straight into the stereo system and get the sound as well as the vision. That's why it's beginning to take off."

And the song?
Keith: "Mick and I have been bashing that one out in hotel rooms ever since Smokey first brought it out. It was something we all knew; we'd warm up with it in dressing rooms. It was a song we'd wished we'd done then. I can't say why we did it now. It was just . . . 'Let's try it out'."

SUNDAY, 13 JUNE 1982

Keith is interviewed in Paris for an MTV broadcast.
Q: "How has the tour gone so far?"
Keith: "We thought we'd take a bit of time getting into it, but it felt like we'd had two days off (since the US dates). From the start the band was red hot. Sometimes we don't tour for three years and that way you can get really rusty."
Q: "What have you been doing in between?"
Keith: "Mick and I worked on our own albums. That's basically what we did – and set up this tour. This is the first time that Europe has really been played on this scale."
Q: "So we can expect a solo record from you?"
Keith: "No, but I enjoy recording solo. I have a huge collection of tracks I'd done on the piano."
Q: "Is home taping killing music?"
Keith: "I can see both sides of it. But if the kids are doing it, that's fine by

me because it's another level of street level demand. They must really like you."

Q: "How do you maintain your street appeal?"

Keith: "Being a junkie keeps you pretty much down on the street – that was one of the things that kept me down to earth."

Q: "How has being off drugs changed you?"

Keith: "It's changed the way I live a lot because I don't have to worry about all that. All my friends aren't junkies any more, which is what happens when you're on that stuff. I was always very conscious when a tour was coming up; I'd always try and clean up. All the parasites start coming round. And you're getting all that energy back from audiences, and working with the crew. To get over a tour takes weeks, sometimes months."

THURSDAY, 24 JUNE 1982

BBC-TV's Newsnight *broadcasts an interview with Keith conducted by Robin Denselow in a late-night Parisian bar, 12 days earlier. Its focus is the Stone's ten-year battle with heroin.*

Q: "Do you live very much at night?"

Keith: "Yeah, it seems to work out that way. I generally keep the curtains drawn."

Q: "You seem to be the mainstay of R&B within the band. Is that a fair comment?"

Keith: "I'd say I'm one of them. Everyone in the band is very well grounded in that area of music. It was almost heresy to play anything else. We wanted to preach the gospel of R&B. Idealistic kids. In this band, everybody happily supports everybody else which is one of the main reasons that we are still together. It's fun for us, a very well paid hobby."

Q: "Did you realise that drugs could threaten that?"

Keith: "Eventually, in Toronto, yes. The very fact that I was a total junkie for almost ten years leaves me now realising that it didn't worry me too much then because of the very nature of heroin. It's heroin you end up appreciating. That's all you want. Nothing else is interesting to you. *Nothing* worries you! It's a very easy thing to take and get into, and incredibly difficult to get off.

"Black market, especially in heroin is very, very dangerous. They're totally unscrupulous, they have nobody to answer to. You could find yourself taking one great big dose of strychnine. That's why there's such a high fatality rate among musicians, especially because it goes along with a musician's life and it always has done – because of the ups and downs, the adrenaline, the energy, making the gig the next day when you're totally drained. It's passed on from one generation to the next. Toronto made me realise that this was it – if I made a break with it, and got out of the court hassle. Another time would be it. I was jeopardising the lives and futures of my children, guys in the band. It wasn't just me; it was gonna affect everybody I care about. In a way, they did me a favour – God bless the Mounties."

Q: "Were the people you were forced to deal with dangerous?"

Keith: "There were a couple of times in New York where these people have incredible set-ups, look-outs for the cops, bullets would flood into the wall . . . 'Oh, forget it, I'll cold turkey!' New York can be real rough. The next time you'd take a gun with you . . . I carried a piece in those days."

Q: "How long did you carry a gun for?"

Keith: "Until I stopped being a junkie. You'd buy the stuff, walk down the stairs, and they'd have their mate down there who'd stick you up again."

Q: "How has your life changed in the last five years?"

Keith: "It's been a gradual rediscovery of the other joys of life. It's given me more time to live a slightly more normal life, follow through interests. Now I can read a book occasionally, and get out and see other acts, rather than be stuck in a basement waiting for the man to come."

Q: "Do you have any ambitions left after 20 years with the Rolling Stones?"

Keith: "I never had any ambitions in the first place. I guess if there's a general one, it's connected with the band. We're still trying to make the Stones a better band, and I guess we are. They go on every night with the idea of making this show a little bit better than the one before, which is admirable. They are very good players."

Q: "What will you do if, or when, the Stones break up?"

Keith: "I don't know. I read the other day that there was no reason why the Stones couldn't be Sinatra or Bing Crosby which I thought was an amazing comparison. In rock'n'roll, nobody's ever done it. I played with Muddy Waters in Chicago and he's no young guy and he was playing as good as ever. And if he can do it, I'm sure that I can – unless I get my hands chopped off."

Keith's new-found smack-free state poses new problems for Ronnie.

Ron: "He's setting more of an example to me these days than I am to him!

307

When I first met him, he was that guy up there somewhere who you couldn't communicate with unless you had a baked bean can and a piece of string. He was hard to get through to if you weren't on his wavelength. I've seen him when he was really heavily into the dope. Now that he's not, he makes me feel guilty if I have too much to drink."

SATURDAY, 26 JUNE 1982

The Stones perform the second of two nights at London's Wembley Stadium. Mick is cornered backstage by Paula Yates for some old-style questioning.
Q: "What do you do when you're not on tour?"
Mick: "I like reading and writing songs. I don't watch telly."
Q: "What sort of girls do you like?"
Mick: "Cheerful ones. I don't like moody ones."
Q: "Would you say you were content?"
Mick: "Yeah, pretty much."
Q: "More than before?"
Mick: "More than I was, say, five years ago."
Q: "Do you see the rest of the band socially?"
Mick: "Yeah."

MONDAY, 5 JULY 1982

Mick is interviewed in Cologne for a German television show, Tempo.
Q: "A long time ago, in a song called 'Ruby Tuesday', you wrote a line, 'Lose your dreams and you may lose your mind'. Now you seem to me to be still a very sane person. Do you still have a lot of dreams?"
Mick: "I dream a lot, yeah, I do. I'm very romantic . . ."
Q: "In what sense?"
Mick: "Dreaming things that may not come true, or fantasising."
Q: "Surely it must be easy for you to make a lot of those dreams come true, and more difficult to find dreams that you can't realise."
Mick: "No, there's always room for you to be very imaginative if you are."
Q: "Which means that you are still very imaginative?"
Mick: "Hopefully, yeah."
Q: "Do you still find you are able to express yourself fully through music?"
Mick: "Not completely. I don't think I'm a talented enough musician to do that."

MONDAY, 26 JULY 1982

With the European tour ending in Leeds the previous night, Mick celebrates his birthday at Langan's Brasserie in London. The last to leave, he is eventually helped out by the restaurant manager, Harry McHugh.
Jerry Hall: "Be careful. Don't drop him. You're carrying £40 million worth of pop star like a sack of potatoes."

SEPTEMBER 1982

It is announced that Mick has been paid a reported £2 million by publishing house Weidenfeld & Nicolson for his autobiography.
Mick: "Writing that book (will be) fun because you delve into things that you've really forgotten about. It's not just anecdotes, it's how you see the time you're in. There's gotta be stories that'll make people laugh. Bill's really into setting the record straight. I'm not. I'm not gonna be defensive about that. It's totally subjective."

He is also asked who might play Mick Jagger in a film version of his life.
Mick: "They're probably not born yet. I could direct it though, and write the screenplay. Do it all!"

OCTOBER 1982

Mick's name has recently been linked to a string of women, including Cornelia Guest, Valerie Perrine and Victoria Vicuna.
Mick: "For any relationship to last, there has to be a bit of playing about."

THURSDAY, 24 MARCH 1983

A full-length in-concert feature film, Let's Spend The Night Together, *shot during the autumn 1981 US tour, is released to British cinemas.*
Press release: "Twenty-five songs spanning 20 years of the greatest ongoing act in Rock'n'Roll."

FRIDAY, 24 JUNE 1983

"I WATCHED AS STAR WAS MURDERED"

Friend and Guinness heir Nicholas Fitzgerald tells the Cheltenham Echo *that he's writing an "explosive" book on the murder of Brian Jones. He maintains he* received a call from a mutual friend who was "clearly upset and said there was something very wrong" at Brian's Cotchford Farm home.

Nicholas Fitzgerald: "When I arrived the atmosphere was very strange – people were standing around like stone statues."

Later that evening, he saw three men beside the pool.
". . . One of whom appeared to have his foot over the water. Richard (Fitzgerald's chauffeur) was also watching. But he only confided to me some years later that he was certain the man had his foot on Brian's head and was holding it under the water. I have since realised that is what I saw too."

After being pushed into a bush by an unnamed man, Fitzgerald "freaked out and left". Now claiming to have evidence that "an order went out to kill Brian Jones", he says he's felt in fear of his life and employs security guards at his remote home.
"I don't need the money. I am conducting a personal vendetta against people who killed a friend and, as a Catholic, I consider that the guilty should be brought to justice."

Det-Supt John McConnell, Sussex CID: "The death of Brian Jones was fully investigated at the time and no subsequent evidence has been forthcoming to cause Sussex police to reopen the 13-year-old inquiry."

SATURDAY, 25 JUNE 1983

Despite having walked out on the mixing of the forthcoming Stones album, Keith maintains a dignified silence, preferring instead to discuss his specialist subject.
Keith: "I don't like to regret heroin because I learned a lot from it. It was a large part of my life. It is something I went through and dealt with. I'd regret it if I hadn't dealt with it, or if I had OD'd. I would definitely regret it then. A lot of my friends, who should by rights be around, aren't because of it. I don't think it makes a damned bit of difference to anyone going to get into it being told, 'Don't'. In fact it sometimes reinforces the desire to take it. Having been on it, I know. If there is anything I do regret, it's its accessibility to very young kids."

TUESDAY, 26 JULY 1983

Mick Jagger turns 40.
Mick: "When you get to my age you really have to work at staying young. You've got to be fit, because rock requires a tremendous amount

of energy and I find that if your body is alive, your mind becomes alive. That's vital in a business that is as fast as this."

Pete Townshend: "(He) will still be beautiful when he's 50, and his talent will still be as strong at 50 because his ambition is not dependent on his youth. His songwriting is not dependent on his own suffering, and his desire to be popular and loved (is) not dependent on his personal security . . . Jagger was into rock'n'roll before me but, unlike me, he still lives for it."

SATURDAY, 20 AUGUST 1983

The Stones sign a world-beating $28 million contract with CBS that commits them to a further four studio albums.

Sheldon Vogue (Atlantic Records): "We hated losing them, but the numbers they were asking just didn't make sense."

Mick: "It's good to have a change. You become part of the furniture after a while."

Keith: "There's more enthusiasm with a new company."

FRIDAY, 21 OCTOBER 1983

Interviewed for German television, Keith is asked about the Stones penchant for "writing songs about sex and drugs and rock'n'roll".

Keith: "We don't know much about anything else. It seems that blood and violence is playing a greater role in the world. We're that great old cliché, a mirror of society. I love clichés, they're so true and so boring, but there are horrible elements of truth in cliché. To me this album is a little bit of a brother to *Beggars Banquet*. When there's too much crap going down, you find yourself writing about it and singing about it. We never stepped out of our way to be political or sociologically interesting. 'Undercover Of The Night' is basically about Central America: 'Oops a daisy, here we go again,' the possibilities and the confusion and the stupidity of not leaving people alone. I was reading something the other day that said, 'If the system's the answer, it must have been a bloody stupid question.'"

Q: "How do you rate yourself as a guitarist?"

Keith: "I'm not into ratings. The day that I'm satisfied with what I do is the day that I give up, 'cos then I've done it. It's the search that's important. The greatest thing that a musician can do . . . it doesn't matter if you're successful or famous . . . is that somebody picks up on it. That's the greatest epitaph: 'Rest In Peace – he passed it on.' "

WEDNESDAY, 26 OCTOBER 1983

Mick and Keith are reunited in Mexico where they begin shooting action scenes for a forthcoming promotional video, directed by Julian Temple.
Mick: "It's not a performance video, though there is performance in it. Tonight we're doing a big shot of these bourgeois people in a swimming-pool. I get taken out of my room in the Holiday Inn, taken off to be done in. I play two parts – a journalist and a rock singer, which is me. It's quite a complicated story; it's very compressed. Julian likes to do dual roles. Keith's one of the real baddies, head of the baddies. I don't think he'll have a lot of trouble!"
Keith: "I'm winging it!"

But is all the effort that goes into video-making more to do with marketing than art?
Keith: "I've no idea. It's a double-edged sword. We've been doing visuals for promotion for years, but now it's almost got to the point that you have to make a movie."
Mick: "I wouldn't call it art. But it's been around for a long time. Lots of bands including this band, broke on television. It gave us a lot of oppor-tunities. That's how we got to be known throughout England. It's the same principal. I'm all for that and I always have been. We did skits, painted ourselves up for a 'Jumpin' Jack Flash' video. It was a bit amateur-ish compared with what's being done now. Rock videos are a testing ground for directors."
Q: "Will videos become as important as your recordings?"
Mick: "It's difficult to say. The two things are tied together. They cer-tainly take a long time to do. The main problem is the funding of them. Most record companies won't fund a whole album's worth of them. But I'd really like to tie the whole thing up with one album."

THURSDAY, 1 NOVEMBER 1983

A new single, 'Undercover Of The Night', is released.
Mick: "It is supposed to be about the repression of violence in our minds, in society's minds, because we get used to it. It's also about repressive political systems, pretty serious stuff, not Top 20 material. It makes a

change from songs about having a party . . . A lot of it was inspired by the things I read about all the people who've disappeared in Argentina."

Mick: "The video sent out with that song makes it easier to understand. It's a bit of a departure for us. We haven't done anything like that since 'Street Fighting Man'."

However, the furore that greets the video almost overshadows the record's release.

BBC spokesman: "It's exceedingly violent and we couldn't consider it for *Top Of The Pops*."

Julian Temple: "It's a story that's been triggered off by the song, which is to a certain extent what goes on in some parts of Central America. More than that, though, it involves MTV because you see the whole thing through the eyes of a couple of kids watching it on MTV."

The Tube co-host Muriel Gray gives the pair a genuine on-air grilling.

Q: "Mick, why on earth did you choose to put such explicit scenes of violence into a promo film?"

Mick: "The video follows the song. It's about political repression, it's about violence. We're not trying to sell the record with advertising clichés. We wanted to make something that was about the song."

Q: "We've all seen the real atrocities of South American terrorists on the news. Doesn't this glamorise it?"

Julian Temple: "When he gets to the age of 21, the average kid in America has seen 65,000 killings on TV and that devalues the meaning of a killing. It makes people immune to it."

Q: "Would you then prefer kids to say, 'Oh, that's like the Stones video?'"

Julian Temple: "The film is asking how we react to seeing this kind of thing. Are we immune to it? The song is the best song for a long time – let's have a video that lives up to the song."

Q: "Mick, is there a danger of glamorising violence? You must see the possibility."

Mick: "No, there's no gratuitous violence in it at all. There's no slow motion . . ."

Q: "Didn't you realise it would be banned by the television authorities?"

Mick: "No, this is the only country that's banned it. It's shown on MTV, NBC. All the other countries are showing it."

Q: "Is this going to help the situation in El Salvador?"

Mick: "We're trying to make a point, not to create a scandal in the newspapers. It's not particularly violent compared to what you see on television. People call it a video nasty, but it's not at all."

313

Q: "Murder isn't usually accompanied by crashing guitar. Can't you see that's a real danger?"

Mick: "We're trying to make something that's interesting and new and has a valid point. This song was a political song and we think that this is the best thing to go with it."

Q: "Are any profits from the single going to help the victims?"

Julian Temple: "That's a stupid question."

Mick: "There won't be any profits from this video. And what I do with my profits is a matter of privacy."

Elsewhere, Mick continues to defend the use of theatrics in rock.

Mick: "There's room for doing simple rock performances and something with a bit more theatre in it. You can either call it gimmicks or theatrics. If it's really good, it's theatrical, if it's rubbish it's just gimmicks. I think it's worth trying."

But what about the song itself?

Mick: "That was originally just me playing guitar and singing, Charlie playing timpani and Bill playing bass. We just added everything else afterwards."

MONDAY, 7 NOVEMBER 1983

Release of the Undercover *album.*

Mick: "There's a lot of funk. It's a very hard record. There's not a lot of romance in it – in fact, there's none!"

Mick: "We didn't have a specific idea in mind, making a romantic album or whatever. Six or seven songs came out and formed the basis of it."

Keith: "The only real difference in the way we put this album together was that for the first time in ten years or so, Mick and I actually got together for a few weeks before the rest arrived. We went into the studio and worked up four or five songs, rather than walking in and winging it."

Some detect a new level of cynicism in the album's lyrical content. Or is it social commentary?

Mick: "I wouldn't say it was uncaring. There are a few songs, particularly 'Undercover' and 'Too Much Blood', which are not about girls and cars which a lot of rock'n'roll songs are. There's some social commentary, more than usual for us. I'm glad it's a bit different, that you get different angles on lyrics and don't just stick to the same subjects all the time."

And the record's fashionably rhythmic flavours?
Mick: "You pick up rhythms when you go out dancing. It was recorded in Paris where you hear a lot of African rhythms – which are similar to Latin rhythms – on the radio in Paris."

'Too Much Blood'
Mick: "It's kind of an anti-violence song, which won't get played on the radio which is a shame. It is anti-violence even though it uses violence to demonstrate that. That song was written and done in one or two takes. The rap was extemporary, just off the top of my head."

The Stones longevity prompts another round of predictable probing. One inquisitor wonders if the Eighties-era Rolling Stones regard themselves – "as a pop group, or like Bob Seger, a blues rock band?"
Keith: "To me they're just the Stones . . . When it comes down to it, I'll be happy with rock'n'roll."
Q: "Is it difficult for you to maintain an edge?"
Mick: "Yeah, well, the street is a very overrated thing to be. You should be smart in street, smart in everything. I don't wanna live a closeted life. I personally don't like that kind of life. It's purely a matter of taste."

Despite the rumours of a falling out prior to the album's completion, Mick and Keith respond to a question about their friendship with a rapport that testifies to its enduring strength.
Mick: "First of all it's the music, and the band itself. Keith and I have directed the way that it's gone. We've had lots of disagreements, though most have been over the band rather than personal ones. The friendship's lasted for 36 years. It's quite a long time."
Q: "What's the biggest musical risk the Rolling Stones have ever taken?"
Keith: "Picking up the guitar in the first place."
Mick: "Writing the first song was a risk."
Keith: "Or giving it to somebody!"
Mick: "We tried it out on other people first."
Keith: "Maybe releasing 'Little Red Rooster' as a single."
Mick: "*Satanic Majesties* was a risk. We're not prone to that many risks. I think going on, playing Philadelphia without playing too many gigs before in 1981, was a risk."
Keith: "Every time you put a record out it's a risk."
Mick: "And every time you do a video is a risk."
Keith: "Life's a risk!"
Mick: "Rock'n'roll's about sex and cars and risks."

Q: "Will the Stones be touring in 1984?"
Mick: "I dunno. We haven't really talked about it much."

MONDAY, 23 JANUARY 1984

'She Was Hot' becomes the second single to be lifted from Undercover.
Mick: " 'She Was Hot' is an on-the-road song. I hate road songs normally but that's your experience so you draw on it. The video of it is gonna be different to the last one insofar that it's gonna be more of a comedy. We got the idea from an old rock movie, and we're gonna do a pastiche of that. It has a big blonde girl with big breasts and she's dancing and driving everyone crazy. It should be funny, unlike 'Undercover' which was serious."

FRIDAY, 3 FEBRUARY 1984

The band's latest promo is broadcast on NBC's Friday Night Videos, *where Mick is asked about the Stones' perennial macho pose.*
Mick: "The Rolling Stones have a pretty masculine stance, but I don't think we've particularly been macho or un-understanding of women. We've written a lot of quite tender songs. People don't think of The Rolling Stones as a band that's made melodies or anything romantic, but I don't think that's true. We don't see ourselves as an exclusively macho rock group, you know, with chains on."

WEDNESDAY, 21 FEBRUARY 1984

Bill Wyman attends a rock awards ceremony at the Lyceum, London – and falls in love.
Bill: "I saw two stunning girls leaving the dance floor and my heart just jumped. She took my breath away . . . I was totally besotted with Mandy (Smith) from the moment I saw her."

MARCH 1984

But out of love – temporarily at least – with one of his long-term partners.
Bill: "I've lost touch with whoever Mick is now . . . I'm sure he has as well. Seven or eight years ago, I could still talk with Mick about books, films and intelligent things, but now I just talk to him in asides. Mick is a very difficult person to know."

MONDAY, 23 APRIL 1984

After Mick testifies against Allen Klein in a Manhattan court, a compromise is reached whereby the Stones drop their lawsuit and Klein pays their half-yearly royalties on time.

Mick: "I wanted to be reasonable and cool, but the moment he walked in, I blew my top and screamed at him, 'Where is my $800,000?' I do not want him in my life. It's like dealing with the Russians."

THURSDAY, 10 MAY 1984

An early draft of Mick's autobiography does not impress Futura, who have the paperback rights.

A Futura spokesman: "No sex. No rock'n'roll. It's just boring stuff about his ordinary parents, and his ordinary upbringing. I was surprised at the poor quality."

Mick doesn't sound particularly thrilled by the project either.

Mick: "I thought I'd get it over with, put that period of my life behind me. I won't remember it in another ten years. It's hardly there now. My perception is an insider's view so it'll be different. Bill wants to write this book that's the truth and I tried to explain that our views are totally subjective. There's a lot about the Fifties in it. I remember that well, the beginnings of rock'n'roll. Books about that era have always been written by erudite music critics."

Mick: "I decided halfway through that I didn't like nostalgia. It was too much living in the past and so I just put it on the back burner . . . It was just boring trying to remember everything. It was just . . . 'Euchhh.' "

Unsurprisingly, the book is cancelled.

Q: "Do you read what others write about you?"

Mick: "No, not much. Some artists become obsessed with their own press, what critics say about you and what they say about your personal life. I think you should throw it away."

Keith prefers sticking to what he does best, telling Lisa Robinson on All Night Long.

Q: "You once said that nobody becomes a musician thinking they're gonna make a lot of money."

Keith: "Just to be famous and make a lot of bread isn't enough to keep you going through all the time you need to learn an instrument. I think all the kids who've taken it up in the last few years have taken it up because

317

there's nothing else to do. There's not a lot of work around – especially in England. There has to be a certain amount of hard work and a drive which you really can't control that makes you wanna learn to play an instrument. You don't end up playing an instrument unless you have this love for it above and beyond the call of duty, success and fame."

MID-MAY 1984

Mick begins a one month stint at Compass Point Studios in Nassau in the Bahamas where he lays the basis for his first solo album.

Mick: "When we signed with CBS, they said, 'We'd like Mick to do two solo albums and we'd like the Stones to do four,' so the band knew perfectly well I was gonna do these albums. After all, I'm the only one of The Rolling Stones who's not done any solo projects. Keith's been out on the road with Ronnie, Keith's even made a record on his own called 'Run Rudolph Run'. Bill Wyman's made several solo albums, and he's had one that was quite a hit. Ron Wood's made countless solo records, none of which have been hits! So I was the only one that hadn't done anything. So I thought, 'Why not?' "

Mick: "I'd just finished *Undercover*, did all the videos for that. I thought, 'I don't wanna go back in the studios again with the Stones, I just spent a year with them. I'll do this on my own.' I hadn't really wanted to do one until then. It was a quick decision.

"I started off working with Sly Dunbar and Robbie Shakespeare on drums and bass, and best known for playing reggae music. They wanted to play rock'n'roll music. Bill Laswell, who'd produced Herbie Hancock's 'Rockit', was keen on using them too. Jeff Beck worked on the early sessions. This was the first little band. After that, we had a revolving door policy."

Mick: "I was very aware not to make a reggae album. I thought that would be a little too facile. I wanted to make a rock'n'roll record with a bit of my blues roots, even though it's modern in some places."

SEPTEMBER 1984

As the year continues with no new Stones records or concerts in the pipeline, Bill begins work on a new project, Willie & The Poor Boys, an all-star fundraising venture in aid of the Multiple Sclerosis-stricken ex-Faces bassist, Ronnie Lane.

Bill: "The Stones are probably the most disorganised band I've ever known. It is an irritant, yes. Timekeeping is non-existent, really, and schedules are of no use whatsoever. It's a miracle we all meet at the same place at the same time for anything. But we do, and that's the way this band works. And it works well when we do get there . . ."

NOVEMBER 1984

Mick flies to Rio De Janeiro, Brazil, with director Julian Temple to shoot a film to accompany his new solo album.

Mick: "I had more freedom, plus a good budget from CBS. Halfway through making the record, we played Julian Temple the songs even though they weren't finished, and tried to find a theme and start writing a movie. It's not a movie *per se*, more a series of promos that runs for sixty minutes."

Mick: "We wanted to take the mick a bit so we used a lot of clichés from the video format. It starts off with this guy going off to Brazil, a glamorous location, like Duran Duran. It was raining that day so we had to rewrite the script. I get these girls in a boat and I'm acting really badly, playing a rock star going to Rio. And this guy's drunk all the time. He doesn't care about music or video or anything. And then there's this dance sequence – *West Side Story* with knives. All very clichéd! He has a row with his girl-friend, then picks up three transvestites who beat him up and chuck him in the back of a meat truck. He gets taken off to the interior of Brazil where no one can understand him. He says, 'But I'm Mick Jagger.' The story is how he copes with this new kind of life. He becomes a slightly better person. It's very light-hearted. It's not moralistic."

Q: "What's the name of the character you play?"

Mick: "He's not me, he's a very bad version of me – and some of my mates in rock music."

And Julian Temple again, a man better known for his work with the Sex Pistols.

Mick: "Yeah. It was the stuff he did with The Kinks that was really good, 'Come Dancing', and Sid Vicious' 'My Way'. I really love that video. Julian is a kind of semi-angry educated young man in the world of the English film director. We got on quite well and did that series of videos for *Undercover* . . . We thought it would be fun to do it more semi-autobiographical, so we started off with this character who's this rock star who's very over the top and he drinks too much and he's surrounded by this entourage. I've met people like that even though I'm not like it myself. I could model it on a few of my mates . . . no names!"

319

DECEMBER 1984

Mick films a segment for the Band Aid fundraising video.
Mick: "I was in Brazil when they did Band Aid, so Bob Geldof called me up and said, 'Okay, get a one-inch video camera and do a video for it,' which I did. It was a very quick idea. It sounds all right. I liked the way it caught on. That was kinda interesting. The original Band Aid thing was a wonderful idea."
Q: "Do you give money to charity?"
Mick: "Yeah, most people do, but not everyone wants to talk about it."
Q: "What do you do with your money?"
Mick: "Spend it. I'm a spender, I don't invest. I don't gamble, which is a good thing because you can really run with a lot of money with gambling. That's a very nasty habit. I spend money on living, on nothing. I like good things but I'm not a collector by personality. I don't collect precious objects and put them in cages. I don't have a collection of art. (*Looks towards camera*) If you come round my house you won't find much!"

LATE JANUARY 1985

The Stones regroup at the Pathé-Marconi Studios in Paris to begin work on their next album. Unsurprisingly, they also bring with them an adjudicator, producer Steve Lillywhite.
Keith: "Mick and I had been saying since *Some Girls* that we should find another producer because we hadn't really had any producer since Jimmy Miller on *Goat's Head Soup* in the early Seventies. We never intended to produce that many Stones albums between us. It's just too difficult a job to be the writer, the arranger and musician and then go into the studio and spend your time dashing between the control room and the studio, putting on your producer's hat and then your musician's hat."
Bill: "It took him (Lillywhite) a couple of days to realise the way to do it. He made a few mistakes, was told what to do, then he sat back and thought about it and he did a very good job."
Ron: "There couldn't have been a better bloke for the job."

SATURDAY, 23 FEBRUARY 1985

The Smiths' Meat Is Murder *album débuts in the British chart at number one.*
Mick: "I'm not sure I wanna hear a whole album about meat."

320

A few months later, New Musical Express *commissions Smiths' guitarist Johnny Marr to interview Keith.*

Keith: "Why are they bringing guitar players to talk to me? It's like me at 21 going to see B.B. King to get some licks. I guess they now regard me as one of their favourite eccentrics . . . I dunno. I shall be very sweet."

MONDAY, 4 MARCH 1985

Mick's solo album, She's The Boss, *is released.*

Mick: "The other Stones might think that if the album did really well it might be the end of the Stones, but I know it won't be. But it was strange working without the others. It's rather like having a wife and a mistress. The Stones thing is like a long marriage. I know them very well, I know their strengths and weaknesses. I almost have telepathy with them after all these years."

Keith: "I thought the timing was very strange, bringing out something like that, an obviously commercial album, just before we were to start work on the new Stones album. I mean, if he'd done his favourite Irish folk songs with a lady harpist or have Liberace accompany him on Frank Sinatra songs, something you couldn't possibly do with the Stones, that would have been fine. To my mind a Mick Jagger album should have been a gi-normous event, not just another record. I told him it was dumb timing and not an inspired piece of work."

Mick: "They weren't very keen, but they've all done things on their own so they couldn't really say anything. Anyway, it's 1985, not 1965 anymore."

The title track is seen by some as a riposte to the accusations of chauvinism that have dogged the Stones' career.

Mick: "Yeah, I suppose it was, subconsciously. The song of that title is a bit of a joke about the whole boring thing of men and women adopting a role rather than getting on with it. I did this song once called 'Under My Thumb' about this girl who used to kick me around, a pushy bird. So I thought it would be fine to call this *She's The Boss*."

Mick: "I don't think I've been badly treated by women. 'She's The Boss' is not really about me personally. It's a humorous song about a kind of relationship that's happening, where the lady goes out to work, and the guy feels horrible – he doesn't have a job and he's at home, or she's out earning more money. It's about readjusting to that different situation."

'Running Out Of Luck' . . .

Mick: "Life's a gamble. I think coincidence and chance are important in life. Most things happen by chance, and you have to grab chance while it's there."

Q: "Was making this album a more disciplined affair than working with The Rolling Stones?"

Mick: "Yeah, much more disciplined in some places; in other places, it was pretty riotous. It's very professional but I wouldn't say it was clinical. The guys put their backs into it much more than I thought. I went home a couple of times at three or four in the morning, and they were still trying things out."

Mick gives several television interviews from Paris to promote the album, including this entertaining encounter with a presenter named Sunie.

Q: "Was working with other people the main reason you did the solo album, or did you need the money?"

Mick: "The money always comes in handy but it wasn't a prime reason. I was just getting away from the pattern of making Stones albums rather than doing anything else musically."

Q: "How do you feel about your image now that you're over 40? Do people want you to be eternally young?"

Mick: "You can't really help getting older. I mean, time goes on. I've been doing this for 23 years. You can't be 19 for ever. It's stupid to play like you could be."

Q: "You still do that youthful thing, running around the stage and looking glamorous. Is that not something that people associate with being young?"

Mick: "Rock'n'roll is not entirely an athletic pursuit. You have to be fit to play rock'n'roll. A lot of the best rock singers I know are very unfit. Look at Meat Loaf!"

Q: "How regular a guy are you?"

Mick: "If you're in California, people are very star conscious. I don't see anywhere else like that. Obviously there are bits that are nice and glamorous and easy – you can have a couple of weeks off in the Caribbean which can be fun. But it's not all like that. I go to the pictures. I like being ordinary. When you're on the road, you tend to have bodyguards. If you want to go out to the football, that can be difficult. There's always somebody with a bit of paper who wants your autograph as a goal's being scored. I support Spurs and Arsenal. I was brought up supporting Arsenal because they come from south of the river. Arsenal used to come from Woolwich, you see. You'd be surprised how long this loyalty goes back. Later on, all my friends got into supporting Spurs, and as Spurs were a more exciting team I got into supporting Spurs. Living away from England it's nice to be able to support both!"

Q: "Who do you love most in all the world?"

Mick: "What a funny question. You tend to say things like, 'Oh my family, my mum and dad.' I see them a lot so I could say that. I love my dog. I don't think you can have more than four or five close friends outside the band. They're close friends who I have a working and business relationship with. There's a slightly different thing. But outside of the band, I do have friends who are 'ordinary people'!"

Q: "Who do you admire?"

Mick: "When it comes down to it, people in the arts. Not many great statesmen come to mind. I always gasp in admiration at people who can draw or paint. Someone like David Hockney or Francis Bacon. I've been lucky enough to watch them and it's such a fantastic facility. I can't do it at all! I admire that very much."

Q: "What people do you dislike?"

Mick: "I dislike lawyers, politicians, tax inspectors . . ."

Q: "Why didn't you get involved in politics?"

Mick: "I got seduced by rock'n'roll and the music thing. I don't think that anyone in England wants rock singers being politicians. You have to take a lot of knocks and there's a very high intellectual standard as well. It's a really tough business and I really don't want to get involved in it."

Q: "Everybody seems to be terribly interested in you and Jerry Hall and whether you're faithful to each other."

Mick: "I'm not gonna talk about that."

Q: "Not a bit?"

Mick: "Or my children."

Q: "Not a bit?"

Mick: "Not even a little bit."

Q: "I didn't realise it was taboo."

Mick: "No, it's not taboo. I just don't feel like it. I'm bored with it all."

Q: "I was gonna ask you something different about it."

Mick: "Nah, you weren't."

Q: "I flippin' was!"

Mick: "I'll tell you if it's different. Go on then, ask me the question."

Q: "I've never read anywhere about what your relationship is like. Whether you're tempestuous kind of people . . ."

Mick: "Catty!"

Q: ". . . or whether it's nice and friendly."

323

Mick: "I've read it's supposed to be a nice friendly arrangement so I guess I'll leave it at that!"

Q: "Aaagh! Turn the page . . ."

Mick: "I hate talking about my private life 'cos that's only what people are interested in. I get bored talking about it."

Q: "What do you do to keep fit?"

Mick: "In the winter I play squash and indoor tennis. I hate running in the winter; it's so boring. I do weights a bit. That makes you feel good."

Q: "Do you follow the pop scene in Britain?"

Mick: "No, not really. It's very changeable. When I'm there I do. It's a pointless exercise to try and keep up. I don't think Spandau Ballet or Depeche Mode are any good. I don't consider Spandau Ballet as anything new. I think Duran Duran have done a couple of good tracks. I think the Thompson Twins are the more talented songwriters, actually. I'm not a 14-year-old girl and so I obviously don't go for a good-looking group unless the music is something. I like much heavier music with more sex in it – vicious, nasty and dirty."

MONDAY, 18 MARCH 1985

Keith's wife Patti Hansen gives birth to a daughter, Theodora Dupree.

Keith: "Even for a hardened old cynic like me, it was a fantastic thing seeing a baby being born. I have to admit I was close to tears. I'm a soft-hearted guy when it comes to kids and things like that. I just love it."

MONDAY, 8 APRIL 1985

Mick continues his promotional assault with an appearance on BBC-TV's Whistle Test *in conversation with David Hepworth, where he confirms that the Stones are still a viable force.*

Mick: "I still think they've got a long way to go. We started a new album a few days ago in Paris. We've been recording for about five days, doing demos actually."

Q: "How do you decide when Mick Jagger material ends and Stones material starts?"

Mick: "There isn't any difference really in terms of the songwriting. I wrote this material in a very short space of time. We'd just finished doing the video for 'Undercover' and I wrote the tunes in a couple of weeks. I worked much faster than normal. I had nothing to do so I went in and did demos. And I thought, 'The demos sound good, the songs sound okay – this is the moment to do a solo album.' "

Q: "You must have quite a lot commercially and reputation-wise riding on this solo record. Does that bother you?"

Mick: "Yeah, I suppose it does. I wouldn't have put it out if I hadn't liked it. I thought it's a good record for what it is. I'm sure the next one will be better."

Q: "You still seem to have a very playful attitude to writing material."

Mick: "Yeah, well I think that rock'n'roll, though it has its serious social comment side to it, if one is so disposed, should be kind of a laugh. I just write what I feel like, so if you're in a boyish, playful mood that's what you write. I hate pretension in rock. I think it's horrible. Yeah, you can make a serious point. Pretension and seriousness are two different things. On this album, it's mostly about personal relationships; there's not a lot of politics. Life is mainly social – concerned with the people we work with, we live with and our family life."

Q: "Do you think it's possible for a song you write now to have the resonance of something like 'Sympathy For The Devil'?"

Mick: "If it's good enough, yeah. But obviously people have heard that now, so you've got to go further. Maybe someone who's been brought up on a song like, say, (Wham!'s) 'Wake Me Up, Before You Go Go', that will change their idea of what popular music can embrace."

Q: "I've got two contrasting pictures of you – one is this genial chap who's a cricket fan, the other is this very powerful rock star you shouldn't mess with. Which is true?"

Mick: "They're both true. I'm not much of a genial cricket fan for much of the time. Some people are very combative, you know, in interviews and in life. If they want to be like that, then I'll play their game. But I don't really enjoy that very much."

Q: "It always seems that in The Rolling Stones, it's Mick who makes the decisions, who is the chap talking on the phone . . ."

Mick: "You have to do some of that otherwise they'll walk all over you – companies, distribution people. You've got to be very careful because everyone gets ripped off at some point in their career."

MAY 1985

Jerry Hall confirms that she and Mick are expecting a second child.
Mick: "I'm looking forward to that. I'd like a boy because I've got two girls." (*Three, actually – Karis, Jade and Elizabeth, born in March 1984.*)

Q: "Are you gonna marry Jerry Hall?"
Mick: "I don't know. Maybe I will, maybe I won't."
Q: "What do you think?"
Mick: "Maybe I will, maybe I won't!"
Mick: "I like to read. I like to watch movies. But most of my life revolves around music. I don't have any passion for gardening, or stamps or butter-flies. I like my family also, you know . . ."

JUNE 1985

As sessions for a new Rolling Stones album continue, Mick is inevitably asked . . .
Q: "How long can the Rolling Stones continue?"
Mick: "It's like jazz. When jazz started, they thought that was a ten-day wonder. When rock'n'roll started, they said it would be over. And it was. Performers in rock'n'roll are very fly-by-night, and some still are. You can carry on for quite a long time. I used to be on stage for half-an-hour when I was 19 and that was easy. Now I do two-and-a-half hours. Anyone who's gonna do a two-and-a-half hour show has gotta be in good shape. It's fun, but if you do it all the time it's soul destroying."
Q: "Is it difficult trying to keep ahead?"
Mick: "I'm not trying to be an innovator. You can be innovative within your own limits."
Q: "What do you think of Britain these days?"
Mick: "I think it's still got a lot of life, though the more it goes on having millions of unemployed young people, the more kind of depressed it will get."
Q: "Are you a Labour man?"
Mick: "Not at the moment, I'm afraid! I'm not a right-wing Conserva-tive, certainly. Labour's never gonna win an election with their present platform. I know that (Labour leader) Mr Kinnock is an old rock'n'roll man, which is typical of that part of Wales where he comes from."

Jools Holland solicits a series of thumbnail portraits of Jagger's fellow Stones for the MTV cameras.
Charlie Watts?
Mick: "Drums."
Ron Wood?
Mick: "Have another drink."
Bill?
Mick: "Quiet."

Keith?
Mick: "Loud."
And – a wild card – Billy Preston?
Mick: "Put your wig hat on your head."

But back to basics . . .
Q: "Will the Stones be touring soon?"
Mick: "End of the summer. I look forward to it because it's been a long time since I've been on the road. We'll start off with America and see how far we get!"

WEDNESDAY, 26 JUNE 1985

Privately, though, it's a different story. The group (minus Wood) convene at the Rolling Stones office in London where Mick informs them that he has no time to devote to Rolling Stones activities for the remainder of the year. The rumour mill begins to turn once more.
Mick: "Rumours like this come up regularly and have done since the Sixties . . . the truth is we're very much together."

SATURDAY, 13 JULY 1985

The transatlantic Live Aid concerts find Mick and Keith performing – albeit separately – at the JFK Stadium in Philadelphia. Mick plays a solo set earlier in the day, with Tina Turner joining him for a closing 'It's Only Rock'n'Roll'. Keith and Ronnie close the show in ramshackle fashion with Bob Dylan, as Keith explains to Mat Snow in New Musical Express.
Keith: "Screw it, man, it was three acoustic guitars and no microphones – you can't play to 90,000 people with three acoustic guitars and no microphones . . . It was only to feed people, you were not trying to prove anything here. Y'know, we could've walked off, but fuckin' 'ell, it was fun."
Mick: "Tina and I got really wrecked afterwards."
Q: "Are you concerned about the Third World?"
Mick: "If the rich keep getting richer and the poor keep getting poorer, at some point you're going to have a collision."
Q: "That's socialism . . ."
Mick: "Well, not really. That's just self-preservation. It's not necessarily socialism. I'm just looking at it from the point of view that if the northern

countries get richer and richer and the southern countries get poorer, you're inevitably gonna get trouble.

Q: "Do you feel you've done enough to help the Third World by contributing to Live Aid?"

Mick: "There's an endless desert to do. I can't possibly say to you, 'Yes, I've done enough, that was it.'"

The day's events did little to heal the ever-growing rifts within the Stones.
Keith: "As the Stones begin to work on more and more solo stuff it becomes increasingly difficult to get the band to meet in the same country, let alone the same recording studio."

MID-AUGUST 1985

Mick, Keith and Steve Lillywhite finish mixing the new album in New York.
Bill: "It was quite hard. We spent an awful lot of time getting into it again 'cos we haven't played for four years. It usually takes 10 days or two weeks to get back into it. This time it took about a month to get that ESP."

Bill: "It took about three months on and off because, some days two of us aren't there, and another day someone has flown back to London to see his kids."

Ron: "There was a lot of covering for each other on this album . . . teething troubles, you know."

Bill: "It's often the case these days that you don't all arrive at the same time at the studio and work on the same tracks . . ."

FRIDAY, 23 AUGUST 1985

Mick's version of Martha & The Vandellas' 'Dancing In The Streets', a duet with David Bowie for the Live Aid project, is released as a single.
Mick: "We've been friends for ten, 15 years. There have been a few ups and downs, fights over girls, usually. We'd always talked about doing stuff together but never actually did it, so this was a real catalyst to get down and do something. We did the video and the record in 12 hours."

THURSDAY, 12 DECEMBER 1985

Ian Stewart – the silent Stone who once said, "I have always disliked the really insincere, greedy, self-congratulatory side of show business" – suffers a fatal heart attack while waiting for treatment in a London clinic. His funeral takes place a week later in Leatherhead, Surrey, where the Stones bid him a tearful farewell.

Keith: "He was the glue that held us all together. Very few people realise how important he was to the Stones. I thought he'd be the one holding the shovel to bury us all."

Jeff Griffin (BBC radio producer and friend): "Stu was unique in that both Mick and Keith listened to him. He was the one person capable of knocking heads together."

Keith: "Stu was in the band and he wasn't in the band, so you could always ask him to arbitrate over an argument within the group, or go to him with a problem. I don't know who I'm going to go to now."

Keith: "Who's gonna tell us off now when we misbehave?"

SUNDAY, 23 FEBRUARY 1986

The Stones ignore their personal gripes and play a memorial show for Stu at the 100 Club in Central London, billed as Rocket '88.

A band spokesman: "The chances of the Stones getting together are 100 per cent better than they were before the gig. It looks as though all the trouble seems to be sorted out. Mick and Keith both left the club with their arms around each other. The band are keen to lay bets that they'll be gigging within 18 months. A week or so ago, I would have said there was no chance at all."

TUESDAY, 25 FEBRUARY 1986

The Stones pick up a Lifetime Achievement Grammy presented by Eric Clapton. Later that evening, Bill and Keith are interviewed for the Music Box *television channel.*

Q: "Are you still able to motivate yourselves?"

Bill: "It's just once every 18 months, two years. It's just a matter of getting back into playing together, a bit of mind contact, and you're ready to go. I always thought that older musicians were there to be admired. That's why I've always loved Little Richard and Jerry Lee (Lewis) and all those people. But that doesn't happen any more in England. They like to blast you if you're over 30."

Q: "Is it fair to say that you're the driving force behind the Stones?"

Keith: "No, I don't agree at all. This is a band; you can't pick it to bits. I hate analysing those things. I'm scared of it. Once it's found it, it's out the window, it's gone."

Q: "Do you believe the hype about yourselves?"

Bill: "Nah, you can't do that. If I believed that I was the greatest bass player in the world, as I've been told by various newspapers over the years, I'd have a real problem now. I know I'm not. I can pick 50 bass players that are better players than me, but they don't play with the Stones."

Q: "What about the knocks?"

Bill: "We've always been used as the ones to knock. That's part of our whole thing and it still is. I'm still the Old Bill. Some people took it very seriously. Brian Jones took it very badly and got really cut up about it. The rest of us dismissed it. We always have the last laugh because I'm still in the band 20 years later and they no longer write for a newspaper or present a TV show."

MONDAY, 24 MARCH 1986

Dirty Work is released. Untypically, the album includes just three Jagger/ Richards songs.

Keith: "It's rare that when an album's released, you know whether you're happy with it. This is one of those rare ones like *Exile* or *Beggars Banquet*, where you think, 'Hey, I done my best and that's a good 'un. I'll stick my name on this.' While we worked on it, I said this one's 'extra Stone'. We went in and did what we're good at. We came up with the right kind of songs for the Stones to play."

Bill: "There's a lot of variety."

Ron: "It sounds more like you would hope a Stones album to sound like."

Mick: "It's a very good Stones album."

Keith: "Normally when it comes to making a Stones album, Mick and I get together and sort the songs out, but this time he just wasn't around. As Ronnie lives pretty close to me, he was coming over, we jammed and a few songs started to come out. Eventually, I said to him, 'Hey, you've helped me write three or four songs here,' and I really wanted him to get recognition for them because he doesn't always get the credit he deserves. I mean, the band still consider him the new guy and he's been with us 10 years!"

One song, 'Had It With You', is regarded as Keith's thinly veiled attack on Mick. "It's such a sad thing . . . to see a good love die."

Another song, 'Fight', isn't entirely innocent either.

Keith: "I wrote 'Fight' when Mick walked out of a session and I got mad. So I guess something good came out of it."

Steve Lillywhite: "I usually like to talk about an album I've just made, but with this, I just feel as though I don't want to say so much. It is Keith's album to a great extent. I mean, he wrote those songs because of Mick's solo commitments."

The album closes with the sound of Ian Stewart playing 'Key To The Highway'.
Keith: "I sorted out a piece that Stu did in Paris recently . . . During the sessions, Stu played this lovely tune on the piano and I found it when I was looking for an exemplary piece of his playing."

On the same day, a cover of Bob & Earl's 'Harlem Shuffle' becomes the first single from the album.
Ron: "We must have limbered up on around 100 songs, a lot of favourites – Jerry Lee Lewis, Smokey Robinson, Eddie Cochran, Al Green, Hank Williams – and out of those 'Harlem Shuffle' took us two takes."
Mick: "I liked a couple of other things, so did Keith, but it didn't get an instant reaction with the kids and other people. 'Harlem Shuffle' did."

Bill and Ronnie attempt to paper over the cracks when asked about the "creative tensions" behind the making of the album.
Bill: "If you've got too many people wanting to do their songs, people are gonna argue."
Ron: "Nothing comes out of anything that runs smoothly anyway. You've gotta have a bit of friction."
Bill: "You gotta get a bit of spirit going."
Q: "Is it true that Mick and Keith recorded their parts in different studios?"
Bill: "Never."
Ron: "No, we never had leads long enough . . ."

Keith concurs.
Keith: "Creative tension? Not 'arf. We rely on it! No more rows than usual. Mick and I have known each other for as long as pre-memory and if Mick and I can't have a row, who can?"

Mick is conspicuously absent from most – though not all – promotional duties.
Q: "How much did you want to do this album?"
Mick (opens arms wide): "This much! I was there. There's a lot of complicated interpersonal relationships involved."
Q: "And your solo album?"
Mick: "Yeah, for a first one, it was great, very quick to make. The next one's gonna be fantastic!"

And there's always another film in the pipeline, as Mick explains on Australian TV's The Meldrum Show.
Q: "What's this about you and David Bowie doing an Eighties remake of 'Some Like It Hot'?"
Mick: "We've talked about that. We'd like to do something and we hope to work on some storylines for that. We wanna do a comedy which has music in it. Films are very fragile things; they can fall to pieces quickly. We have the studio that wants to do it. Who knows? If we get it together by the end of this year, that'll be quick for films."

Meanwhile, Keith attempts to explain his enduring love for rock'n'roll.
Keith: "It's a cliché, but the more you find out about it, the less you know. What else am I gonna do? Build model aeroplanes?"

TUESDAY, 15 APRIL 1986

Mick reportedly tells Keith that he won't be touring with the band this year because he will be recording a second solo album.
Keith: "If Mick tours without us, I'll slit his throat."

Shortly afterwards, speaking on BBC Radio 1's My Top Ten, *Keith exercises a little more restraint.*
Keith: "It's difficult to do anything at the moment, let alone tour. I was talking to Charlie the other day and he's still waiting for Stu to come bouncing through the door. It hasn't sunk in all the way yet. We're all so used to seeing him then not seeing him for a few months that it just feels like a gap right now. I guess we'll have to get used to it eventually. For the band it was a big wallop and, as I say, we're still in semi-shock."

However, that doesn't stop him from finding a new name for his errant partner.
Keith: "In Paris, I live around the corner from the English bookshop. There was this book in there and in great gold letters it said Brenda Jagger. So he became 'Brenda' for a bit."

SATURDAY, 19 APRIL 1986

The Charlie Watts Orchestra plays the first night of a week-long residency at Ronnie Scott's club in London's Soho district. The shows provide the catalyst for Charlie to clean up his quiet descent into private hell.
Charlie: "After two years on amphetamines and heroin I was very ill. My

daughter Serafina used to tell me I looked like Dracula . . . I used to take a lot of things that kept me awake then moved on to other things . . .

"I nearly went round the bend. I'd never been one for drink or drugs but I think I must have gone through some major crisis of identity. It just didn't suit me. I'm not a good drinker or a drugger and I nearly lost everything including the most important thing in my life, Shirley. That was what turned it around for me. I woke up one morning, I had a broken ankle, a wife on the verge of leaving me and a gig at Ronnie Scott's in two months' time. I knew then I had to get myself straightened out and that day I just stopped and, thankfully, I've never gone back."

On a happier note, Keith's recently rekindled relationship with his father Bert is flourishing.
Keith: "(We're) the terrible twins. Forty-two bottles of beer under the bed and the old man's going round telling everyone he's given up drinking. He just wanders off when he feels like it . . . He comes back here (to England) to his favourite local and then goes to Long Island when all the stories run out. The old man's at home, looking after Marlon. I think grandparents are great, and he and Marlon get on really well."

SATURDAY, 26 APRIL 1986

Indie mavericks Psychic TV release 'Godstar', a eulogy to flamboyant ex-Stone Brian Jones – with, says the band's frontman, a little help from beyond the grave.
Genesis P-Orridge: "The atmosphere in the studio went very cold. We heard the exact rhythm of the chorus of the song, 'And you were so beautiful, you were so very special'. It was a strange metallic noise. I'm sure it was Brian . . ."

CIRCA MAY 1986

The Stones gather round a table in Amsterdam for a business meeting. Later that evening, Mick and Keith have a few drinks.
Keith: "We had a great time and at five in the morning, Mick came back to my room. Mick was drunk and Mick drunk is a sight to behold. Charlie was fast asleep, but Mick rang his room, saying, 'Is that my little drummer boy? Why don't you get your arse down here?'

"Charlie shaved, put on a suit and tie, came down, grabbed him and went, 'Don't ever call me your drummer again. You're my fucking singer!' BOOM! Charlie dished him a walloping right hook. Mick landed in a plateful of smoked salmon and slid along the table towards the window. I just pulled his leg and saved him from going out into the canal below."

MONDAY, 7 JULY 1986

Keith plays on and co-produces Aretha Franklin's version of 'Jumpin' Jack Flash'.
Keith: "It was great. I really enjoyed doing it. The amazing thing about Aretha is that voice, which is like a national monument in America. And she's chain-smoking when she sings. Dionne Warwick's another one who literally lights a new one with the old one. And they've both got these voices!"

SATURDAY, 12 JULY 1986

Keith meets Chuck Berry in St Louis with a view to participating in a full-length documentary film about the rock'n'roll legend's life.
Keith: "I wanted to set Chuck up with a good band. I've never seen him play in tune. I'd been so disappointed with Chuck Berry's live gigs over the years . . . He didn't give a damn, and he's managed to get away with it. If anybody is gonna do it, I want it to be me."

Keith concedes a rare deference to his musical mentor.
"He's the only guy who's hit me that I never got back. Maybe I'm saving it! It was in a dressing room. He'd done a show in New York. I went up to say hello and he was just leaving with a little bit of white tail. I made the mistake of tapping him on the shoulder . . . He turned round and gave me a full shot right in the face. I was very proud that I didn't go down."
Keith: "I felt I owed him so much. I pinched virtually all his riffs when I started, you know."

SATURDAY, 28 JULY 1986

Keith and Patti's second daughter, Alexandra, is the latest addition to the fast-growing number of Rolling Stones offspring.
Q: "You're family men now."
Keith: "It's nothing new. I've got a son of 16 and a daughter of 14. I was expecting to be a grandfather before I got to be a father again. But you roll over in the middle of the night, and boy, there you go."

e Stones in the mid-Eighties. "We needed a break. Mick needed to find his own feet and see what it's like... easy to go a little crazy inside the Rolling Stones bubble if that's all you do." (*Michael Putland/Retna*)

The Stones line-up backstage, US Tour, 1981. "We're still trying to make the Stones a better band, and I guess we are," said Keith. "They go on every night with the idea of making this show a little bit better than the one before, which is admirable. They are very good players." (*LFI*)

Bill Wyman's 'Je Suis Un Rock Star,' released in 1981, was the first significant solo success for a Stones member. "I thought the song had a strong potential but I wasn't prepared to do it because I didn't want to make solo records anymore." (*copyright unknown*)

Mick at 40. Pete Townshend: "(He) will still be beautiful when he's 50, and his talent will still be a strong at 50 because his ambition is not dependent his youth." (*copyright unknown*)

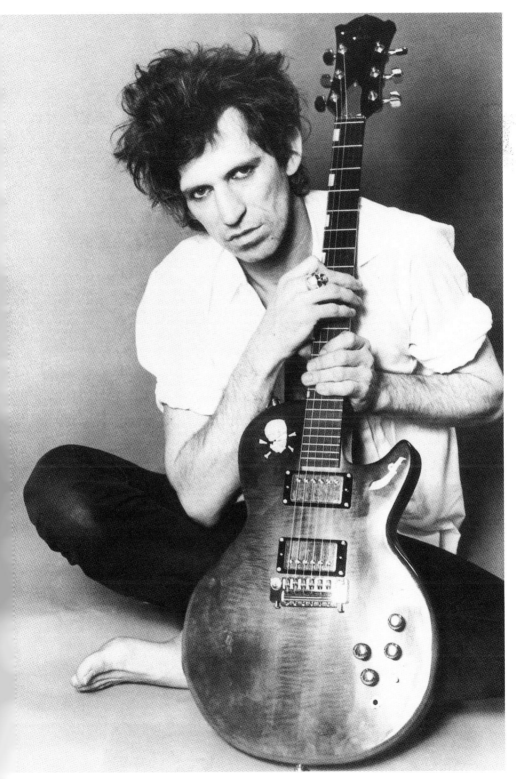

eith with the guitar given to him as a wedding present. He and model Patti Hansen married on Keith's 40th
thday, December 18, 1983. "I'm not into ratings," he said. "The day that I'm satisfied with what I do is the day
t I give up, 'cos then I've done it. It's the search that's important." (*LFI*)

Live Aid, July 13, 1985. (Back l-r) Keith, Daryl Hall, John Oates, Ron. (Front l-r) Tina Turner, Mick, Madonna, Bob Dylan. Mick: "Tina and I got really wrecked afterwards." (*LFI*)

Bill with Mandy Smith. "She took my breath away... I was totally besotted with Mandy from the moment I saw her." (*LFI*)

Shattered Stones, during the video shoot for 'One Hit To The Body', Elstree Studios, May 1, 1986. Keith: "If Mick tours without us, I'll slit his throat." (*Michael Putland/Retna*)

Mixed Emotions. The Stones hold a press conference at New York's Grand Central Station to launch their *Steel Wheels* album and tour, July 11, 1989. "After 25 years with the same cats, the idea of starting again from scratch was scary," said Keith. "But suddenly I had another band in the making, a great band." (*Redferns*)

...ay from the Stones, Charlie concentrated on his ...st love: jazz. Shirley Watts: "I think Charlie was ...ays a 50-year-old man. Charlie's tastes were never ...e same as the rest of the crowd. To tell you the ...th, I was always surprised he was a part of that ...d." (*Redferns*)

Bill Wyman announces his departure from the Stones after 30 years, January 1993. "I really don't want to do it anymore... When I joined this band, we thought we would last two or three years with a bit of luck and come out with a few shillings in our pocket." (*Camera Press*)

A publicity shot to promote *Voodoo Lounge*, 1994. The album was arguably the Stones' strongest since 1978's *Some Girls*. (*Virgin Records*)

Brixton Academy, London, July 1995, with long-time associate, Bobby Keys on sax. "Playing those places is how we test ourselves," said Keith. "You know, if we can't rock a club, baby, then I'll toss it in and take up golf." (*LF*

Bridges To Babylon, 1997. Mick: "I want to ask the Rolling Stones a very original question: 'Is this going to be your last tour?'" Keith: "Yes, this and the next five!" (*Brian Rasic/Rex*)

Mick and friends. "It's very odd, the relationships that men have with women... After all this time, men still like to find women mysterious." (*LFI*)

A rejuvenated Ronnie onstage, 2002. "None of us gets out of here alive, but I do realise I was tearing the backside out of it... I'd better nip it in the bud or I may be dead in six months." (*LFI*)

Forty Licks – The Rolling Stones four decades on. Keith: "After 40 years, still doing two-and-a-half hours onstage every night, that's the biggest last laugh of all. Maybe that's the answer: 'If you want to live a long life, join the Rolling Stones'." (*LFI*)

Q: "You're family men now."
Bill: "I've been a family man since 1959, what are you talking about?"

SUNDAY, 3 AUGUST 1986

"STONE IN SEX PROBE OVER GIRL OF 13"

'Family' newspaper The News Of The World *exposes Bill's affair with Mandy Smith.*
Mandy Smith: "My mother approved of my relationship with Bill. It was an unusual one."

The Star *picks up on the story the following day.*
"Detectives were studying reports that beautiful blonde Mandy Smith lost her virginity to the rock star, who will be 50 in October . . . Mandy claims that the two-and-a-half-year affair began after she met Wyman at a trendy disco. She alleges she lived with him as man and wife, doing the housework and sharing his bed."

WEDNESDAY, 8 OCTOBER 1986

Keith leaves for St Louis where he spends a week rehearsing for the forthcoming Chuck Berry movie. The vintage rocker lived up to his reputation, forcing an exasperated Keith to play the intro to 'Carol' repeatedly until he got it right.
Keith: "This must be the most difficult gig. If I can handle this, I can handle anything . . ."
Keith: "I'm trying to show the band that, in order to get this gig together, I am gonna take some shit that I wouldn't take from *anybody*. I'm *not* gonna let Chuck get to me that much. Anybody else, it would be toilet time."
Keith: "Chuck Berry is the only cat who can do that to me. I had to show the rest of the band that I was serious."
Keith: "He's probably the hardest guy to work with, and I've worked with Mick, you know, so at least I've had some experience. There's a lot more to him than he wants to show. There were a couple of times in rehearsals when he'd be the greatest guy in the world. Then he'd freeze, like he'd given too much away. He's a very shy guy. He's always scared of giving something for free."

THURSDAY, 16 OCTOBER 1986

Keith's all-star band back Chuck Berry for two filmed shows at the Fox Theatre, St Louis.

Keith: "We're in the middle of 'Roll Over Beethoven' and Chuck comes up to me in the solo and says, 'After the chorus, we're gonna change the key from C to B flat'! I said, 'No.' I don't think many people say that to Chuck. Even when it's going great, he'll come in with a potential screw-it-up. That's just him. When you're working with him, you gotta be prepared for anything."

Keith: "I'm walking out of this gig feeling very happy. I wanted to serve Chuck up with a good band, and I did it. That was my gig no matter what happened! I cannot dislike the guy even though he's given me more headaches than Mick Jagger. I've done what I wanted to do for him. Now I'm gonna sleep for a month!"

SUNDAY, 19 OCTOBER 1986

"ROLLING STONE CONFESSES TO ROMANCE WITH 13-YEAR-OLD"

Claiming that the romance is now over, Bill comes forward with his side of the story.

Bill: "I love her very much. She's a very special person . . . What makes it special is that we get on very well. I enjoy her company and she's got a lovely body . . . For the first time in years, I'm trying to cut down on the number of women I'm sleeping with – that's how I can tell that Mandy has got to me.

"I suppose I see myself as an explorer. Every woman is like discovering a new continent. They're all different and I want to discover as much as I can about each of them, and as many of them as possible. That's why I find new encounters very difficult to resist, because there's such a sense of excitement. It's something that doesn't die down when you get older; you just want to try every one. I've always believed that one of the greatest pleasures in life is taking a girl's clothes off for the first time. There's nothing to beat it."

His voracious sexual appetite was, he explains, prompted by difficulties encountered in his first marriage.

Bill: "It was my first big affair. (Diane) was the most perfect girl within a two-mile radius. But within a year it was all over. Sexually the relationship was a complete disaster. It was all rather sad. It was probably because of that that I've overindulged in sex ever since. The first three years after Diane I went completely mad . . . I'd love to settle down and live a normal family life. But I don't know whether I'll ever stop wanting to be an explorer."

AUTUMN 1986

As a new breed of synth pop acts, including The Communards and Pet Shop Boys enjoy chart success, a perceived lazy reliance on technology dismays an old Stone.
Keith: "The thing that strikes me as strange is that as more and more possibilities present themselves, the more records sound alike, and I think that's wrong. Technology is supposed to be a tool that widens the spectrum to make more possibilities available, but at the moment it is working negatively. I think people are getting frightened by the number of possibilities and are sticking with formulae they know to be safe."

The Stones might not be busy, but Keith insists he's not been idle.
Keith: "I probably have enough material already recorded for a solo album but whether or not I'll release it this year depends on what the Stones are doing. At the moment, it doesn't look like we'll be touring but if I were to release a solo album it would immediately be construed as my reply to *She's The Boss*. I don't want to start fighting him through records, too! I don't want an extension of this public row we're having on vinyl. I can take care of him myself."

WEDNESDAY, 21 JANUARY 1987

Jerry Hall is arrested and charged with importing 20 pounds of marijuana into Barbados. After a four-day trial the following month, she is cleared of the charge.
Jerry Hall: "I have been through a nightmare, but I want to tell you that we must never forget the presumption of innocence. Ninety-nine out of a hundred people who are charged and sentenced are guilty people . . . I am happy to be one of the innocent ones."

MONDAY, 2 MARCH 1987

Mick takes his battle for the heart of the Stones to the Daily Mirror *where he claims that Keith wants to run the band "single-handedly".*
Mick: "I love Keith, I admire him, but I don't feel we can really work together anymore."

TUESDAY, 3 MARCH 1987

The Sun carries a retaliatory interview with Keith that accuses Mick of being "obsessed with age" and claims – spuriously – that he's already lined up the Who's Roger Daltrey as a replacement.

Keith: "He should stop trying to be like Peter Pan and grow up . . . I'm not sure when it all started to go wrong. Up until the beginning of the Eighties, you could have called me up at the North Pole and Mick at the South Pole and we would have said the same thing. We were that close. I didn't change but he did. He became obsessed with age – his own and others. I don't see the point of pretending that you are 25 when you're not.

"Until this time last year, there was still a chance. Mick could have said, 'Let's do it,' and it would have happened . . . He has told me to my face that he cannot work with me but he cannot say why. I don't think he knows himself."

Q: "So no chance of a reconciliation, then?"

Keith: "You'd better ask the bitch."

He continues his offensive elsewhere.

Keith: "You can't sit down with Mick over a bottle of whisky and thrash things out until you find out what is really bothering him. He just reacts in a juvenile way, changing the subject or retaliating with some counter-charge. That's very easy with me – you just call me a junkie. He's done that."

WEDNESDAY, 18 MARCH 1987

When in doubt, call up the bass player.

Q: "So, Bill," asks *Music Box*, "are the Stones finished?"

Bill: "It looks that way. I think the time comes when all good things must pass. It's a pity we didn't go out with a big bang. Instead we went out with a whimper . . . I don't know if we'll ever go back on the road. That depends on the 'glamour' twins becoming friendly again. They're the problem . . . Mick is the guilty one. He has decided to do his own thing and be famous in his own right."

After the initial broadcast, Wyman's office successfully lobbies MTV to prevent the interview going out a second time. "Misquotes, off-the-cuff remarks that were taken out of context and blown out of proportion," says a spokesperson. "There's no story."

A little later, Keith confirms that there was indeed a story there.
Keith: "It was Mick deciding that he could do . . . I don't know whether 'he could do better' is the best phrase, but he felt that The Rolling Stones were like a millstone around his neck – which is *ludicrous* and I told him so.

"It's a hard job, being the frontman. In order to do it, you've got to think in a way that you're semi-divine. But if that feeling goes a little too far, that you think you don't need anybody . . . Mick lost touch with the fact of how important the Stones were for him. He thought that he could just hire another Rolling Stones, and that way he could control the situation more, rather than battling with me."
A spokesman for Mick: "There's no official end to the group. You know the Stones – they go through these tribulations. Hopefully, things will settle down to where people can talk again. You can never write off The Rolling Stones."

THURSDAY, 11 JUNE 1987

Mrs Thatcher lands the Tory Party its third successive General Election victory.
Mick: "I can't say I was overjoyed. All right, Mrs Thatcher's politics may benefit people in my income bracket. I don't want to appear hypocritical, but paying more than 60 per cent tax is a bit of an imposition. People might say, 'Rich sod,' but it's still a lot to pay. But I still don't have to approve of her victory. I don't think I am a right-wing person. I was certainly brought up with liberal principles."
Q: "Is politics part of your music?"
Keith: "Only in an indirect way. I don't think rock'n'roll music is at its fullest when it gets too involved with politics and tries to preach and say, 'You must do this,' or 'You free him.' I think rock'n'roll's real power is far more under the surface."

WEDNESDAY, 17 JUNE 1987

Keith signs a deal with Virgin Records as a solo artist.
Keith: "When I announced that I was going to do a solo album, a lot of people were saying to me, 'Yeah, but who's gonna sing on it?' And, you know, I've made a few records, and some I've sung on . . . It's not alien to me."

SATURDAY, 20 JUNE 1987

Mick is in New York filming the promo video for his forthcoming single. But he's still dreaming of that grander cinematic project with David Bowie.

Mick: "We've developed it between us. We did the deal with UA and saw 50 writers . . . We've still got a lot of work on the script. It's great to do it from this perspective rather than be asked to play a role in a film, then get sent the script and think, 'I don't really like these lines.' The film's called *Rocket Boys*, but that might change. It's so long until it comes out that I hate to talk about it. I mean, it'll probably take two-and-a-half years . . ."

Q: "Has the video business encouraged rock stars to imagine they are film stars?"

Mick: "It's a fantasy of everyone to be a film star."

Q: "But why do all rock stars flop as film stars?"

Mick: "Because they're probably not good actors, or because the films they made are vehicles for them. Very few people have made a string of movies. Sometimes they've worked and sometimes they haven't. As far as I was concerned, I had to say, 'I'm gonna be an actor or I'm gonna be involved in music.' It wasn't a hard choice."

SATURDAY, 22 AUGUST 1987

Mick Jagger's tour, scheduled for October, is cancelled after a row with guitarist Jeff Beck.

A spokesman: "He had been rehearsing the tour for a month. Jeff is well known for being difficult to work with and tempers finally snapped. But the tour has been postponed because Jeff is a brilliant guitarist and will be very hard to replace."

Jeff Beck: "I quit the tour because Mick only offered me peanuts to play with him. It was laughable, an insult. I wanted to teach him a lesson because I believe if you want the best you have to pay for it. The kind of money he offered is what you pay an ordinary session musician. Mick's problem is that he's a meanie. He is no better than a glorified accountant. He counts every single penny. For someone with his money, I can't believe how tight he is. I'd still love to go on tour with the old geezer. He's just got to make me a proper offer."

Q: "I hear that Jeff Beck is not an easy person to work with."

Mick (laughing): "He's not! He's well known for being quite difficult. Actually in the studio he's quite easy to work with. All musicians have their quirks, and you have to get to know them. That's important. It's fun to do that with different people."

LATE-AUGUST 1987

Keith begins work on his solo album, as he tells Francesco Adinolfi.
Keith: "It took me a long time to find the right guys to work with, a real bunch of friends. For instance, I've known Waddy Wachtel for more than 12 years and I was sure that we would work together some time in the future. He's been in and out of bands with Linda Ronstadt and Stevie Nicks and I think he was a little frustrated working for the ladies all the time. He came to me and said, 'Keith, I wear the panties.'

"Me and Mick (Taylor) were like ships in the night and one night we met. Mick was doing some session work with Johnny Johnson, Chuck Berry's piano player, and he asked me if he could come down to the studio. I said, 'No, if you really want to, pick up the guitar and work with me.' I couldn't use any of the Stones otherwise there would be too many grey areas."
Keith: "The key was to find myself a bunch of guys that could feel and sound like a band. Because rock'n'roll is really about interaction. It's not about just pushing buttons and letting machines do all the work. You might make a record that sells a lot that way, but it certainly has nothing to do with making a good rock'n'roll record. It's really about the interesting tension and communication going on between one guy and another. It's that indefinable thing. You can't find it on any meter in the studio. It's a feeling, a spirit that comes across, and it's those moments that we're capturing on this record . . . It's an organic approach to composition, basically the same approach the Stones took on all their classic cuts. I never really sat down and tried to compose something on paper. I can't walk into a rehearsal and say, 'It goes like *this*.' Songs, to me, come through osmosis. All the best songs are basically beautiful accidents."

As was his key relationship during the making of the record . . .
Keith: "Steve (Jordan) and I didn't even know we were gonna write together. He figured I'd write them all, but the more we got into it, we both had our fingers in the air at the same time. The ideas just started to flow and we figured we didn't need an outside producer."
Steve Jordan (co-writer, co-producer): "When you look him in the eye, you know you're not going to bullshit this man. And when you're going to bullshit him, do *not* look him in the eye. There's only one way he likes

to say things, and that's (by being) brutally honest. He's not going to preach to you, but he does have this moral code of honesty and loyalty and sincerity."

Keith: "I grew more confident about singing as we got on with rehearsals. I was used to having only one or two tracks to sing every three years with the Stones, and suddenly I had to sing a whole album's worth. But, like anything else, the more practice you have at something, the more you find room to manoeuvre and find out what your limits are and how to overcome them. During rehearsals, I began to remember things my choirmaster had taught me. I was a soprano up until my voice broke at around 13 . . . I could hear this little voice of my old choirmaster echoing in the back of my head, telling me all the things I had learned from him about singing some 300-odd years ago. But the voice has changed a lot since I sang in Westminster Abbey, so it became a question of, 'Well, what can I do with this goddamn voice?' "

MONDAY, 31 AUGUST 1987

A new single, 'Let's Work', is lifted from Mick's forthcoming album. New Musical Express *isn't convinced.*

" 'Let's Work' has got to be one of the flimsiest songs Ole Rubber Chops has ever recorded. A sort of tribal beat and Jagger's warbling refrain of 'Let's Work!' are the flesh and blood of this horror. Produco-mafia man Dave Stewart tarts it up a bit and makes Mick sound as though he's auditioning for the Eurythmics. No chance!"

Q: "Isn't the message of 'Let's Work' to work your way to the top?"

Mick: "No, the message of 'Let's Work' is that if you don't work for something, you're not really going to get it."

Q: "Isn't that a message suitable for Margaret Thatcher as well?"

Mick: "Margaret Thatcher? She's like a nanny. I'm not a nanny!"

FRIDAY, 11 SEPTEMBER 1987

Peter Tosh, 43, is murdered at his Jamaican home by robbers.

Mick: "Yes, that's pretty sad. I last saw him about two years ago, he's been living in Jamaica for a long time. He never left."

Q: "There's a problem with rock and death."

Mick: "Death is a problem. Rock is less a problem. There's a high casualty

342

rate in show business because people are always travelling, driving late at night while they're tired or drunk. They take a lot of drugs to keep awake, or go to sleep, or just to put them out of their misery. Most are accidents."

MONDAY, 14 SEPTEMBER 1987

The release of Mick's second solo album, Primitive Cool, *is virtually over-shadowed by the continuing war of words with Keith. Songs such as 'Shoot Off Your Mouth' and 'Kow Tow' are obvious barbs in the guitarist's direction.*

A spokesman: "Mick is very bitter about the row with Keith. He's had a real go at Keith and hopes he listens to the album and realises the significance."

Mick: "Keith sees The Rolling Stones very much as a conservative rock'n'roll band with very strong traditions, and as he gets older, his ideas have become more conservative. I see it that way too, but his traditional view is so strong that I can't function only within that. I used to tell people that I would never need to make a solo album because I could do what-ever I wanted to do within the band, but it started to get narrower, so I no longer felt that. I like to be a bit more open-minded about things."

Keith: "Mick is more involved with what's happening at this moment – and fashion. I'm trying to grow the thing up, and I'm saying we don't need the lemon-yellow tights and the cherry picker and the spectacle to make a good Rolling Stones show . . . He had to go backwards and compare himself with who's hitting the Top 10 at that moment."

Mick: "I'm very much a traditional rock'n'roll person. I like to play with sounds a lot, but when I come to make the records, I go about it in a much more traditional way. I like to use drum programmes, but I like to use drums as well. I love drums because they're so physical. I like to watch drummers play and to interact with live drums when I'm singing in the studio too. You can't interact with a programme in the same way. I prefer timing that moves. 'Honky Tonk Women' starts off at 100 bpm and ends at 130. All music now starts at one beat and ends with the same beat. Everything has become more set, mainly through the use of machines."

Q: "Why call it *Primitive Cool*?"

Mick: "I just thought it was a good title."

Q: "In the song, the child asks the father what it was like in the early days. Are you getting old?"

Mick: "Well, the child talks about what was it like to live in the Fifties, whether it was all just fashion? Because when kids look back at what happened 30 years ago, often all that's left are the funny shoes or skirts."

'War Baby'
Mick: "When we were kids we used to march for CND, 'Ban The Bomb' and all that. People in America don't really know first-hand about war. They've never really had a war since the Civil War 200 years ago. They know they had husbands and others in the Second World War but they didn't really come to them directly. Sometimes they get a bit gung-ho to have another one, and this song's really about people who were brought up after the Second World War who don't want another one very much."

Q: "When you sing, 'When I was born in the war/They call me a war baby', it sounds autobiographical. How much is autobiographical in your lyrics?"

Mick: "The further down from where it comes makes a lyric more meaningful. On the other hand, I don't think you should sing songs just as autobiography. Other people aren't that interested."

Mick: "No, this solo album doesn't mean that The Rolling Stones have broken up. No, I don't know when or if we'll get back together again. Yes, there have been problems among the group. No, I don't want to go into them, it'll only cause grief. We've been together for nearly 25 years, that's longer than most marriages . . . (It) was done very quickly. It was very flippant, very tongue-in-cheek; I was coming straight from the Stones album for which I'd written a lot of dark material, so I thought I'd do something very different and very upbeat . . . I wrote a whole batch of songs quickly, straight off, in a three-month period."

Mick: "As a singer, you're the one who's inventing the melody – it's very rare that the guy who works out the chord structure actually writes the melody. He'll usually say, 'Look, I've got this idea,' and then go 'chang-chang-chung!' but that's not really a song. I wrote the lyrics with Dave (Stewart), sometimes to my own melody, sometimes to something that he had a melody idea for. It's very hard to analyse who wrote what."

It's only rock'n'roll but is it ageing as well as its most famous frontman?
Mick: "Rock'n'roll still has a tremendous amount of naivety. Probably one of the biggest difficulties is to retain that naivety. Rock'n'roll has never had maturity because the musical form was never mature – but it's older now than it was 20 years ago, so it's got history and a sense of tradition. You're pushing the frontiers all the time, unlike other forms of popular music like jazz, which doesn't rely on lyrical content, so it's very

hard to draw analogies with rock music. It's just a 30-year-old thing and nobody really knows how it's going to develop. So everyone who's out there actually doing it is pushing it on."

Including . . . The Housemartins?!
Mick: "Every time a new band comes along, it seems to go back to zero again and they become like glorified skiffle groups – just three guys on guitars and you think, 'Fuckin' hell! . . .' It's good and bad. You come up with a group like the Housemartins, God bless them. I mean, where are we going? The Housemartins sound like a skiffle group, and so that is regenerative in a way because it's very simple to do. You just pick up a guitar and you don't need anything else other than what was needed 30 years ago."

With sales of Primitive Cool *paling in comparison with those for* She's The Boss, *Mick is obliged to maintain a busy press schedule. Come in, Scandinavian TV . . .*
Q: "Are you tired of being famous?"
Mick: "No, not really. It comes with the job. But there are parts of the world where you can go where no one knows you if you want to."
Q: "Can you go out on the streets without people hassling you?"
Mick: "Yeah, you can do that if you know what you're doing. I think it's important to stay around, to do things on your own and not always rely on other people to fetch and carry for you all the time. When you're working, yes, it's very convenient. But when you're not, I like to do things in a very ordinary way. It keeps your feet on the ground."
Q: "Rock is seen as a rebellious thing. Is it still important for you to have rebellious spirit to your music?"
Mick: "I think it should have a questioning attitude. To play at rebellion is fine when your 14 or 15, but I don't think it sits well when you're older. I don't think that rock music has a very rebellious attitude at the moment. It has an attitude of excess, which has always gone with it, but nothing more than that.
Q: "You've released two albums as a solo artist. Has it been difficult to establish an identity for yourself apart from the Stones?"
Mick: "I think people have associated me so much with the Stones that I don't know really how they see one from the other. On this album, the attitude is different and the stretch of the material is broader than on the last couple of Stones albums, which have been very mainstream rock with that old-fashioned Stones attitude. With this album, I've tried to get away

from that a little bit because I felt that the last two Stones albums have been in that vein. There's no point in me coming out with the same."

Q: "What drives you to keep on performing and releasing albums?"

Mick: "I think it's your own creativity. You have it inside you and you don't really know why or how. It's just an urge to do it. The same urges that started you off in the first place."

Q: "What inspires you?"

Mick: "Everything you see around you – a beautiful face, a nice landscape, a drunk person on a street, someone being sick on the pavement."

Q: "You are able to reach young people with your music and you have a certain responsibility towards them, do you feel that you have to say positive things to wake them up to what's going on in the world?"

Mick: "I don't think one should take too much responsibility on your shoulder. I think people have to make up their own minds about things. All you can do is say what you see. If you believe in something, and want to write about it, that's fine. You should be true to your own feelings."

Q: "Do you write other things apart from songs?"

Mick: "I tried writing short stories, and obviously verse. The short story is a really hard form to write in. I just do it for my own amusement."

Q: "If your children came to you and said they wanted to become famous pop stars, what would you say?

Mick: "I'd tell them to go into real estate."

Hello again, Sweden . . .

Q: "What motivates you?"

Mick: "I think if you have a creative instinct, you just want to keep exercising it. You don't feel any different from the way you did at the beginning. If you feel the urge you should just do it."

Q: "And the money?"

Mick: "Money? You think we get paid?!"

Q: "Has the rebel transformed into a yuppie?"

Mick: "The mentality of the Eighties is really the acquisition of more money. I think that material things are necessary. I don't really believe in just money values. When we started in the early Sixties the acquisition of material things was very important, everyone wanted them. But I think acquisition of money in the Eighties has become the prime mover for everyone."

Q: "How is the male sex symbol of the Seventies doing when AIDS is around?"

Mick: "I think sex symbolism in pop music has been going on since the

Fifties. There have always been people coming on the scene who are really pretty, a bit androgynous, who stand there with a guitar looking beautiful, 19 years old singing nice songs and having a good body. That's never going to go away; that's part of what pop music is. But I was never a male model. I was lucky to be able to get by just by looking a bit different."

Q: "You're probably the most written-about artist of today, and yet we don't know much about you. How do you keep Mick Jagger to yourself?"

Mick: "There's a whole shelf of books! You have to have some kind of interior privacy."

Q: "The song 'Primitive Cool' is about your children asking you what it was like when you were young. What kind of life are your children living today?"

Mick: "I don't really wanna talk about my children and what kind of life they're living. The song's a fantasy. It's set in the future. They never ask me questions about it."

Q: "Are you a good father?"

Mick: "No, I'm a terrible father! I beat them all the time. They like it!"

Q: "Do they like the music?"

Mick: "Don't know. I don't ask them."

Q: "You've lived quite a rough life. What do you tell your children when they ask you about it?"

Mick: "They never ask me."

Q: "Would you like them to live the same life?"

Mick: "If they wish to, why not? I doubt very much that they will because this is a very different time."

Q: "Releasing a second solo album is another reason for the press to shout that the Stones are over. Isn't it time to split up?"

Mick: "I don't know. I think that the Stones have a lot of musical validity. I think they should carry on working."

Q: "Are you going to tour?"

Mick: "I would like to think so."

Q: "Are you gonna tour on your own?"

Mick: "I might like to do some shows."

Q: "Who taught you to dance?"

Mick: "Well, Tina Turner always claimed she did. I learnt from all these different people like Little Richard, James Brown, Tina. I kept my eyes open. If I had to learn steps, I couldn't dance at all."

Q: "How do you think people will remember you when you're gone?"

Mick: "As someone that added some bricks to the wall of popular music.

They'll probably think, 'He was the one who sang 'Satisfaction',' or something like that."

Q: "How would you like to be remembered?"

Mick: "As a songwriter. Songwriting is the most permanent thing that I've done, and I've done quite a lot of it."

. . . and Dutch TV . . .

Q: "You rhyme a lot. Do you have a rhyming dictionary?"

Mick: "Oh, yes. I was given a rhyming dictionary by this old English musical composer, Lionel Bart. He wrote in it, 'Do not let this aid to rhyming ruin your talent or your timing.' What he meant was don't use the rhyming dictionary unless you're really stuck. All writers use these tools, but they have to be used very sparingly."

Q: "What's the difference between the Stones sound and your solo sound?"

Mick: "People associate The Rolling Stones as a driving rock band which is what it is a lot of the time. But the Stones also play ballads, and the sounds can be changed in the recording process. The Stones is two guitars with a straight 4/4 backbeat and a lot of walking bass – that's what it is. The Mick Jagger solo sound is a lot wider. It has a lot of keyboards in it. But I'm yelling all the way through – and as soon as you hear the voice, it takes up so much of the record. And the drums, too, they're the main things, with the guitars on the sides, so that's where you get the similarities."

Q: "What books are you reading?"

Mick: "I read trash, pulp novels, detective stories. Sometimes I read magazines."

Q: "You don't like the books written about you."

Mick: "It's not that I don't like them. I am myself. Why would I wanna read someone else's version? I might get confused! A lot of these books are just crap."

Q: "Would you resurrect your autobiography?"

Mick: "I don't think I ever would because it's much more important to live your life rather than write about it. Perhaps when I'm very old I might . . . I'd done a lot of work on it, the research and a lot of talking. A lot of the work is done, but I'm not really interested in writing a straight autobiography. I think it's rather dull. There's so much known about me that all the facts are not new. I'd like to find another way, another style."

Q: "Are The Rolling Stones playing again in the future?"

Mick: "I hope so. Why not? I think it's a viable band. I can't give you 100 per cent."

SATURDAY, 3 OCTOBER 1987

Keith attends the premiere of Hail! Hail! Rock'n'Roll *– the Chuck Berry movie – which takes place at the New York Film Festival.*
Keith: "Asshole that he can be, I still love him. I'm still fascinated by what he does. I wouldn't have missed it for the world."
Steve Jordan: "It was something that plagued Keith. He *had* to document the real thing before Chuck died and he did. Maybe I'm reading too much into it, but having played with Keith before and after, I think he's more himself now, more comfortable, like he feels entitled to make his own mark."

FRIDAY, 9 OCTOBER 1987

Bruce Springsteen's new studio set, Tunnel Of Love, *is released. It immediately tops the charts on both sides of the Atlantic.*
Q: "The American writer Armistead Maupin has a theory that every generation creates a male artist that straight boys are allowed to be queer about. In his latest book, *Significant Others*, he writes: 'It used to be Mick Jagger. Today it's Bruce Springsteen. Straight guys would go all the way to serve the boss.' What do you think?"
Mick: "It's an old theory. Elvis was the first androgynous singer. I don't see Bruce Springsteen as an androgyne. He's much too butch. What straight men like in a man is someone more feminine, and to me that doesn't really suggest Bruce Springsteen. Butch people like Bruce Springsteen always have an attraction for people, but what you're talking about is much more complex."
Q: "What do you think of Bruce Springsteen?"
Mick: "I don't really know that much about him. He's a very hard working rock singer from New Jersey who for many years had a band on the road before achieving any kind of international success."

FRIDAY, 1 JANUARY 1988

Keith confirms publicly that work is under way on his first solo album in an interview with Kurt Loder for MTV.
Keith: "A lot of what I'm gonna do is gonna sound like the Stones. All you need is one of those intros and it's The Rolling Stones; it's just the way I play."

He also discovers a new form of Keith-speak.

Keith: "There doesn't have to be a correlation between the age of the player and the music. It's a matter of, 'Can you put the stuff out? Can you transfer that ingredient, that one extra piece, that you can't read on all the meters; that has the magic of transferring the feeling, so that every time you push Play, that magic's gonna come out as fresh as the day it was put down?' For me that's art, that's magic, and that's fascinating – and that's what can be done."

He finds comfort in a new wave of guitar-based rockers . . .

Keith: "The public'll let you know when they're sick of something and they're sick to death of push–button drum kits. If you got Guns N' Roses out there, then all power to 'em, 'cos what the public's telling you is that they want some guys there who play together, with the music as a human thing."

. . . and made his peace with the ageing process.

Keith: "One day you too will be proud of getting this old and still be able to do your gig. I mean, I never wanted to make 30 either once. That was when I was 20. When I was 30, I never wanted to make 40. But once you hit 40 you think, 'Right, now I'd like to hit 100!' "

TUESDAY, 8 MARCH 1988

In anticipation of his first solo tour, which begins two days later, in Osaka, Japan, Mick gives a press conference in Tokyo.

Q: "Is this your first visit here?"

Mick: "Yes, it's my first visit to Japan."

Q: "I thought you might have dropped by incognito."

Mick: "No, I never did. I went to the airport once."

Q: "How's Japan?"

Mick: "It looks very clean and ordered compared to New York."

Q: "What about a new Stones album?"

Mick: "After the Japan tour, a Stones album I hope very quickly! We'll probably start a project by the end of this year."

Keith: "The idea of saying I wanna go out there and make a solo record, and break up The Rolling Stones and then end up playing Rolling Stones records sucks. I mean, I ain't saying anything to you that I haven't said to him . . . And quite honestly, I don't give a shit. That's the way I feel about it . . . It doesn't make sense to me. It's dumb. He's selling out. Come back when you're clean."

However, Keith doesn't discount a Rolling Stones reunion.
Keith: "This thing's bigger than both of us. The Rolling Stones will do what they're gonna do, and the forces of nature will take over."

APRIL 1988

Keith completes work on his solo album.
Keith: "I haven't recorded this because I was bored. I'm a musician and I need to work. If The Rolling Stones were together, then I would be doing it with them. At the moment, they're not. I think soon they may be. I have to work. What else would I do? Lie in bed and go mad?"

Keith: "We recorded the whole thing basically like we would with the Stones, with everyone playing live in the studio which apparently now is a novelty. I don't know why. To me that's one of the essential things about making a rock'n'roll record."

Keith: "The enthusiasm from the other guys is incredibly important, and these guys gave it to me all the way. They would never let me indulge myself. For instance, with the Stones, if I'd stop playing, everybody'd stop playing, go off for a drink and a phone call and, an hour later, come back and try it again. With this lot, if I stopped, they'd just carry on. They'd look at me: 'Pick it up, pick it *up*, man!' 'Why, you goddamn nigger!' *Nobody's* kicked me up the ass like that."

TUESDAY, 26 APRIL 1988

Mick is cleared after accusations that his 1985 single, 'Just Another Night', was plagiarised from a 1982 LP, Just A Touch Of Patrick Alley.
Mick: "My reputation is really cleared. If you're well known, people stand up and take shots at you."

WEDNESDAY, 18 MAY 1988

The Rolling Stones meet in London to discuss plans for an album and tour in 1989.
Keith: "Mick suddenly called up: 'Let's put the Stones back together again.' I'm thinking, 'Just as I'm in the middle of an album. Now what are you trying to do, screw me up? Just *now* you want to talk about putting it back together?' But we talked about it. I think you'll find a new album and a tour next year from the Stones."

SATURDAY, 2 JULY 1988

'Don't Believe The Hype' gives Public Enemy their first British Top 20 single, confirmation that a new form of black music is making a radical impact on contemporary pop. However, Keith is less than impressed by what he's been recently hearing.

Keith: "To me the disgusting thing about popular music at the moment . . . and I'm especially disappointed with you black guys, just pushing buttons and shit. They are really fucking up. You set up a drum kit and say you're gonna use a live drummer and the engineers go, 'What? How do we record a thing like that?' Music's got to do with people, not pushing buttons. To me, it's kind of weird that George Michael is number one on the black charts. What happened to Little Milton? What happened to the soul?"

There is a subtext to Keith's outburst.

Keith: "It's an indication of the difference between Mick and myself at this particular stage. He's very much into synthesisers and computers and I'm not."

SATURDAY, 16 JULY 1988

Mick takes a break during rehearsals for the Australasian leg of his solo tour to tell local television reporters that there's life in the Stones yet.

Mick: "We plan to do something in 1989. What that's gonna be I don't really know. I've written around 15 songs for the album."

Other topics under discussion include . . .

Going solo . . .

Mick: "If you've been married to the same girl for five or ten years and then you go with another one, it's a little bit strange but you get used to it."

Live shows . . .

Mick: "I haven't done live shows for years. This is very much a rock show. It's not a hugely produced Las Vegas revue where I stagger on in an old white suit and belt out a lot of old favourites before I croak off to the dressing room."

Fitness . . .

Mick: "I don't think when you get to my age that you should do so much exercise. You might fall down dead! You've got to be careful. None of this running round a track or playing football. Just a gentle swing of a tennis racket'll do."

The family . . .

Mick: "My parents were very strict and they used to beat me every night whether I was good or bad. It made no difference! And it's very difficult for me to be different to that when you've been brought up with a strict discipline. I try and be more modern and understand people's psychological needs. Different styles of potty training have been tried."

Q: "You said you couldn't see yourself on stage at the age of 40 belting out 'Satisfaction'."

Mick: "No I didn't. I said I couldn't see myself on stage when I was 50 doing it. Didn't I?"

Q: " 'Satisfaction' was recently voted as the best rock'n'roll song of all time . . ."

Mick: "It's great, very gratifying. Very pleased with that. It's not really one of my favourite songs but it's a great song. There've been some great versions of it – Aretha Franklin, Otis Redding."

TUESDAY, 23 AUGUST 1988

Mick and Keith hold a summit meeting in New York to firm up plans for 1989, as Keith tells Top *magazine.*

Keith: "Our battle is not just about two rich rock superstars indulging in power struggles and ego games. It's about us trying to find each other at this point in our lives. I mean, I love the guy. I love to work with him. There are certain things about him that piss me off . . . nothing more than what goes down between any close friends, really. If you can't lean on your mate or tell him when he's fucking up, then you're not really his friend, right?

"Mick and I are still testing each other out. But we have always been able to work together, no matter what we thought of each other at certain times. We'll see. This is just an interesting time. Maybe what we've found out is that Mick really needs The Rolling Stones more than The Rolling Stones need Mick. We all love the band, but I don't think that Mick thought he needed the Stones. He's probably realising now that he does, which is why we're talking about putting it back together . . . at *his* request, not mine. I'm busy with my own band at the moment."

THURSDAY, 29 SEPTEMBER 1988

A book of Ronnie Wood's paintings, The Works, *is published. It includes many portraits of the band.*

Ron: "Keith is easiest because he's always there! Mick is the hardest one to capture and Bill is the deceptive one. Charlie is the most pleasurable to draw."

SATURDAY, 1 OCTOBER 1988

Keith Richards' first solo album, Talk Is Cheap, *is released.*

Keith: "I enjoyed making this record, but I fought against the idea because to me it meant admitting I couldn't keep my band together, that I *had* to work on my own. My sense of failure."

Q: "What's the difference between a Keith Richards album and a Stones album?"

Keith: "Mick Jagger ain't on it! I would write certain songs because I would say, 'Well, Mick would sing it like this.' So I would write in a slightly different way. I make a few different moves for myself. I try and break the rhythm up, whereas for Mick I'd write more . . . march music!"

Keith: "This one has an identity that with the Stones is impossible to maintain all the time, for God knows what reason. It's an elusive thing. I had the feeling this one might be special as we were progressing. It was incredibly easy to make. Those are usually the ones that come out best . . . I think one of the worst things you can do in rock'n'roll is think about it."

Keith: "The album is called *Talk Is Cheap* because if we were able to talk about music there would be no need for music. Music performs a function that can only be provided by the very fact that it *is* music. And to talk about it – which is what we have to do – becomes very difficult 'cos you can't put music into dialogue. It performs a function that is totally separate from anything else."

'Whip It Up'

Keith: "There are a lot of little tributes on this album. Hats coming off here and there. There's even a little one to, bless their souls, the Fab Four. That's on 'Whip It Up'. It's a deliberate early Beatles way of doing things on the harmony vocals."

'You Don't Move Me' was a tribute song of sorts – to Mick's apparent treachery . . .

Keith: "I'd written about 40 songs for this album and I just dried up. Steve

354

(Jordan) turned around, looked at me, and said: 'When in doubt, write about Mick!' . . . In ten minutes, I'd written the whole thing."

Keith: "He's heard it, but I don't know if he's actually listened closely to it. Mick's heard the whole album a couple of times . . . talked all the way through it, but then he probably talks on the job! From what I hear, he likes the album. But I'm not sure he will enjoy the meaning of that particular song."

Keith: "For many years, Mick and I have been very close; we both had the same ideas. You could call Mick in Australia and call me in America and ask the questions and we'd give the same answers. Since 1982–83, Mick started to have a power struggle with me. And it only takes one person to create a power struggle.

"All lead vocalists, the more they do it, the longer it takes them to realise that they are not semi-divine. Eventually, they go to sleep, and next morning they still believe they're semi-gods. If you're a player, you always lean back on the band, on the music. I'm happy. I have many friends both inside and outside the Stones . . . Mick is a very, very lonely guy."

Keith: "There's no joy in punching a wimp. I like him, and I say these things, and they come out and they sound kind of cruel but I've known Mick since I was four years old. And despite myself, I do love the guy."

Keith: "I don't mind him reading this shit, because this is part of my attempt to help him along. What's so *hard* about being Mick Jagger? This exaggerated sense of who you are and what you should do and worrying about it so much. Why don't you just get on with it and stop trying to figure all the angles?"

But there is the occasional conciliatory tone.
Keith: "I love Mick. Most of my efforts with him go to trying to open his eyes: 'You don't need to do this – you have no problem, all you need to do is just grow up with it' . . . I tip my hat to Mick. I admire the guy enormously."

And despite the bile, Keith maintains that the Stones are set to return.
Keith: "There will be a record and a worldwide tour in 1989. I don't think it will be difficult to come back with the band. Mick and I are not in total agreement about everything but that doesn't mean working together is impossible. Sometimes conflict and tension can be very creative, and because the Stones have laid off for two or three years there should be a lot of energy about. We still need each other. It's like Mick and I are married and can never be divorced. Even if The Rolling Stones never played

another note in their life, Mick and I would still have to deal with each other."

Keith: "Charlie wants to work. He hasn't played for a year. I'm trying to get the boys to practise if they're serious about next year. Maybe I could use this to transmit the message once again about how important it is that *Bill and Charlie start playing now!* Because it'll be so much easier next year if they start practising now. They've heard this speech before, and they'll hear it again. I've got Ronnie working them, if he can just pull the moral weight to get them together and start juicing them up."

THURSDAY, 24 NOVEMBER 1988

Keith and his band, The X-Pensive Winos, kick off a month-long tour with a show at the Fox Theatre in Atlanta. Rona Elliot asks him if he feels a sense of betrayal performing on stage without the Stones.

Keith: "That's how I thought I would feel. That was one of the reasons why it was difficult to do. But it's like a lot of things – the idea of doing something is far more horrific than actually doing it. Basically, I had to admit to myself that the thing I always thought I could do, which was to force the Stones together, I couldn't do that right now. I had to recognise I'd failed. After 25 years with the same cats, the idea of starting again from scratch was scary. But suddenly I had another band in the making, a great band. One is a miracle. To be able to put two great bands together in a lifetime . . . you know, somebody's smiling."

And, as the New Year begins, how is the situation with Mick?

Keith: "I like to think of it like going through growing pains. We really need some ventilation and there's no point in going head to head . . . for what? We are great friends and that's why we fight. I'm the only one that can say no to Mick, nobody else can do that. In a way, I suppose he resents that. I see him surrounded by yes men and I'm the only one that can steam in there and upset things."

THURSDAY, 12 JANUARY 1989

Keith: "If Mick's albums had been blockbusters, it would be very unlikely that I would be leaving tomorrow to start a new Stones album. It's fun to work with Mick. Mick and I can work together like nobody's business. We know each other so well. This album might surprise people – it's already surprising me."

FRIDAY, 13 JANUARY 1989

Mick and Keith meet in Barbados for a reconciliation. Over the weekend, they write three new songs, including 'Mixed Emotions'.

Keith: "I said to my old lady, 'I'll either see you in two weeks or in two days, because I'll know if it'll work the minute I get there.'"

Mick: "I never said I wouldn't work with him again. Last autumn when he was slagging me off, he was just using that to get some publicity for his record. In typical English fashion, I took no notice."

Keith: "We needed to clear the air. It was more difficult to organise than the Moscow summit. But before we knew it, we had a tape full of songs."

WEDNESDAY, 18 JANUARY 1989

The Rolling Stones are inducted into the 3rd Rock'n'Roll Hall Of Fame Awards at the Waldorf-Astoria in New York City. It is Mick and Keith's first public appearance together since the spat. Ronnie Wood and Mick Taylor join them to accept the induction.

Pete Townshend: "There's some great artists here tonight, but the Stones will always be the greatest for me. They epitomise British rock, and even though they're all my friends, I'm still a fan. Guys, whatever you do, don't grow old gracefully. It wouldn't suit you."

Mick: "You know, it's slightly ironic that tonight you see us on our best behaviour, but we're being rewarded for 25 years of bad behaviour. I must say I'm very proud to work with this group of musicians for 25 years. The other thing I'm proud of is the songs that Keith and I have written.

"I'd like to pay tribute to two people who can't be here tonight. Ian Stewart, a great friend, a great blues pianist, whose odd but invaluable musical advice kept us on a steady, bluesy course. And to Brian Jones, whose individuality and musicianship often took us off the bluesy course, often with some marvellous results. Jean Cocteau said that Americans are funny people. First you shock them, then they put you in a museum. So on behalf of the Stones, I'd like to thank you very much for the award."

TUESDAY, 7 MARCH 1989

Keith: "I can be 'Keef' any time. That's easy. But there are other sides to me that are there for myself. I don't want to sound ungrateful but that image – 'I'm Keef and I'm stoned out of my mind all the time' – can be like a ball and chain. Now and again, I try to enlighten people that there is another side to it all. I mean, do you have kids? They bring you right down to earth. At home, I'm just 'Dad' or 'Darling'.' "

But there's only so much 'Dad' and 'Darling' that Keith can take.
Keith: "I live in a household of women, which sometimes can drive me totally round the bend, which is why I need to work and get on the road. I love 'em all, but it's weird to be living with a load of chicks – it doesn't matter what age they are. For a guy, the only guy in the house, you gotta call up another cat and say, 'Hey, come over, or I'll just drop over there!' "

Though, as Keith tells German television, home is where the muse is . . .
Keith: "Songwriting is as much a mystery to me as it is to anyone else. I mean, the best songs to me are the ones I write in bed. That means I don't even have to move. The guitar's always next to the bed, the tape recorder's always next to the bed, and if I wake up and without waking the wife up and put a little song together . . . that's luxury to me!"

WEDNESDAY, 29 MARCH 1989

The group arrive at AIR Studios, Montserrat in the West Indies, and spend a month recording their new album.
Mick: "Apart from one song I did last year and one Keith did last year, all the songs were written in this rather compressed time frame. We had got into a terrible habit of meandering and being disorganised. I sat down with Keith and he said, 'We're never going to do an album.' Well, maybe we won't but there isn't any harm in trying . . . The only way it's going to work is if we come in, write the songs, do the arrangements, have it all ready and go into the studio. It does sound very professional for The Rolling Stones and to be honest I never thought it would work . . . but it did."

FRIDAY, 31 MARCH 1989

Back in London, news breaks concerning another Stone's domestic arrangements.
Mandy Smith: "Bill asked me to marry him on Easter Sunday and I accepted immediately. It was really romantic. I'm delighted and so is he."

MAY 1989

The diaries of artist Andy Warhol, who died in 1987, are published.
Mick: "Life's too short to read something that long. Jerry's read it all, but then she's more of a lady of leisure than I am. Trouble with Andy was that

he virtually had no sex life at all, so he lived vicariously through others. He wasn't the ideal dinner companion. Jesus, he was so boring. All he'd ever say was, 'Woow, I'll have a vodka,' and then talk to his dachshund, 'Ooooh, great.' But he was great to work with."

WEDNESDAY, 17 MAY 1989

Bill Wyman opens a burger restaurant, Sticky Fingers, at 1a Phillimore Gardens, off Kensington High Street, in West London. The walls are covered in Stones memorabilia from his personal collection. And on the menu?
"Beggars Banquet – a spectacular feast . . . for those with BIG appetites" . . . £9.75
Brown Sugar dessert . . . £2.75 and a Honky Tonk cocktail . . . £3.95."

WEDNESDAY, 31 MAY 1989

Keith picks up a 'Living Legend' award, presented by Eric Clapton, in New York. Inevitably, he is quizzed on the current status of the Stones.
Keith: "I can't answer that."
Q: "Why not?"
Keith: "Why should I?"
Q: " 'Cos we're all interested."
Keith: "So stay interested."

FRIDAY, 2 JUNE 1989

Bill marries Mandy Smith at Bury St Edmunds Registry Office. The Stones attend a lavish reception three days later at the Grosvenor House Hotel, London.
Ron: "Mandy is a lovely girl, but the fact is I'm just too young for her."
Eric Clapton: "I've bought him a pair of navy blue silk pyjamas, £129 from Harrods. At Bill's age, you shouldn't be hopping into bed unclothed."
Keith: "I feel really bad. I forgot to buy them a wedding present."
Mick: "We could make lots of jokes about Mandy keeping him fit for the tour. And we will. It's so showbiz, innit? When I heard it was really happening, I found it hard to believe, after all she did – telling her story, running off to Spain with someone else. Still, that's *lurve* in the land of rock'n'roll."

Several weeks later, Bill was still full of the joys of matrimonial bliss.
Bill: "On a good day, she's the most beautiful, the most charming, the

kindest and most generous girl I've ever met. Even on a bad day, she's nearly there. It's amazing, but since we got married it's worked better than either of us expected. I mean, we thought it would work successfully and nicely, but it's worked brilliantly."

Meanwhile, another Stone is about to celebrate his 25th wedding anniversary.
Shirley Watts: "I think Charlie was always a 50-year-old man. Charlie's tastes were never the same as the rest of the crowd. To tell you the truth, I was always surprised he was a part of that band."

TUESDAY, 11 JULY 1989

The Stones call a press conference at Grand Central Station, New York City, to announce details of their first tour in seven years.
Q: "Is this the last time?"
Mick: "I don't see it as that. It's the Rolling Stones in 1989."
Q: "Some commentators say that the only reason you're doing it is for the money."
Mick: "What about love, fame and fortune? Have you forgotten about that?"

THURSDAY, 31 AUGUST 1989

The Stones' Steel Wheels tour gets underway at the Veteran's Stadium in Philadelphia. The grandest tour ever undertaken by a rock'n'roll band, much publicity is given to the elaborate set design by Mick Fisher.
Mick: "It's supposed to be a run-down industrial plant. But when it goes from day to night and the whole thing gets lit, it takes on a more romantic, mysterious light."

MONDAY, 11 SEPTEMBER 1989

Steel Wheels, *the first new Stones album in three years, is released. But who is the dominant partner this time?*
Keith: "It's much more 50/50."

One song, 'Continental Drift', is particularly notable in that it revisited an unlikely moment from the band's past . . .
Mick: "We have one kinda North African track, a continuation of the 'Paint It Black' theme. I went to Morocco to record some of it, where Brian went with Brion Gysin to record the tribesmen. I was writing this

song and remembering their harmonics and thinking, 'Wouldn't it be great to have them on the track' – and a letter from them arrived . . . It turns out that the seven-year-old boy Brian met when he was there, the chief's son, is now the chief and he invited us over to record. I went up to the village – it's about two hours away – by donkey. But we couldn't do any recording there because there was no electricity, so we had to bring them to Tangier."

Unnamed eyewitness account: "There was a terrific atmosphere – the music was all very Arab sounding. Even Mick's voice was more nasal than usual. Everything was on a natural high. There was no drinking and no smoking of anything illicit. And the only women around were some tribeswomen and Ronnie Wood's wife, Jo. The guys were thrilled that some of the local musicians remembered them from the other visit. There was a lot of back-slapping and joking. It was emotional because they all got to thinking about Brian – and remembering the last time they were all there together . . . When the band finished playing they just sat around gazing up at the sky, deep in thought. It was obvious they were reminiscing."

Bill: "It's like family. Coming together after all these years is like seeing Uncle Fred and Auntie Edith again."

Mick: "I play a lot of guitar on this album, more than I've ever done before. Keith's helped me on that . . ."

But, 20/20 magazine asks, who is the real leader?
Mick: "Me. But it's still very democratic. They all have a veto on what we do, really . . . There's bound to be rivalry. There's always been a bit of to-ing and fro-ing and everyone likes to have their say. It's not just a question of keeping Keith happy – everyone is such a fucking prima donna. Charlie and Bill like to have their say about this and that, this keyboard player, that backing singer, Coke or Pepsi, but it all came out in the wash. We sat down, rowed like crazy for a day and stopped slagging each other."

Mick: "It's very nice if people think I'm a country gentleman or something. I don't mind that because there's always been a part of me that loves England and Englishness, and there's another part of me that thinks it's fuckin' ridiculous and makes me laugh. It's a very funny place when you step away from it. It's got this creeping obsession with royalty. Last time I came here there was some stuff in the papers about Princess Anne's nanny or something, some incredible garbage and now it's front page news about Lady Di comin' second in the egg and spoon race. So she should, she's fit enough."

361

WEDNESDAY, 27 DECEMBER 1989

25 x 5: The Continuing Adventures Of The Rolling Stones, *a television special for BBC's* Arena, *yields plenty of rare and unseen footage, as well as a string of impeccable one-liners from Keith.*

On the departure of Brian Jones . . .
Keith: "Hey, cock, you're fired."

On why he has no regrets about hiring Allen Klein . . .
Keith: "I figured it was the price of an education."

On the Toronto bust . . .
Keith: "I looked at the old lady and said, 'See you in seven years, babe.' "

And on the split . . .
Keith: "We needed a break. Mick needed to find his own feet and see what it's like . . . It's easy to go a little crazy inside the Rolling Stones bubble if that's all you do."

5

No Expectations

SUNDAY, 4 MARCH 1990

"MANDY AND WYMAN: IT'S ALL OVER NOW"

It's announced that Bill Wyman has filed for judicial separation after just nine months of marriage. He's also hinting – again – that his days with the Stones are numbered.

Bill: "There comes a time in your life when you know there's other things to do. When I started playing music, everybody thought it was a two or three year thing. We'd get a nice little house, nice car, find a nice lady, settle down and then do all the things we really want to do, like write books or photography or astronomy or archaeology. Here we are, 28 years later, and I still think maybe next year I can go and do all those things. But time's running out. I've probably only got 20 to go now and you've gotta start thinking."

He also suggests that his motionless and expressionless on-stage stance symbolises his estrangement from the group.

Bill: "I've always thought the music comes first. It doesn't come naturally so I don't try to do it because I would look foolish. I have great fun, but I don't feel like I'm part of the band. I feel like I'm watching a show on my right, which is the band, and I'm watching this show in front of me, which is the audience."

THURSDAY, 22 MARCH 1990

Dates for the European leg of the tour are announced at a press conference at the Tabernacle Club, West London. Out goes the cold and grey Steel Wheels concept in favour of a colourful Urban Jungle theme. The press conference begins with a speech from the tour's sponsors.

Budweiser spokesman: "Today, The Rolling Stones are drawing millions of fans to stadiums on each continent they visit. We at Budweiser see a parallel between The Rolling Stones' commitment to their fans and our own commitment to producing the best-selling beer in the world. Consequently, we at Budweiser are proud to support The Rolling Stones' tour on this or any other continent. We know it's a great partnership. Ladies and gentlemen, thank you."

Mick: "I'd like to apologise – the rest of the band couldn't be here today. Bill Wyman has a sort of love/hate relationship with the British press. He's in France. Charlie Watts and his wife are spaying wild animals in Africa. Ron Wood is losing money very heavily, I've heard – that's why he's had to do this 'European in Ireland' – on racehorses. And Keith is in America with his family, and he told me, 'Don't forget music, there will be music.'"

Q: "Is there any reason why the States took to the last Stones album and we didn't?"

Mick: "Maybe because we weren't here. But we're here now, so maybe they'll buy a few more."

Q: "How do you feel being, not only a rock'n'roll band, but, as well, something done as big business, with sponsorship . . .?"

Mick: "Well, we're all in this business together, I think you'll find. We've got our sponsorship, you've got your advertising in your magazine. Rock'n'roll's been big business for a long time. I'm afraid the days are gone of it being an amateur thing, and I don't even remember those days, I'm afraid. Underneath all the bullshit and the fanfare which is what we're doing today, it's still the same music underneath it all."

Q: "Why the title 'Urban Jungle'? Is it bullshit or is there a message?"

Mick: "Probably a bit of both . . ."

Q: "How do you keep fit for the tour?"

Mick: "I can't reveal that! I've sold my secrets to the *Daily Mirror*. I don't work very hard and I eat a lot."

Q: "Have you got a punching bag?"

Mick: "The old lady! Nah, you set me up for that one!"

FRIDAY, 18 MAY 1990

The tour begins in the Feyenoord Stadium in Rotterdam, Holland. While diehard fans debate the set-lists, the media seems more interested in . . .

Who's coming . . .

Mick: "You can't choose your audience. You're pleased if anybody at all will pay money to come and see you. But I am happy that it is not just old people turning up to relive their youth. Every night on this tour I've seen some very, very young ones down at the front."

. . . and Mick's fitness regime
Mick: "Physical preparation is very important. (I do) an hour and a half: you could do more. I start off with some weights, say ten minutes . . . light jogging, stretches, then some sprinting, warm downs and then some more weights . . . Before these European dates, I was already in good shape, but I still went through some four weeks intensive training, specifically designed for this . . . The diet is pretty much what I eat anyway, a mixed one, high in carbohydrates, rice, pasta, potatoes, which help muscle efficiency from dropping off, plus quite a bit of protein."

For a more detailed breakdown of Mick's physical preparations, his journalist/ musician brother Chris watches him in action with personal trainer, Torje Eike.
"A typical session starts with a 15-minute warm-up, followed by aerobic and anaerobic training, or a combination of both. The aerobic component would be a steady pace run for up to 30 minutes, to keep the pulse rate steady at about 70 per cent of the maximum heart rate. The anaerobic work would typically involve 'interval' training for up to 15 minutes. Weight training builds upper body strength, improves posture and prevents back problems. Mick also had a daily dance class, and up to 14 hours a day rehearsing with the band."

WEDNESDAY, 4 JULY 1990

The Stones play the first of a three-night run at Wembley Stadium.
Guy Fetherstonhaugh (fan, aged 35): "The last time I came to Wembley was to see the Pope in 1982 and I haven't been to see a pop concert since Elton John at university. It is nostalgia, I suppose."

SATURDAY, 18 AUGUST 1990

The Stones are entertained by Czech President Václav Havel and his wife before a benefit concert in Prague.
Keith: "That was an amazing gig . . . A lot of the reason you've got major shifts in superpower situations in the past few years has to do with the past 20 years of music. You'll never get rid of nationalism and so-called patriotism, but the important thing is to spread the idea that there's really this one planet – that's what we've really got to worry about."

FRIDAY, 24 AUGUST 1990

The four-month Urban Jungle tour closes with two rescheduled shows at Wembley Stadium, London.
Mick: "After this, we'll need a bit of a break from each other. It's great the band is getting on so well, but to be honest, it's nice to go and play with some other musicians for a bit. That's what I'd like to do."

Or play something completely different . . .
Mrs Eva Jagger: "Mick likes listening to good music, too. When we go to his home he always plays lovely classical music."

Mick's dietary change was particularly welcome, too.
Mick: "After a year of pasta every day I could hardly look at the stuff. I ate quite a lot of fish and chicken. I found the best time to eat was some four hours before the show which meant I was ravenous afterwards. It was a revelation to find I wasn't tired at the end of the day."

WEDNESDAY, 24 OCTOBER 1990

The first volume of Bill's long-awaited autobiography, Stone Alone, *is published. While richly detailed in all aspects of the Stones' Sixties career, inevitably the press pick up on a detail tucked away on page 355 where Bill reveals that by 1965 he had already 'entertained' 278 girl fans.*

Asking 'Who The Hell Does Bill Wyman Think He Is?' on behalf of Q *magazine, Mat Snow wonders whether "the frisky fellow" is still counting.*
Bill: "Of *course*! I know *exactly* where the tally stands. I'm not telling you, though . . . It's four figures . . . I'm not going any further. I'm a married man now."
Keith: "I couldn't, in all honesty, get through Bill's book because I got fed up with each chapter ending up with his bank account. 'And after all that I only had £5,000 in the bank.' Anyway, Bill's not really telling anything. He's saving the real one for later."

MONDAY, 18 FEBRUARY 1991

Mick begins filming Freejack, *his first film in 21 years, in Atlanta, Georgia. It also stars Anthony Hopkins.*
Geoff Murphy (director): "Using rock stars in films is a risk, but I don't

see it with Jagger. He can do the job, looks incredible and has big commercial quality. He is charismatic and magnetic."

MONDAY, 11 MARCH 1991

A new song, 'Highwire', recorded in January, is released. A rare pop at political expediency – in this instance, the sale of arms to the Middle East – it walks straight into controversy due to the war being waged in the Gulf.

Mick: "We were completing work on our live album (*Flashpoint*) and wanted to put a new studio track on it. I thought this would be a good opportunity to address a current issue. I do like to occasionally touch on political issues at a time when they are what people are talking about. Pop music has a role there. It should address as broad a range of subjects as possible – not only sex and cars."

Mick: "In the first part of the song, I'm criticising the situation that has led up to this inevitable war. The scale of the war is because of the past 20 years of high-tech sales from the West and Soviet Union. The chorus voices the concern I have for our troops, and indeed all the troops in the Gulf, that the war will not be long and drawn out with thousands and thousands of soldiers and civilians being killed."

Mick: "There are the total pacifists who disagree with war at any cost, and there are the gung-ho militarists, who love the idea of battle. In between, lies almost everyone else. I'm right in the middle; I try to present a pretty balanced view."

MONDAY, 8 APRIL 1991

Flashpoint, a live album of the recent Steel Wheels/Urban Jungle tour, is released. Otherwise, it's a quiet year for the Rolling Stones, though Keith is simply pleased that the band is still a functioning unit again.

Keith: "The Stones have got too big for their own good, in that the way they work is on a gigantic scale and you're either doing that or you're doing nothing for two years. And that, as any musician will tell you, is not a good thing. If you wanna make music, good music, you really have to do it regularly. In a way, we thought we were fighting about whatever we thought we were fighting about. In fact, we just needed to get out. That could have broken the Stones forever or it could have given the Stones strength. And in putting *Steel Wheels* together, we found that what we did separately actually helped. The minute Mick and I got back together and started laughing about all of these things, now that was a positive thing."

MID-APRIL 1991

Keith attends a John Lee Hooker session in New York. He plays guitar on a version of 'Crawling Kingsnake', which ends up on Hooker's Mr Lucky *album.*
Keith: "I'm very respectful, but I put in my little bit. I wanted his foot. He wasn't gonna do it, but I got a piece of wood. I wanna hear *my* John Lee . . . It's an honour. To play with guys that I used to sit at home and listen to and wonder how it was done – it's amazing. I got to work with all of my heroes. I'm eternally grateful to work with all of those guys because they taught me an awful lot about what it is to be a musician. You don't stop. You just keep going, I mean, John Lee Hooker: he's 78, and he's got 15 girlfriends. We should all be so lucky!"

TUESDAY, 23 APRIL 1991

Ex-New York Dolls guitarist and lifelong Keef clone, Johnny Thunders dies.
Keith: "Guys that don't really know me, they're more likely to be the child of my image. That's something I have to think about, because I'm not exactly just like that. Chasing an image is a dangerous game."

JULY 1991

Mick buys a huge family home, Downe House, on Richmond Hill, on the out-skirts of London.
Mick: "People find it hard to accept multifaceted people – that you can be a person who has children, but yet you can go out and get wild and crazy and mad and drunk, and then go out on the road and be completely sober because that's what you have to be. I don't find life quite so simple, that everyone's just got these tiny personalities and that they can only behave in one kind of way."

FRIDAY, 25 OCTOBER 1991

A new concert film, Rolling Stones At The Max, *shot during the last stages of the Urban Jungle tour, is premiered worldwide. It utilises the new IMAX system that, says Julian Temple, "not only puts you in the front row, but on stage".*
Mick: "It's not a documentary about a tour, or being on the road or how it all works, or what happens when you go back to the hotel. That's been done so many times. I thought it would be better to just film it as a concert."

Michael Cohl (Executive Producer): "The band's basic position was, 'We've done too many (concert films). It's always flat on the screen and never works.' My point was, 'I've got an idea that overcomes that.'"

Keith: "You can't get this on an ordinary movie screen or television."

TUESDAY, 19 NOVEMBER 1991

The Stones sign a £25 million, three-album deal with Virgin Records.

Richard Branson: "I first saw the group as an 18-year-old in Hyde Park . . . The Stones are the greatest rock'n'roll band and I am honoured they have chosen Virgin."

With the deal in the bag, rumours circulate that Bill's departure from the band is imminent. Keith worries about the future on behalf of the other members.

Keith: "Let's find out. The one thing I don't wanna do is quit early and then sit around for the rest of my life wondering what would have happened had I carried on. That would be a regret and I don't like them."

Keith reveals that he'd yet to discuss the matter with Bill.

Keith: "I can't talk to him about this stuff on the phone. I've worked with the guy 30 years. I gotta look him in the eyeballs – just tell me, man, one time. I don't wanna change the line-up unless I have to. And I don't wanna drag Bill in at gunpoint either. I wanna see him in the next few weeks and figure it out once and for all. If he's determined, then I will have to figure out who could possibly step in his shoes."

Whatever happens, Keith insists that it's business as usual for the Stones in 1992.

Keith: "Mick and I are getting together next February or March and start a new record. I've a feeling that the Stones have got something very interesting in them. I still wanna see what the Stones can do. That's what interests me."

TUESDAY, 26 NOVEMBER 1991

Keith Richards And The X-Pensive Winos' Live At The Hollywood Palladium, December 15, 1988, is released on CD and video. It includes a trio of Stones favourites, 'Time Is On My Side', 'Happy' and – from the 1967 Between The Buttons album – 'Connection'.

Keith: "When I told the Winos that we're going on the road, they said, 'Great, but we've only got ten songs to play. We gotta half hour show.' Okay, let's do the songs I do with the Stones – 'Happy', 'Before They

369

Make Me Run', 'Little T&A'. I've got Sarah Dash singing with me so we can do 'Time Is On My Side', 'cos that was originally an Irma Thomas song. We needed a couple of more songs, so we got the reggae one on *Dirty Work*, 'Too Rude'. And it struck me that 'Connection' had never been played live with the Stones, and it's such a nice rocker, so interesting to play. So it crept in. If I'm gonna do Stones songs, I'm gonna do ones I sing or songs the Stones have never done."

Keith also reveals that more Winos material is probably on the way.
Keith: "The Winos have been writing all summer. We've got some grooves and we're gonna put them down . . . The Stones are still together as far as I know."

As part of the promotion, Keith entertains two German journalists, Christian Kammerling and Andreas Lebert, in his New York apartment. They spot that his stereo is still turned on . . .
Q: "What have you been listening to?"
Keith: "A really old James Brown CD. I go through phases. I listen to a lot of classical music and folk music. In Europe last year, I picked up some Portuguese fado music, which is very nice, some nice gypsy stuff in Czechoslovakia and some really good flamenco in Spain."
Q: "What do you think of today's music?"
Keith: "I have the feeling it's all experimentation. Sometimes experimentation takes over what's really any good. Pop music has become a lot more complicated now – that's always a sign of decadence. It usually signals the end of a style . . . Each generation has its own rhythm. Our parents had swing, we have rock and the kids of today are taking our stuff and interpreting it for their time. We'll see where it takes us. They've got typewriter rhythms, people pushing buttons with fingers. But maybe that's the feeling this generation has."

Noting that their host has already finished his first bottle of whisky, and that his ashtray is completely full and it's just two hours after breakfast, they ask about survival.
Keith: "You're beginning to sound like my wife. She's always asking, 'Why are you lighting up another cigarette?' I tell her it's because the last one wasn't long enough. I've taken worse things than cigarettes and whisky . . ."

Interviewed for French television show, Rien A Declarer, Keith explains that his solo work gives him an unexpected insight into his relationship with Mick.
Keith: "I learnt a lot about Mick's job, of being the focus of attention the

whole time. With the Stones I got it easy. I can do as much as I want, then I can pull back and sneak around, have a drink! He probably found the same thing when he started doing his solo stuff. You can't just hire a bunch of musicians and expect them to back you in the way the Stones do. You live and you learn."

But it hasn't curbed his desire to collaborate.
Keith: "I don't like working alone. I always like to hang with friends. I always have ideas, but they're gonna be a lot better if I can bounce them off someone else. I like the give and take, yelling at each other and sitting around on the floor scribbling. Why do it alone when you can do it with friends? If I did it all alone, it would take me ten times longer, and then I'd have to start arguing with myself. And I don't like to do that."

THURSDAY, 5 DECEMBER 1991

Mick joins Lenny Kravitz on stage at Wembley Arena, London, where they duet on a version of the Stones' 'No Expectations'. Later, they tried to write a song together for Mick's third solo album.
Mick: "All we did was get completely stoned and go out dancing. We didn't come up with a single idea, so we did 'Use Me' instead."

SUNDAY, 12 JANUARY 1992

Mick attends the birth of Georgia May Jagger, in London.
Jerry Hall: "It's a miracle we've managed to stay together so long . . . It's difficult in the entertainment business because there's always attractive people around and so many young girls who chase after Mick."

A month later, he is seen holidaying on the Indonesian island of Phuket in the company of a teenage girl.
Jerry Hall: "I confronted him and asked who he was with in Thailand . . . A man is supposed to be with his woman when she's just had her baby."
Keith: "I hope the man comes to his senses. He should stop that now, the old black-book bit. Kicking 50, it's a bit much, a bit manic."

WEDNESDAY, 15 JANUARY 1992

Has he, or hasn't he? The official line is that "Bill Wyman has made no decision as to his future with the Rolling Stones."
Keith: "I wouldn't want to change the line-up at this stage. It would be a

wrench. But as long as you've got Charlie Watts and Mick and me and Ron . . ."

Mick, though, hints that it's a fait accompli.
Mick: "I think Bill's had enough of it, really. He's got enough money and I suppose he feels he's done it. We haven't really talked about it, but I don't think I'd be out of order in saying that I doubt we'd actually get someone new in the band who'd be a permanent Rolling Stone. We'd make a record, do a tour and see how it works over a two-year period."

WEDNESDAY, 12 FEBRUARY 1992

Mick joins Arts Minister Timothy Renton on the stage of the Royal Festival Hall in London to announce a new government-sponsored initiative, National Music Day, planned for 28 June. The Rolling Stones, Eric Clapton and Elton John are all tipped to take part.
Mick: "The idea started in France with [French Arts Minister] Jack Lang and their National Music Day was full of a lot of people having a great time. So then I met our Arts Minister at a cocktail party and I said, 'Hey, why don't *we* have a National Music Day?' "
Tim Renton: "Actually, it was not at a cocktail party, Mick, it was in the Nubian Room at the British Museum."

SATURDAY, 15 FEBRUARY 1992

Keith inducts guitar maker Leo Fender into the Rock'n'Roll Hall Of Fame.
Keith: "The basic idea of it (the Hall Of Fame) is very good, but it just ends up being showbiz, everyone doing a lot of business telling everybody how much they love each other. I like the original idea, of being able to learn how to record, learn how to mix. That was the idea. But there's too much fame and not enough whore."

SUNDAY, 23 FEBRUARY 1992

Mick flies to Los Angeles to continue work on another solo album.
Mick: "It was recorded in a very seedy area of Hollywood, with a soup kitchen on one corner, a transvestite pick-up on the other. (Producer) Rick (Rubin) and I would always go and listen to mixes in his Rolls parked in the street. We couldn't decide which version of 'Sweet Thing' to choose, so all the local bums surrounded the car and gave us their

opinion – not always politely – of what they liked the best. I still think they were right."

MID-MARCH 1992

Keith bites the bullet and begins work on a second solo album.
Keith: "My problem with this was if I write a song, do I keep it for myself or do I give it to the Stones. I never wanted to split myself like that. Why should I? I realised that whatever I was working on, that's where it'll go. The most important thing is to keep working so that you're not on a lay-up for two years and then have to go into maintenance for six months. That is daunting. This way, I know we're all ready to go. *Steel Wheels* proved that."

SUNDAY, 28 JUNE 1992

National Music Day takes place with 1,500 events, including a Celebration Of The Blues at Hammersmith Odeon, where Charlie Watts and Ron Wood join Mick for two songs, including a version of 'I Just Wanna Make Love To You'.
Mick: "The idea wasn't to take people's tax money away from existing events, and I didn't want the whole thing to get too politicised . . . Raising money in public for charity is something that grates on my Hassidic sensibility. I mean, enough already!"

MONDAY, 14 SEPTEMBER 1992

A new Ronnie Wood solo album, Slide On This, *is released in the States.*
Keith: "I like Ronnie's record. It's very good. Usually I'm involved with Ronnie's thing, but I think Bernard Fowler did a great job with it. They're all working, that's the important thing. It means that when the Stones get back together, they don't have to go through this, 'What happened to the greatest rock'n'roll band ever? Well, they sound crap.' It usually takes six months to wind it all up again."

TUESDAY, 20 OCTOBER 1992

Keith releases a second solo album, Main Offender. *Its original title was* Blame Hound, *because, he says, "I always seem to get blamed for everything."*
Keith: "It's nice to get out of the rut. I realise that I've been writing songs for 25 years for Mick to sing. This gives me the opportunity to write songs

for myself to sing. It gives me the chance to stretch the songs a little differently."

And be stretched in the studio.
Keith: "With the Stones, I guess I'm more like the boss, at least in the studio, where we're writing the songs and putting the tracks together. If I stop in the middle of a take 'cos I'm not happy with it, everything stops. They wait for me to put it back together. With the Winos they glare at me and keep going."

A Dutch television interviewer asks Keith if there's a major difference between this and the first solo record.
Keith: "Yes, there is definitely. Mainly because I've managed to retain the same people, that makes a lot of difference. I sense a certain growth and identity between these guys. I couldn't define it. I like records to feel fresh, so if there's a mistake or two I'd prefer to leave that in rather than do another take that doesn't quite have that edge. I want the take that has the spirit, the feel. You don't get a measuring stick. You have to go by instinct."

With each new release, Keith becomes increasingly philosophical about his trade.
Keith: "If you're a musician, then silence is your canvas. I don't care what the meaning is, I wanna know if it gives me the shivers. If it's done that then it's done the job. Everything has come out of what I've needed to do to make the music. So if it takes skulls and hell and everything else, then you go through it and see if you come out."

Keith tells Ira Robbins for Pulse! *magazine . . .*
"I'm not an autobiographer. I write songs, I don't write a diary. I'm not baring my soul. I'm trying to distil things and feelings that I've had through my life and I know for damn sure that other people have had, and I try and evoke them. The only songs that interest me could mean anything to anybody. You can take what's happening to you and relate to it, and it will have a totally different meaning to you than it will to somebody else. I never think a song is finished being written just because you've recorded it and put it out. Now it can grow, because other people are going in to hear it. That's when it takes on its real meaning."

This time round, Keith and Steve Jordan nominate guitarist Waddy Wachtel for additional duties.
Keith: "Steve and I are very black-and-white in obvious ways. We tend to yell at each other and, meanwhile, nothing is being done. Great

argument, but no record! We needed a breaker and Waddy has a mathematical brain, he can step in between Steve and I. It's a perfect gathering. Being able to pull the guys together for another round is great."

Despite recent hopes, Keith expresses his disappointment at the news that 1993 is going to be another quiet year for the Stones.
Keith: "It's very important that if you write songs and make records, you gotta take it on the road because that's the only way you're gonna figure out what you're gonna do next. On stage, there's only one take and you gotta do it every time. The whole spirit of the band is elevated and concentrated, and that's when you get ideas for the next thing."

'Wicked As It Seems'
Keith: "It's a collection of images. I'm just waiting for everyone to tell me what it's all about. I don't really care what the meaning is. I just want it to give me the shivers. If it's done that, it's done the job. The only way I've changed is that I don't lose my temper in the quite spectacular ways I used to. I can't get off now and chicken out. I'd be sitting on the kerb wondering where it's all gone. I'm in it for the long run. I told you I was sick . . ."

SATURDAY, 7 NOVEMBER 1992

Keith Richards and The X-Pensive Winos kick off their worldwide tour in Buenos Aires, Argentina.
Keith: "With the Stones you get two years with nothing much to do. To me, that's death."

In fact, he goes even further about his devotion to the Stones . . .
Keith: "It's a kind of bubble there. You can stay inside and be insulated, but I don't think it's really any good for you. Some of the things I've done in my life have probably been like a vain attempt to break out of that."

WEDNESDAY, 2 DECEMBER 1992

Keith and the Winos' tour stops off at the Marquee Club in London.
Keith: "I now have two great bands. This also lets me do things on a smaller scale. With the Stones, everything is enormous. You're always playing football stadiums where God joins the band in one form or another – with either rain or snow or wind or heat! To play in a controlled environment – you know, four walls and a ceiling – is a joy."
Keith: "The Stones try doing secret gigs but basically you're pushing against a business. If there's that many people want to see you, and you put

on a tour of stadium–sized venues, you're kind of locked into that. We're always looking for new ways of doing things, but it's a hard fight."

But, says Richard Jobson, a club show affords no hiding place.
Keith: "Mistakes? That's what this music's about! You can learn and profit by them."

THURSDAY, 3 DECEMBER 1992

Mick and Keith both confirm the rumour that Bill is leaving the band.
Keith: "In the last few months, I've been trying to leave the door open for Bill. Maybe he's had enough. It's a drag. I really didn't wanna have to change anything. But at the same time, I certainly wouldn't want a reluctant Bill in the Stones. It's gonna be a task to find the right guy but I'm sure he's out there somewhere."

Former Who bass player John Entwistle?
Keith: "I doubt that very much! He's a good player, but I don't hear him with Charlie Watts!"
Mick: "Bill has decided he doesn't want to carry on. For whatever reasons he doesn't want to do it anymore, so we are looking for a new bass player. I don't think it will faze us too much. We'll miss Bill, but we'll get someone good, a good dancer."
Keith: "I was pissed as hell when he went because the rule is, no one leaves except in a coffin. But Bill realised before we did that he didn't want to do it 100 per cent. I mean, you try flying from Chile to Johannesburg."
Bill: "They said, 'You can't leave'. Like school bullies. Mick and Keith got very uptight. For six months they said the nastiest things they could possibly say. It was really bitchy, cruel in a way. But it's the control thing, isn't it? It hurt me after 31 years giving my all. People were asking Mick, 'What are you going to do about a new bass player?' He was quoted as saying, 'It can't be that difficult. I'll play the bass.' Keith said, 'No one leaves this band unless they're in a coffin.' And nasty faxes. And then I sat with Charlie and Mick one night and talked. I said, 'I don't want this life any more. I've got other things I want to do. I want to have a new family.' And after about six months they were fine."

FRIDAY, 11 DECEMBER 1992

With Keith still out on tour, and Mick filming a promo video for his forthcoming solo single, some wonder if the pair's relationship has sunk to a new low.

Keith: "It's far more stable than it was six or seven years ago. Mick and I had a big fight, a family squabble, and the crunch came with the *Steel Wheels* record. If that hadn't have come off that maybe would have been the end of it. We've grown up because of it. It's probably a necessary clearing of the air, and I think we both appreciate each other's position to each other now. I certainly understand more about Mick's job by doing my own solo stuff, by standing up the front all the time. And Mick has realised that you can't just go round the corner and hire a bunch of musicians, no matter how good they are, and expect to get the back-up that he did with the Stones."

In fact, he's looking forward to the next Stones sessions . . .
Keith: "The Stones still have some good records in them. If Mick and I can come up with the songs, I still sense another golden period."

But hasn't he used up all his best songs on the solo album?
Keith: "Songs aren't like that. When I'm writing with Steve Jordan and working with the Winos, those songs come out of that process. The Stones songs are not written yet. Songs don't keep. You can't put 'em in the freezer and pull 'em out when you want them. They have to be fairly fresh."

THURSDAY, 17 DECEMBER 1992

Keith talks drugs to Kerrang! *magazine.*
Keith: "I never felt I was jeopardising future operations. Maybe I was testing myself . . . maybe the dope was my way of keeping my feet, uh, in the air!"

But, when quizzed on Scandinavian TV about a local musician's recent suggestion that drugs should be freely available in order to solve the problem, he takes a different tack.
Keith: "No, I don't think so. I mean, given by whom to whom? I mean, drugs are never free. Somebody's gotta pay. I remember when I thought that. He'll grow up, don't worry about it."

And that old 'Keef' mythology?
Keith: "Image is like a ball and chain, a long shadow. You always drag it round with you and it's always five years out of date. But, you know, keep piling those myths on."
Q: "There's an image of Keith as the guy who lives and breathes rock'n' roll, while you are the calculating businessman."

Mick: "If only it were true. I really don't enjoy business. I never do business apart from The Rolling Stones. I'm not interested in playing the market. I find that very dull. But you have to do a certain amount of business, or you just get ripped off, or end up having to do things that you don't realise you were asked to do. Keith's a great family man. He takes them all on the road, his mother-in-law and whatever else. He's not generally perceived as such, but he is very family-oriented."

Keith: "I need family, I love family. I don't see what's so incompatible about that. Everybody's adaptable. You don't have to rule that out of your life just to play rock'n'roll."

Mick: "I'm not like that. When I go on the road, I like to be on my own, otherwise I can't concentrate. I love my family and I love to see them. But I don't think I would like to live like Keith."

So what's all this about you being a control freak?

Mick: "You can't be in control of everything. Sometimes you want to lose control of everything. You can only control very small areas of your life. That's a mistaken idea to think that performers are in control. I think the audience like the idea that he's not in control, and there's a certain element of chance in the performance. That makes it more interesting."

Q: "But you have a choreographer, train every day, and don't drink at all. That's extreme discipline."

Mick: "It has to be very disciplined. I can't do it for a prolonged period of time at my age unless I'm very disciplined. When I was younger, tours weren't so long, and the shows were only half an hour."

WEDNESDAY, 6 JANUARY 1993

It's official: after 30 years' service, Bill Wyman leaves the Rolling Stones.

Bill: "I really don't want to do it anymore . . . When I joined this band, we thought we would last two or three years with a bit of luck and come out with a few shillings in our pockets. Now here I am, 30 years later, and I haven't done any of the other important things in life. I have a very successful restaurant, I'm working on a new book, I've just released a solo album. I do archaeology in an amateurish way. And I have a private life to deal with as well."

A little later, he adds . . .

"I left because I didn't see anything new happening in the future. I realised if we played for another 10 years I'd still be playing 'Jumpin' Jack Flash', 'Honky Tonk Women', 'Street Fighting Man' until we packed up."

Mick: "He's been telling us for a long while and I know that Keith didn't really wanna believe it. We hoped that he was gonna change his mind, but I didn't really think so in the end. He's told me so many times. We'll find someone else and, hopefully, we'll make a virtue out of a necessity."
Q: "What kind of bass player will you be looking for?"
Mick: "Beautiful legs, a great dancer! We're looking around."

So who's in line to audition?
Keith: "I don't think the Stones do it like that."
Mick: "You're gonna have to audition, Keith!"

FRIDAY, 15 JANUARY 1993

Mick's forthcoming album is previewed with a new single, 'Sweet Thing'. Immediately, comparisons are made with the Stones' 'Miss You'.
Mick: "That's because it's more dancey, but if you listen to them back to back, they don't sound anything like each other. There are certain similarities, I suppose, but I'm still the singer and that's the thing that's gonna be most apparent."

How careful is Mick to avoid comparisons between his solo material and the Stones' work?
Mick: "I consciously reject things that I think sound like the Stones would do them best. And I don't write songs on a five-string guitar – that always gets a Keith-style sound. It is slightly different because I wander off the norm and bring myself back. If some of the numbers sound like the Stones, so what? As long as they're good."

SATURDAY, 6 FEBRUARY 1993

Mick plays a butler in a spoof sketch about the British royal family for NBC-TV's Saturday Night Live.
Mick: "Part of the reason the royal family exists is to be seen doing nothing but to be seen. So if they have a baby, they have to show the baby because it's gonna be heir to the throne. It would be churlish not to show that baby . . . People in England would be very hard put to swap to a republican system. But (they've) been such a mess recently. There's not a lot you can say in their support. They've shot themselves in the foot. I'm finding it a bit tiresome now."

MONDAY, 8 FEBRUARY 1993

Wandering Spirit, *Mick's third solo album, is released.*
Mick: "We were in a pretty funky studio. The guy who owns it is a complete nut for the late Sixties/early Seventies, so all the equipment is this big old stuff. I couldn't quite work out where I was. I didn't consciously want to make an album from 1972 or whatever. I don't think in the end it sounds like that, but there are nods in that direction."

'Wandering Spirit'
Mick: "The idea is that a lot of people in our society are very deracinated, both geographically and physically. That song is about someone looking for the next thing, where he finds his spiritual ending. That sounds very complicated . . . it's just a straight gospel song!"

'Mother Of A Man' is Mick's response to the recent riots in Los Angeles, sparked by the local police's beating of a black youth, Rodney King.
Mick: "A lot of my friends went out and bought guns and joined local gun clubs. I was around for the (1965) Watts riots. But this time they were not contained in just one neighbourhood. Nowhere was safe. It didn't go into Beverly Hills, but that's what everyone was worried about."
Q: "Do you carry a gun?"
Mick: "Noooo, though there have been some situations where I've carried one."
Q: "What kind of situations?"
Mick: "Dangerous situations."

The producer is Def Jam legend Rick Rubin.
Mick: "When I first met him six or seven years ago, he was producing LL Cool J records, but he wasn't a purist. He had other artists on his label, Sir Mixalot, as well as these garage bands, so I thought he might have a different view than other, more musical producers. I thought we'd work well as a team. We had a few disagreements along the way, but they were good disagreements. We sorted them out without coming to blows."
Keith: "It's not something to gloat about, but it just doesn't sound like Mick had his hand on it. He was letting other people channel him, and the only people who can really do that are me, Charlie and Ronnie. The way Mick works, if he doesn't like the way a track's worked out, the guy's fired. One of my assets is that I can pull a bunch of guys together. I'm working for them as much as they're working for me."
Q: "What's the difference between making a solo album and working

with the Stones, apart from the fact that you can work with other musicians?"

Mick: "That's the obvious difference. With the Stones it's much more collaborative; you have to work as part of a team. As a solo artist you listen to everyone's opinion, but you don't have to act on that. If you're working as part of a committee, as with the Stones, you end up making compromises."

Q: "Is success as important to you as it was 30 years ago?"

Mick: "Yeah, but when you're young you want absolutely everything, and when you're older you get a bit more philosophical. Not everything works; not every gig is going to be wonderful."

Q: "What are your good days?"

Mick: "Show days are good days. That's very euphoric."

Q: "What's your biggest achievement? Becoming a superstar?"

Mick: "Not really. The thing that I enjoy most is writing songs. The other thing is being on stage. It's an achievement to have written a lot of songs."

Q: "What are you most looking forward to?"

Mick: "Getting this record out of my heart so I can get on with the next thing."

Which, when Mick and Keith get together in March, looks to be another Stones album.

Mick: "I want the next Rolling Stones album to be the best one we've ever made."

Keith: "He doesn't talk about it, but I would say that the solo thing has been a dash of cold water for Mick. It's made him realise that it's in front of the Stones that he falls into place with the public."

Q: "Are you idealistic?"

Mick: "I think everyone is. People still fantasise. They're brought up on a romantic diet whether it's on TV and at the movies, or in fairy stories where the prince marries the princess and falls in love forever. That's what we all aspire to. The thing is, everyone knows there's another side to it; that it doesn't always work out. People know that but they still want it to be perfect and fairytale."

Q: "Do you find it hard conducting your private life under the glare of publicity?"

Mick: "Yeah, it's a bit of a drag really, because sometimes they write things that are very upsetting. I'm very thick-skinned about it because I've been doing it since I was 19, but for some people it not only destroys their relationships but it destroys their psyche."

Mick: "British journalism is mean. They're in a cut-throat world, and if they don't write mean and cynical, they lose their jobs. They're in the rat race more than anyone. What I find objectionable are people who aren't in the public eye being set upon, victims of some sort of tragedy, not people that are famous or politicians. Suddenly, they're door-stepped and photographed and whatever else."

WEDNESDAY, 21 APRIL 1993

Bill Wyman marries designer Suzanne Accosta in the South of France.
Bill: "The sunshine today is like the sunshine in my heart."

He tells the Mail's *Nina Myskow that it is by no means a whirlwind romance.*
Bill: "I actually met Suzanne back in '79 in Paris, when we were recording there and she was a model. She was 20. We had a little fling for a few weeks, kept in touch, stayed friends, wrote, occasionally called each other. So when I cleared all that garbage out of my life, suddenly there was this lovely world out there, and I was all lightweight and bouncy. I thought, 'I want to get settled down, forget all the womanising. Who do I know that I'd be happy to be with for the rest of my life?'

"I phoned Suzanne up in the States, and said, 'How do you fancy coming over for a holiday?' The buzz was still there, the same original little spark. While she was over, I said, 'Would you like to get married?' She said, 'No! Certainly not the way you behave. I know you too well. I'm never going to marry you until you change your ways.' I don't blame her. She knew what I was like. Even when I was seeing her in Paris, I was seeing someone else. I said, 'I'm willing to give up everything to marry you'. And three days later, she said, 'If you mean it, then yes.'"

WEDNESDAY, 2 JUNE 1993

Mick and Keith are inducted into the Songwriters Hall Of Fame in New York.
Keith: "There was really only one song ever written. That was by Adam and Eve. We just do the variations . . ."

FRIDAY, 16 JULY 1993

"THE GREY AND GLITTERING STONE"

Mick celebrates Bastille Day and his 50th birthday — neither of which fall on this date — with a 250-strong party at Walpole House in Twickenham.

Prime Minister John Major: "I'm glad to see another cricket fan join me on 50, in fine form and with no sign of fading away for a good while yet."

But there's little evidence that he'll be taking up the ultimate retirement sport.
Mick: "I hate golf!"
Q: "How do you deal with this Granddad Jagger stuff?"
Mick: "Only in England!"
Q: "How does it feel being in a band, part of a bunch of boys? Does it defer your maturity?"
Mick: "Definitely. Being with a gang of guys in a band is like being in permanent adolescence. It's not quite as bad as when you were 19, but it's the gang syndrome. You tend to rely on one another, watch each other's backs. One person's responsible for this, one's the quiet one, here's the noisy one, one's drunk you have to control . . . When you stop doing that and go back to family life, you have to change your behaviour. It's definitely not a normal lifestyle."
Q: "What is there left for you to do now?"
Mick: "Nothing. It's all finished! I enjoyed doing this record. I've got one or two things I'd like to do in the movies, produce some things. I don't really project myself 10 or 15 years ahead. I only project myself a year or so ahead, so I'm quite happy with what I'm doing."

Adam Sweeting writes of Mick in The Guardian *that "Few celebrities offer such an impenetrable exterior and remain so unknowable". He then solicits the views of several friends and associates.*
Tony King (ex-personal manager): "I would think Mick feels hideous about being 50. Probably one part of him shrugs it off, but when you're 50, you know you're older."
Andrew Oldham: "Well, honey, I'm glad I didn't have to work that hard because I would hate to have those lines in my face. You become a revisionist of your own life if you're not happy with it, and I don't believe he is happy with it. You can't have anyone around you who can eventually tell you the truth."
Imran Khan (cricketer): "Mick's not a conformist, yet he's pretty conservative in a lot of ways. He's . . . a very balanced man . . . When the time came to play he played, but he had the self-denial and the strength to work."
Keith Altham (ex-PR): "They're very selfish people. You think about the amount of charity concerts other artists have done over the years, but

the Stones don't do anything . . . There's all this stuff about 'Mick does a bit behind the scenes'. It's a very little bit, is all I can say."

EARLY SEPTEMBER 1993

The four Stones regroup for sessions at Ron Wood's house in County Kildare, Ireland. They are joined by "a cacophony of bass players" including Doug Wimbish, Pino Palladino and Darryl Jones.
Keith: "I said to Charlie, 'I'm gonna leave this to you, you're the rhythm section, you decide.' We auditioned 20 bass players in five days, all the top session players, including a couple of chicks who were very good. But the minute Charlie and Darryl started playing together, that was it."

Invariably, Mick and Keith don't see eye to eye as the creative process kicks in.
Keith: "These days Mick and I find it easier to go through Charlie rather than talk things through face to face. The trouble I find with Mick is that he's got ants in his pants. He can't lie in a hammock for the afternoon. He hates introspection. To dispense with that he'll leap at the fax machine and start making phone calls. He dissipates his energy and really gets up my nose, contradicting everybody, creating confusion."

And the drummer's looking anxious, too . . .
Charlie: "I probably have as many rows with Mick and Keith as they do with each other . . . We've never been that sociable as a group. It's quite normal for us not to speak to each other for six months. Keith very rarely answers the phone, and he never rings anybody up."

Attempting to keep the peace this time round is co-producer Don Was, who later interviews Mick for Ireland's leading rock magazine, Hot Press.
Mick: "To write things from an adolescent point of view would be stupid, but I don't think it would be great to write things from an ageing point of view either. That's not really what I feel at the moment. It's a very fine line. You've got an hour on this record: time to express immaturity, maturity and everything in between – social comment and silly songs about girls that really say they're about cars! Most of the writers I learned from were blues writers – John Lee Hooker, Muddy Waters, Sonny Boy Williamson, Howlin' Wolf, Willie Dixon – and they were all in their forties when those songs were written. Those guys were not particularly young or particularly old . . . They just wrote as they felt."
Keith: "Producers are like gurus – you don't find them, they find you. I read Don my usual riot act, you know: 'Are you sure you wanna be the

meat in the sandwich?' Because most of the guys we've used are scared to step in between Mick and me. It doesn't happen so often now, but when it does, it flares. I'd be like, 'What are you doing singing a song called 'Attitude' with your feet up on the sofa, man?' And Don would instantly step in and break it up."

SATURDAY, 18 DECEMBER 1993

Keith hits 50.
Keith: "I was surprised to see 30, even more surprised to see 40. But you go through that and you're still there, so you think, 'Better carry on.' I don't feel any different about age. I've enjoyed growing up; it gets interesting. After 50, it should get really good. I'm looking forward to it."

EARLY 1994

After almost 20 years in the band, Ronnie Wood is finally granted fully fledged Stone-status on financial terms.
Keith: "When we're on stage Ronnie Wood is one of the Rolling Stones. But if you wrote it all down on typewritten paper and took it to court, then they would say he's an employee. I've fought against that over the years. I think Ronnie's levity overshadows his musical abilities. And I know Charlie Watts hates the idea of Ronnie being employed by the rest of us."

MONDAY, 21 FEBRUARY 1994

Keith guests with George Jones on 'Say It's Not You'.
Keith: "I did the Jones duet for Gram (Parsons). That's a song he taught me and which we used to play endlessly, even when we were supposedly being cured. We'd be in cold turkey and playing would be our therapy. After a few days we'd say, 'Okay, we're clean, that's it,' and off we'd go, stay clean for a week or two. Those were the days . . . silly days."

SUNDAY, 3 APRIL 1994

"ROLLING STONE MURDER SENSATION"

Two books, Who Killed Christopher Robin?: The Truth Behind The Murder Of Brian Jones *by Terry Rawlings and* Paint It Black: The Murder Of Brian Jones *by Geoffrey Giuliano, claim to have solved the mystery of Brian*

Jones' death. Inspired by the new research, the police reopen the case, but it is closed soon after when nurse Janet Lawson could not be found. Rawlings prints a deathbed confession from Frank Thorogood, the builder who was with Brian at the time of his death. The confession was told to Tom Keylock, the band's ex-gofer.

Frank Thorogood: "There's something I have to tell you. Promise me you won't say a word while I'm still alive. It was me that did Brian. I just snapped. It just happened. That's all there is to it." *Thorogood dies the next day, aged 69. Giuliano's evidence comes from 'builder Joe', who 'admits' to holding Brian's head under water with some pals. The latter, though, is discredited when the Rolling Stones fanzine,* Shattered!, *claims the 'revelations' were based on a spoof interview 'done for a laugh'.*

TUESDAY, 5 APRIL 1994

Nirvana frontman Kurt Cobain, the first genuine new rock idol of the Nineties, kills himself with a gunshot to his head.
Q: "What did you think of Kurt Cobain's suicide?"
Ron: "He was on a death wish."

Mick elaborates in a rare interview for New Musical Express.
Mick: "It was inevitable, I mean, Jesus Christ, he tried it several times. I blame his immediate friends and, er, managers. I think he had none – maybe he was so obnoxious he had no friends. I don't know. I never knew the guy. I was in that position but I was never expected to commit suicide . . . just expected to OD. There's a very slim line there – it's almost the same thing. He showed some promise but you only had to listen to his songs and a couple of interviews to see this guy is certainly not suited to be in a game like this one. He was out of his depth."

TUESDAY, 3 MAY 1994

"IT'S WY-MAN OVERBOARD . . . AS DINOSAUR STONES HIT THE ROAD AGAIN"

The Stones hold a press conference for the forthcoming Voodoo Lounge tour on the Honey Fitz, a boat that once belonged to ex-American President John F. Kennedy. It's also announced that Darryl Jones and keyboard player Chuck Leavell will join the band on the tour.
Q: "Why is there so much excitement about the Stones after all these years?"

Keith: "Just look at us, darling."

Q: "Are you and Mick still fighting?"

Mick and Keith: "All the time!"

Q: "What would you say to people who believe you are only doing it for the money?"

Mick: "What about all the beer you can drink and all the girls down in front?"

Keith: "First things first, boys."

Q: "Will you play Woodstock II?"

Mick: "We weren't invited to the first one, and we're not going to the second."

Q: "To what do you attribute your longevity?"

Keith: "That's rather a personal question."

Q: "Have you ever slept with David Bowie?"

Mick: "Of course . . ."

Q: "Is this going to be the last tour?"

Mick: "I hate that thing where you say it's the last tour and beg for sympathy. 'If you don't come, you're never gonna see them again.' I'm not gonna say it's the last tour. I think it's a mistake to say that."

And, finally, one question is directed to the ever-reticent Charlie Watts.

Q: "Will the personnel change affect you in any way?"

Charlie: "No."

The crowd erupts into spontaneous applause.

MONDAY, 4 JULY 1994

'Love Is Strong' becomes the first new Stones single in three years.

Keith: "I started that one. To me, it's intimately related to 'Wicked As It Seems' (off Keith's *Main Offender*). All of our songs are like, this one's the cousin of that one. They are all offshoots of themes and motifs."

Mick: "We ran through it a bunch of times and I was playing harmonica, and I started singing through the harmonica mike, so you get this strange sound. Then I started singing down an octave, so you get this breathy, sexy tone. When we were in rehearsal, I'd come in early in the afternoon and put on a bunch of CDs and play harmonica along with them for my homework, 'cos like any instrument you can't just pick it up and play it. It was good to put harmonica on a track like this. You always think of playing it on a 12-bar blues, and it's fun to put it on one which isn't."

MONDAY, 11 JULY 1994

The Stones release a new album, Voodoo Lounge.

Mick: "We said at the start of this record that we were going to try and make it a bit simpler and less overdubbed."

Keith: "This album is full of things that we used to do well and have deliberately not done, because the Stones are always wary of repeating themselves obviously. We're the guys that don't play 'Satisfaction' on stage very often, you know?"

Mick: "Don (Was) is a very easy person to get along with. He's quiet, he's efficient, he's got no axes to grind. And he's one of those people who has very wide interests outside of rock music, so you don't just have to talk shop, which is good for friendship."

Keith: "The focus is definitely back. This time it doesn't just sound like the Stones, it *feels* like the Stones. I think our records in the Eighties all reflected a frustration at being locked into the juggernaut routine. The interesting thing, now that we've re-found ourselves as a band, is to see how much further it can be taken, especially since nobody has ever taken a rock'n'roll band this far before. To me it's a case of how can it grow up without seeming like a parody. I like the challenge."

'Sparks Will Fly'

Keith: "We had a big bonfire going one night out in Ronnie's garden. I was throwing all these logs on it, and these sparks started flying. I started running back to the studio – 'I've got one! Incoming!' Charlie was the only guy there, and he and I played the thing. Nobody else was allowed to play it for months until we'd got it right. It all has to do with the rhythm and the guitar, and after that the rest of it fell into place. Charlie's laying down the law on that one. You've got to know a guy well to play that tight together. It's unspoken, because it's all going by in front of you in three seconds."

Charlie: "Keith Richards is the easiest person in the world to play with, and so we just played like we normally play. I start off and he comes in, or he'll start off and I come in. And we'd do three goes at it, look at each other, and he'd say, 'Let's try it tomorrow.' He's writing the thing, and he knows if it's right or wrong."

Mick: "Keith and Charlie had never heard the vocals on that, and when they finally did, they were sitting around going, 'Did he say that? I can't believe he said that.'"

(A reference to the line "I'm gonna fuck your sweet ass")

'The Worst'

Keith: "It's funny but a lot of these songs were written in kitchens. I wrote this in the kitchen in Barbados, and I thought, 'That's a pretty melody,' but I didn't know what to do with it. I guess that's where Ireland comes in, because it has its own traditional music and it's not country music as such, but it's the roots of it, you know? It's that Irish feel."

Mick: "That's very country, isn't it? Keith sings very pretty on that. I do his backgrounds and it sounds so Okie. When I listened back to it, I said, 'Is that really me singing?' It's really strange."

'New Faces'

Mick: "There's some tracks you can't help but notice that they sound like old ones. 'New Faces' sounds very 'Lady Jane'-ish. Maybe it's the harpsichord."

'Moon Is Up'

Mick: "Everything on that track is put through some sort of device. I'm playing harmonica through a harmoniser and whatever other pedals I had, and Keith is playing acoustic guitar through an amp which is put through something else. So everyone has an effect. And the voice has got an effect. And it's all put in one great sweltering echo to make it all sound like it's all in one room."

Keith: "That song had been around since Ireland, and everybody was fascinated with it. The song was suddenly there, you know, and what are we gonna do with it? To me, it was all tied in with Charlie. If Charlie Watts is willing to experiment in the studio, then I'm the happiest man in the world. It so happened that as we were trying this track out in different configurations, I put an acoustic guitar through a Leslie cabinet, Ronnie was playing pedal steel through some tiny little amplifier and Mick was singing through the harp mike. The drums were the only thing that sounded real because they were real. So we fished around a bit and I said, 'What about playing on a suitcase outside?' Before I knew it, Charlie Watts is out there in the stairwell, with a garbage can and brushes, and that's the sound. After that, it was very hard to keep him out of the stairwell."

Charlie: "We've often done things like that, in loos or corridors. It's easier to do that than to do it with echo chambers, you know. It's sometimes not so good for an engineer, 'cos you've got this sound and you can't get rid of it. Whereas if you record it dry you can always add things. But this was good."

'I Go Wild'
Mick: " 'Waitresses with broken noses' – that's Ronnie's speciality. He knows every waitress in Dublin so I put that line in for him."

'Sweethearts Together'
Keith: "Mick and I were singing straight into the mike together, which we haven't done for a long time – mainly for technical reasons, we would do harmony separately. Don Was said, 'Go and do it together.' "
Ron: "The great thing is that Mick and Keith are getting along so much better now. Whenever they felt a little feud coming up, they would say, 'I guess we better do 'Sweethearts Together' to cool things down.' "

'Suck On The Jugular'
Keith: "Mr Watts again. I mean, it's all drums. The arrangement is all to do with the drums. Charlie laid down that beat and I said, 'Well, if you can keep that up for several minutes, we've got a track.' 'Hey, no problem.' And he always makes it look like it isn't."
Charlie: "It used to be called 'Holetown Prison' and we did that in Barbados near Holetown. That's what we would loosely term a groove song; I like those a lot. We did a whole bunch of those type of songs, but a lot of them didn't get on the record because it wasn't the right time to use them. I like those songs more than our ballads."

'Blinded By Rainbows'
Mick: I was writing this at the end of the *Wandering Spirit* album and I thought, 'This would be better suited to the next Rolling Stones album.' It's pretty strong. It's good to have one like that on the record. It shakes you up a bit. Otherwise all the songs are about girls and cars and immaturity."

'Thru And Thru'
Keith: "It's a bit of a departure. I don't know where it came from. I was in Barbados one night with Pierre de Beauport, my guitar man. We got back around four or five in the morning and I said, 'Let's go into the studio. Incoming, incoming, Pierre.' Something just clocked in the car on the way home, and if I let it go, it's gone. It all came out at once. You love 'em when they come out like that. I didn't think it would turn up on this record. It would've probably been a back burner job if it hadn't been for Charlie once again, saying, 'Lemme take the drums down in the stairwell.' I had nowhere for this song to go, but Charlie provided me with the whole means of getting through it and out the other end."

Despite its merits, Voodoo Lounge *wasn't quite the success it should have been.*
Mick: "I think it sold pretty well . . . we sold five million records. I don't think that's disappointing after 34 years."

In all probability, Mick is more concerned with the Stones' latest venture into new technology, namely the accompanying 'Voodoo Lounge CD-ROM', which, for example, gives fans the opportunity to 'hang out' with the band in a New Orleans bordello or watch the Stones carouse with half-naked women.
Mick: "Keith and Ronnie never even watched the presentation of what a CD-ROM was and what to expect of it. They thought it was such rubbish and walked out. I'm not saying this to put Keith and Ronnie down . . . they didn't get it at all. But slowly they came to get more involved, seeing how fascinating it really was, looking at the screen and talking about putting these blues singers in that room."
Keith: "I'm not a hi-tech fan. I can turn on an amplifier and I can use the knobs on my guitar but a computer man I'm not. My problem at the beginning was, 'Is this a toy or a tool?' As it developed I got more and more interested. This one happens to be about the Rolling Stones and the blues. This could be your *Encyclopaedia Brittanica* of the future. You can push that button and see what's in the door, so it's like a game and exploring, but you're learning at the same time."
Mick: "We were faced with two things. It was gonna be a historical piece about the Rolling Stones where we could have a lot of footage and you could see it chronologically. Or we could do it on a more fantasy level. I opted for the fantasy version. I thought it should be a more inventive piece than a 'looking back' documentary because a documentary doesn't give the medium a chance to shine as much.

"The original drawings went back and forth between Patrick Woodroffe, Mark Fisher and me at the beginning. And then slowly the rest of the band got involved. And of course it was so delegated that I got tired of it in the end because there were so many versions coming at me. But I'm very pleased with the result."

Prior to the tour, Keith reveals that he's kicking the booze.
Keith: "It isn't because of the tour. I gave up the hard stuff some time ago. I often do. People always think of me as a boozer and that's the image, but I got fed up with that old elbow-bending routine. I never used to get drunk anyway, and having given up heroin it was no big deal to stop drinking."

But he's not softened his rap attack, as he tells the NME.
Keith: "I can't imagine anybody buying their 20 favourite rap records in a

391

few years time, y'know. But at the same time rap's a loud expression that's come over the streets. I mean, it's like, 'What are you saying, man? Good God! You're falling apart at the seams!' But it's an honest expression of rage and frustration. It's down there and it's down there serious. I know the brothers and they have a legitimate complaint. I just wish they wouldn't drill it in my head, 'Bom, bom, bom, ya, ya, ya', y'know. I'm into music, I'm not into trying to preach to people. I think music says more by its musicality than whatever you say."

MONDAY, 1 AUGUST 1994

The Voodoo Lounge tour, nicknamed 'The Storm', gets underway at the RKF Memorial Stadium in Washington, DC, before winding its way through the United States and Canada to, during 1995, Australasia, South America, Asia and Europe.

Two key on-stage additions are . . .
Darryl Jones: "There are a thousand bass players who can play way faster than me and who know a lot more tricks than I do. I deal with the fundamentals, and I play rock-solid bass. That's what I love to do. I mean, I can dig a solo, if the musical genre is appropriate for it. But that is not my first love. My first love is laying down the bass line, and it's the same thing I did with Herbie Hancock and Miles Davis, and the same thing I'm doing here."

And a backing singer whose earlier work on Mick's solo records have given her an insight into working with him.
Lisa Fischer: "You're on the edge every minute. Because you're not quite sure what he's going to do, you have to keep on your toes. But within that 'edginess' there's a sense of calm, because you know the boundaries, and there's a comfort in that knowledge. And Mick is very exciting to watch. During rehearsals he's great, but on stage, he's a raging fire! The Stones work hard when they work, and they play hard when they play. There's no middle ground."

Once again, though, the staging threatens to upstage the band. With two criteria in his mind – "That Barbra Streisand shouldn't be able to sing on it, and that Prince Charles shouldn't like it" – designer Mark Fisher comes up with a concept that blends 21st century "cyberworld" technology with ancient superstition.
Mark Fisher: "The Stones are fearless and powerful people who will make a statement and stand by it. This intense, explosive attitude can

392

translate into a tremendous visual statement . . . They have this feeling that, as a kind of show band, they ought to get in front of something unique . . . Steel Wheels was a bit more referential, you could look at it and say, 'This reminds me of a steel mill or an oil refinery.' I don't think many people are going to stand in front of this and announce what it reminds them of. They've never seen anything like it."

Keith: "We'll use the lighting and scenery to make it not just one huge structure all of the time. We can change it – make it a little smaller at times, gigantic at others. What we're looking for is a bit of dynamics instead of a great big grand slam show."

Mick: "This time it's more clean and open than before, and is a metaphor for turn-of-the-century technology. The trick is not to let the stage over-whelm the music."

Patrick Woodroffe (lighting designer): "To Mick, this is a giant play-ground. He wants as many places to go, as many different things to see and play with and lean against and pick up and run across."

Keith: "These days, you can't just hang up a curtain and put your amps down."

The shows are well received. And so is the drummer . . .
(Audience): "Char-lie! Char-lie!"

Mick feels he knows 'em all.
Mick: "It's not as anonymous as people would think. There's quite a lot of people that just follow us around so we get to know who they are by their flags and banners and the way they look. You can even hear them shout."

MONDAY, 26 SEPTEMBER 1994

'You Got Me Rocking' becomes the second single extracted from Voodoo Lounge.
Mick: "It's about someone who was becoming a disastrous failure until he woke up. You know, the butcher that cuts himself, the surgeon who shakes, the pitcher that's in a slump, the tycoon who loses all his money."

MONDAY, 28 NOVEMBER 1994

'Out Of Tears' makes it a hat-trick of strong singles from Voodoo Lounge.
Mick: "There's no set way to write songs. I used to say, 'Now we're writing songs, I'm gonna sit at my desk,' and 'Out Of Tears' was a little bit like that. I was sitting at the piano in Ronnie's studio going 'Da da ding, da

da ding.' Then you go and listen to it, and it's got this really good mood because it's you on your own. No one else was there and you're creating the mood. There's a very sad mood to that song. The Stones are mainly a guitar band, but I think with a ballad sometimes it's nice to move away from that. When a song is written on a keyboard you get a different melodic structure."

Keith: "Both Mick and I like to do that. You can have an idea for a song, and you play it on guitar and it just doesn't work. And then you try it on piano and suddenly it starts to make sense to you."

TUESDAY, 29 NOVEMBER 1994

"VOLKSWAGEN PRESENTS ROLLING STONES VOODOO LOUNGE TOUR 1995"

It is announced that the second half of the tour will be sponsored by Volkswagen.
Jennifer Hurshell (Volkswagen spokeswoman): "Pop *Voodoo Lounge* in the tape deck and hit the road – cars and rock'n'roll were made for each other. Working with the Stones allows us to reach an international audience with an irresistible message."

Mick: "We can't wait to bring this show to Europe. It's down and dirty and spectacular."

Keith: "On any given night we're still a damn good band. I got news for you – we're still a bunch of tough bastards. String us up and we still won't die."

MONDAY, 6 MARCH 1995

The Far East leg of the tour begins in Tokyo. But the Stones' plans to perform in China are thwarted.
Keith: "The letter we got from the Chinese authorities was hilarious. It went through 30 objections, starting with 'Will cause cultural pollution.' I thought, 'Yeah, that's the general idea.'"

THURSDAY, 25 MAY 1995

"JAGGER'S ANTIQUE!"

The first ever recordings by the embryonic Rolling Stones sells at Christie's for over £50,000. The mystery phone bidder for the reel-to-reel tape of Mick and Keith's teenage bedroom band, Little Boy Blue and The Blue Boys, is Mick Jagger.

Unnamed friend: "There was no way Mick was going to let anyone else get their hands on them. He was very wise to keep his bid anonymous. The asking price would have gone through the roof had it been known he wanted them."

SUNDAY, 16 JULY 1995

Journalist/author, Salman Rushdie, who skived off school to see the Stones in September 1963 on their first UK tour, catches up with them at Wembley Stadium.
"The point is that the Stones were amazing. Their force, their drive, the sheer quality and freshness of Jagger's singing and the band's playing . . . this music has sunk so deep into our blood that we may even be able, by now, to pass the knowledge on genetically to our children, who will be born humming, 'How come you dance so good' and those old satanic verses, 'Pleased to meet you, hope you guess my name' . . . The Rolling Stones may not be so dangerous now, they may no longer be a threat to a decent, civilised society, but they still know how to let it bleed. Yea yea yea WOO."

The piece enlivens the letters page in the following week's edition of The Observer.
"It is also good to know that someone as intelligent and erudite as he can write with unbridled enthusiasm about such a relatively 'low' form of artistic expression. However, didn't he get carried away just a bit?

"What the Stones did in the Sixties was to take the songs of black American blues singers, give them a sharper, more regular beat and deliver them with a sexy stage show for white audiences. And they've never really made any advance on that. So when Rushdie says he is satisfied that they 'haven't fallen into the Bob Dylan trap of murdering their old songs', what he is overlooking is that their lack of creativity doesn't allow them to do their songs in any other way than they always have.

Howard Moss, Swansea."

Another notary attends one of the Wembley Stadium shows.
Bill Wyman: "It was my first Stones gig. I'd never been to a Stones show before. I enjoyed the concert but I didn't miss for one minute being on the stage. I'm not into that egomaniac, fame, up-front thing. I was always in the shadows at the back, out the way and just doing me duty. Same as Charlie. It's been so nice since I left that I often wonder why I didn't leave earlier."

WEDNESDAY, 19 JULY 1995

The Stones play to 3,000 ecstatic fans at London's Brixton Academy.
Keith: "Brixton? Well, you looked down and thought, 'It's just like playin Richmond Station Hotel in 62 and 63.

Mick: "Welcome to the Brixton Academy. We loved to play Wembley, it was really great and I don't know if any of you went there. But this is a bit of a laugh, we'll have a bit of fun."

Keith: "Brixton Academy was brilliant. I loved playing London: they were sweet to us, bless their hearts. It's taken them a long time to fall back in love with us but they did it this year – bless 'em."

Keith: "Gimme my little Fender amp and forget all the distractions of hi-tech stage stuff and computers. It's always a challenge to be eyeball-to-eyeball with the audience and just see how you feel about it now, see if you can do it. Playing those places is how we test ourselves. You know, if we can't rock a club, baby, then I'll toss it in and take up golf."

WEDNESDAY, 30 AUGUST 1995

The Voodoo Lounge tour winds up in Rotterdam.
Keith: "What am I gonna do tomorrow?"

Keith: "I was so impressed with everybody. Darryl Jones – a new engine down there, that's helped enormously. That's not to knock Bill. It's that you've gotta give it more than the proverbial 100 per cent. Today, I take my hat off to Bill for bowing out at the right time."

Well, there's always the option of discussing the Keith Richards 'legend' with Neil Spencer in The Observer.
Keith: "Now that is a part of me, the part that people are going to remember, but no one is that one-faceted. I'm a lot of different guys. In fact, the mythical Keith Richards is the one that no one wants to meet, including myself. I can pull him out if I have to, if something gets me going, but most of the time I'm the same as anyone else. I'm just one of the lads."

Or, of course, relations with the singer.
Keith: "The armistice is signed and the deal is sticking. Mick is a lot more open and easier to work with now. We're like any family, we have our crises."

And the state of the band?
Keith: "The way I judge the band is that if Charlie Watts is smiling and

Mick's confident enough to change four or five songs each night, I don't have much of a problem."

MONDAY, 30 OCTOBER 1995

A version of Bob Dylan's 'Like A Rolling Stone', recorded at Brixton (19/7), is released as a new Rolling Stones single.
Keith: "It's taken us nearly 30 years to have the balls to play it. Been playing that song ever since I first heard it. What a construction, what a lovely song. If only it didn't say, 'How does it feel (to be) a Rolling Stone', I'd have cut it 30 years ago! But even ten, five years ago, it would have seemed gratuitous. Now, I think, is the time for it. Now it doesn't feel obvious. It feels right. Mick can sing the hell out of it, he puts a new feel on it with the harp. Because, I tell you what, that Mick Jagger can blow harp, man. Shame about the rest . . . Sorry, Mick!"
Mick: "Remembering the lyrics was a challenge. I cut one verse."

MONDAY, 13 NOVEMBER 1995

Stripped, a semi-Unplugged hits collection, recorded in rehearsal and at various club shows, is released.
Mick: "This album is not really an album of the tour. It's the antithesis of that because the Voodoo Lounge thing was very big stages and so on. By the time we got to Europe we got the idea that this record should be much more intimate and personal."
Keith: "It's not a live album. It's an album cut on the road. There are some live tracks and the tracks that are not cut on the stage are cut in a room. One or two takes, no overdubs. It's the band playing without an audience, relaxing and enjoying some songs that maybe they wouldn't have played again otherwise. We found a few new roots, it's just growing up, you know, we got a very slow metabolism."
Mick: "We were wracking our brains over how to do a different record on the road. I always liked the Jackson Browne one that combined live things with new songs from hotel rooms. So maybe, we thought, we could work up eight-track versions of songs from *Voodoo Lounge* when we're in the hotel room. In the end, that didn't happen. Then we started to do this acoustic set when we were in America . . . The original idea was to record the acoustic songs in a large place, but I had my reservations about that. So I thought if we start off the European tour with a club gig and we do a couple more. And I always thought we should tape the

rehearsals because you sometimes get a good feel there. So we did those things and came up with about 50 songs . . ."

Keith: "I was expecting a disaster but I thought it was worth a try. And I was amazed; it came out just like a record, as if we were playing live but there was no audience. One, two takes, no overdubs, no fancy work. I don't think I remember people recording like this since Louis Armstrong and The Hot Five."

Keith: "I believe it's definitely the best sounding live Stones record there is. People always throw *Ya-Ya's* at you, which was damned good in spirit, but soundwise it was early days. I think with a bit of luck people might agree this is *Ya-Ya's* but better recorded."

Mick: " 'Shine A Light' was one of the ones I found in this internet list. The funny thing was that I don't think anyone else played on the original record apart from me."

Keith: "I never thought I'd play 'The Spider And The Fly' again. It was not on the top of my list, but when we played it . . . 'Hey, yes!' "

MONDAY, 4 DECEMBER 1995

The Beatles release a 'new' single, 'Free As A Bird', the flagship for their extensive Anthology *multi CD/video project.*
Mick: "One day, everything will be put onto one tiny CD."
Keith: "John (Lennon) speaks to me still every other day. I speak to John. I miss him a lot, I still do. I was speaking to Farmer George (Harrison) about it the other day because he was at Brixton Academy. He was bemoaning the fact that he was not in a band. I love George. I dunno what it's like singing with a dead man. I've never done it. Don't call my coffin . . ."

TUESDAY, 26 DECEMBER 1995

Nicky Campbell gives Keith a Boxing Day grilling on BBC Radio.
Q: "Where do your songs come from?"
Keith: "You think if I knew that I would tell anybody? The fact is I don't know. All I know is that they fly in right through the room, they go through concrete, they go through the air. I think everybody now knows that my attitude to songs is that I'm an antenna. I wait, I sit down and play an instrument. The only bit I do is knock it into shape."
Q: "And so anybody who thinks they write a song is . . ."
Keith: "They think they're God. And that's a very bad mistake!"

Guitars . . .

Keith: "Maybe one day a week, I don't touch it, but at some time during the day you've gotta stroke the baby . . . You hear something up here and you run to it and say, 'I wonder if that'll actually work.' That's the lovely thing about music, and especially the guitar. You know, you look at it, and it's a . . . tennis racquet, but the more you find out about it, the more you don't know. Which is great because it means you've still got more to find out. How can you be bored with a guitar? Everybody should be born with a guitar – there'd be far less suicides."

Q: "Well, quite a few suicides have come from people playing the guitar . . ."

Keith: "Yeah, they were right."

Q: "In what way?"

Keith: "They obviously couldn't play properly!"

Q: "What about your health kick?"

Keith: "Yeah, can't you tell? Ha! Ha! Ha! It's the idea that life is a regime, of trying to be this way or that, is ludicrous. Everyone is different and I think everybody should take their lives and bodies in their own hands and get to know it. Mine likes to be abused, preferably by myself. I can run around that stage for over two-and-a-half hours with a Fender strapped to my neck. I can do the splits, stand on my bloody head, run three miles if I have to, swim underwater. I'm in good shape. Would I feel any different if I ate nuts and peas?"

Q: "You might be more regular."

Keith: "I am very, very regular, I'll have you know. There are two things in this game – one's called bowel movement and the other's called vowel movement."

He also has some advice for the Britpop generation.

Keith: "Yeah, take up another job! Nah, I haven't heard a lot. It's that 'pop' thing I'm worried about."

Campbell plays Blur's 'Country House' . . .

Keith: "They're pretty, too, right? That helps. It's the most original thing I've heard in my life! Hey, I don't wanna knock guys. They're okay. They can get a pub gig."

The DJ then plays Oasis' 'Roll With It'.

Keith: "Boys having a bash. Like the English Byrds. There's rockin' and there's rollin' . . . It's not called rock'n'roll for nothing. You've got to hit the thing hard sometimes but the rock is only good if you've got the roll.

It is not a matter of pounding something to death. You're not working in a quarry. It is the contrast, otherwise you might just as well play a pneumatic drill."

Q: "How much money have you got?"

Keith: "I've got enough to buy off questions I don't wanna answer."

EARLY 1996

Jerry Hall consults divorce lawyer Anthony Julius.

Ron: "Jerry is not going to take any more. This time it really looks like it. She has known what's been going on for a long time, she's not stupid. She's known all about Mick's flings but she has been prepared to brush some of them, not all, under the carpet."

As life off the road starts to bite, Keith warns Jane Stevenson in the Toronto Sun *of trickier times ahead . . .*

Keith: "I never heard Mick Jagger sing better, play better and operate better than he has done in the last couple of years. He impressed me immensely, but it doesn't get him out of jail. There's a little remission coming up."

SATURDAY, 27 APRIL 1996

Keith retires to his house in Jamaica where VH-1's Anthony DeCurtis catches up with him in characteristically relaxed mood.

Keith: "Coming off the tours, your metabolism gets used to it. Voodoo was the longest tour I'd done. I have a couple of places that are laid back to try and get the metabolism to slowly calm down. Later on, in the evening, around dinnertime I get ants. Something inside goes, 'Where's the show?' The body clock does that. I'm prone to habits!

"I have a great life, man. I found what I wanted to do very early, and I got very successsful at it very early and the people around the world like what I do. What's so hard? What's so difficult? Everyone has struggles in their life. I had a baby die. Been busted, threatened with jail and death and all kind of things. But . . . who hasn't, in one form or another? That's life. It was other people's projections that I was at death's door. I make sure; that's why I'm still here. Really, number one on the list? Look out, cock, I'll be around!"

Mick . . .

Keith: "How do friends go through life working with each other? You go up, you go down, sometimes you disagree. Mick always thinks I disagree too violently, and I always think he's too smooth. But what do brothers do? Brothers always fight off and on. It's just that we have to do it in public. In some ways, it keeps changing and evolving, in other ways, it's the same as when we're in the playground when we were four or five years old."

Bettering themselves . . .
Keith: "Some people are like, '*Beggars Banquet* to *Exile* via *Sticky Fingers* and *Let It Bleed*. They'll never get there again.' No, of course we'll never be there again. It doesn't mean we'll not be somewhere else."
Q: "What legacy would you like for the Stones?"
Keith: "About 50 billion dollars! We made a lot of good music. We went through a lot of stuff to do it. We got remunerated very well for doing it. If you had a good time listening to a Stones record that'll do for me . . . especially if you got laid to it!"

MONDAY, 10 JUNE 1996

Charlie, newly installed at Number 347 in The Sunday Times *Britain's richest list, returns with* Long Ago And Far Away, *the latest album by the Charlie Watts Quintet.*

Being a Broadway-inspired set, what would the younger Charlie have made of it?
Charlie: "I might have sneered at the principle of the thing. But not after I'd heard them. It's kind of schmaltzy, a bit Hollywood, but it's very well done schmaltz and it sets 'Bird' up wonderfully."
Charlie: "It's very daunting because you know that anything these players were asked to do musically they could do, and a lot of things I might be asked to do, I know I couldn't. Technically, I'm very limited. People tell me I'm part of rock'n'roll. But the tight jeans and the big stages, that's not my world at all. My world is the Blue Note club in Paris, or Birdland in New York. That's where I would go to see someone play."

The title track is sung by Stones backing singer Bernard Fowler, whom Charlie packed off with a pile of Sinatra records, prior to the session.
Charlie: "He's such a wonderful talent . . . He has such a poignant quality to his voice. Every time I hear 'Long Ago And Far Away', I cry. My mother died during the making of the record, and it's a song that she used to sing."

The dapper drummer turns up to the interview wearing Tommy Nutter and Hermes . . .
Charlie: "My suits are one of my biggest pleasures. If I have a big argument with my wife, she sometimes threatens to cut all the sleeves off. That's the ultimate threat."

MONDAY, 14 OCTOBER 1996

The Rolling Stones Rock'n'Roll Circus *is released on video and CD.*
Keith: "I quite liked seeing it again, more than I did when we did it. We had a very dim view of our performance which is why it went on the shelf. Brian was a basket-case by then. He didn't have much longer to go, and that was probably another reason why we scrapped it at the time."

NOVEMBER 1996

Bill Wyman opens a second branch of Sticky Fingers, this time in Manchester. According to The Guardian *food critic Matthew Fort, it is "steakburgerribs'n' chicken'n'fries'n'salad, fingerlickin', kidsjustluvit country". However, a fellow food critic Sophie Grigson describes the hamburgers at the Kensington branch as "the best in London".*
Bill: "Food's just refuelling to me. I don't think about it . . . I can't deal with those chicken vol-au-vent things. I like plain roast chicken."

And for the taste of nostalgia . . .
"My gran used to do rabbit. Rabbit was like chicken is these days. Chicken was for big meals, like Christmas."

THURSDAY, 14 NOVEMBER 1996

It is reported that Mick and Keith were involved in a mid-air crisis after the Concorde in which they were flying suffered engine trouble over the Atlantic.
Jon Ronson (Passenger): "It was terrifying. We were over the Atlantic when the engines seemed to stop. I thought we were going down and that my number was up. But Keith didn't seem at all bothered. He just lit up another ciggie and knocked back a Jack Daniel's. Mick was just the same. He didn't seem at all concerned."

JANUARY 1997

The Stones begin sessions for a new album. Rumours circulate that Mick and Keith are refusing to record together during its making.

Mick: "We always spar."

Keith: "People love it. Everybody else watches. 'There he goes again.' You watch me in action, yelling and screaming. I couldn't dream of making a record with people and not going, 'You're totally wrong, man! That tempo is crap!' Because that means people care. You need the passion. People that go, 'Okay, one, two, three, four' might as well be doing jingles."

Keith: "*Steel Wheels* was a miracle that we got back together. *Voodoo Lounge* was consolidation and this one, we're pushing out a bit again."

Mick: "Miles Davis used to do it by changing his band totally. But with a band it's much more difficult. I thought if we at least had some different producers we would stand a chance of not sounding exactly the same on every track."

Ron: "There was quite a collection of different heads involved and that accounts for the variety of sounds. Mick had particular treatments for songs like 'Gunface' and 'Juiced', while Keith had his own vision for 'How Can I Stop' and 'Lowdown'. So we got the Dust Brothers, Danny Saber and Babyface to bring their personality into the process."

Don Was is also on hand to mediate again – and to observe and contrast Mick and Keith's writing styles.

Don Was: "Each guy has his own unique writing style. Mick can sit down with a pad of paper and a guitar and deliver a song, but Keith needs to play with other musicians. He hammers out a song by playing it over repeated sittings, with at least Charlie sitting behind the drums. Then he improvises stream-of-consciousness lyrics over a period of time and culls from the best of those."

Charlie impresses Was even more.

Don Was: "Either I've learned how to listen to music better or something dramatic has happened to this guy! You don't have to spend much time in the studio to realise that Keith's personality is huge. And if you see Mick Jagger onstage, you understand how far this guy projects. What I've discovered on this album is that Charlie Watts has a personality that looms as large as those guys – he's just more soft-spoken about it."

Keith: "The Stones make better records under pressure. There is a certain immediacy about this one that I like, a certain feeling of moving on. I've never lost weight making a record before! This one cost me 10 lbs that I could ill afford. But we're getting it back on!"

Keith: "We were in three different rooms in the studio at once. You'd pass Charlie in the corridor and say, 'I can't stop now, I have to do an overdub in Studio 7,' and Charlie then going, 'Well, I'm off to put some percussion on in Studio 1.' It was nuts – high pressure, but fun to make."

Ron: "I eventually set up my own room in Studio 4 with Charlie and Jim Keltner and we did an alternative album at the same time!"

Charlie: "It was very peculiar 'cos what we usually do is that when every-body's in the room, we all play. That's how Keith's songs are done. With this, the guy mashes it up."

Mick: "Charlie loves doing it. He's able to do both things now – be traditional, play with the band, and do loops and experiments. When you actually listen to it, it's not like (Miles Davis') *Bitches Brew*, we're not going off into the stratosphere. It's just different grooves, but I also think the songwriting is better, which is what makes it in the end."

Keith: "To me, it all counts on Charlie Watts. He's such fun to play with and he's so *on* right now. You look at the guy and it's as if he's having a cup of tea. Effortless . . . elitist and arrogant. I admire that!"

WEDNESDAY, 4 JUNE 1997

Ex-Faces bassist Ronnie Lane loses his long battle with multiple sclerosis.

Ron: "I shall miss the old sod. Ronnie was a very solid player who laid down a great foundation. I was watching a video of a gig of (The Faces) at the Roundhouse. He had such a big sound. We used to call him 'Plonk' – but he was very reliable."

SUNDAY, 6 JULY 1997

Tribute band The Rolling Clones say they have received a fax from the Stones' management threatening legal action unless they stop using the band's 'lapping tongue' trademark and change their name.

Mick Haggard (singer): "When we got the fax we just couldn't believe it – we thought it was a joke. I hope the Stones don't know anything about this situation. We reckon Mick and Keith themselves just wouldn't have anything to do with it."

A Stones spokesman: "The Rolling Stones have lost a lot of money over the years through people using things like the tongue-and-lips logo.

They don't mind tribute bands, but when people start cashing in on their trademarks, the solicitors step in."

MONDAY, 18 AUGUST 1997

The world's press gathers under Brooklyn Bridge as the Stones announce details of their forthcoming Bridges To Babylon *tour. Mick drives the band over the bridge in an open-top red 1955 Cadillac convertible.*

Mick: "That's the first bit of driving I've done on such an empty Brooklyn Bridge in my life. Wonderful it was."

He then walks into the crowd of journalists and teases . . .

"When I was very young, before I got involved in music, I kind of fancied myself as a tough, original investigative journalist. There's one thing I've always wanted to do. I want to ask the Rolling Stones a very original question: 'Is this going to be your last tour?' "

Keith: "Yes, this and the next five!"

Q: "Did you ask Bill Wyman to play on this tour?"

Mick: "Bill is very busy. He has got his own young family now."

Q: "What about your forthcoming baby?"

Mick: "The tour was booked before the baby was booked! Yeah, I'll be there . . ."

Q: "How do you keep coming up with new songs?"

Keith: "We don't write 'em. They come to you. It's a thing you gotta do. You receive. You transmit. You don't create them."

Q: "How are the tours different from, say, touring the States in the Sixties?"

Mick: "We do do a lot of the same songs, but it is different. Some things are better and some things aren't. Instead of by van, we travel by plane . . ."

Mick: "As far as the music's concerned, we're going to do some old favourites, we're going to do some new things and we're going to do some unusual things. And the tour's a mixture of gigs. There's going to be lots of stadiums, some theatres and some pubs on the tour. I think it's going to be a different tour than Voodoo Lounge."

Keith: "It's hard out there doing the big things. You want to touch where you come from, the smaller places . . . For us, it stops it from becoming rote."

Bill: "I cannot see them ever stopping unless someone dies. There is very little else they do. What are they going to do? They are going to say, 'Let's do another tour.' "

SUNDAY, 31 AUGUST 1997

The death of Princess Diana in a car accident in Paris while being chased by photo-journalists prompts much debate about the role of the paparazzi.

Keith: "You set yourself up in this game. You're supposed to worry when they're not there. You're up for grabs out there. I've been living with that for most of my life. I don't think it's enough to die for. I don't think you should run away. Hey, just stop. It was handled just very badly. Circumstances all came together in that tunnel. It was a real amateur job. Somebody wasn't taking care of business."

Mick: "It's certainly got worse. They didn't use to exist at all, except in Italy, thus the term. It's an Italian thing. But then money screams and they're more and more invasive. People start getting ladders and taking pictures of you at home. It's very unpleasant for the children of people that are well known."

Keith: "I never met the chick. How hard is it to be the Princess of Wales? I'm still trying to correlate how important she really was in relation to things. I hate riding on bandwagons, but at the same time, it's a focal point of the English."

Elton John reworks his 1974 hit, 'Candle In The Wind', for the funeral.
Keith: "I find it jars a little. After all, it was written for Marilyn Monroe. This is writing songs for dead blondes."

The royals' favourite ivory tinkler doesn't take too kindly to the remark.
Elton John: "He's so pathetic, poor thing. It's like a monkey with arthritis, trying to go on stage and look young. It must be awful to be like Keith."

Keith: "The only reason Elton spoke out like that in response to something I said is that I guess the truth must have hurt. I was talking about a funeral, and the rest of it doesn't bother me. He's got to live with it, not me."

Keith: "To me, the monarchy is not that important. I tell you, none of them is getting near me with a sword. I kneel for no one."

SEPTEMBER 1997

Readers of long-running Stones fanzine, It's Only Rock'n'Roll, *vote for the songs they most want to hear on the forthcoming tour. Revealingly, the top 10 songs all date from the band's first decade.*

1 'Angie'
2 'Sympathy For The Devil'
3 'Gimme Shelter'
4 'Midnight Rambler'
5 '(I Can't Get No) Satisfaction'
6 'Ruby Tuesday'
7 'Can't You Hear Me Knocking'
8 'Paint It Black'
9 'Under My Thumb'
10 'Wild Horses'

Ron: "There are these lists going around on the internet of favourite Stones tracks. And if people continue to vote on them, we might just take some notice."

THURSDAY, 18 SEPTEMBER 1997

The band warm up with a show at the Double Door club in Chicago.
Q: "How's the band sound now?"
Keith: "Better than ever, thanks to Charlie Watts."
Ron: "I get as nervous, if not more, in a little club."
Mick: "It's kinda sweaty. People grab hold of your ankles and pass you requests and you say hello to them between songs. And no one's gonna notice when we screw up."
Keith: "They're ready. All we gotta do is figure out what to do with the big stage. They need an audience. I've been keeping them busy for a couple of weeks! 'C'mon boys!' . . . You're always on the cutting edge with this stuff. Every time you go out there there's new stuff to play along with, and you try and figure out how to make it better."

MONDAY, 22 SEPTEMBER 1997

'Anybody Seen My Baby?' is issued as a single – though not without some controversy.
Mick: "I was in England a few weeks ago and I was playing it in the front room and my daughter arrived with her friend in the kitchen and it's wafting through the house and they started to sing (kd lang's) 'Constant Craving' over the top. It was, 'Oh, time to make a phone call.' It was no way a deliberate thing. We don't need to steal songs; we've got enough."

kd lang: "I've always been a fan of the Rolling Stones and take it as quite a compliment."

Mick: "I don't think it really sounds like it, myself. It's just a lot of nervous lawyers . . . I think she's great. I've seen her on telly. She sounds great, but I don't have any kd lang records."

TUESDAY, 23 SEPTEMBER 1997

"IT'S ONLY CROCK'N'ROLL"

The 10-month Bridges To Babylon *tour kicks off at Soldier Field Stadium in Chicago. Having rehearsed some 60 songs, the Stones are well prepared for the internet winners which are flashed up on a screen midway through the set.*
Keith: "Either we'll die in the attempt or it'll be fantastic."

So, Keith, you're still with us . . .
Keith: "I would suggest that other people worry about their own health, quite honestly. I'm 54 and kick ass. People ask me if I work out. What, me? I play for the Rolling Stones. That's enough of a workout . . . There's only one really fatal disease, I've concluded. It's called hypochondria. And it is deadly."

As the tour progresses, the Stones intersperse the stadium shows with a few club gigs.
Mick: "I suppose people miss the kind of closeness of it. I don't mind where I play really. I don't care. I like to play in clubs. If I could play half-a-dozen clubs and make as much money as I can playing 100 stadiums, I'd do the half-dozen clubs. Let's put it that way."

A feature of the stadium shows is a small secondary stage at the end of a 200-foot catwalk.
Ron: "The stage was so small there wasn't even enough room to swing a guitar round. I could hardly turn around without knocking into Charlie's drum kit."
Ron: "I love playing on the big stage, but my favourite is going over the bridge to the small stage."
Mick: "You're surrounded 360 degrees by people. You get this feeling that you're being examined from all angles. I don't enjoy it that much. For three numbers, it's fantastic. Playing in the round is really strange because as a performer you feel there's nowhere to retreat to, you feel very open, vulnerable."
Keith: "The 'B' stage makes you more accessible. So far nobody's been

pulled off – couple of close ones here and there. It brings things down to a much smaller crucible. It's almost like two shows. You do one show up there, then a little show down there . . . I found it one of the best inventions we've come up with."

Charlie: "The sound's better on the big stage."

Ultimately, Keith doesn't mind what stage he's on.
Keith: "It's where I get most peace! That's where the phones don't ring, where nobody can come up to you. It's your turf, and when you play with a band like this, it's really your own playground. Ronnie and I always say: 'Right, time for some peace – not quiet.'"

He even has an 'offstage stage', too, his 'Baboon Cage' which he transports from hotel room to hotel room.
Keith: "Unless there's a sign on the door saying, 'Cage closed', it's open. It's where anybody in the band and friends in town that we know can come up and kick around ideas. What usually happens is that loads of people talk and yell at each other, and then start to play some music. Suddenly it's ten in the morning and there's bodies on the floor. That's a fair description of the Cage."

MONDAY, 29 SEPTEMBER 1997

The new album, Bridges To Babylon, *is released.*
Keith: "It's full of fance – that's funk and dance put together."
Keith: "Mick brings the pop element. He's more interested in what's happening now. I'm more interested in keeping the Stones as they are and not following trends. A third of the stuff Mick had doing his way, synthesised things. There was a third that we worked on together, and another third that I put together."
Ron: "I compare it to something like *Beggars Banquet* or *Let It Bleed*."

'Flip The Switch'
Keith: "It's the fastest track the Stones have ever cut. Or any other rock'n'rollers. It even beats 'Rip This Joint'; it comes roaring out. The record starts and ends with Charlie Watts."

'Gun Face'
Mick: "(It's) quite a provocative song. It's about a guy who wants to kill his girlfriend's lover. Most of the songs are of a personal nature, but 'Gun Face' isn't a first-person song!"

'How Can I Stop'
Keith: "It's cut just like old soul records – a little Chi-Lites and Stylistics."
Charlie: "Keith always does those poignant 'How Can I Stop' things. Fantastic."

Citing Keith's 'Locked Away' and 'Thru And Thru', MOJO *writer Barney Hoskyns sees 'How Can I Stop' as continuing a rich strand in the Stones' more recent work.*
Keith: "I wouldn't have been able to write songs like that 10, 15 years ago. I wouldn't have been able to put it over with the right attitude. I guess a lot of the earlier stuff is just a hard shell – 'Before They Make Me Run', and so on. Never forget that one of the first ones was 'Happy', which should explain some of the lines on this face. Even when the cops are waking you up again, you somehow have to laugh."

'Might As Well Get Juiced'
Ron: "Just wait 'til you hear it live! We're reinventing ourselves a bit with that one. We thought it would be different to do a tip-of-the-hat to techno. It's one of the new tracks that we've definitely earmarked for the tour – if we can get around to arranging it properly."
Keith: "They ruined a good track. I have a better one in the can – one that Mick and I had done previous to the Dust Brothers spending six months making it. It's still a very interesting track, but I have a burning, radical version."

And the album title?
Keith: "It's a Rastafari concept. They use it to designate the external world. Babylon is business, deals, 'Yes boss, no boss,' the commercial world. I have been to Jamaica for many years and was able to breathe spiritual fresh air there – not as something religious, more like a connection with the earth, the sea and all that surrounds us. I try to make things as simple and pure as possible, and have a great time."

Paul Sexton, who conducts the band interviews for a tie-in promotional disc, wonders what it is that keeps the band going.
Keith: "We still feel we're getting better and we have things to offer. We ain't the Beach Boys, some nostalgia band, you know."

OCTOBER 1997

Keith's Wingless Angels *album, recorded with the Nyabinghi Rastafarian drummers from the Jamaican hills, is released. This self-styled "project by Keith*

Richards and brothers in Jah" appears on Keith's own Mindless label.
Keith: "When we'd finished *Exile On Main Street*, I came up from Kingston to hear what they're doing . . . It's taken 25 years to get this together. We used to do it for fun every night. Then we got so good, I thought we ought to record it on something better than a cassette with a rusty microphone. It was done in my front room with a local Jamaican ambience – bullfrogs, crickets and loads of rum!"
Keith: "They sing like angels but they can't fly."
Keith: "They're full of energy. I've seen them on their ups and downs for 25 years. Three years ago, we tried to take it into a studio in Kingston. I'd given up the idea of recording this."

WEDNESDAY, 15 OCTOBER 1997

Keith is quizzed about rock's latest bad boys, Oasis' Gallagher brothers.
Keith: "These guys are just obnoxious. Grow up and then come back and see if you can hang. I don't hear anything there, it's all just retro to me."

But there is an element of pity . . .
Keith: "I would hate to be a rock'n'roll star just starting off now. Get laid and you're gonna get Aids. You can't do what we did. The worst thing we could get was a dose of clap. Vietnamese Rose was the worst you could get. It did bite a little, but you could get rid of it."

THURSDAY, 23 OCTOBER 1997

Noel and Liam Gallagher challenge Mick and Keith to a punch-up while inter-viewed live on air by Steve Lamacq for Radio 1's Evening Session.
Liam Gallagher: "I'm gonna shoot me mouth off here . . . All these snakes coming out the closets, all these old farts. I'll offer 'em out right here on radio. If they wanna fight, be at Primrose Hill Saturday morning at 12 o'clock. I will beat the fucking living daylight shit out of them. That goes for George (Harrison), Jagger, Richards and that other cunt that gives me shit. If any of them old farts have got a problem with me then leave your zimmer frames at home and I'll hold you up with a good right hook. They're jealous and senile and not getting enough fucking meat pies. If they want to fight, I'll beat them up . . . We've just done a cover of the Stones' 'Street Fighting Man' just to piss Keith Richards off 'cos he's been slagging us off."

WEDNESDAY, 26 NOVEMBER 1997

Bent, *in which Mick plays a transvestite club owner Greta/George, opens in New York.*
Mick: "I was not attracted to play the part because she has glamorous costumes and silky underwear. It is the depth of the character and the arc that I bring to pass in the role that I felt was a challenge to my cross-dressing abilities."

TUESDAY, 9 DECEMBER 1997

"MICK'S NEW BOY"

Jerry Hall gives birth to Gabriel Luke Beauregard Jagger in a London private hospital while Mick is in Atlanta, Georgia, touring with the Stones.
An insider: "Jerry's lived in London many years, but she's a Southern girl at heart and wanted that reflected. Beauregard's always been a popular name in the South."

It seems that the Stones have entered a new phase of domestic bliss – though nothing's changed in the Watts household.
Shirley Watts: "I love Charlie even more than when we married. I'm so mad about him. He has an incredible depth of sweetness in his nature . . . Actually, the most irritating habit he has is chewing his nails. He never ever criticises me so he's never told me what I do to irritate *him*. That's frustrating, too. It's a side of him I can't get to grips with."

JANUARY 1998

Keith continues to find new ways of insisting that he's not ready for retirement just yet.
Keith: "It would almost be, like, to get off the bus before it got to wherever it was going. So what? You'd be standing there in the road, a cloud of dust, and you'd wonder what it would be like to still be on it. Maybe Bill Wyman feels like that."

MONDAY, 26 JANUARY 1998

'Saint Of Me', the second single from Bridges To Babylon, *is released.*
Mick: "I didn't know what I was doing sometimes when I was sitting in

the Dust Brothers' studio in Silverlake. I'm sitting there playing my key-board and playing 'Saint Of Me' and thinking, 'Sounds like shit, this is terrible.' It was quite slow, very low-tech and I didn't know how it was gonna build."

Ron: "Some of the stuff the Dust Brothers do was quite new to me. They don't look at a song particularly musically. They look at it on a computer or a laptop, you know, and they say, 'You wanna see your guitar?' instead of 'Do you wanna hear it?' "

Mick: "I was playing keyboards, emptying the cigarette butts, emptying their bong and asking for coffee which they didn't have. They were pretty straight when I worked with them. Probably when I left they fell to pieces. I certainly don't do loads of drink or drugs when I'm working."

Charlie: "They are very nice young men. And it was very interesting. But it takes a lot of work on their part."

On the rumours that Keith didn't get on with the Dust Brothers
Mick: "He doesn't really get along with people very often. He takes a stand against people."

FEBRUARY 1998

"HER SATANIC MAJESTY REQUESTS"

Ex-Prime Minister Margaret Thatcher tells reporters that she recently entertained Mick and Charlie at a hotel in Hawaii.
A Thatcher spokeswoman: "She was delighted to have them up to her hotel room. She thinks they are a great British export."

Martin Newell couldn't resist penning a witty rhyme in The Independent *to mark the summit meeting.*
"And passing round the Hob Nobs/ While a maid brought in the teas/ She asked, 'Shall I be mother?'/ As Charlie mumbled, 'Please.' "

MONDAY, 2 MARCH 1998

Mick Jagger interrupts the Bridges To Babylon *tour to catch the English cricket team being routed by the West Indies from the vantage point of the Guyana Bank of Trade and Industry hospitality booth. Cue more broadsheet amusement, this time from B.C. Pires in* The Guardian.
"You had to have Sympathy for the poor Devil. He must have been Shattered. An English cricket fan needed a Heart of Stone or a heavy dose

413

of Sister Morphine or some form of Emotional Rescue to avoid a Nineteenth Nervous Breakdown while watching England Exile on Regent Street, a match that ought to have been a Beggar's Banquet."

Mick: "You should have listened to me. Who said that the West Indies attack was too old? They were famous last words. The truth is it's all over for England. It was really fun yesterday and there was a time when things were going well, but England did not get up and at them as we expected this morning. The keenness went out of our attack and they let the West Indies linger on too long."

SPRING 1998

Charlie Watts meets his public thanks to an AOL-hosted Q&A session.

Q: "Hiya Charlie, I'd just like to say you're a great drummer. And why don't you like to make music videos?"

Charlie: "Because they're boring . . . bloody boring."

Q: "The other Stones have long credited you with being the glue that holds the Stones together. How have you done it?"

Charlie: "I've got no idea. I don't think about things like that."

Q: "We have heard that you draw a picture of every bed you've ever slept in on the road. Is this true?"

Charlie: "Yes, it's true. Since about 1968 or '67. Out of boredom, really. It's like a visual diary."

Q: "Do you feel that the band is playing better than ever?"

Charlie: "Yes."

Q: "Is this your first time ever online?"

Charlie: "It's my first time ever looking at a computer like this. Except with Mick and the cricket."

Q: "Do you ever see yourself retiring, being a 'country gent' and enjoying your grandchildren?"

Charlie: "Yes. Soon."

Q: "You've been called 'The Best-Dressed Stone'. Any comment on that?"

Charlie: "No, not really."

Q: "How is it that even with Keith and Ronnie's chugga guitar playing, you're able to keep such steady grooves going? They both tend to throw in chords on off-beats when they feel the need to. How difficult does this make your job?"

Charlie: "They don't throw me in any way. It's very easy to play with

Keith. He's one of the best rhythm guitar players, actually. So it's very easy."

Q: "You are often cited by other Stones members as being the inspiration for the 'Rolling Stones Sound'. Yet you have always shunned this idea. Will you ever take credit for your contribution to rock music?"

Charlie: "No, I'm not interested."

Q: "Charlie, I have always been intrigued by your enigmatic smile. What is it that makes you smile that way?"

Charlie: "Indigestion, usually."

Q: "What do the Stones do when they're not practising or touring?"

Charlie: "I've got no idea what they do."

Q: "If you could have been in a different band other than the Stones, who would it have been?"

Charlie: "Duke Ellington's."

Charlie: "I am not interested in computers or the internet but Mick is. Mobile phones? I think they're a pain in the arse but most people think they're fantastic. I don't know what Mick would do without one! But I am more of a dinosaur than he is."

MAY 1998

Mick announces that work has already started on his début production for Jagged Films, the production company he launched in November 1996.

Mick: "I don't think the best producers hang around on sets too much. I've been pretty hands on so far, getting it from the stage of being just an idea to getting the money, the cast and working with (scriptwriter) Tom Stoppard on three drafts. He's so fantastically bright that people are afraid of his intellect. They don't want to tell him, 'Wait a minute, we need a much bigger ending!' I don't mind doing that."

TUESDAY, 19 MAY 1998

The European leg of the Bridges To Babylon *tour is jeopardised when Keith breaks a rib in a fall at his Connecticut home. The accident, which took place in Keith's library, gives new meaning to his "I'll do it 'til I drop" claim.*

Jane Rose (Keith's spokeswoman): "He sustained injuries to his ribs and chest after falling off a ladder. Tomorrow, doctors will give promoters of the tour a clear indication of Keith Richards' recovery period and an announcement will follow about European concerts that are affected."

415

WEDNESDAY, 3 JUNE 1998

"GIMME TAX SHELTER"

It is revealed that the Stones have been lobbying Parliament for several months after learning that the Treasury plan to close a loophole that allows high earners to avoid paying tax on overseas earnings while resident in the UK.

Joyce Smith (the Rolling Stones tax adviser): "My clients fully understand that it is the government's policy to introduce anti-avoidance measures and to close tax 'loopholes'. What we consider deeply unjust, however, is the retrospective nature of this particular change."

SUNDAY, 7 JUNE 1998

The Stones controversially cancel four British stadium shows in August and reschedule them for June 1999. The tax reforms that came into effect on 17 March would have meant that if the shows had gone ahead, they would be taxed on the entire European tour. That's because Chancellor Gordon Brown had scrapped the Foreign Earnings Deduction, which allowed tax-exiled earners 62 working days back in the UK each year.

Bernard Doherty (Stones PR): "The Stones made an appeal to the Government. They were halfway round the tour and 75 of Mick's crew complained they were losing out financially. The band met and agreed to cancel the British dates as a business decision. Mick was particularly furious that Gordon Brown moved the goalposts. It's not just the money earned from the UK leg but also money collected from earnings abroad."

Mick: "It's been a very difficult decision to make. I was tempted to bite the bullet but I'm not the only one affected. A Rolling Stones world tour is a two-year project and there are over 200 people involved. I'm really sorry and apologetic to all those who've now got to wait until next year to see the shows. We would have played for charity but the Inland Revenue couldn't bend the rules. It is a shame. I'm not attacking the Labour government. They have every right to change the tax laws. I don't have an axe to grind, I'm not a party political animal, and the government isn't run for my convenience . . . We send our apologies to all the fans, especially those in the UK, but we are looking forward to the shows next year."

Mick: "This wasn't some tax loophole. It's a scheme that was set up by Denis Healey, a Labour Chancellor, and has been in use for 20 years. We would have expected the new rules to have applied at the end of the year, not to take effect in the middle. If we did the UK shows it would have meant that the entire European tour ran at a loss."

Clearly riled by the press reaction – the Daily Mirror *ran a story with the headline, 'Dumping Jack Flash' – Mick pens a 'Right To Reply' piece for* The Independent.

Mick: "Whatever the Treasury says, these changes are being introduced retrospectively. This is highly unusual. The government has every right to change the tax laws but we would have expected the new regulations to come into effect at the end of the tax year, not in the middle . . .

"It is not just the band who are affected. Our crew signed up on the basis that their earnings would be free of tax in Britain because they were hardly in the country. Already the manager of an American act has told us they may not hire British technicians because they won't want to work in the UK, which is a vital part of any European tour. This was a very difficult decision for us. It is not a tax protest."

Jonathan Freedland, writing in The Guardian, *sees some contradictions at the heart of the matter.*

"The Rolling Stones have done us all a service, illuminating the odd lattice-work of prejudices and politics that governs our attitude to wealth . . . Those who profit from making us happy can earn as much as they like with barely a squeak of dissent. Alan Shearer and Elton John pocket millions because they supply an entertainment we demand. Tom Cruise, David Hockney and John Grisham are in the clear because enough people believe they brighten their day. The Rolling Stones should have been in that group, too. But the Labour spinners skilfully bumped them into the fat-cat bracket, branding them not as self-made entrepreneurs but as parasites on 'the support of British fans' – as if their vast fortunes aren't really theirs at all."

A Treasury spokesman: "Gordon (Brown) will not be lectured by tax exiles. It's unfair that people who pay their fair share of tax should have to subsidise those who pay no tax at all."

Bernard Doherty (Stones PR): "The Stones hate the term 'tax exile'. It sounds like someone sitting by a pool sipping a pina colada. We're talking about a hard-working band."

Charlie: "I could have murdered him, greasy-looking sod."

Ron: "It was like, those greedy Stones, but it wasn't like that at all. It wasn't about us losing money from our own pockets. It was everybody involved in the tour who would have lost out – right down to the make-up girl. We all would have been taxed – the crew, all those trying to save some money would have got hit hard. It just made sense to call the tour off – it would have been a massive loss-making exercise."

THURSDAY, 18 JUNE 1998

Six months after its launch, Mick's Jagged Internetworks web company broadcasts the second Cornhill Test match between England and South Africa. The company also announces that it recorded 2.7 million hits when it broadcast a match between India v Australia in April.

Mick: "Here's one instance where the net is living up to some of the hype. The figures not only show how popular the game of cricket is on the Internet, but also how the Internet has changed the way the game is seen and heard."

FRIDAY, 31 JULY 1998

As the Stones hit Sweden, Keith's patience wears thin as he is asked yet again about the band's longevity.

Keith: "I'm not gonna get any younger and neither are you, you know . . . and if you're lucky, you get as old as me, and get older maybe, with real luck. But try to get there first and leave us alone and let us find out how old rock'n'roll can get, you know. Because we're the only ones that can tell you, because all the others are in graves."

Q: "Do you think teachers or insurance agents at your age envy your life and would like to copy your lifestyle?"

Keith: "Well, put it this way: I certainly don't envy theirs. I wouldn't know about them envying mine, and if they tried to do my job for a couple of weeks, I think they'd be happy to be teachers and bank managers. You have to start very young to do this, and then hope to stay alive."

TUESDAY, 11 AUGUST 1998

Thirty years after their first attempt to perform in the old Soviet Union, the Stones play Moscow. The country's tastemakers had deemed the band unsuitable for Communist youth after witnessing a performance in Warsaw in 1967.

Mick: "They thought the show was so awful, so decadent, that they said this show would never happen in Moscow."

Keith reveals that it's not only fans' votes that can influence set-lists, as he tells Dean Goodman in It's Only Rock'n'Roll.

Keith: "I always judge how Mick's feeling about a show by how many songs he's willing to change in a night. I don't make the set-list up because he's got to sing them. If there's four or five different songs from the night before, I know that he's really feeling like on the ball. But if it's like, 'We'll just keep it the same, we'll change that one' – I know something's up. Is it the throat? Has he just had an argument with Jerry?!"

MONDAY, 26 OCTOBER 1998

Ernst Hofacker for Musik Express *in Germany tells Keith that Ray Davies (of The Kinks) has one problem with the Stones . . .*
Keith: "That he's not in it!"
Q: "He thinks that people simply come to the show to see the pyramids."
Keith: "They come for the music, brother! With a few lights thrown in, a well-lit rock'n'roll show. I like Ray but he thinks too much. Too much of an intellectual for rock'n'roll."

MONDAY, 2 NOVEMBER 1998

Over a pint (or three) of Guinness in a Dublin hotel, Ronnie Wood tells Victoria Newton in the Sun *about his insatiable capacity for booze.*
Ron: "I've always said I must have hollow legs to cope with all the drink I get through. I just don't seem to put any weight on. I can drink about ten pints of Guinness now – then I have to move on to the shorts. It's not as much as I used to get through, thank goodness . . . I've got me own pub at the bottom of the garden. It's great because I don't have to go out to get drunk and have a good time. Now I just pop down the garden instead. I have the local landlords come to service the Guinness and lager taps to make sure they're okay. The only problem is I have a few loonies turning up at 3 o'clock in the morning for a drinking session. I think there's about 22 pubs near me anyway, so you never have to stagger too far."

That same day sees the release of No Security, *recorded during the early part of the* Bridges To Babylon *tour. Two fans are plucked out of the crowd for the sleeve.*
Mick: "They look kinda like 'Us and the world'. It looks like life holds no security for anyone. It's something in their faces."

The band discuss the tracks with promo interview disc inquisitor, Paul Sexton.
Ron: "It's a good live album, probably our best."
Ron: " 'Respectable' . . . always reminds me of Green Day crossed with the recent problems in the White House. It's very relevant considering it was written so many years ago."

'Saint Of Me'

Ron: "We have a couple of songs that have become instant standards, like 'Saint Of Me'. The audiences just pick up on them as though they were 'Satisfaction' or 'Brown Sugar' , , ."

Mick: "It seemed to take on a different dimension because the crowd used to sing along with the end of it. It seemed to happen every night and it became like a football song."

'Out Of Control'

Keith: "It's basically Mick's construction. His idea was to have the enormous contrast between the verses and the manic chorus. It's a great song to play and it just got better. In fact, I prefer the live version to the record version, but that's not unusual with me. You write a song and you record it, and everybody takes that as being *the* version, and in actual fact you're only still exploring it. When you take it on stage, suddenly you find all these other possibilities, different nuances and different ways of dealing with it, and you realise that you never actually stop learning a song. I'm still learning 'Satisfaction', quite honestly, so 'Out Of Control' has a long way to go."

FRIDAY, 27 NOVEMBER 1998

News breaks that 29-year-old Brazilian model Luciana Giminez Morad has been telling friends that she is pregnant with Mick Jagger's child after an eight-month affair. The couple met after a Stones show in Rio de Janeiro.

Jerry Hall promptly banishes him from their shared home in Richmond, calls him a "lying, cheating, no-good slimeball" and, rumour has it, is now talking to lawyers.

Shortly afterwards, Morad flies to London (on a Virgin Boeing 747 named Ruby Tuesday) for a legal briefing. She also hooks up with New York lawyer Raoul Felder, who has also spoken to Jerry Hall. He predicts that "Jerry and Mick will be getting divorced and it will be pretty nasty".

According to a friend, Mick tries some damage limitation.

"He's calling Luciana all the time. The last thing he wants is Luciana to team up with Jerry. But she is determined to have the baby and his relationship with her is getting strained."

Mick: "I never intended to be a sex symbol. I never really wanted to sort of get into pushing that particular aspect of myself because I thought of myself as a serious musician. I didn't want to be a stripper. But then I turned out to be one. Just another girl on the runway."

WEDNESDAY, 9 DECEMBER 1998

Despite all the recent controversies concerning sex and tax, bookies William Hill install Mick as a 10–1 candidate for a knighthood in the Queen's next Honours List.

Graham Sharpe (a spokesman for Hill): "He's done as much for music as Cliff Richard and Paul McCartney, and both are knighted."

JANUARY 1999

Keith: "The end of the century is always weird because people go berserk about the zeros. For some reason there's a mass psychosis. In the 1890s, they were mad, too, you know. The best advice I can give anybody is just don't fly because these computers ain't got it together yet. Walk, and walk softly."

FRIDAY, 15 JANUARY 1999

Jerry Hall petitions for divorce, asking for a rumoured $30–$70 million of Mick's reputed $150 million fortune in light of his "committing adultery with an unnamed woman".

TUESDAY, 19 JANUARY 1999

Mick's response is swift.

Bernard Doherty (Mick's PR): "To avoid any misinterpretation and speculation, Mick Jagger's lawyers, Smyth Barkham, wish to state they will be contesting Jerry Hall's divorce petition on the grounds that Mick Jagger and Jerry Hall are not, and never have been, married."

Bill: "We had Jerry over for lunch with the children last weekend, actually. It was pretty good. She's in quite good spirits. I think she's going ahead with the divorce. I think she's had enough, you know. It's just so many times. That's all I have to say . . . I had a very similar problem, you know, but I took care of it and I found someone in my life that I wanted to marry and have children with and be done with the rest of it. That's what I've done. Let's hope he does the same thing."

But will the disaffection spread to the Stones themselves?

Bill: "Charlie is probably the one most desiring of that. But Charlie won't let anybody down. He is indispensable in that band. If Charlie retired, then I think the band would fold, where I knew when I left that wouldn't happen. They can always replace the bass player."

SUNDAY, 7 MARCH 1999

Meanwhile, something strange is happening down at the farm, Charlie and Shirley's Halsdon Arabians stud farm near Dalton in North Devon, that is.
A Devon & Cornwall police spokesman: "A man and a woman were arrested on suspicion of theft and false accounting in relation to an allegation of financial irregularities. They were interviewed and released on police bail without charge pending further inquiries."

Ron is having better luck with horses, picking up the Small Breeder Of The Year, awarded by the Irish Thoroughbred Breeders' Association.
Ron: "That meant as much to me as being inducted into the Rock'n'Roll Hall Of Fame."

SATURDAY, 3 APRIL 1999

As personal troubles mount, Mick is happy to discuss lighter matters on From Station To Stadium, *a BBC Radio 2 documentary hosted by Mark Hagen.*
Mick: "I just signed this picture for someone where I was wearing the most horrific pink suit with a fluffy thing on it. I suppose at the time it didn't look too bad because that's what you did. It wasn't really that out of line. And now it looks ridiculous. But you tend to step out at certain moments and why not?"

And does he still possess any of these sartorial antiquities?
Mick: "Not all of them, but I've got quite a lot. Actually I've got them out again, because they're going mouldy so I got this lady I know to kind of try and see if she could take all the damp out of them so they'll last a little bit longer!"
Mick: "I'm still exactly the same. I can fit into all my old clothes. I've got a 28-inch waist and a 31-inch inside leg."

SATURDAY, 10 APRIL 1999

As the band prepare to hit Britain, the Stones elaborate on the build-up to a show for the benefit of BBC listeners.
Charlie: "There's usually a lot of waiting around."
Keith: "I hang with Ronnie in the string section room. You start to hear

the first band go on, then you hear the crowd through the walls, and you know that time's approaching. It's not particularly exciting. You go do your thing, go to make-up, to wardrobe, we're very professional in that way."

Ron: "If I haven't got my glasses on I can only see the first couple of rows. I'm like waving at these imaginary people 'cos I need glasses for long distance. The other day – you know, people hold various signs up in the audience – I went up to Mick and I said, 'What does it say on that sign there?' And he said, 'Oh I think it says Woody's rubbish . . .' "

Keith: "I'm one of those guys who didn't want a big screen a few years ago! I've learnt to work with it and realise that if you're playing places of this size in summer in open air, it's actually a real help to you on stage."

Mick: "Even the most basic thing is technologically driven."

Keith: "The art of it is to create, for two hours, your own country, Stonesland – for you and several hundred thousand people."

Keith finds new metaphors to describe his interaction with Ronnie.

Keith: "That's the string section. That's the ancient form of weaving. Ronnie and I pride ourselves on people saying, 'Who played that, and who played that?' Because we figure we're playing well and nobody can tell who's doing what; that's what it's all about."

Meanwhile, the crowds continue to laud the unsung drummer with mass choruses of "Charlie, Charlie".

Keith: "To me it's one of the happiest moments in the show. Charlie is the most modest, the shyest man . . . the idea of stardom horrifies him, but he's managed to live with it. It's not often that the drummers get the recognition."

The Keith Richards fan club isn't far behind, though.

Don Was: "Keith is a paradigm, the connection between emotion and art. He is the musician that all musicians should aspire to emulate."

Keith: "Don, I love you! I guess he's talking about attitude. I know as a musician I've got a long way to go. I know my limitations. I have a feeling that Don means it's a certain spirit, a morale thing in that you can get the best out of everybody whether it's sweet-talking or kicking their ass. I do love my music . . . I sleep with the guitar, you know what I mean?"

Charlie: "Keith is the most interesting, the most different of us all. He's a man of vision, and one of the few people who hasn't really changed over the years. Wherever he goes, whatever he does, he's always Keith. He'll be in his room and all the stuff that makes him Keith will be there. The music's going, the wine's there, his guitar's there, and he'll be sitting in the middle of it all like some wonderful sultan. It's fantastic. It's not a new thing, it's the way he's always been."

SUNDAY, 2 MAY 1999

"MY ROLLING STONE LOVER BRIAN WAS MURDERED"

Anna Wohlin, Brian Jones' girlfriend at the time of his death, breaks her 30-year silence with the publication of a book, The Murder Of Brian Jones.
Charlie: "All that about Brian being knocked off is rubbish. I know a lot of people would have willingly knocked him off, but it didn't happen. Brian was just very weak. He was asthmatic, unhealthy. The stuff he took – uppers, downers, leapers, bleepers, whatever they were – were too strong for his body. He couldn't take it. And his swimming pool was about 70 degrees or something – it used to shimmer with heat. You'd drive down there on a spring morning and the heat would be rising off the top. And he got in there, and I suppose it was like getting into a warm bath, and he fell asleep. And that's how he died."

SATURDAY, 8 MAY 1999

A month before the Rolling Stones' Bridges To Babylon/No Security *tour rolls into Britain for four dates in early June, a documentary helmed by Chris Evans is broadcast on Channel 4.*

It provides the very latest on several familiar topics, such as the Mick and Keith feud . . .
Keith: "We don't fight anymore. The only fights I have are when someone tries to jump on the stage. There was this guy a while back who was coming at Mick. I looked round for security but they were way back. I didn't know whether this guy had a knife or a gun or just a piece of paper for him to sign. I didn't want to spend time thinking about it, so I just whacked him one with my guitar. I whacked him pretty hard, but it had to be done. Charlie was a bit upset that I sent him sprawling over his drum kit, but that was his problem. I was just protecting our territory."

Backstage necessities . . .
Mick: "We know what we want and we take it with us, whether it's Marmite or shepherd's pie for Keith, or incense candles for Ronnie. We make it as comfortable as we can."

The view from the back . . .

Charlie: "I love it when it suits me. I have a very different view of the Rolling Stones than anyone else in the world. I'm the drummer. All the Rolling Stones look like to me are three skinny guys, one with a little behind and two with mad hair."

. . . and that old drum-stool cynicism.

Charlie: "I'd never go and see a band playing a stadium gig, which is what we have to do. I'd only ever want to see someone play in a little club. My wife is more of a fan of this band than I am. She likes rock'n'roll and dancing, and I don't. Given the option, I'd just sit at home and do nothing. I can spend weeks doing nothing at all, which is why I hate going out with Mick. He can't stand still for a second. He's always wanting to do something else."

Charlie: "Part of the reason we're still going is we're all still fit to go and I suppose we'll keep going until we keel over doing it."

MONDAY, 17 MAY 1999

Luciana Morad gives birth to a son, Lucas.

Jerry Hall: "He told me about the pregnancy the day before he knew it was going to be in the papers. I found that difficult. I was very upset . . . I like babies and this boy is the children's half-brother, so he's a blood relation. He's family and I have a very strong sense of family. Mick's seen the baby and, when I told him I'd be happy for him to bring him to meet our children, he cried."

FRIDAY, 4 JUNE 1999

In a cruel twist on the usual 'Old Stones' stories, Scotland's leading cosmetic surgery hospital, Health Care International, costs out facelifts for the Frowning Four.

Catherine Knowles (Surgery assistant): "Jagger's craggy, rangy looks are his main attraction so we won't smooth him out too much. Jagger fans expect a bit of rough but pinnaplasty is a must because it'll pin back his Spock ears . . . I reckon Mick can expect a couple of hundred quid change from £7,000."

She also reckons Keith requires Mick's treatment plus some work on his upper lip. Total price £8,000. Recommended "rhinoplasty" nose jobs for Ronnie and Charlie would set each back around £2,200.

Bill: "All I know is I look a bloody sight better than they do, and I'm seven years older. I think until you feel good inside and at peace with yourself, you don't look good, you don't behave good, and you're not a good person . . . The last seven years have been the happiest of my life."

TUESDAY, 8 JUNE 1999

The group play to an audience of friends, family and fans at the Shepherd's Bush Empire in West London. The inclusion of 'Some Girls' in the set list is ironic, in light of Mick's current domestic difficulties:

"Some girls give me children I never asked them for!"

JULY 1999

Mick agrees to pay Jerry Hall £3 million as an annulment settlement after the dissolution of their 21-year-long relationship. She also gets to keep the property on Richmond Hill, though it is later revealed that Mick isn't too far away.

A friend: "After they split, Jerry stayed in the Richmond house with the kids and Mick just sort of wandered around the world. He spent a lot of the summer in France. But London has always been Mick's home town and it just didn't seem natural to him that he should live at a different address to his family. Whatever problems he has had with Jerry, Mick remains her best friend and he is a devoted father to his kids. The Richmond house is big enough for all of them. So Jerry has let Mick have his own quarters. Everyone is very happy with the arrangement, especially the children."

TUESDAY, 27 JULY 1999

Although Mick initially denies that he is Lucas' father, a DNA test confirms his paternity.

Jerry Hall: "It's not my problem. Mick has to sort it out. I have no animosity towards the baby or towards her. I said to Mick that any time he wanted to introduce the baby to our children, I would be supportive."

Luciana praises the father.

"Mick is a very decent man and he loves all his children. He does not blame Lucas for being born. He is a very loving father and, as fathers go, Lucas couldn't be luckier."

Anita Pallenberg, who has recently passed a fashion degree at St Martins School of Art in London, is less impressed by the band.

Anita Pallenberg: "Keith gives me a certain amount of money as the mother of his children, but I managed to change my lifestyle radically . . . I don't think the Stones are so amazing. They're just human beings. They might be amazing when they have a guitar and sit up there on stage, but on a daily basis, it's not that extraordinary. It's not words of wisdom every five seconds. They can be pretty stupid . . . I'm quite happy someone else looks after (Keith) now. It's a relief I don't have to be babysitting some-body . . . Even my son has problems communicating directly with Keith unless he actually goes there and stands in front of him."

But, by his own account, Keith is a changed man . . .

Keith: "I made a determined effort after the tour to get up with the family at 7 a.m. After a few months, I was allowed to drive the kids to school. Then I was allowed to take the garbage out. Before that, I didn't even know where the recycling bin was. I read a lot. I might have a little sail around Long Island Sound if the weather is all right . . . Patti and I go out once a week if there's something on in town – take the old lady out for dinner with a bunch of flowers, get the rewards . . ."

SATURDAY, 14 AUGUST 1999

Mick and Jerry's marriage is officially declared null and void, thus formally ending their relationship.

Jerry Hall: "The final straw was when my children began to take on a mocking, disrespectful tone. They're smart and they know everything. They realised our relationship was wrong because there was an imbalance of power . . . I had public humiliation and private heartbreak, but I loved him. I still love him . . . He's got amazing personal charm. He's very intelligent, witty and fun to be with, so he's an irresistible package. The thing is he's not committed . . . He wants us to be together like we were and I could never do that again. He says that this time he'd be faithful, but I don't believe him. He's promised too many times . . . He had so many affairs he had to weave a web of intrigue and confusion to keep me off balance. And living like that is exhausting . . . I still find Mick very attrac-tive. When I go with him to a party, he's the best-looking, most charm-ing, interesting man there. If I didn't know him so well, I'd definitely want to go out with him. But sexual promiscuity leads to chaos and now he's getting a lot of ribbing."

WEDNESDAY, 3 NOVEMBER 1999

Keith receives the Q Magazine Special Merit Award from Bob Geldof at the annual Q Awards in London.
Keith: "It's a pleasure, really a pleasure. I'm all right on stage but this is embarrassing. Bless you all."

WEDNESDAY, 29 DECEMBER 1999

The Stones are confirmed as the top grossing touring band of the Nineties, raking in £500 million while playing to 12 million fans over some 333 shows. Languishing behind them are the Grateful Dead (£190 million) and U2 (£180 million).
A spokesman (for *Amusement Business* magazine): "The Stones generate revenues that would likely top the GNP of some Third World countries."
Keith: "The thing we all had to learn is what to do when the passion starts to generate money. You don't start to play your guitar thinking you're going to be running an organisation that will maybe generate millions."
Mick: "I'm not first and foremost a businessperson. I'm a creative artist. All I know about business is what I've managed to pick up along the way."

THURSDAY, 30 DECEMBER 1999

"GEORGE HARRISON STABBED"

Keith: "What George really went through was not in the papers. I spoke to Ringo about a month after it happened and he told me exactly what went on. It was horrific. George was stabbed about 40 times. It happened outside his bedroom on the landing. He would have been dead if he'd been lying in bed. He wouldn't have been able to fight. The man was slashing him everywhere. George's wife hit him again and again on the head with this brass lamp, but he just wouldn't stop. There was blood everywhere. I think George is still going through trauma. He's bound to – he's lived in that house for 30 years. It's just so shocking that it should happen to a guy who's so inoffensive. George has never been nasty to anyone. He's only ever preached love and peace. He's not like John Lennon: he's never made statements or anything. He's just a very nice guitar player."

6

On With The Show

It is reported that Mick has registered his name as a trademark in a bid to prevent others exploiting it and producing products such as clothing and perfumes in his name.

Bernard Doherty (PR): "He had to protect the name Mick Jagger, because there were a few loopholes to be closed, with his face and name being used. One of the ideas he came up with, jokingly, was to register it as a trademark for a Mick Jagger lip balm, but I can confirm he has no plans whatsoever to enter the world of cosmetics."

FEBRUARY 2000

Mick begins recording demos for his fourth solo album.

And Keith?

Mick: "I don't think he was mad at all. I don't think we ever intended to do any touring this year. We were always talking about working next year and we've been planning what we're going to do. We're going to be working next year which is coming up to our 40th anniversary."

Mick: "I love the writing process. That's what is so much fun about making this record. I'd sit in my house in France, in the little recording room, and write the songs. I'd put them down and then lay down some beats on the computer and play the guitar. That feeling – or the actual guitar – ended up on the finished record. So the writing process is in the grooves, so to speak."

Mick: "I had a lot of good times making it. My family was always around. Matt Clifford was always around. And I worked really closely with Marti Frederiksen on the five tracks that I did with him. And Pete Townshend kept saying, 'I want to play on this.' Pete lives 20 yards away from me in England, so one day I said, 'Pete, can you come today?' "

THURSDAY, 30 MARCH 2000

Mick opens the £2.25 million Mick Jagger Centre For The Performing Arts at his old school, Dartford Grammar, Kent. His parents, Mr and Mrs Joe and Eva Jagger, Jerry Hall and their three children attend the ceremony. A school band, Cherry Sunburst, played versions of 'Brown Sugar', 'It's Only Rock'n'Roll' and 'You Can't Always Get What You Want'.
Mick: "It was pretty good. In fact it sounded excellent."

Days earlier, he'd been reported as saying the school had "extremely petty rules" and a headmaster who was "an iron-fisted disciplinarian, totally cold and unapproachable".
Mick: "I loved my school days. Each morning we would sing our hymns and either be praised or damned for our behaviour . . . I hope I didn't give the impression that this school was a mixture of 'Blackboard Jungle', 'Dotheboys Hall' and 'St Trinians'. I had many wonderful teachers and I have a lot of good memories of the place. It is true that the school I went to was very different from the school of today. There are shatterproof windows in the new block to prevent damage from footballs, there are salads and chips for lunch, and tweaked ears by maths masters are instantly reported to Childline . . . When I was here, there was no doubt that the serious stuff of education was maths, science and Latin. Music and the arts were pushed to the margins, a nice little optional extra in your spare time. An interest in playing music, or in the theatre or even worse, trying to earn a living as a musician, was a bit like having an embarrassing illness. You kept it to yourself."

Before leaving, he scrawls "I was back" on a wall.

FRIDAY, 14 APRIL 2000

Mick rushes from the Cannes Film Festival to be by his mother's side at the Parkside Hospital, Wimbledon.
A friend: "Eva is seriously ill, and it seems that the doctors can only do a little amount for her. She has a heart condition and isn't getting any better. Mick is devastated."

TUESDAY, 25 APRIL 2000

It is revealed in court that the manager of Charlie Watts' stud farm had stolen £9,199 from the Stones drummer between September 1997 and December 1998.

Shirley Watts (to the court): "We always travelled first class abroad (together) on stud business . . . There were bank accounts and my husband and myself transferred money over when it was needed to top up the accounts . . . (By 1998) it was costing more and I was not able to ascertain why. I would ask, but I could not get to the bottom of it."

Paul Atkinson is subsequently found guilty on three charges of theft and sentenced to three years' jail. His wife Joan is jailed for a year.

THURSDAY, 25 MAY 2000

The first volume of Andrew Oldham's autobiography, Stoned, *is published by Secker & Warburg. Living in Bogotá, Colombia, for many years, he reveals it's been five years since he's touched any kind of drug, and two since he turned to Scientology.* The Independent *gives its readers the opportunity to fire some questions in his direction.*

Q: "Which of the Rolling Stones would you most like to have round to tea today?"

Andrew Oldham: "Brian Jones. When I arrived in Colombia in 1975 and realised I was home, I was so happy. I looked up at the sky and said, 'Brian, you fool. Why did you have to take it all so seriously? You should have stuck around for the good times.' Anyway, that was when I was 31, it's 26 years later and I know a little more. I'd have time for him now whereas then he just got in the way, and being young and invincible and struggling to keep this thing we'd got going, we pushed him aside and let him drown in all senses of the word. Brian was obviously seriously disturbed. So was I, but less seriously."

Q: "Are you as bad a man as you'd have people think?"

Andrew Oldham: "I've never set out to have myself thought of as bad. I just lay the facts out as flat data. Truculent, obstinate, teenage, excessive . . . yes. What do you expect from a 21-year-old kid driving around in a Phantom V who hasn't paid his taxes? But bad? Not at all. My universe is clear and I'm an asset to it."

Q: "Would you let your daughter marry a Rolling Stone?"

Andrew Oldham: "I was sure not to have daughters so as to avoid dilemmas of that sort. A friend once told me that if I'd had daughters I'd have packed them into a plane and I'd be at the gun turret aiming at all incoming genitalia."

Q: "Met any good Svengalis lately?"

Andrew Oldham: "The true Svengalis of the day are the artists who basically manage and divine themselves daily – Ricky Martin, Madonna, Tom Cruise, Mariah Carey are some. This brand of artist all have business antenna that make your actual Svengali, such as the likes of Malcolm McLaren and those who followed me, redundant."

FRIDAY, 26 MAY 2000

"JAGGER SINGS FAREWELL TO HIS MOTHER"

The funeral of Mrs Eva Jagger, 87, takes place at St Andrew's Church in Ham, Surrey. Ron, Charlie and Keith sing 'Morning Has Broken', while Mick joins his brother Chris for a version of 'Will The Circle Be Unbroken'. Keith had flown in from New York early in the morning to join the 200 mourners.

A spokesman: "Keith is extremely upset as well, because he was very close to Eva. He has known her a long time."

On a lighter note, Bill Wyman reveals that he's always had a "little complex" about his height (he's 5' 7"), but remains bullish about his general health.

Bill: "I've always been skinny. I always weighed about eight stone, into the Seventies and early Eighties. I'm up to about 10 now and starting to get a little tum. I'm not too keen on it, but I haven't done anything about it. I've never had a fitness routine. I ignore all that. I don't look after my diet, either. Eat red meat. Crisps for lunch. Don't do any of that vitamin thing. I just have whatever I fancy – bars of chocolate, cream cakes, whatever. 'You bastard!' that's what everyone says. I'm very healthy. Never been in hospital in my life, only for an appendix when I was a kid. I've been smoking since I was 17 – I'm 63 now – no problems. My chest is clear. It's something in the genes."

Bill is also revelling in the exotica of everyday life.

Bill: "I love to do ordinary things. I change the light bulbs, do a bit of hoovering, change the toilet rolls. If you don't, you end up with nothing to do. You get bored. Get into alcohol, drugs or whatever. Everything flows nicely. I don't need anything else. Houses, cars, I don't adorn myself with riches. My greatest achievement is my family. I have felt, for a long time, at peace with myself. I don't have any fears of death. I don't want to die, but when the time comes, it'll happen. I'm comfortable in myself. I just wish most people were like that. If everybody felt like I feel, there wouldn't be any problems in the world. Or wars. Just the joy of being alive. I just enjoy every part of it. It sounds pretentious, but in all sincerity, I believe that. What more could I need in my life?"

He does, however, rue the day he stopped trying to kick smoking.
Bill: "I started 46 years ago, and I smoke 40 a day. I gave up four years ago for eight days, and then I was stupid and had one. I have every intention of giving up, and I have all those bloody patches and things, but I get all dizzy and almost hallucinate. It is a drug, after all. I see colours I haven't noticed before. A bit more oxygen to my brain, I suppose! But it's not healthy. I should stop as soon as possible."

JUNE 2000

Brian Jones' Fan Club members are notified that Alastair and Harriet Johns, the current owners of Cotchford Farm, intend to sell tiles from the pool where Brian drowned.
"Over the years they have had a constant battle with frost affecting the tiles on the side of the pool in winter. Many tiles fall off and it has become a problem having to cement them back every spring. We have been asked to advertise the tiles for sale to fan club members when work commences on replacing them this summer. We have given much thought to this idea, and although there will undoubtedly be some who feel the idea is macabre, we feel that it is another opportunity to own something connected so closely with Brian."
James Phelge (Honorary Member): "We are selling the tiles to generate money for a statue of Brian to be erected in his hometown of Cheltenham. We are not profiting from his death. They are just tiles after all – just concrete that would otherwise have ended up in the rubbish."

It is announced that Jerry Hall is to star in The Graduate *on a West End stage later in the year. The lead role of Mrs Robinson involves her appearing nude.*
The aspiring actress also reveals that Mick – now stepping out with Ortensia Visconti, niece of Italian film director Luciano Visconti – has bought the mansion next door to her on Richmond Hill.
Jerry Hall: "Mick and I love each other, and we're great friends. He's a wonderful person. He's not a mean person. He's a good father, he's clever, he's funny, he's attractive, he's great to be with. We are always laughing. But I'm single and I'm independent. And I'm certainly much happier now."

433

Jerry Hall: "It takes two to make a marriage work and I am more than willing to share the blame for why it didn't work. He's very nice to me, he's a very nice person. Just because you divorce someone it doesn't turn them into a horrible person. They've said so many really mean things about him in the papers. I had people come up and say that I've inspired them to try and have a friendly divorce, and that's quite a good thing."

Mick: "I've never been deeply, madly in love. I'm just not an emotional person."

THURSDAY, 29 JUNE 2000

"BOOZE NEARLY KILLED ME"

Ronnie checks into the £4,000-a-week rehabilitation clinic, The Priory, in West London. He confesses to downing two or three bottles of Vodka a day, washed down with copious amounts of Guinness, and was recently spotted binge-drinking at Ascot and Wimbledon.

Ron: "My kids were like, 'Dad, you've got to do something.' None of us gets out of here alive, but I do realise I was tearing the backside out of it . . . I'd better nip it in the bud or I may be dead in six months."

MONDAY, 3 JULY 2000

Mick attends the wedding of his first daughter, Karis, to Jonathan Watson on an island in San Francisco Bay. Also in attendance are Karis' mother Marsha Hunt, Mick's father Mr Joe Jagger, Jerry Hall and their three children, Elizabeth, James and Georgia, and Mick's daughter from his marriage to Bianca, Jade Jagger.

A friend: "It was incredibly romantic. I saw Mick wipe away tears."

TUESDAY, 11 JULY 2000

After two weeks in the clinic, and three-and-a-half weeks without a drink, Ronnie talks about his battle to Alison Boshoff (of the Daily Mail*).*

Ron: "I woke up one day and thought I should check myself into hospital. I was really drunk at Ascot, but in the back of my mind, I thought, 'I can't keep this up – I've got to stop while I've still got my health.' They said it was a good thing I did because if I had carried on at that rate for the next six months, I may have died. They were surprised at what good shape I was in. The only weakness they could find was the liver. If I give it a break, they think it will mend."

He maintains that it was the Stones' recent tour that finished him.

Ron: "I do think I was an alcoholic. I never went anywhere without a drink. It was my little crutch. I was on Guinness all day, then on to the hard stuff before showtime and then afterwards, all night, every night, thrashing it. Then it's hard when you come off tour.

"I miss the taste of it. It's lovely stuff . . . I don't regret the coke. I had a great innings on that. The thing is they all turn you into a depressive in the end. You think you are getting high, but actually you are just boring everyone to tears."

Keith sends a Fifties cartoon fax: "Rehab is for quitters. Welcome home, Love Keith."

A friend: "Ronnie will be taking it extremely easy for the next few weeks. He's not as young as he used to be and realised his drinking was out of hand. It will be hard for him to obey the doctor's orders, especially with a pub at the end of his garden, but he's determined to try."

TUESDAY, 18 JULY 2000

It is announced that Ron has begun to dismantle the pub he'd built at his home in County Kildare, Ireland, where the draught Guinness had flowed freely on tap.

Guinness spokesman: "Ronnie called to cancel deliveries. He also wanted the old kegs picked up and the beer taps removed."

Months later, it is reported that Ron has turned to organic gardening in a bid to overcome his battle with the booze.

TUESDAY, 1 AUGUST 2000

A court rules that Mick must reveal his finances in a net worth statement in the ongoing child support case relating to his new son, Lucas.

David Kirshblum (Manhattan Family Court Examiner): "Show me the money."

WEDNESDAY, 7 FEBRUARY 2001

The court rules that Mick must pay an "undisclosed amount" towards the upkeep of his son, Lucas, until the boy reaches the age of 21.

Luciana Morad: "I'm glad this is over. I feel I've done the right thing for my son."

TUESDAY, 24 APRIL 2001

Ronnie, owner of a 75-acre stud farm in County Kildare, Ireland, sees one of his mares, Zayta, win her first chase. The pursuit is also proving good for his health.
Ron. "I love to go to Ireland, the peacefulness around the horses does a lot for the constitution."
Jessica Harrington (trainer): "Ronnie gets a serious kick out of his horses, which says a lot for a man who has seen and done so much in his life."

TUESDAY, 8 MAY 2001

"JAGGER IS DAD IN A MILLION"

Luciana Morad: "Lucas is still a little shy around Mick since they haven't spent a lot of time together. I wish he could see his dad every day. Right now, Mick only sees Lucas when I go to London or we meet in New York. But Mick is a great father – whenever I need his advice, he's only a phone call away."

And, guess what, he's a chip off the old block.
Luciana Morad: "He loves pretty girls, especially dark-haired ones. If he's in a room with eight-year-old girls, you can't drag him away."

MONDAY, 4 JUNE 2001

Charlie Watts, "the most handsome Englishman of his generation", according to Pete Clark in the Evening Standard, *plays the first night of a two-week stint with his new 10-piece group at Ronnie Scott's club in Soho, London.*
Q: "Are the Stones coming?"
Charlie: "I might leave their names on the door."

He also inadvertently lets slip the fact that the Stones are likely to tour in 2002.
Charlie: "This is the most adventurous thing I've ever tried. Before, I'd always said, 'No, ooh no, no,' but this time when it came up, I said that I would try it. Also, at the time that I accepted, I didn't know that the Stones would be going on the road next year. It's like, as soon as you say you are going on holiday, something important comes up. If you never say you're going on holiday, nothing ever happens."

And that great leadership battle?
Charlie: "Well, (Mick's) not, actually. He might say the most, but he's not the leader."

Getting older . . .

Charlie: "I've always been comfortable with whatever age I'm at, and now I'm about to be 60. But I do feel I'm getting a bit old for whatever it's called that I do for a living."

Q: "But you can't still do it for the money?"

Charlie: "Oh, I do do it for the money!"

Ron: "Every so often, I get a call from Charlie pleading: 'Ronnie, we've got to get back on tour. We need to pay for these bloody horses!'"

Charlie: "There's a lot more interesting people around than rock'n'roll bands. There's this huge cult grown up around rock'n'roll, but I never saw it myself. I don't mean I never saw it going on, I mean I just didn't get it.

"All the musicians I love look beautiful. The way a man looks as he plays, his style, is very important to me.

> Marvin Gaye: The coolest-looking man – the epitome of a black American.
>
> Elvin Jones: Beautiful!
>
> Duke Ellington: Stylish.
>
> Kenny Clarke: Chic, like Fred Astaire."

Charlie: "I hate doing things like this: interviews, videos, pictures, all of it. I'd prefer Keith to do it for me, but he can't really, can he?"

No, because Charlie has a record to plug, the Charlie Watts/Jim Keltner Project.

Charlie: "I don't know how to judge this record, really. I just find I like it, but I don't know why because it's not what I normally like. Each time I've done a recording I could say, 'Well, I don't care if you don't like it because Gershwin wrote that beautiful song and I think we do it beautifully.' Whereas with this, I don't know what to think. It's kind of uncharted territory. But I'd like to think of it as sounding 'tomorrow' rather than 'yesterday'."

Charlie: "My wife doesn't like it, though," he smiles. "She prefers the Stones."

SATURDAY, 16 JUNE 2001

Promoting his latest Bill Wyman & The Rhythm Kings' CD, Double Bill, *Bill receives a jolt of nostalgia when Angela Hagen steams in with one of those 'What's your favourite colour?' type pieces for the* Daily Mirror.

Favourite Films: "I rarely go to the cinema because people are always coming up to me wanting to talk. But *Gladiator* was amazing and I also liked *Enigma*, which was Mick's film."

Favourite TV: "I do like *Panorama*, *Newsnight* and documentaries about early cultures or UFOs. I'll also watch any football, no matter who's playing, or cricket. I like that *Time Team* programme too because that's about archaeology and history, which are my real passions."

Favourite Food: "Lamb cutlets with mint sauce and mashed potatoes – you can't beat it, especially with a nice drop of red wine."

Favourite Friend: "Suzanne. Once we got married and had kiddies I didn't even look at other girls. I still don't. Suzanne is the most positive woman I've ever met. And I've never been happier in my life."

Favourite Hobbies: "I love watching out for UFOs. I think I saw one 18 months ago in the south of France. We spotted this orange disc hovering in the sky for half-an-hour and I filmed it with a movie camera. I also like metal detecting. I've found more than 200 old coins, 17 Roman brooches and an axe blade from 1700 BC."

Favourite Book: "I'm reading *The Day After Roswell*. The US government has always denied any incidents with UFOs at Roswell, except it turns out that they've got millions of documents relating to them and this book is all about that."

SUNDAY, 1 JULY 2001

It is announced that Ronnie Wood is working on an epic painting of A-list patrons of London's celebrated restaurant, The Ivy. The 15'×8' work, titled 'London Dining', executed in the manner of the grand Victorian-era society scene, was commissioned by theatrical impresario Andrew Lloyd Webber. Among those depicted are Elizabeth Hurley and Hugh Grant, Elton John, Pet Shop Boy Neil Tennant and broadcaster, Janet Street-Porter.

Andrew Lloyd Webber: "I thought it would be difficult to persuade them to give up their time and sit for an artist unless he or she was, well, a bit exotic."

Ron: "I always had the knack but was never sure what direction it would take. As it turned out, the music side of things turned out well but my art has never been far away and I have been painting regularly all my life. Although we had never met before, we soon got talking and Andrew told me about The Ivy project. It appealed to me enormously, so I accepted the challenge."

THURSDAY, 23 AUGUST 2001

Mick appears on the cover of the latest issue of Saga, *the magazine for the over-50s.* "His face is heavily creased, grey is emerging deep amid hair dye and the body looks as if it has been through a few too many debilitating diets. But, at 58, Jagger is still taking on challenges."

Mick: "I don't think enjoying life is an exclusive prerogative of young people. I think it's stupid to behave like you're 17. But that doesn't mean to say you have to be an old fart sitting in the pub talking about what happened in the Sixties."

Paul Bach (editor): "Some of our detractors wrongly think that *Saga* relates to old age and feebleness. But if you do your sums you will quickly realise that people of 60 or 70 would have been in their teens themselves when Jagger was beginning to make his mark on the world."

MONDAY, 24 SEPTEMBER 2001

Enigma, *Mick's production début, premieres in London. A film version of the Robert Harris novel, the movie stars Kate Winslet and Dougray Scott.*

Mick: "I didn't want to make teenage comedies, and I didn't want to make really trashy films. I wanted to make films that were a bit challenging. I thought this was a good example of that . . . I'd have loved to have been all the parts. I could have done them all brilliantly. There's no doubt about that. But I wasn't allowed. That bloody director!"

Mick: "I find the business side of it all boring and ghastly. I just wanted to make the movie. I put in seed money, not heavy stuff. I made a rule when I started this that I was not going to be heavy-handed. I did not want to come on to the set very often. And when I did, I wanted to be encouraging. Since it was my idea, it is very tempting to have a lot to say. But I have learned when to keep my mouth shut. I believe in British films and British talent. We've had some of the best technicians and film crews around for years. We are now getting a crop of strong young actors coming through who are acceptable to Americans. I am not against having an American actor in any film, so long as they are good. Where it goes wrong is having to employ an American who is no good just to keep the financiers happy."

THURSDAY, 4 OCTOBER 2001

"STONE AGE SURVIVOR"

Bill's latest book, Bill Wyman's Blues Odyssey: A Journey To Music's

Heart And Soul *is published. He explains the idea behind the project to Kieron Grant of the* Toronto Sun.
Bill: "I think as a musician, researching and writing about the history of the blues lends this book a bit more credence. I played with a lot of these people, recorded with them and saw them live. I just wanted to write a book that everybody could read and make it totally illustrative. You see where the railways were, where Highway 61 was. It gives it a whole new interesting way of getting into it. It de-mystifies it."

Bill also reveals that his favourite blues track is Howlin' Wolf's 'Going Down Slow'.
Bill: "It's him on his deathbed and the vocals and playing on it are just amazing."

And his perfect blues combo?
Bill: "I would have Little Walter on harmonica, Howlin' Wolf on vocals and guitar (or maybe harmonica) and Muddy Waters playing guitar behind him. I'd play bass and I'd have Georgie Fame on organ and James P. Johnson on piano."

But in promoting 'real music', Bill launches a tirade against the music industry within earshot of Daily Mail *journalist Tony Bonnici.*
Bill: "Record companies see one success and everyone jumps on the bandwagon. It's become obsessive and there's no room for anything else. The industry is obsessed with youth. They are not real musicians. They are just pretty young people someone has discovered. They don't write the songs they sing, most of the time they mime when performing live and most can't play an instrument.

"You would be surprised just how many people agree with me, but they won't talk about it, because they are afraid of adverse publicity because these bands line the pockets of record industry bosses. If you can't perform live you should go and get another job. I saw a bit of Hear'Say on TV once. They were just five plumpish boys and girls who were miming. I didn't see any creativity. At least when I see Robbie Williams, I think he can sing and play an instrument."

Mick is inclined to agree, as David Fricke finds out.
Q: "Is pop music interesting to you now?"
Mick: "Not really."
Q: "What's missing?"
Mick: "Outrageous personalities with a great tune and a different sound. I'm sure one will crop up soon. I'm very patient. Everyone said, 'You

must hear the Ryan Adams record.' I thought it was all right. It's very old-fashioned music. But it is appealing . . . Pop music is the kind of thing you catch yourself whistling in the bath: 'Oh, it's the Cher record! I'm whistling the Backstreet Boys! Oh, fuck!' Everyone does it, and it's cool, because no one's listening – hopefully."

Even the Stones' ex-manager weighs in.
Andrew Oldham: "A group without songs is an aeroplane without parachutes. As for advice, if you are not prepared to get screwed the first time around and remain standing, then find another game. The system functions on giving you one slice of the cake and then inviting you to eat away at yours. Of course, if I was 19, I'd jump right in again regardless."

Onto more important matters, does Bill Wyman care about getting old?
Bill: "It doesn't bother me at all."

But you do dye your hair, don't you?
Bill: "Of course I do. I don't know why, it just looks better. My greyness is in patches. Mainly round the back. And then there are other bits that aren't and it's sort of blotchy, that's the trouble. I'd end up like a dalmatian dog."

Unlike the four remaining Stones, Bill at least comes clean about his political persuasions – he admits to voting Tory.
Bill: "Yeah, because I remember what Labour's all about. I remember having to leave the country in '71 because tax was at 90 per cent. Never trust 'em. I vote Tory because that's where I come from."

With the bit between her teeth, Observer *writer Sabine Durrant wonders what Bill would think if his five-year-old daughter Katie was to date a 57-year-old in eight years' time?* ·
Bill: "Won't happen because my Katie won't start going to pubs and clubs and night habitats when she's 10, so when she's 14 she won't look like a 20-year-old. That's the difference. I want them to be as normal as possible. I never encouraged my son to be a drummer or guitarist. I let him do what he wanted. And he did really well. He got 10 O-levels, two A-levels, and a degree, with honours, in business studies."

SATURDAY, 20 OCTOBER 2001

Mick, who has just sold his New York apartment, performs 'Miss You' and 'Salt Of The Earth', with Keith at the Concert For New York City, held at Madison

Square Garden, to benefit the firemen killed in the September 11 catastrophe.
Mick (to crowd): "If there's anything to be learned from this, it's that you don't fuck with New York."
Mick: "I don't know why 'Salt Of The Earth' just jumped into my head because we haven't done it very much, but I thought it was good for the moment. 'Miss You' was a song about being in New York. It seemed to work out."
Mick: "I was very pleased to do it because it was, first of all, something I felt close to and a good cause. It also sounded like it was going to be a fun evening. I lived there for a long time so I have a huge sympathy with the town. I identify with it perhaps more than any other city in the United States. You feel a great closeness especially when there's trouble. I mean I was in New York from the mid-Seventies onwards when it was really terrible – garbage piled high in the streets, and you didn't like walking around. Now it's slightly on the up-and-up."

Keith joins him by surprise.
Mick: "He decided he wanted to do it at the last minute and I always wanted to do it with him so I was very pleased. I gave him a ring and said, 'It's all coming together,' because the thing about these events, you never know what they're going to be like. It's a bit hit-and-miss sometimes."
Keith: "Mick and I were wondering what songs to play, and Mick said, 'Oh, how perfect would it be for 'Salt Of The Earth' and I said, 'I can't think of a better one, Mick.' It seemed like it was written for the occasion . . . Over my years living in New York, I know a lot of those guys. Cops and firemen, they're some of our biggest fans. If I'm walking in New York City and it's (raining), I've often been picked up by the cops. They say, 'Hey, Keith, wanna lift?' I love New York, and New York loves me."

WEDNESDAY, 24 OCTOBER 2001

Bill celebrates his 65th birthday. He is now eligible for a concessionary bus pass and a state pension.
Bill: "I have to run a tight ship. I've got three little girls coming through school. That's going to cost me 20 grand a year, and it ain't going to come from Stones' royalties. They reduce all the time because fewer people are buying the old stuff."

He is also out and about with the Rhythm Kings, but that's not going to swell his bank balance.
Bill: "We don't do this to make money or to do a career move. We do it

because we love playing the music . . . It's a 12-piece band, so with travel, food and the hotels there's not much left."

FRIDAY, 2 NOVEMBER 2001

Keith's manager Jane Rose gives the strongest hint yet that the Stones are set to play a 40th anniversary tour in 2002. The pair already have, she says, "a bunch of ideas".
Jane Rose: "They're in discussions, which is step one. Nothing is confirmed. Even in the planning it's not confirmed. They're just talking about it. Things look good."

For the time being, though, Keith, a compulsive bibliophile, is currently reading James A. Michener's Alaska *while he waits for Mick to get his solo album out.*
Keith: "I don't know anything about the place, but at least I now know a little bit. The last author I read was Dostoevsky. I like Dashiell Hammett, who I think is a brilliant writer. And Raymond Chandler. I read, like, four books at once. I read everything. It's the same with music. I listen to Mozart, and I listen to AC/DC."

MONDAY, 19 NOVEMBER 2001

Mick's fourth solo LP, Goddess In The Doorway, *is released.*
Mick: "The Goddess is the ideal woman. She is the one who is tantalising you. In Greek mythology, she is like the siren, she is very dangerous, she is very beautiful, she comes and goes at her own will, so she is very tantalising. She is very difficult to find, when you want to see her. She is like the elusive woman. She is never gettable, she is always a little bit out of reach. Then some women are always there and they never go away."

One song, 'Don't Call Me Up', is immediately linked to Mick's recent domestic troubles.
Mick: "Well, you can put any interpretation on it you want, but actually it was written before all the press about it started rolling. People like to put their own gloss on it, so that's nice. You can interpret it any way you want. But that is actually the oldest song. I wrote that halfway through the last Rolling Stones tour."

A new website, mickjagger.com is launched at Virgin's behest in a bid to make Mick more palatable to the teenage market. It claims: "Over the years, Mick Jagger has been many things . . . rock superstar, sex symbol, cultural revolutionary, musical poet, tabloid subject and all-around pop culture provocateur."

Bernard Doherty (PR): "Mick logs on all the time when he is bored on tour. He spent two years on the road writing these songs and decided to record them in Paris, but we all know these days that even he can't just send a single to the radio and hope they play it."

The promotion inevitably takes in an internet Q&A . . .
Q: "How do you compare the sound and style of it with your previous work?"
Mick: "It's a contemporary record without being slavishly trendy."
Q: "What do the other Stones think about it?"
Mick: "Charlie said he thought it was a bit pop. Ronnie liked it very much. But I haven't heard from Keith yet. I'm not holding my breath."
Q: "Any special vocal workouts to maintain your voice?"
Mick: "I don't drink alcohol very much. And I don't smoke, which is, I guess, pretty sensible for a singer."

Several big name celebs are roped in to help. Bono lends a hand on 'Joy' . . .
Mick: "When you've done so many records for so many years, you have to give young people a go."

But was 'Joy' written with Bono in mind?
Mick: "No. I've known Bono since I can't remember. We've always had singsongs. When I'd done 'Joy' – though I hadn't finished all the vocals – I thought it would be great to do with him. U2 were playing in Cologne, so I took my little recording system to his hotel room and we did it."

Lenny Kravitz helps out on 'God Gave Me Everything'.
Mick: "He wrote the chord structure and then we wrote the top lines together. I said, 'Do you have any lyric ideas?' He said, 'Absolutely none.' So I went into a corner in his *Clockwork Orange* house in Miami, wrote the lyrics in about ten minutes, and said, 'Well, I hope this is going to do.'"

'Hideaway' benefits from the assistance of Wyclef Jean.
Mick: "That started in the Sam Cooke style, but when we did the demo it got more dancey and Al Green-like. I thought that Wyclef (Jean), who I'd met quite a bit and hung out with, would do it slightly differently – he changed it somewhat, but he kept it in the Al Green groove."

Also audible are two not-yet-so-famous names, his two youngest daughters, Elizabeth and Georgia Jagger.
Mick: "I wrote 'Brand New Set Of Rules' sitting on my bed one evening.

It's a very simple song with a very innocent premise. It's sweet and I have my two daughters singing background on it. They sing marvellously in tune."

There had been suggestions that the album was going to be heavily accented towards R&B.
Mick: "Not really. I've never met with (top R&B producer) Timbaland. I mean I like his beats and all that, but I never met with him about it. I do know Missy Elliott, and I did ask her if she wanted to do a rap (on 'Hide-away'), but she never showed up. That's what Missy's like."

Did he miss Keith?
Mick: "Not really. I work with a lot of good people on this record. I don't really miss anybody. I know that I'm going to work with the Stones guys again, so I'm happy doing this . . . It's a lot easier without the so-called democracy. Democracy in music is not always a good thing."

Within a week, it is reported that the album has sold in handfuls rather than in the expected thousands.
Mick: "Well, I'm not going to live or die by the record sales. You want three things when you do something, and you want to be pleased with the result. You don't want to put out something you're not happy with which can happen. You want critics and friends to like it – people that actually listen and take it in. And thirdly you want some kind of commercial success."
Keith: "He's not very good without me, is he?"

The title prompts some to ponder Mick's largely hidden spiritual side.
Mick: "I have a spiritual side. Everyone has one . . . I've written about it before in songs like 'Just Wanna See His Face' and 'Shine A Light' (both on *Exile On Main Street*). 'Joy' is more fleshed out. It is about the joy of creation, inspiring you to a love of God."

Perhaps, asks his Dotmusic inquisitor, it is time to make a blues record?
Mick: "I would love to do a blues record, either with the Rolling Stones or on my own. But the songwriting limitations upon the blues are rather too much of a structure, you know, a real forced-into-a-corner kind of style. It's difficult to be forward-looking in that genre, and that's a really tough one. I like to be a little bit contemporary."

With the band's 40th anniversary approaching, Mick is asked whether it's time for the Stones to assemble their own Anthology *project.*
Mick: "I think that would be interesting for some people. For others it

would be the ultimate in boredom. I'm interested in hearing the result, but sifting through the tapes? I mean, no! None of the Rolling Stones are all that interested. The only one who liked that kind of stuff was Bill; he had that librarian sort of mentality. He's the diary-keeper."

Invariably, some journalists attempt to draw Mick on his personal life. Elizabeth Vargas from ABCNews.com fires away on a variety of private matters.
Those seven children . . .
Mick: "I think you play good cop, bad cop with your children, to a certain extent. On some occasions you've got to be quite disciplinarian and other occasions you've got to be easygoing."

Sex . . .
Mick: "It's always a difficult subject telling your children about sex. I don't think you can sit them down and tell them everything about sex in one go. You know, you just tell them sort of little things as you go along and don't make it a big deal."

Women . . .
Mick: "In our society, we're supposed to be monogamous, but we're not. In other societies, you don't have to be monogamous, and we're all human beings, so supposedly we've evolved all these different systems for dealing with this. It's very odd, the relationships that men have with women . . . After all this time, men still like to find women mysterious."

Ever been truly in love?
Mick: "I really can't answer that question."

Going to marry again?
Mick: "You never want to say never. Whatever you say is going to be wrong, isn't it?"

Thinking of retirement?
Mick: "I think I can write songs for quite a long time. I like to perform in a very physical way. I don't know how long I'll be able to do that."

Keith explains his parenting skills elsewhere.
Keith: " 'Do as I say, don't do as I did,' and I give them a few good reasons why not. But they're smarter than that, their mother raised them right."

446

THURSDAY, 22 NOVEMBER 2001

A documentary, Being Mick, *made by Mick's own production company, is broadcast by Channel 4.*
Q: "Does any theme connect all the films you'd like to make?"
Mick: "They're all hopefully intelligent, that's the theme. But nobody wants to give you the money for them. Everybody wants lots of set pieces and explosions and sex. Nothing wrong with it, but it's just not my thing, bombs and bottoms!"

Wandering into the Stones' tape vault, where old tapes are being dug out for the following year's reissue campaign, Mick is asked how it feels to be surrounded by so much history.
Mick: "Fine! It's just like having a library and going in and getting a book out."
Q: "Proud?"
Mick: "I suppose you do. It's not my first emotion. What we're doing here (now) is what I'm more interested in."
Q: "Are you a moral person?"
Mick: "Yeah, but I think like most people, my morals tend to be pretty fuzzy . . . Yeah, I have values for relationships, but I'm not gonna talk about them. I don't necessarily believe that for all people, marriage is the perfect state. I guess I have a pretty ordinary, bohemian attitude towards love and marriage. You always have a go at it, try things, and sometimes they work and sometimes they don't."

Pete Townshend, who is shown adding some incendiary guitar to 'Gun' during the Goddess *sessions, proffers some neighbourly advice.*
Pete Townshend: "If I've got meetings in London now, I just get on the fucking train! Sometimes people engage me in inane conversations. But they're very, very short inane conversations. If you had a security guard with you, you should do it one day because it is so fast . . . it's like doing a helicopter run."
Mick: "Do they have carriages with six people?"

Jade, who is wrongly supposed to have introduced her father to model Sophie Dahl, also drops by.
Jade Jagger: "See you later, dad. Don't bring any of those women. Nobody younger than me, please!"

Mick is shown gesticulating wildly as he goes for another vocal take.
Q: "How important is all the physical stuff you do while you're singing?"

447

Mick: "I don't have to. It's emotive. It's part of the emotion. You've got to get into the character."

FRIDAY, 30 NOVEMBER 2001

George Harrison dies.

Keith: "He was really a lovely guy. What he didn't need was . . . the knifing. I think he probably would've beaten the cancer if it wasn't for the blade. John was my first mate among them, because George was a bit quiet. Now I think, 'One by gun, one by knife.' For such pleasant guys, who made such beautiful music and never did harm to anybody, to have to go through that kind of violence – I mean, I'm used to it. I've been stabbed several times, and the bullet wounds are healing.

"George left his mark, man. I don't think I can say anything else except, 'George: Miss you. Bless you. And we're still listening to you.'"

DECEMBER 2001

Ron Wood releases yet another solo album, Not For Beginners. *Recorded in his Kingston home studio, it features guest appearances from Rod Stewart, Kelly Jones from the Stereophonics, various siblings – and, as he tells Will Hodgkinson in* The Guardian, *Bob Dylan.*

Ron: "I was working on (Bob Dylan's) album. Every day he'd have about 10 different songs, and I'd say, 'That's great, let's cut 'em!' While we were at it, we cut a few of mine. He's a Gemini, like me, so I understand him more than most people, who think he's this freak who says nothing. You have to get him in a certain frame of mind, then he's a funny guy."

Ron: "Instead of me working with a Bernard Fowler or a Bobby Womack, this is totally my brainchild. There's lots of slide on it and lots of pedal steel, much more than I've ever done before on one album, and about every four tracks, there's an instrumental which breaks it up nicely. (My son) Jessie plays guitar on a lot of the tracks, and Leah, my daughter, sings on 'This Little Heart'. She's got a great voice and features on another song that I dug up from the past called 'Leaving Here'. I recorded that with my first group, The Birds.

"I'd rate this right up there with my first album, *I've Got My Own Album To Do*. Keith said to me, 'You'll never make an album as good as *I've Got My Own Album To Do*,' so I can't wait for him to hear this. I think he might even like it."

Uncut magazine publishes a list of the Top 40 Rolling Stones songs as chosen by a celebrity panel that includes Sir Bob Geldof, Marc Almond, Mick Hucknall, Ian Astbury and film director Steven Soderbergh.

1 'Gimme Shelter'
2 'Street Fighting Man'
3 'Sympathy For The Devil'
4 '(I Can't Get No) Satisfaction'
5 'Tumbling Dice'
6 'Paint It Black'
7 '19th Nervous Breakdown'
8 'Jumpin' Jack Flash'
9 'Play With Fire'
10 'We Love You'

Ronnie goes for 'Sister Morphine'; Mick backs the winner, 'Gimme Shelter'.

FRIDAY, 7 DECEMBER 2001

"POLICE MISTAKE STONES STAR FOR STONED JUNKIE"

It is reported that Keith Richards' limo was surrounded by six armed guards at the New York premiere of Gosford Park.

Keith: "It turned out that the limo was thought to have been stolen, but you should have heard the rumours at the theatre. In the crowd behind us, my wife Patti and I could hear these gossips saying, 'Oh, isn't it a shame Keith is back on the smack?' We just turned around and said, 'Hey, you idiots, we're sitting right in front of you. Now shut up and let us watch the movie.'"

TUESDAY, 7 MAY 2002

The Stones announce what is widely expected to be their last ever world tour, a jaunt that neatly coincides with their 40th anniversary. As the band hover in an airship high above Van Courtland Park in New York's Bronx district, details circulate about the format for the shows – which take in a variety of different sized venues.

Keith: "It's the Fruit Of The Loom tour – small, medium and large (venues) . . . It's fun to play clubs and not play the same size all the time. We can play stuff that doesn't work in stadiums. Garage (rock)."

Mick is reminded of his 1972 promise to "commit suicide" if he was still singing 'Satisfaction' at 40.
Mick: "Who says we're going to do 'Satisfaction'? That was cheap."

There are complaints that ticket prices are fixed at prohibitively high prices, from $50 to $90, with around 5 per cent of the seats set aside as deluxe "gold circle" tickets.
Paul McCartney: "Mick doesn't exactly need the money, does he?"
Mick: "There's more of us."

SATURDAY, 15 JUNE 2002

It is announced that Mick is to receive a knighthood in the Queen's Birthday Honours list on the recommendation of Prime Minister Tony Blair.
Mick: "Yes, the rumours are true. Today I've become a knight. Totally unexpected. I've been teased mercilessly ever since the rumours started – people waving plastic swords around and kneeling in front of me. Gabriel now thinks I have to wear chain-link body armour every day!"

Officially speaking, though . . .
Mick: "It's great recognition of what the band's achievements have been over the years we've been together . . . It's nice but it's something you should wear very lightly. You should learn to accept compliments grace-fully, but that doesn't mean to say that you should become swollen-headed or put on airs and graces."
Keith: "I have to revert to a Stones point of view. These are the guys who tried to put us in jail in the Sixties and then you're taking a minor honour. Also, to get a call from Mick saying, 'Tony Blair insists I take it' – this is a way to present it to me? . . . It's anti-respect to the Stones. It would have been a smarter move to say thanks, but no thanks. After being abused by Her Majesty's Government for so many years, being hounded almost out of existence, I found it weird that he'd want to take a badge."

But there is a price . . .
Keith: "Within the Stones, it's probably made him buckle down a bit more because he's being disapproved of . . . We have other names for him apart from Sir."

TUESDAY, 3 SEPTEMBER 2002

The Stones' year-long Licks tour across four continents kicks off at the Fleet Centre in Boston.
Keith: "I love Boston. What a place to warm up in!"

The band throw in an unexpected version of The O'Jays' 'Love Train'.
Mick: "We've never let that one out in public before. That was fun."
Keith: "My biggest addiction, more than heroin, is the stage and the audience. That buzz – it calls you every time."

The show is even more remarkable for Ronnie, for whom "recovery has become reality".
Ron: "I'm looking at life through a straight viewpoint now. That was my first gig the other night that I'd done straight and it was a real eye-opener."
Keith: "Ronnie was getting a bit out there, and to his credit he recognised it himself. I've been amazed at his focus. He's really helping us forge this immense machine."

And he isn't the only one impressing the Stones' five-string taskmaster.
Keith: "There's this amazing spark of total opposites that we have, and, like many people, Mick has lots of sides, not just the one he shows the world. I think we've proven now that yin and yang can hang."

But there are still some games to play.
Keith: "You know, there are demons in me, 47 at last count, and the only time they get out is when we're on stage."
Mick: "(Keith) likes to make out he's still a very rebellious 59-year-old. That's all right, that's the role you play."
Keith: "I mean, I don't know the man (Mick) for nothing. Once in a while he needs to be put in his place. We've known each other since we were four years old. We are very different people in many ways. We know when to stay apart and when to let things bring us together. We can't get divorced. You can get rid of the old lady, but I can't get rid of Mick, and he can't get rid of me."
Charlie: "Mick and Keith are like brothers today. They argue, but you cannot get in the middle of them otherwise they'll agree. They both have definite views on things, and they both embrace strong positions."
Keith: "We couldn't get divorced if we wanted to. We are kept together by our babies – which are all of our songs!"

THURSDAY, 26 SEPTEMBER 2002

As the Stones roll into Madison Square Garden, the band reprise the press' pet subject for the benefit of Bernard Weinraub for the New York Times.
How do you (still) do it?
Mick: "Rock'n'roll requires a certain amount of energy. You just can't do

rock'n'roll sitting on a bicycle going 10 miles an hour. You really have to wind the energy level up – that's part of the main ingredient. It's not like you have to be a brilliant musician, but you need an explosive musical energy to play rock'n'roll well. And we have that."

Keith: "I want to do it like Muddy Waters – till I drop. This is not something you retire from. It's your life. Writing songs and playing is like breathing – you don't stop."

Charlie: "I think about the age issue. It doesn't upset me when journalists talk about it. I do know that I saw Duke Ellington when he was in his 70s, and he was fabulous. And he toured every day of his life. We lead a cushy life by comparison."

MONDAY, 30 SEPTEMBER 2002

A 2-CD greatest hits set, 40 Licks, *is the first that documents all eras of the band's career on one package. It also includes four new tracks, which pleases Keith, as he tells Paul Sexton.*

Keith: "It was important to me to have cut these new songs. I really like the guys to work on new stuff before we come to rehearse, or that would mean we really hadn't done anything new, and I hate that feeling of regurgitating, like The Beach Boys or something. It worked beyond our wildest expectations."

Keith: " 'Don't Stop' is basically all Mick. He had the song when we got to Paris to record. It was a matter of me finding the guitar licks to go behind the song, rather than it just chugging along . . . A lot of what Mick and I do is fixing and touching up, writing the song in bits, assembling it on the spot. On 'Don't Stop', my job was the fairydust."

Mick: " 'Stealing My Heart' is a garagey tune, 'Keys To Your Love' is more of a soul tune, and Keith sings a slow ballad called 'Losing My Touch'."

Q: "Is that a commentary on his skills?"

Mick: "You better ask Keith!"

OCTOBER 2002

Lucas Jagger attends his first Rolling Stones show when his mother takes him to a concert in Chicago.

Luciana Morad: "He was excited and enjoyed it very much. I am very proud that Mick Jagger is the father of my son. He is so nice, law-abiding and hard working."

TUESDAY, 1 OCTOBER 2002

"YOU BETTER MOVE ON"

Keith wins a battle to divert a public footpath from his Redlands home in West Wittering, Sussex. He cites "privacy and security" as his reasons for the re-routing.
Philip Couchman (Chichester Harbour Conservancy): "We do not need to be reminded of George Harrison, who lived in a virtual fortress and was still attacked. There is a history of fans trying to get into the house and groups of fans waiting on the boundary for the occupants."
Bill Acraman (Rights Of Way committee chairman, West Sussex County Council): "Famous people, whether they are the Prime Minister or a pop star, are more vulnerable than you or I. We are well aware of what the paparazzi do. We are well aware of what nutters can do. I strongly feel we should be prepared to go the extra mile in such cases."

MONDAY, 7 OCTOBER 2002

It is announced that Mick has donated £100,000 to his old school, Dartford Grammar. It goes into the Red Rooster project for the school's Mick Jagger Centre, which encourages children to work with music from an early age. The Centre has two state-of-the-art auditoriums, a 16-track recording studio and several practice rooms.
Mick: "I believe we should encourage children to sing and play instruments from an early age. I was really impressed with the facilities and the staff when I first visited the centre and I hope that my contribution will help this great work continue and allow even more children to experience the thrill of making their own music. It is so important that they have somewhere like this where they can share their musical ideas and vision and be able to practise for as long as they like."

SATURDAY, 12 OCTOBER 2002

As the band hit Detroit, Ronnie repeats another regular on-tour mantra.
Ron: "It is a better band now. We're thinking more as a unit, from my point of view, instead of the old 'eyes-down, I'll meet you at the end' approach to songs. There's a lot of thought going into it, a lot of creative energy, and a lot of feedback from the audience. Keith and I are weaving together better than normal. I know it sounds corny, but there's something magic that's kicked in on this present tour. We've raised the bar musically."

MONDAY, 21 OCTOBER 2002

Twenty-two vintage albums from the Decca era are reissued by ABKCO, in conjunction with Universal Music, on standard CD and high-definition Super Audio Compact Disc formats.

Keith: "I was amazed. When I heard these new mixes and new mastering, I was hearing little things that we put in there that you can't hear on the originals; they've actually enhanced them. This is amazing stuff because some of that stuff is 40 years old and tape doesn't last forever. But they managed to pull it out and from that point of view I was very impressed by the new system. It was another leap in audio excellence."

Charlie: "They're fantastically remixed, very interesting. But I don't write or produce records, thank God, so I prefer our records untouched, as we do them in the studio. I don't think our records ever sound better than that first time you play them back."

Ron doesn't appear on any of them, but he doesn't let that dampen his enthusiasm.

Ron: "It's great to hear them like new, isn't it? I was listening to some of them with Keith and Charlie the other week, and we noticed all kinds of strange extra fuzz guitars and sitar."

Mick: "I'm not involved in it. I personally can't be bothered with it all."

The same day sees the publication of Bill Wyman's sumptuous new book, Rolling With The Stones.

Bill: "There are 1,500 to 2,000 items featured. I tried to keep the humorous things in there. I didn't get into private things so much this time. That gets bandied about in all those scandal books. I've got about 200 books on the Stones in my collection, and I'd say 90 per cent are based on heresay. A lot of it is gleaned from previous books that got it wrong."

Bill reckons his documentation is infallible.

Bill: "I kept diaries all that time. If you asked me to find a press clipping from Phoenix in 1966, I can go to that trunk in my archive and just pull it out. I'd pick up a programme, a badge or ticket stub and everybody else thought I was mad. They don't now."

But, as he tells Lester Middlehurst in the Daily Express, *Bill is happier still when discussing his wife, Suzanne.*

Bill: "She has made me open up emotionally. She taught me to accept someone saying, 'I love you'. I never had that as a kid. I come from a family that never showed affection and so any display of love has always been an embarrassment to me. When my children come home from school they jump on me with their arms open and give me a big hug and say, 'We love you, Daddy.' In the past, I'd have got embarrassed by that and told them to go away and play but now I say, 'You're the best huggers in the world. Give me another kiss.'

"Everybody thought I would die a death when I left the Stones because nobody could imagine me having a life without them. But the Stones were always a part of my life rather than the whole of it. Suzanne, my daughters and all my other interests are my life now. I can truly say that I have never been happier."

As if marital bliss isn't enough, a package duly arrives at Wyman's office.
Bill: ". . . a big cardboard box full of T-shirts, programmes, posters, badges. There's a little letter in there: 'Dear Bill, I thought you'd like this to add to your collection. Love, Charlie (Drummer of the Rolling Stones).'"

Has the gesture prompted any thoughts of a for-old-times'-sake get-together when the Stones play Britain in 2003?
Bill: "I don't think there'll be a Stones reunion gig. I've no desire to go raking up the past like that again."

NOVEMBER 2002

Caroline Winberg, a 17-year-old Swedish model, claims that Mick – "He is as old as my grandfather" – has been bombarding her with phone calls, requesting her presence on the band's US tour.
Mick: "This is completely untrue. We have spoken on the telephone several times. She said she was coming to the States in the autumn and asked if I could get her and her friends some tickets for a concert. To suggest I have pestered her in any way is absolutely ridiculous."

An American journalist named Bill Wyman – born in 1961, three years before George William Perks became 'Bill Wyman' – suggests that he's been approached by the ex-Stone's lawyers demanding that he desist from using the name.
Bill: "There is no legal action at all being taken . . . All I've done is ask him to make it clear he is not me when he criticises Rolling Stones books or records. If my name was Michael Caine and I was talking or writing about films, people would assume it was the actor. I just want him to make the distinction between our identities clear, that's all."

MONDAY, 2 DECEMBER 2002

The Stones announce their first British shows in four years, including dates at the 73,000-seater Twickenham Stadium, Wembley Arena and the Astoria Theatre in August 2003. The shows will form part of a 220-city European jaunt.

Mick: "We'll be doing three different shows with different formats with different songs, although I don't want to give it all away. This way we don't get stuck in a rut. Charlie and I get off on designing the sets. We're always after new things. I have been screaming and shouting for new things for the European shows – I'm like a child like that."

Ron: "It's a good test for the band, to keep us on our toes. I always love doing the clubs – but there are great advantages with the stadiums as well. Sometimes we'll do an *Exile On Main Street* evening or a *Sticky Fingers* night or a blues and reggae night."

Have the band devised any pre-gig rituals during the tour?
Keith: "I don't go in for superstition. Ronnie and I might have a game of snooker. But it would be superfluous for the Stones to discuss strategy or have a hug. With the Winos, it was important. They were different guys. I didn't mind. But with the Stones, it's like, 'Oh, do me a favour! I'm not going to fucking hug you!' "

Or grown tired of some of the old hits?
Keith: "No, they usually disappear of their own accord. That's the thing about songs – you don't have to be scared of them dying. They keep poking you in the face. The Stones have always believed in the present. But 'Jumpin' Jack Flash', 'Brown Sugar' and 'Start Me Up' are always fun to play. You gotta be a real sourpuss, mate, not to get up there and play 'Jumpin' Jack Flash' without feeling like, 'C'mon, everybody, let's go!' It's like riding a wild horse."

A standard feature of each Stones show continues to be the huge ovations for Charlie when Mick introduces him.
Keith: "Charlie's quite an enigma – the quiet conscience of the Stones. Charlie is a great English eccentric. I mean, how can you describe a guy who buys a 1936 Alfa Romeo just to look at the dashboard? Can't drive – just sits there and looks at it. He's an original, and he happens to be one of the best drummers in the world. Without a drummer as sharp as Charlie, playing would be a drag. He's very quiet – but persuasive. It's very rare that Charlie offers an opinion. If he does, you listen. Mick and I fall back on Charlie more than would be apparent."

Q: "Describe the state of your friendship with Mick. Is friendship the right word?"

Keith: "Absolutely. It's a very deep one. The fact that we squabble is proof of it. It goes back to the fact that I'm an only child. He's one of the few people I know from my childhood. He is a brother. And you know what brothers are like, especially ones who work together. In a way, we need to provoke each other, to find out the gaps and see if we're on board together . . . He'll never lie about in a hammock, just hanging out. Mick has to dictate to life. He wants to control it. To me, life is a wild animal. You hope to deal with it when it leaps at you. That is the most marked difference between us."

Not forgetting, of course, Mick's endless stream of phone calls.
Mick: "There's the ex-wife, then there's the ex-ex-wife, then there's . . ."

JANUARY 2003

As America and Britain prepare for war, Keith pitches in.
Keith: "I say to Osama and the boys, 'Bring it on, evaporate me.' If it gets to the stage where these guys are dictating if we rock or not, then forget about it."

Drugs.
Keith: "I have no problems with drugs, but I have problems with people who deal them. If you didn't have to go down to the bloody gutter to get it, and meet the people who live there, it wouldn't be so bad."

SATURDAY, 18 JANUARY 2003

Cable network HBO broadcasts the Stones' Madison Square Garden show. Several days earlier, the band promote the tie-in with a ten-minute satellite interview from Montreal, Canada.
Q: "Mr Jagger, when I was in high school, about 1970, I heard you interviewed on the radio. You said that you couldn't imagine that when you were 30 years old, you'd still be up on a stage singing '(I Can't Get No) Satisfaction' . . ."
Mick: "What a question to start with . . . I didn't hear you, I'm sorry."
Q: "What's the difference between you and other Sixties bands where so many of the members have died?"
Keith: "We're alive."

Q: "So much has been written about you. Has any of it seemed at all profound?"
Mick: "Very little."
Ron: "I can't think of one thing."
Q: "Are any of you envious of Ozzy Osbourne?"
Keith: "Have you ever *seen* Ozzy?"
Q: "How did you decide on your sound?"
Keith: "We flipped a coin."
Q: "Is there any way Bill Wyman could play with you again?"
Keith: "He could come back as a funeral director."

SUNDAY, 16 FEBRUARY 2003

The Stones hold a press conference in Sydney, Australia, where 200,000 anti-war protesters had recently lined the city's streets. Keith changes tack.
Keith: "They're out in force, right, all over the world, which is very peaceful. We're zooming around this globe and all this stuff's going on. We keep a close eye on it. Let's hope it gets resolved sensibly."
Ron: "I hope the governments are taking notice . . . My favourite banner is 'Fight plaque not Iraq'."

Mick ducks the question.
Mick: "(Australia's) always been a very warm place for us. People are very, very friendly here and take you to heart. We always feel very welcome and at home here . . . it's a good place to slip into."

SATURDAY, 10 MAY 2003

It is exactly 40 years since the release of 'Come On'. Keith warms up for the anniversary.
Keith: "It is going to be laid on us, and in many ways the band are very proud of it. Who else has done it? In one way, it still puts us on the cutting edge."

Is this really the last time?
Ron: "That's even harder nowadays to answer. A couple of years ago, I would have said, 'One or two more years.' But now the sky's the limit. It's rocking better than ever."
Mick: "It could well be the last tour. We might not even do this one. We might all get killed in a car crash tomorrow. You don't know what's going to happen in life."

On behalf of the Daily Mirror, *David Fricke asks Keith if he ever contemplates his own death.*

Keith: "The joke is that in spite of every drink and drug you've ever taken, you will outlive cockroaches and nuclear holocaust, you'll be the last man standing. It's funny how that position has been reserved for me . . . I never tried to stay up longer than anybody else just to announce that I'm the toughest. It's just the way I am. After 40 years, still doing two-and-a-half hours onstage every night, that's the biggest last laugh of all. Maybe that's the answer: if you want to live a long life, join the Rolling Stones."

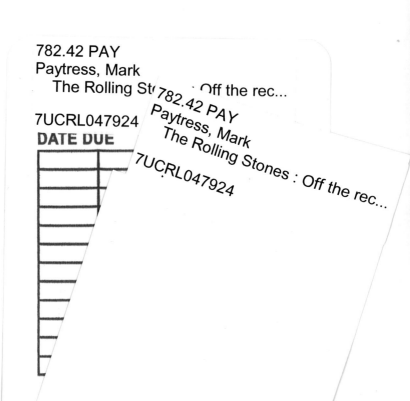

782.42 PAY
Paytress, Mark
  The Rolling St   Off the rec...

7UCRL047924

DATE DUE

782.42 PAY
Paytress, Mark
  The Rolling Stones : Off the rec...

7UCRL047924